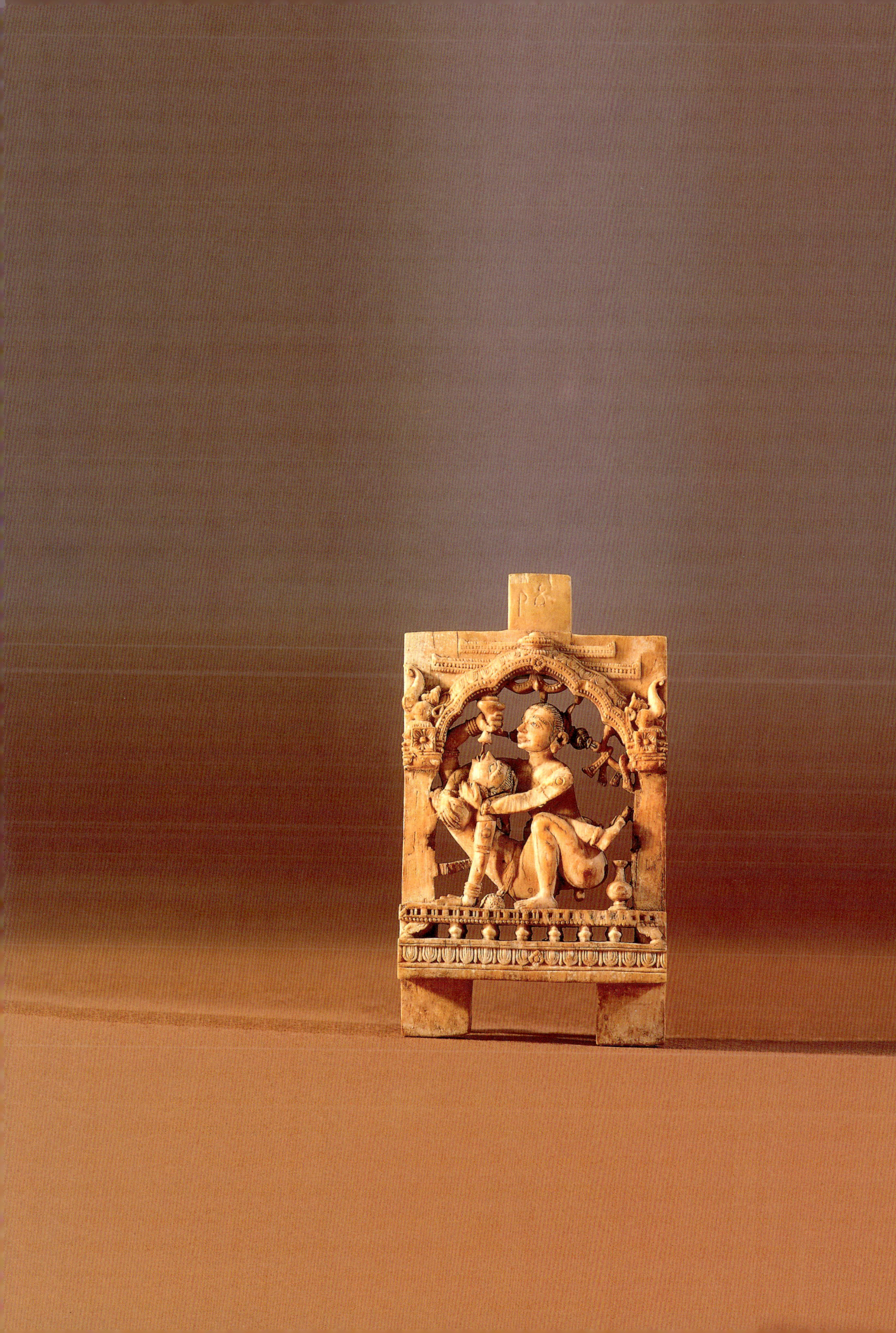

Indian Erotica

Indian Erotica

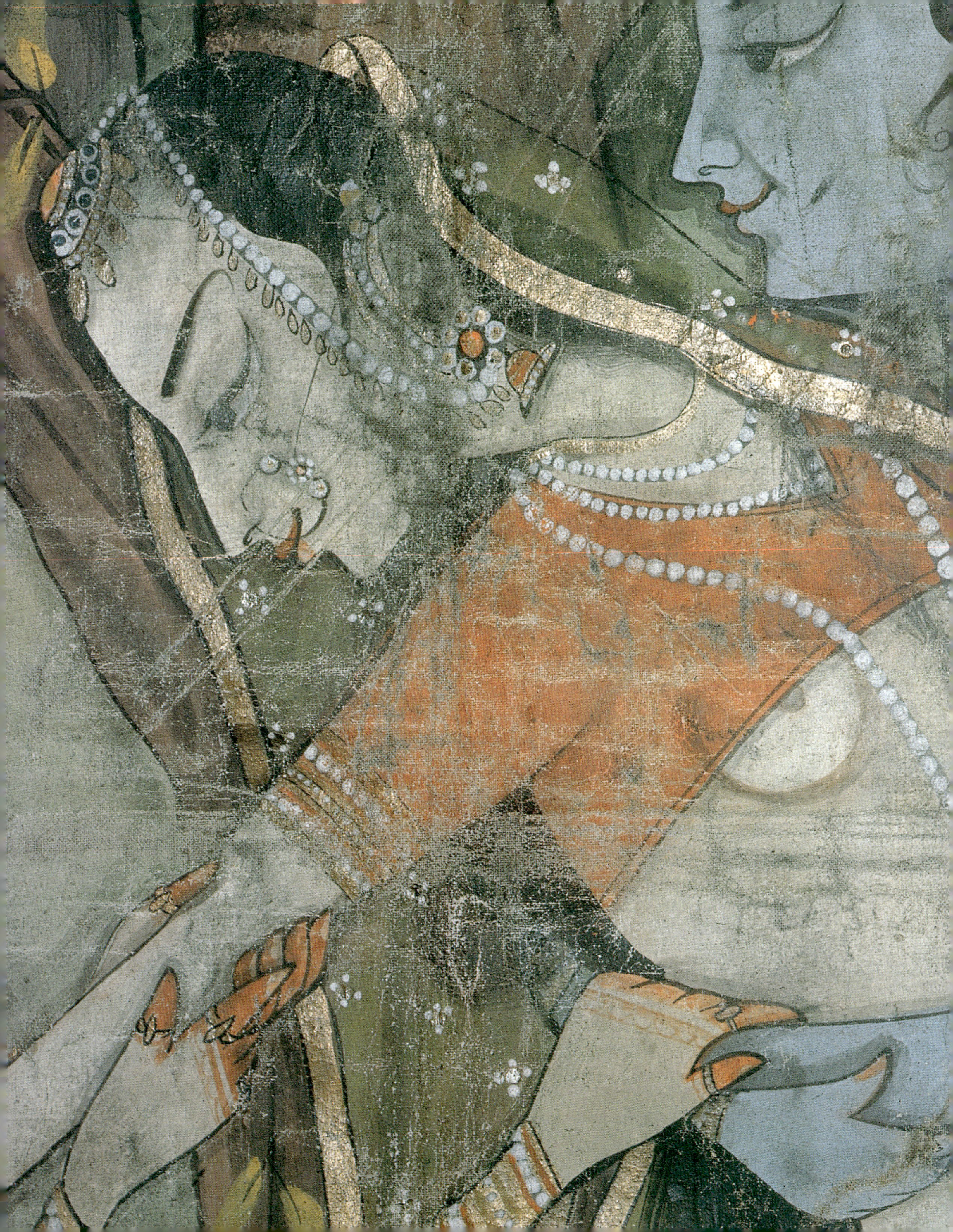

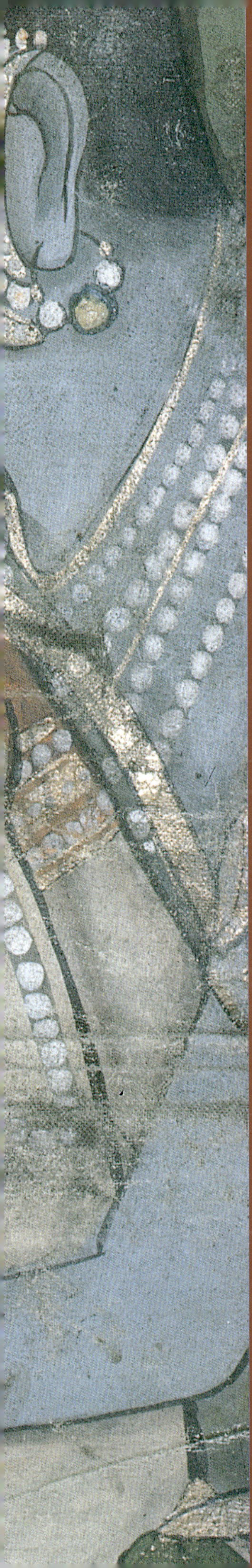

Indian Erotica

Indian Erotica

Text: Dr Alka Pande
Photographs: Lance Dane

Lustre Press
Roli Books

Acknowledgements

The unveiling of the mystique of Indian erotica has been a transcending of the mind and body into a completely different dimension. This rich experiential journey – at times tedious but always challenging and satisfying – would not have been possible without the help and support of my friends and family.

I want to begin by thanking Veena Baswani, chief editor with Roli Books, who initiated the study. Thanks also to Pramod Kapoor, the publisher, who thought of the idea; to Lance Dance, the photographer, who was a constant companion. To Anushree Somany, my research assistant who sat through back-breaking hours of work and also worked as a sounding board. To my daughter, Mandakini Devi, who always added insight into the book. My husband Mukul Joshi who, as always, has been a pillar of strength and provided an incisive evaluation. To Jehanara Wasi who gave me valuable tips. To Pran Neville, Sapna Sundari, Rajesh Singh and Kailash Mishra.

My friend Dona Suri who was the first to encourage me to pursue the study.

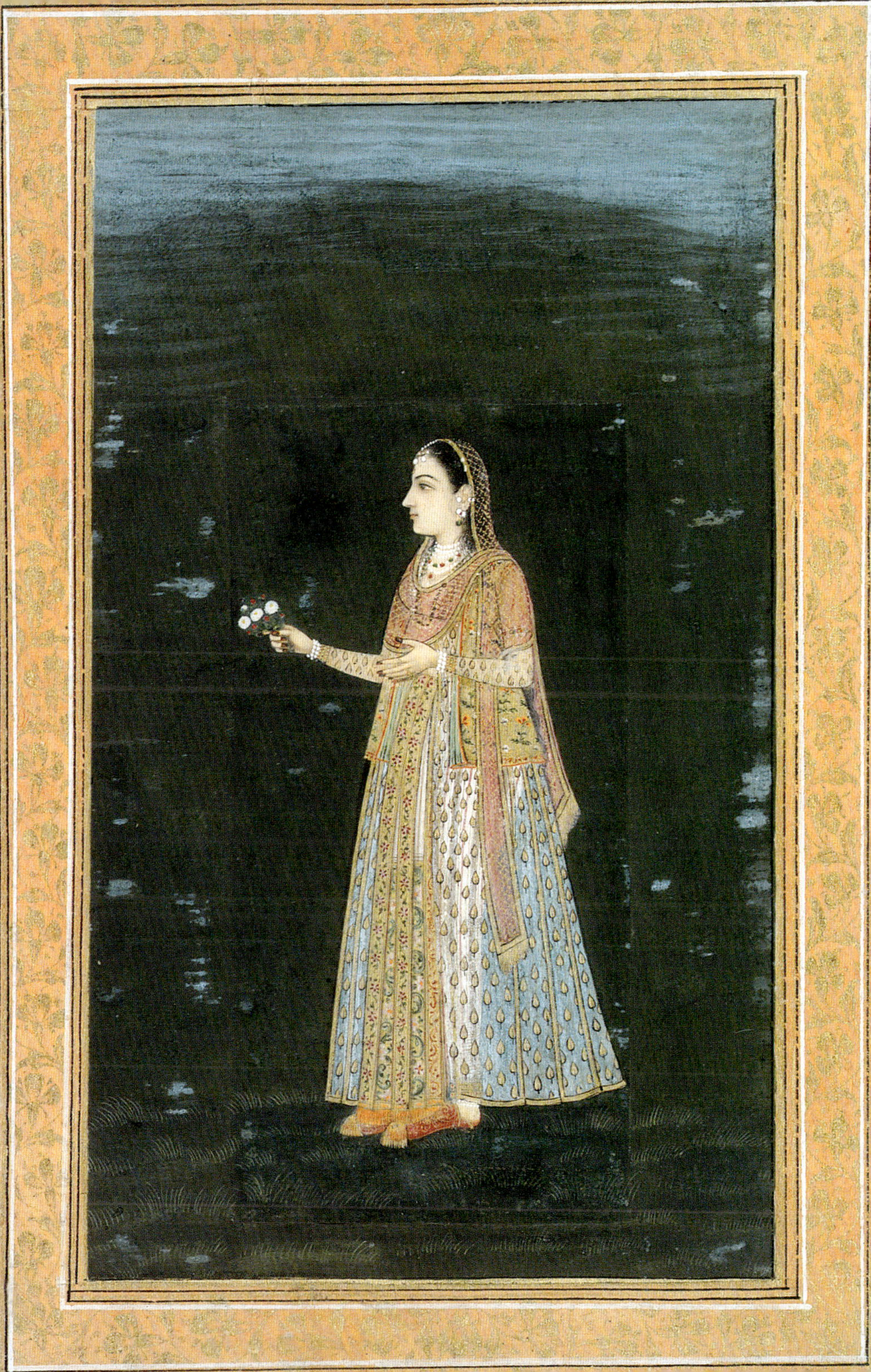

Preface

This work has in the end turned out to be a collaboration between a very knowledgeable photographer, Lance Dane, and I. Dealing with a subject as diverse and challenging as Indian erotica and putting it in a single text was an ambitious task. There were times when I was snowed under with material. Always, discussions with Dane helped.

Having a limited knowledge of Sanskrit, and knowing fully well that Sanskrit texts are the largest repositories of erotic texts, I knew my research would emanate from secondary sources. There was no dearth of these but it was like working in a vast area with one's hands tied behind one's back. This handicap may prevent the book from being profound. But my aim has been to study the production of erotica in Indian visual imagery in an art-historical manner and to present a point of view.

Practitioners of dance and music were some primary sources. Listening to the exposition of *thumris* (a classical style of singing) by singers of different *gharanas* ('schools' of music with characteristic styles), and talking to dancers, helped me understand the performative aspect of erotica. *Shringar*, one of the *navrasas* (nine elements) of Indian aesthetics, leads to one of the rati *bhavas* (emotion) of *vilasam* or pleasure, which emerges from the physical union of man and woman. *Ananda* or *vilasam* (bliss) is a component of erotica that cannot be manifested in the plastic arts of India. They are intangible and experiential, and are transferred through the performance of the artists themselves.

The study is a collation of some astounding pioneering work by a number of scholars who have laboured exhaustively in the field. My contribution has been the development and 'fixing' of the idea of Indian erotica as the skeleton on which this body of work has taken shape.

Right from the representation of erotic symbols, which predate history, to the erotic imagery, which screams out in print and electronic ads, continuity is evident. Tracing Indian erotica has been a journey that has sprung a number of surprises along the way. From the Mother Goddess and cultic fertility symbols to an exploration of the human body and alternate sexuality, *Indian Erotica* expresses the social reality of the period in which its images were formed. Then Tantric religious practices changed the status of women and affected their participation in sexual-religious practices.

The study shows continuity in the importance of *Kama* right from the dawn of civilisation. The profusion of erotic symbols and images, especially in temples all over India, particularly during the tenth to the fifteenth centuries, presents, at times, a paradox in Hindu culture. But in India, the text and its visual counterpart have always moved hand in hand. Sex and religion have always had an intimate connection in primitive and civilised societies. Sex has also played a role in magic-religious rites. It is believed that sex which generates life, also rejuvenates natural forces, and that is why it is conceived as a creative, force with the power to revive, and is linked, obviously, to fertility.

Starting with Vedic literature, the magical aspect of sex assumed an important role as was evident in the Asvamedha *yagna*. This ritual, a horse sacrifice, lasted for a complete year in which a monarch displayed his power over neighbouring kingdoms. Ritual copulation and sexual dialogue were an important component of the rite. The wives of the king participated; the chief queen was

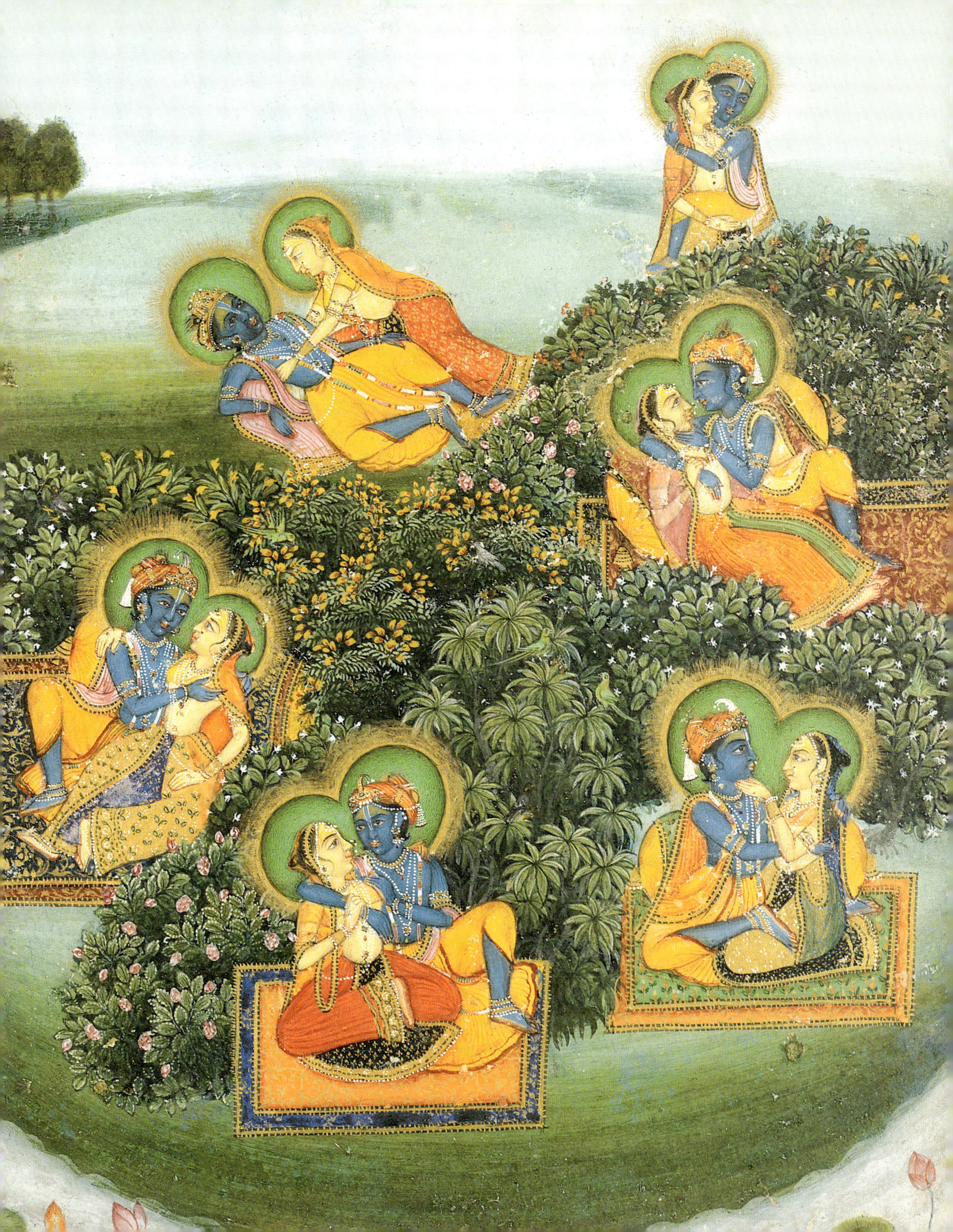

made to lie with the horse while the other queens used abusive language. This was part of an agricultural theme. Yet another rite enjoined restraint, with the king being made to lie between the legs of his favourite wife, without enjoying her.

During the medieval period, tantrics influenced a number of cults. Tantric literature and beliefs gave an impetus to the worship of gods along with their consorts. Gods and their consorts were shown in amorous and sometimes explicit poses. Ithyphallic Siva is shown in erotic play with his consort Uma in a number of Eastern Indian temples.

The Tantrics believed that the state of *advaya*, *sahaja* or non-duality could be achieved through the union of the male and female principles. The male and female principles were centred in the human body as Shiva in the *Sahasrara chakra* (*chakra* denotes spinal centre; *sahasrara* the brain) and Shakti in the *Muladhara chakra* (at the base of the spine). This is represented in art as Kundalini, coiled like a snake, traversing through the six *chakras* to the *Sahasrara* of the yogin's body. It is also represented as a *mantra* or two triangles with a *bindu* (point) in the centre.

At a more popular level, that of folk and tribal art, erotic motifs and symbols are recurring themes. In both forms, erotica again plays a dual role: it is seen in cultic, religious practices and in the recreational activities of communities. Visual representations are also an expression of social reality and the images can be decoded to present a picture of social practices.

There has been a constant interplay between the religious and the recreational when it comes to sexual motifs in Indian art. One instance is the tradition of the *devadasis* (girls who danced for the gods). Popular in the religious life of the medieval period, the *devadasi* tradition made erotica a part of the performing framework of music and dance. The dances were a subtle unveiling and left a lot to the imagination unlike modern dances. Since the patrons during this period were kings and princes, they were often shown participating in sexual activities. Pictorial albums were made especially for the rulers' recreational pleasure. These picture books – meant for private circulation – had explicit sexual scenes and were, probably, both instructional as well as recreational.

The British brought in a culture of Victorian prudishness. While the Indian tradition of the dancing girls and musicians continued in royal courts, visual culture was influenced by imported primness. Pretty landscapes, portraiture and wildlife became the norm.

The turn of the century saw the establishment of British academies of art, and traditional Indian art took a back seat. Post-independent India saw a surge of artists following western ideals of art. But in the last two decades a certain rootedness in contemporary Indian art has taken place. The present generation of artists is now looking at its traditions for inspiration. Contemporary Indian artists are part of globalisation that exposes them to both inside/outside views. They are increasingly conscious of their own ethnic identity in a rapidly growing, cosmopolitan world. They are also more confident of their own expressions.

Aesthetic sensuality, part of visual representation in Indian art, is taking a back seat in the contemporary visual culture. I have tried to show the beauty of sexual representation that took place with utmost restraint in old films. Now, of course, the explicit display of lurid images rather than any revelation of the beauty of the feminine form is proof of the commodification of women. Erotica that started out by giving visual pleasure is now, unfortunately, degenerating to a crude, coarse and tasteless display.

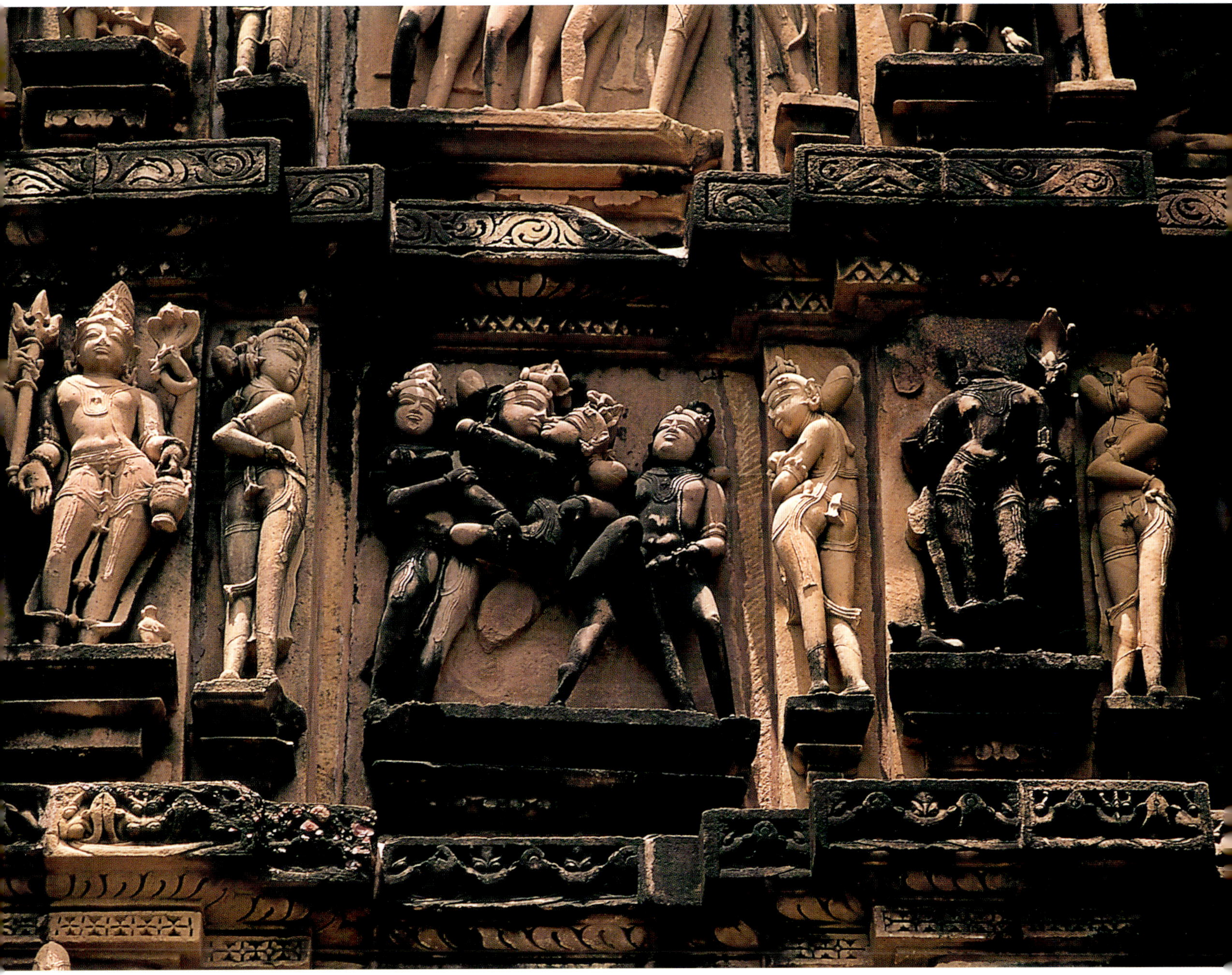

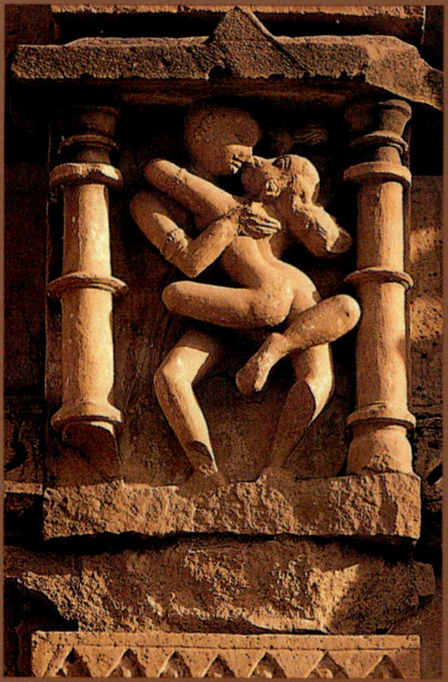

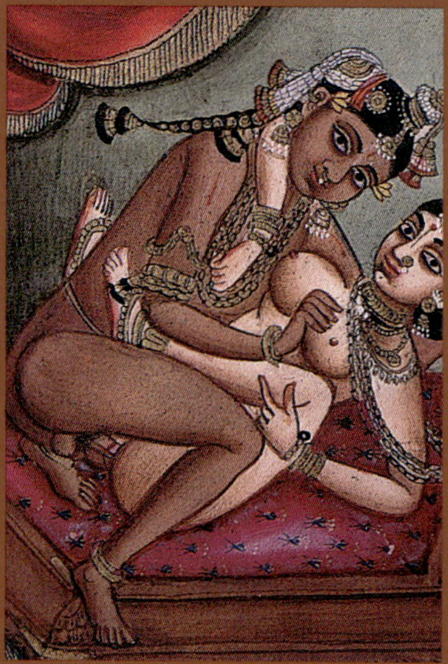

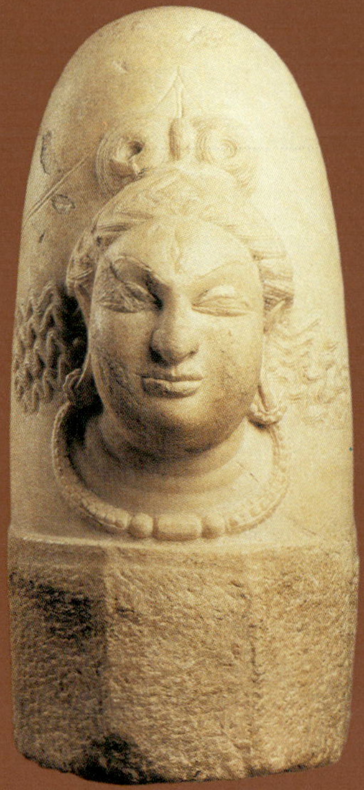

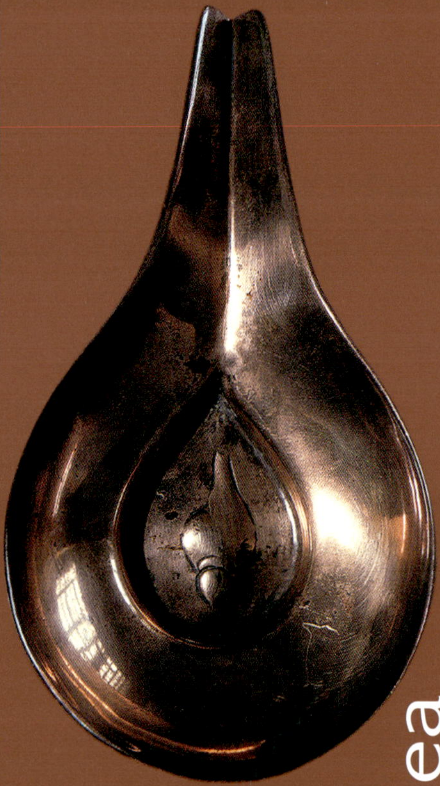

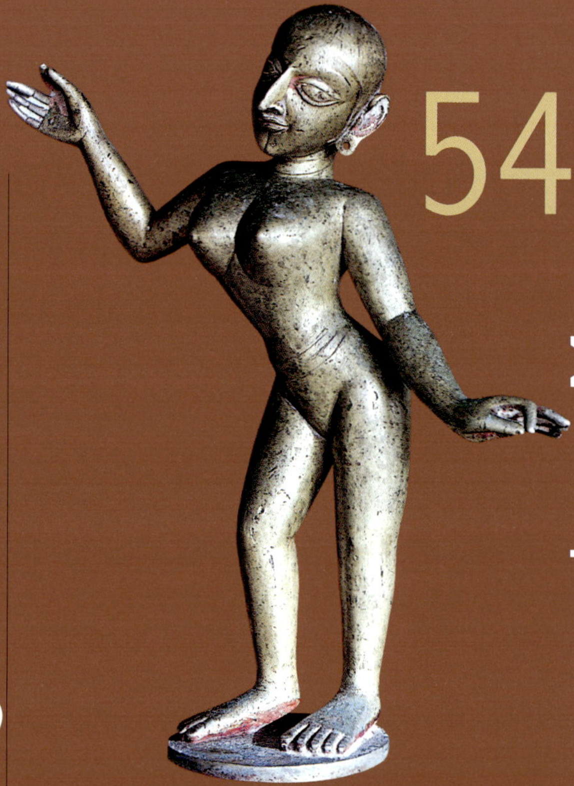

ISBN : 81-7436-172-3

Published in India by Roli Books
in arrangement with Roli & Janssen BV
M-75, Greater Kailash-II (Market)
New Delhi-110 048, INDIA
Phones: (011) 6442271, 6462782, 6460886
Fax: (011) 6467185. E-mail: roli@vsnl.com
Website: rolibooks.com

Text: Dr Alka Pande
Photographs: Lance Dane

Design
Yogesh Suraksha Design Studio

Printed and bound in Singapore

Contents

First thoughts

First thoughts

What do we mean by erotica? It is distinct from love, passion and lust. Erotica means that which leads to *kama* or the sexual act; it is not in itself a straight sexual act. In ancient Indian thought, *Kama* – the Indian love god – is akin to meditation. It is philosophical, the act itself being elevated to being nothing less than a metaphor for unity with Godhead. The *bhakti* or devotional tradition is the showpiece of this theme. Here, the eternal love of Radha and Krishna parallels the union of the *jivatma* (individual soul) with the *parmatma* (supreme or cosmic soul).

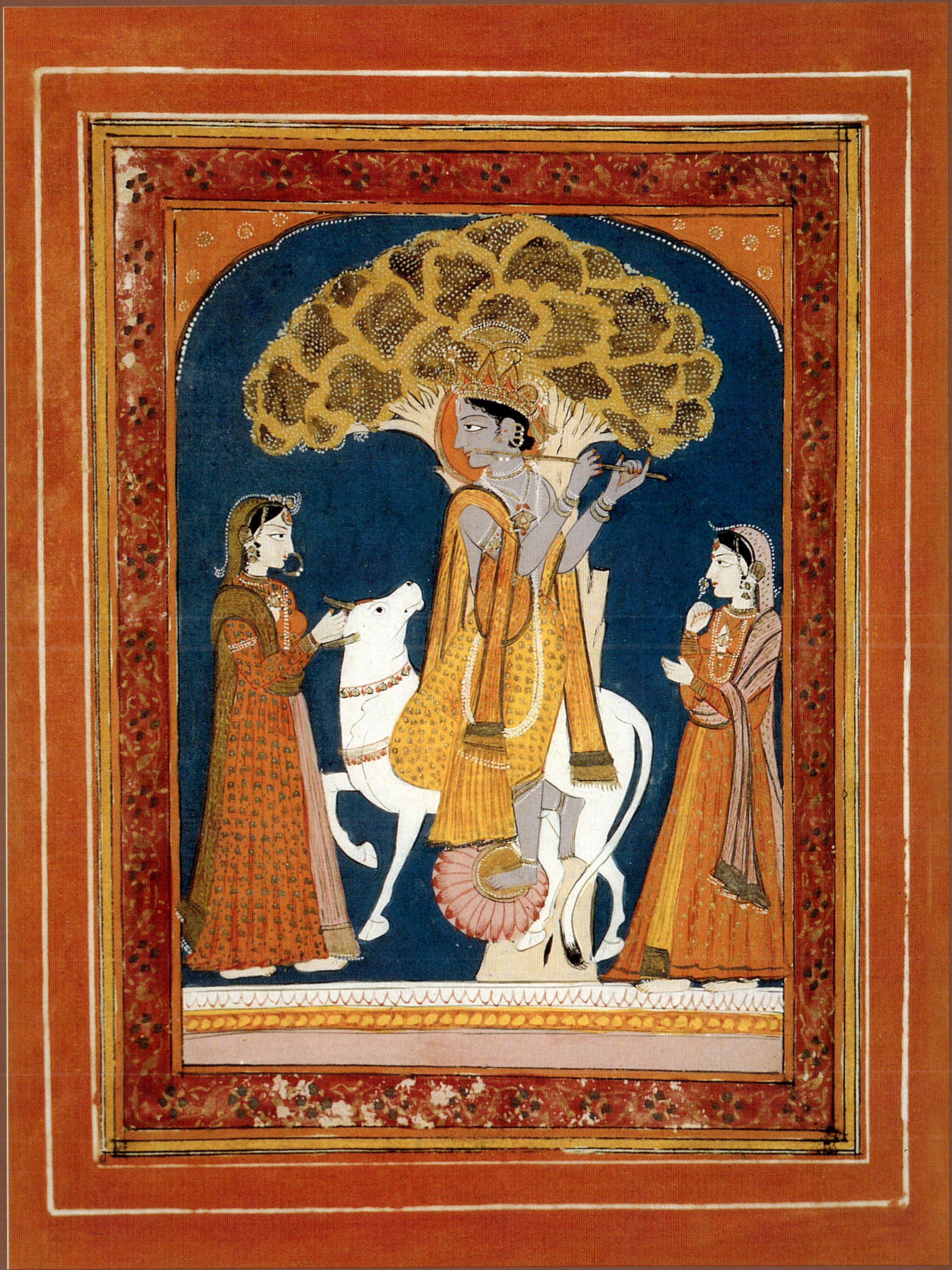

Erotica does not distance itself from what is expressive of sexual love. The mild gesture of stroking the face manifests the erotic as much as the various sexual postures seen in the facades of Indian temples and miniatures. Erotica also includes the essence of the man-woman relationship, the portrayal of men and women in auto-erotic attitudes, and relationships with the same sex.

As a word, erotica has a western connotation. It is derived from Eros, the name of the Greek god of physical desire, whom the Romans called Cupid. But the word came into force as late as the nineteenth century. Booksellers who wanted to give respectability to a category of books that police could otherwise confiscate for pornography used the word. In the process, they unwittingly exposed a vital if somewhat fuzzy faultline that divided the erotic from the pornographic. It was only in the twentieth century that artists openly produced erotica.

In art, the erotic is distinct from the pornographic in two ways. 'First, pornography lacks any artistic intent. Second, its main aim is not only to stimulate the spectator sexually but to degrade, dominate and depersonalise its subject, usually women,' is a crisp definition by Jerrald Levinson. Often, erotica has a deeper meaning; pornography, on the other hand, sticks to the surface, incapable of looking beyond the physical plane.

When contrasted with the *kamasastra*, erotica is art with sexual content that has two uses: one, to merely stimulate sexual thought and feelings; and two, to arouse such desires almost by the way, without intending to. Although there is more than one sense in which a work can be classified as being erotic, all work must succeed in evoking sexual thoughts, feelings and desires. A work can be classified as mildly erotic or highly erotic, depending on the degree of sexual arousal it can sustain. Yet erotic art also reflects the state of the artist.

The divine pleasure

In ancient India, erotica was conceived as a sexual impulse which generated divine pleasure and led to union with the superior being. One of the earliest representations of sexual motifs in religious art was found in sculptures from the Buddhist period, in the form of *dampati* scenes. The next watershed occurred in the Gupta period when the culture and lifestyle of the aristocrats began to appear in literature and art forms. The period also saw the composition of

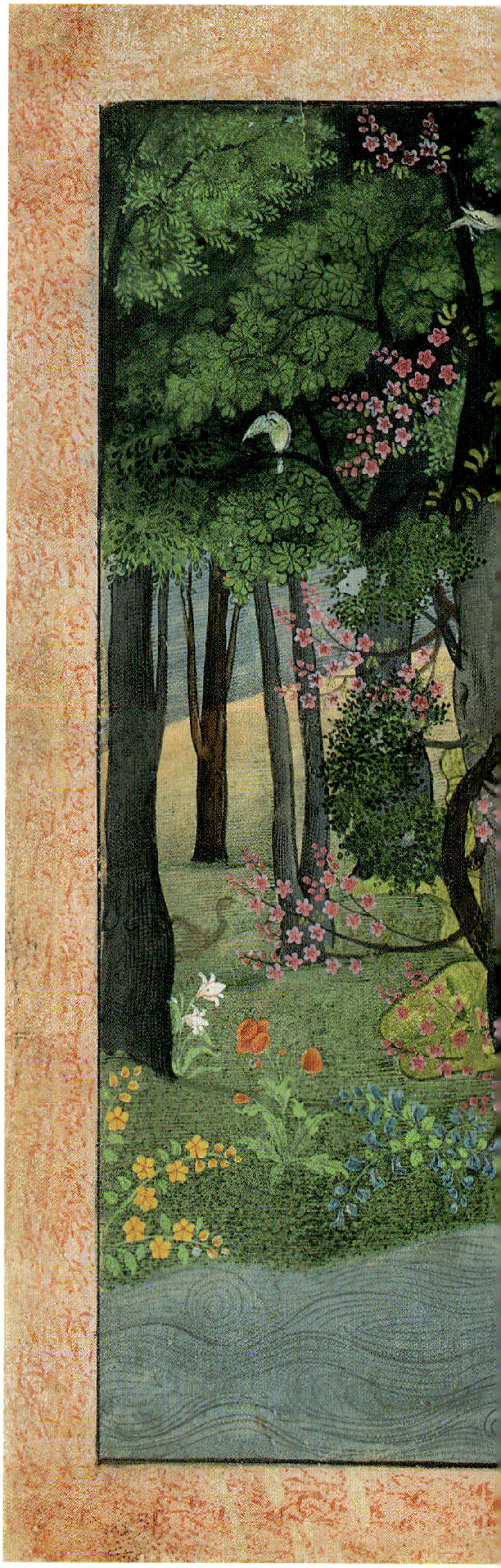

A miniature from the Pahari school depicts Radha and Krishna in divine embrace. *Previous page:* A Rajasthani miniature showing the divine couple's love play.

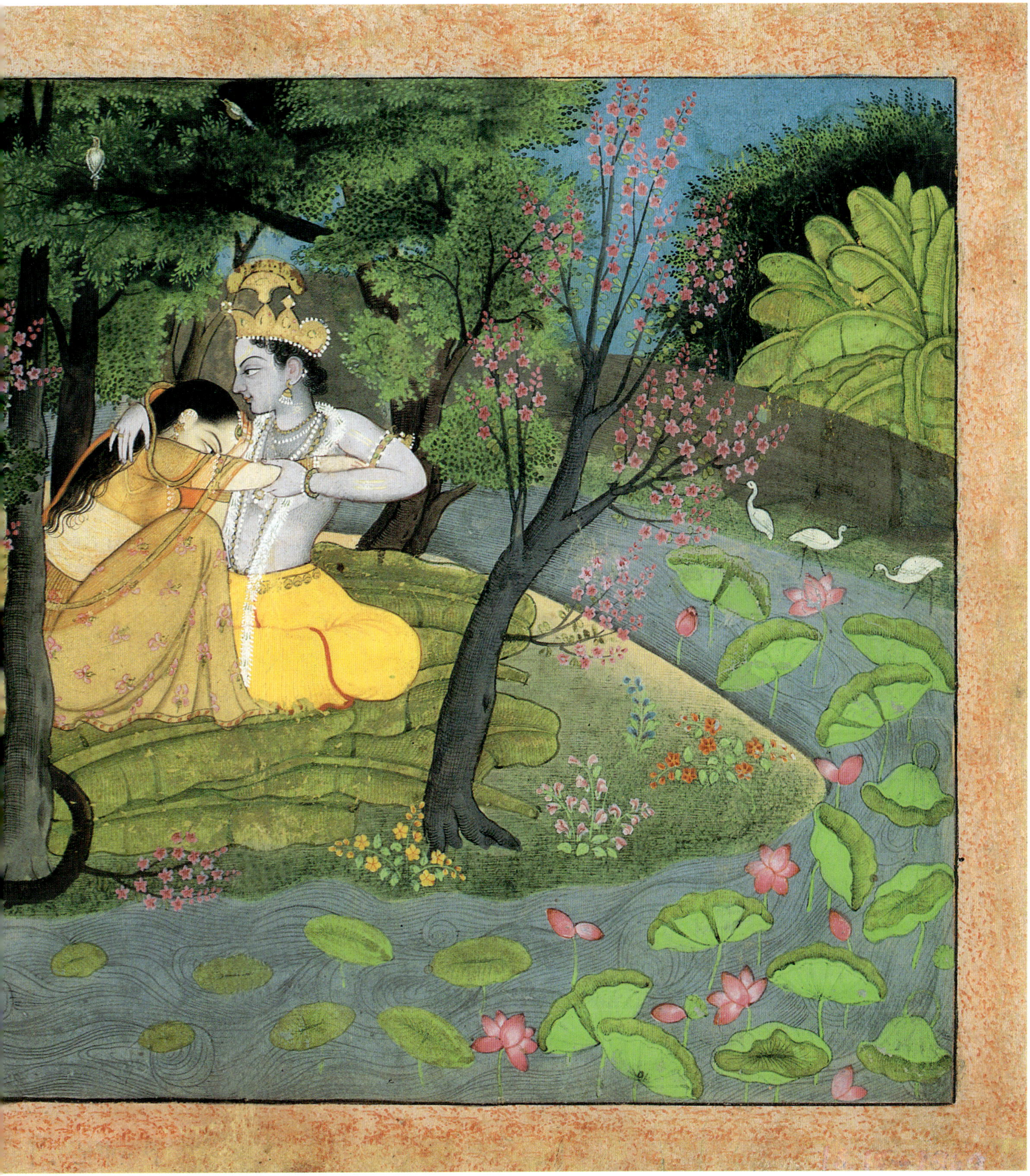

Vatsayana's *Kamasutra*, which will be discussed in great detail later.

At this point a shift could be seen in sexual representation with the motifs not being restricted to cultic theories or the principles of procreation, regeneration, fertility and energy. The position was that *kamasastra* did not just embody the positions of sex but spoke of and for a free and creative mental attitude during *kama*. This would then lead to perfection, something the sexual motifs also depict. However, *kama* was not divorced from desire and pleasure.

Another strain involving the principles of *kama* is the tradition of tantra. Tantra ideology has a highly developed spiritual ritual with its practice embedded in sexo-yogic postures. Eventually, eroticism in art came to yet another turning point with the coalescence of sex and religion, shown in portraitures of Krishna and Radha, especially in the Rajasthani miniatures and those from the Punjab hills. This gave sex a whole new meaning, one attached closely to religion through the union of the human-self with the divine. Sexual and sensual desires turned from being ordinary and common to divine, leading to *ananda* or heavenly pleasure.

The depiction of these desires went hand in hand in literary and visual imagery. This can be seen in the Vedic

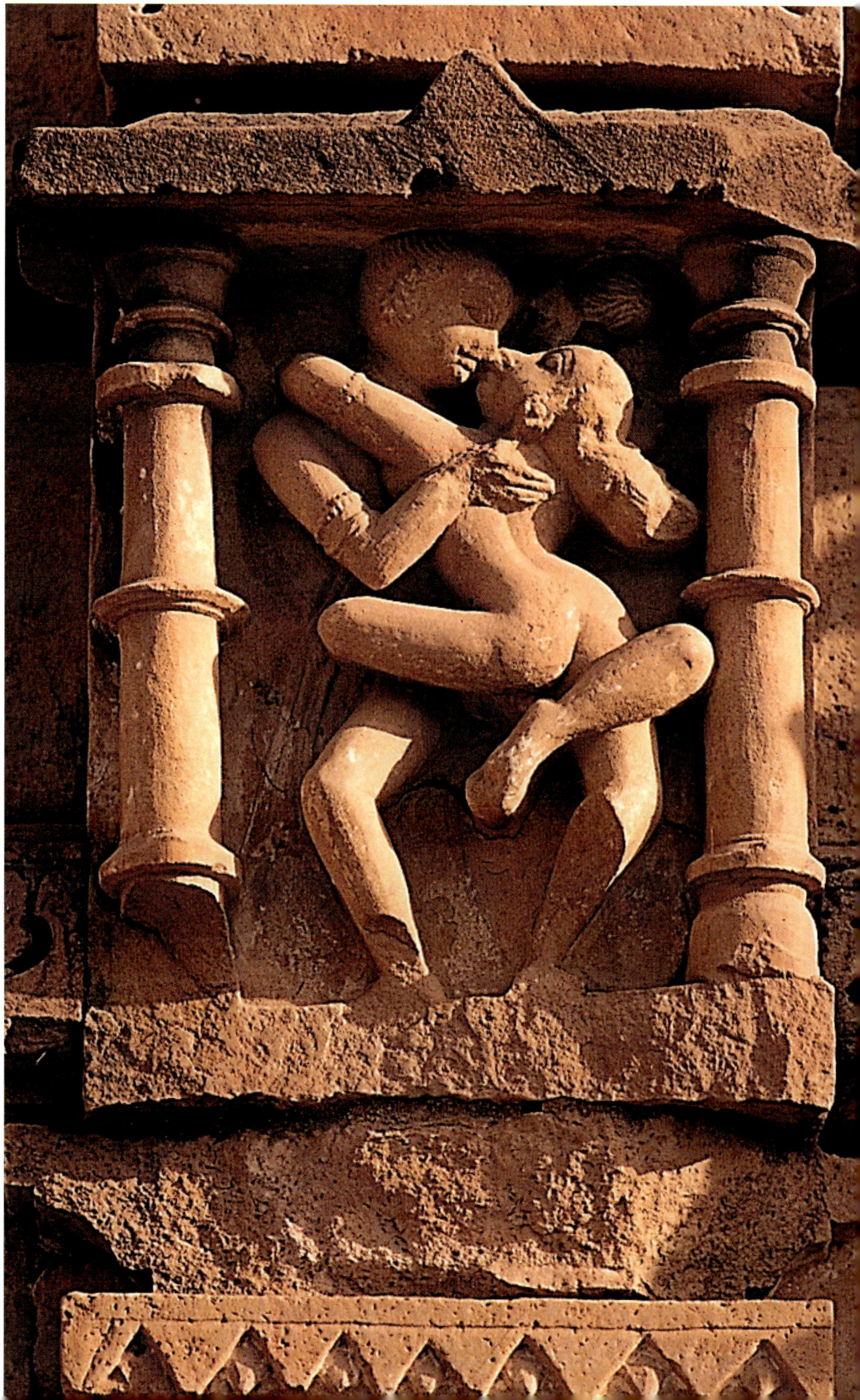

texts and in the contemporary literature of Indian authors, both in their homeland and outside. The *Rig Veda* is full of erotic imagery. Take, for instance, the description of Usha, the goddess of dawn in the *Rig Veda: 'handsome maiden, proud of her form; oh goddess! You come towards the god who is longing to meet you. You, a young lady full of sweet smiles, shining brilliantly, you expose your breasts to the full view of the world. In a charming experience, you, like a young lady groomed by her mother, present the charm of your body to the full view of the world.'* (Kunhan C. Raja's *The Quintessence of the Rig Veda*.)

In the last chapter of the *Brihadarankya Upanishad*, the concept of the mind and the earth imagery is related to the bliss of coital union. The philosophical base of the idea rests on *samkhya* dualism. The tantric texts too place considerable importance on erotic ideas. Erotica is found indispensable in Hindu temple rituals and practices and in the performing of the plastic arts.

On a more individual level, erotica is part of the very identity of the person. If you have not used it, you have not lost it. Sexual prowess and skill cannot be measured by the frequency of the act. In ancient Indian tradition, sex was one of the primary aspects of a true aesthete and a sophisticate. It was one of the 64 arts which made a perfect man. Indeed, as we move into the twenty-first century, the position of the *Kamasutra* as one of the greatest treatises of love universally remains unchallenged.

Shiva and Shakti

The primordial Indian god, Shiva, epitomises the high point of Indian erotica. He is at once the *mahayogi* and the *mahabhogi*. Within Shiva resides the strictest ascetic and the playful lover of his consort Parvati. Shiva and Parvati are also accepted as the primordial parents.

The great poet, Kalidasa (fourth century), likened Shiva and Parvati to word and meaning, each being unable to survive without the other. The erotic aspect is clearly seen in a few lines from Kalidasa's book *Kumarasambhava*. The poet talks of *'the pair of beautiful breasts, with their dark nipples in the centre, so close together, rubbing against each other, that even a fibre of a lotus flower cannot pass between them.'*

In fact, breasts seem to be important to many artists as they are not just part of being a woman or merely a form of beauty; they are symbolic of motherhood, fertility, womanhood and the power of reproduction.

While Shiva and Parvati are accepted as the primordial parents,

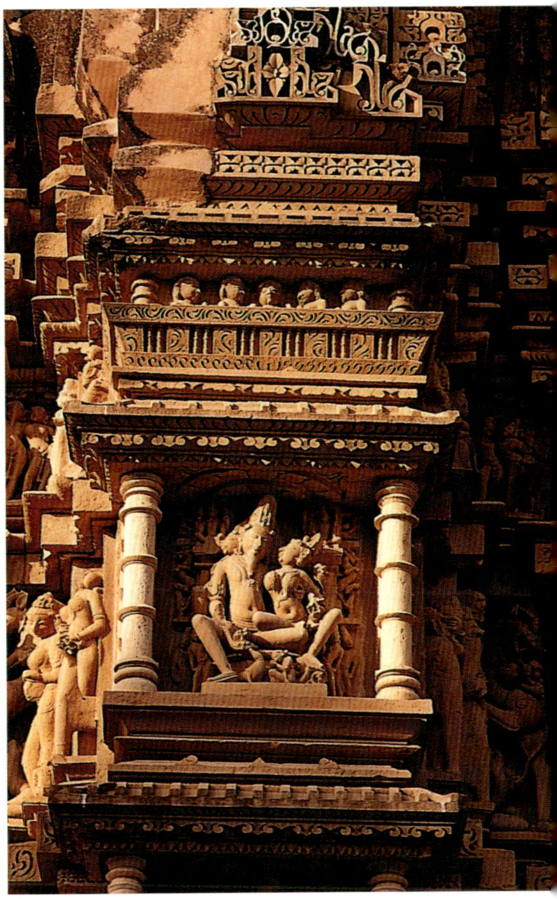

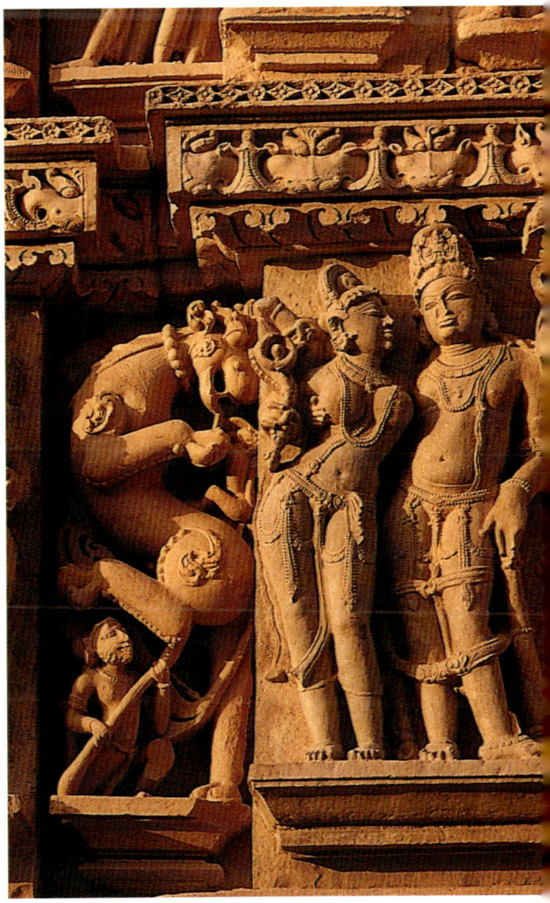

Top: Brahma with his consort Sarasvati from the Chitragupta Temple in the Khajuraho complex. The complex is replete with erotica using the body metaphor voluptuously.
Bottom: Vishnu with his consort Lakshmi, from the south-facing lower bands of Parsvanath Temple.
Facing page: An amorous couple from a small niche in the lower band of the Vishwanath Temple.

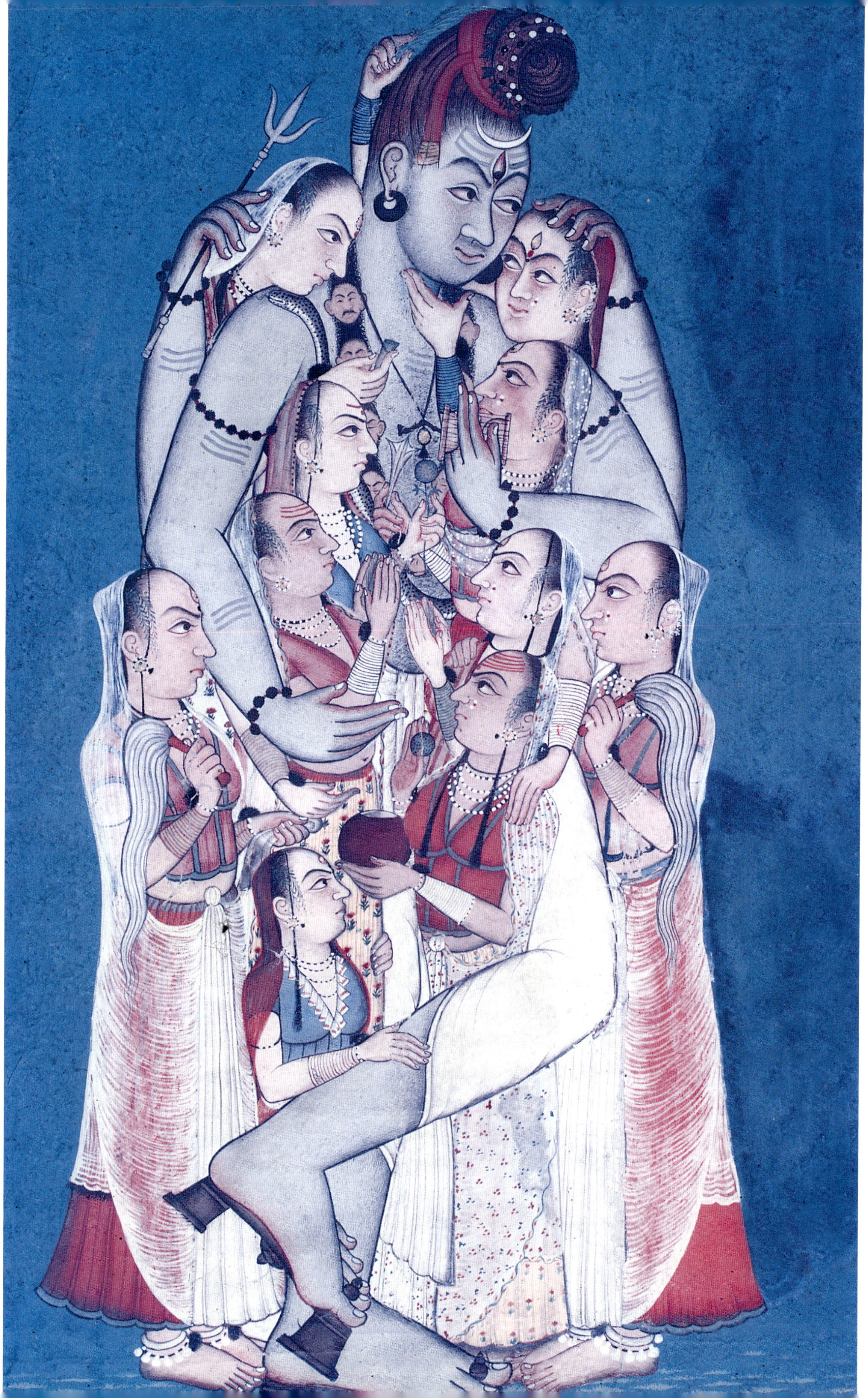

where the generative principle takes a dominant stance, the divine couple Radha and Krishna symbolise pure *shringara* or the recreational aspect of sex.

Kamasutra: The recreational attitude

The very mention of the book conjures up exotic erotica. The most versatile and convoluted of acrobatic positions and contortions form the backbone of the visual imagery of this classic love manual. It is said that the sage Vatsyayana composed the text as part of his religious duties. Written originally in Sanskrit, the *Kamasutra* is accepted as a science of love and comprises 1,250 *shlokas* or aphorisms.

Each *sutra* is an aphorism or the briefest way to state a principle. Part of the oral tradition, the *Kamasutra*, if looked into deeply, is an attitude towards life. It is actually a charter of social graces. It is an amalgamation of the three guiding principles of the Indian way of living: *dharma*, *artha* and *kama*, that is, duty, meaning and action.

The *Kamasutra* is a seminal event in the rich tradition of Indian erotica. It talks of happiness and sexual equality for both men and women. It emphasises the importance of singing, dancing, conversation, dressing and living well. It also talks of the sixty-four sexual positions for fulfilling and gratifying sex. Thus the *Kamasutra* becomes one of the most important documents of recreation, in which the pleasures of life are fully experienced.

Over the years, the most popular portion of the *Kamasutra* has been the section titled Sixty-Four, in which the knowledge of these sixty-four segments goes a long way in making the perfect individual. The eight subjects it deals with are embracing, kissing, scratching with the nails or fingers, biting, lying down, making various sounds, playing the part of the man, and the mouth congress. Each of these subjects is of eight types, and, therefore, this *Kamasutra* chapter covers over sixty-four topics, and gets its name from there.

Tantra: Magic in the air

Another tradition that sees sex as a part of Indian society is tantra. Tantricism was a merger between primitive magic and evolved spiritual concepts that existed in Indian society. Tantric *vidya* (knowledge), in fact, has been an inseparable part of Indian

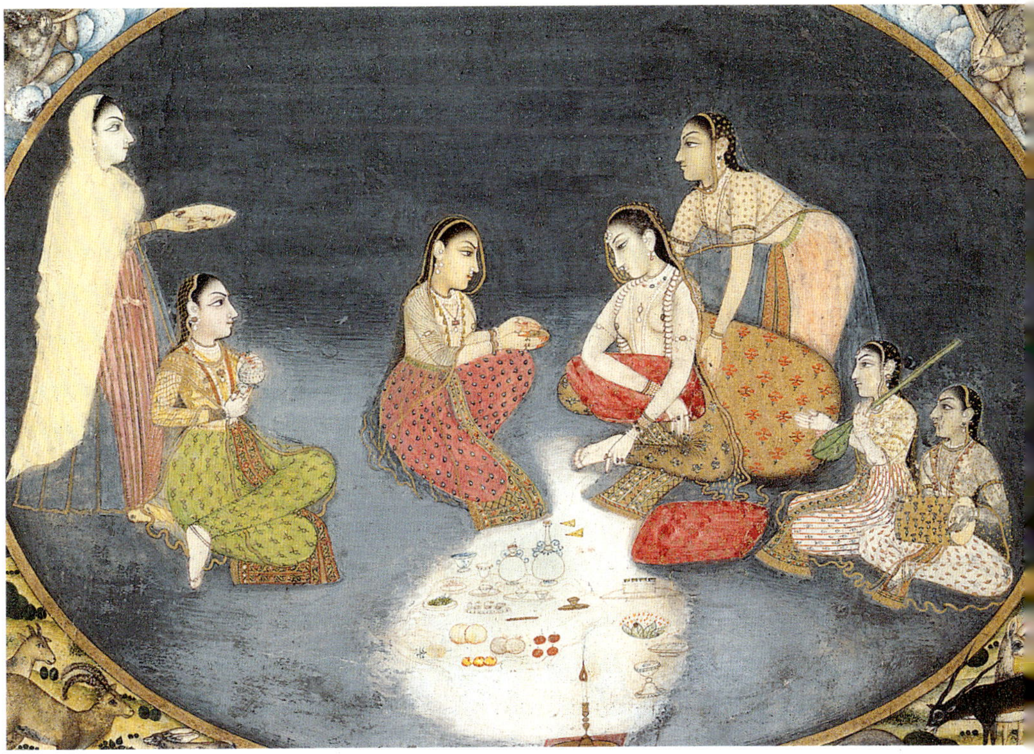

A ladies' toilette being prepared. The *Kamasutra* mentions in exhaustive detail all the different preparations that go into this ritual. *Facing page:* Lord Shiva shown as the quintessential *yogi* and ascetic lover, with devotees clambering around him. The whole image is in the form of Shiva's icon, the *lingam*. The Mandi Kalam school.

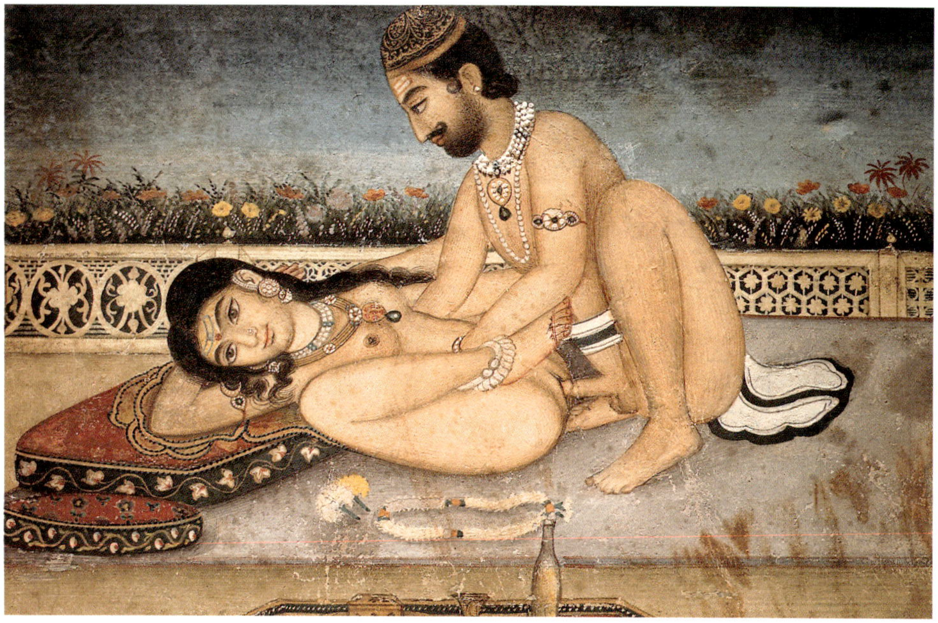

rituals and culture. Often associated with what is called 'black magic', tantra connotes negative aspects. Yet, tantricism is merely a form of magic in relation to religion. It gave sex and lovemaking a whole new dimension.

Tantricism merged with Buddhism to give birth to the *Vajrayana* (Vehicle of Thunderbolt) school of that religion, a type dominant in Tibet from the eighth century. The arts produced were wall paintings, which were brightly coloured and had representations of golden couples seated together in sexual union.

Tantra has four central features – the goal of non-duality, yogic practices, *maithuna* (the sexual act), and other *makaras*.

The aim of non-duality or *advaya* in tantric *sadhna* (practice) is the recognition of the *atma* and *paramatma* to gain *moksha* (liberation). Tantra does not focus on discipline to reach this stage but concentrates on the use of magical and psychological aspects to achieve *moksha*. The state of non-duality focuses on the merging of polar opposites – the positive and negative, the static and dynamic. Ultimately, it focuses on the union of the male and female to gain eternal bliss.

Erotic as essential

It would be misleading to form an impression that erotica is only a part of the sacred in India. It informs the profane too. In fact, ancient India was preoccupied with sex not just for procreation but also for recreation. Unsurprisingly, a vast body of courtesans and mistresses grew up who enjoyed royal patronage and were a part of respectable society. Since then they have inspired many literary works, right from the Mauryan text *Mricchakatikam* to Rabindranath Tagore's *Binodini*.

It is important to note that erotic art has always maintained its *numero uno* position through periods of subversion and emergence in popular culture. Erotica was a part of the Brahmanical, the Buddhist and the Jain tradition, and reached its high point in the tantric tradition.

It also covers a wide canvas, stretching from folk art forms to tribal forms, from the rural to the urban. Erotica is part and parcel of Indian art, thought and literature. It has its own story to tell – a strong narrative that envelops every aspect of life, from the basest of human desires to the most sophisticated of human expressions. In India, it is a way of life that does not find a parallel in any other civilisation of the world.

Sex was an important component of religious art. Here, it is shown in its recreational aspect. *Facing page:* Equal participation in the sexual act was an important point of emphasis in the oldest manual on love, the *Kamasutra.*

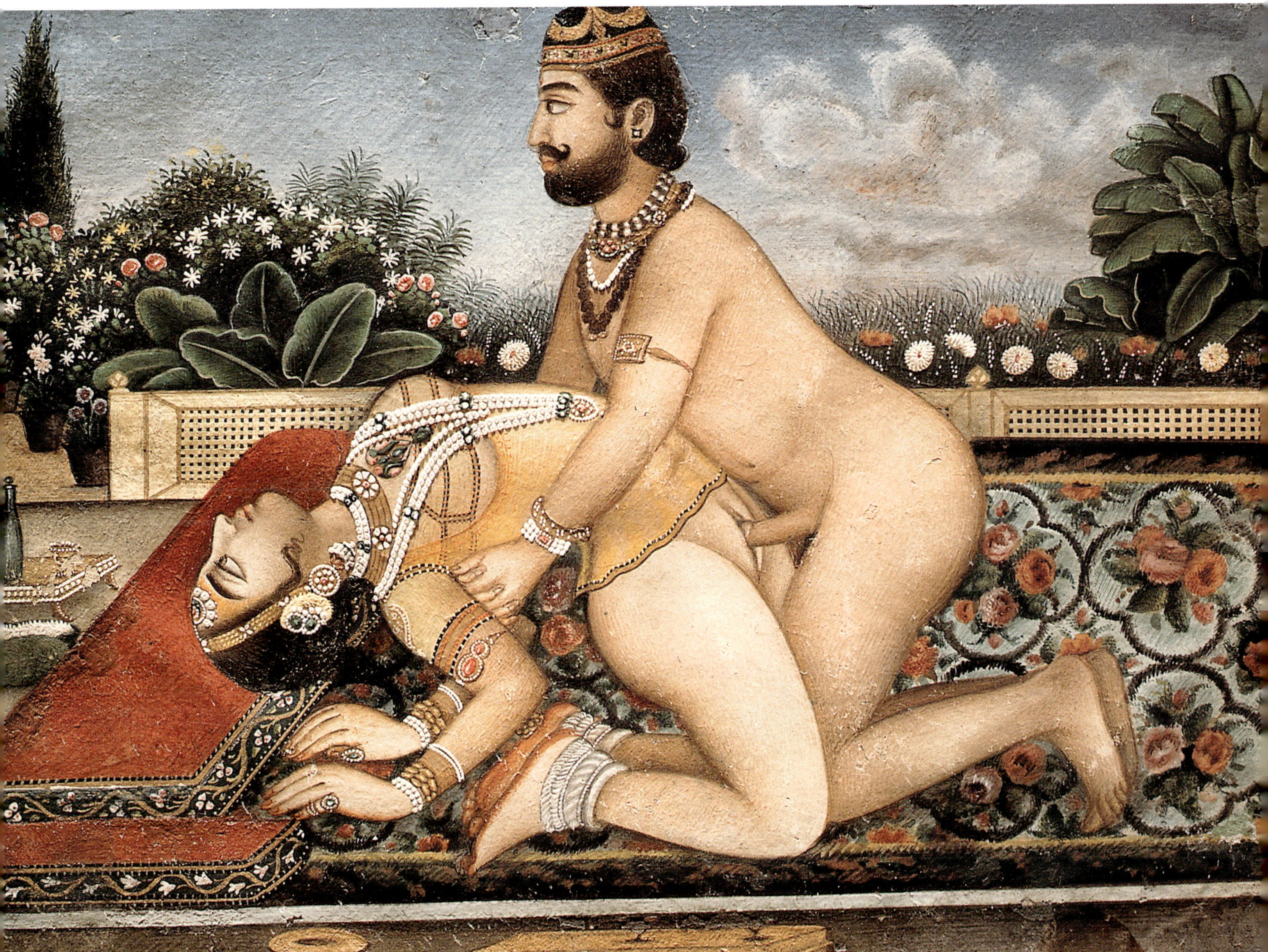

Fixing the Idea

Fixing the Idea

The erotic images of Hindu art, architecture, literature and everyday life, are not specific to an era. They are symbols that have continued up till the present with artists of successive ages drawing on what came before them. So the medieval artist succumbed to the charms of the imagery of the ancient period, as do contemporary Indian artists who reinvent erotic myths and legends from the ancient past.

We do not only look at the artist for reading the persistence of sexual motifs and metaphors in India's literary and visual culture. All the major religions of the country, Hinduism, Buddhism and Jainism, are full of erotic motifs. Sex seems to have played an important role in the religious life of early communities; it was never moralised upon or suppressed. Undoubtedly, sexual representation is a pan-Indian cultural feature.

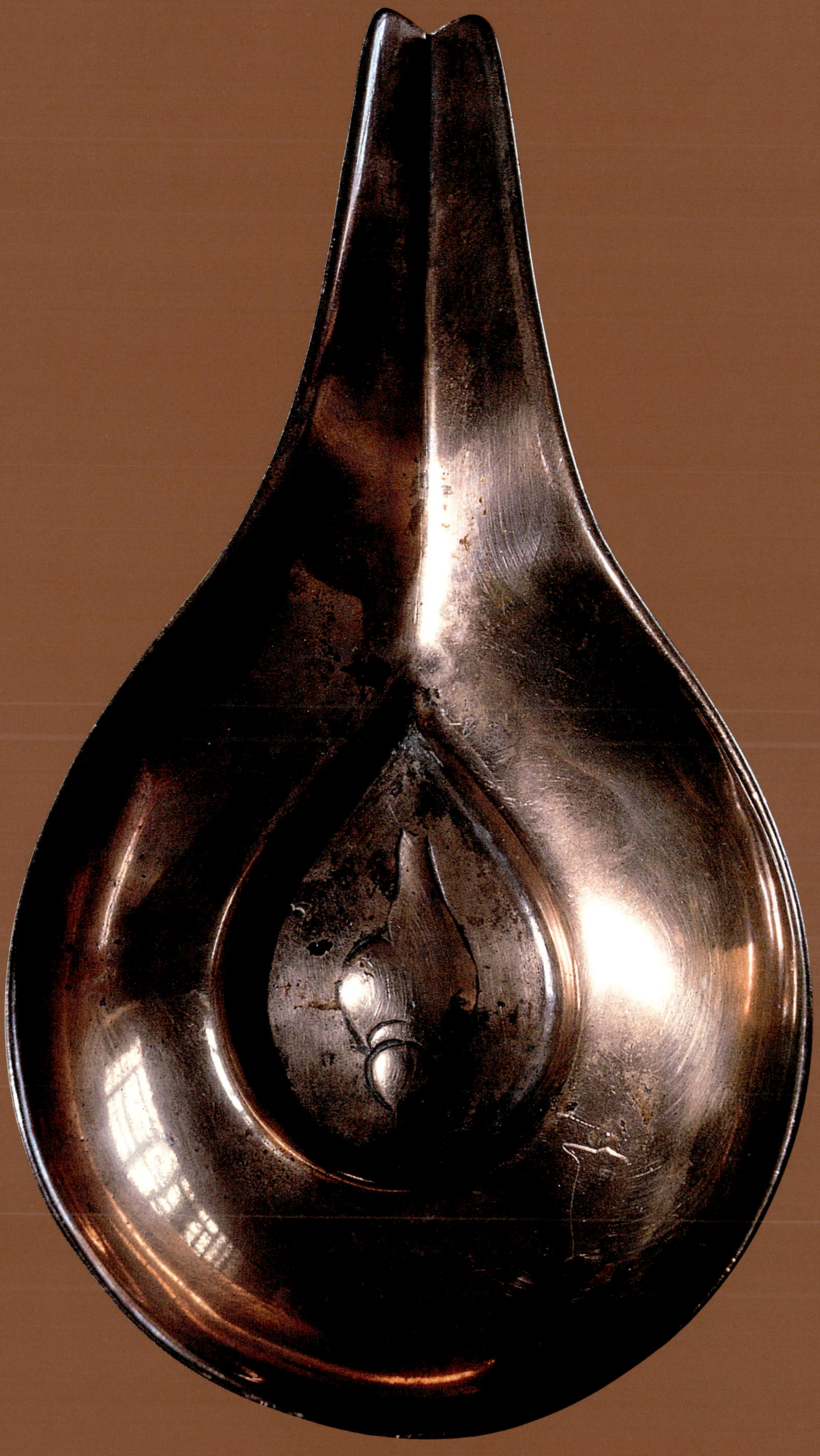

Motifs can be found abundantly in the Indus Valley civilisation, the crucible of Indian culture. Its images were, in turn, based on cultic practices. And even though these changed significantly later, they still followed the same framework of ideas and are based on theories of generation, creation, destruction, plenty and fertility.

Archaeological finds on erotica that go back to the Indus Valley have unearthed phallic and ring stones, images of the mother goddess and of the male ithyphallic horned god in association with animals – the prototype of Lord Shiva. One of the Indus Valley seals has a plant-bearing female figure on a seal, which represents the vegetation goddess, akin to the Puranic goddess, Sakambhari.

One of the earliest depictions of *maithuna* or the sexual act is on a pot from the Chalcolithic period, from Daimabad in the Ahmednagar district of Maharashtra. The human figures are portrayed through a stylised, linear rendering. The phallus and the feminine breasts are clearly evident in the painting. Probably cultic, clearly the visual representation was neither of an artistic, decorative or of a sensual nature.

On a more idealistic level, sexual expression has been interpreted as symbolising eternal bliss or as being an overt manifestation of *kama*, the third *pursartha* (aim) of life. But this explanation does not jell in cases where visual portrayals of orgies and bestiality have been represented.

Whatever may be the interpretation, sexual magic and fertility rites have been associated with Indian culture. From explicit sexual postures to a wide variety of the feminine form – lavishly explored by artists – erotic motifs have been an extremely popular visual tool from the mythic past to modern times.

One of the most important figures has been that of the mother goddess. Let us remember that a whole range of scholars – Moti Chandra, Ananda Coomaraswamy, Mircea Eliade, D.D. Kosambi and D.P. Chattopadhyaya – have recognised the importance of her worship. From their external appearance, three kinds of mother goddesses or votive fertility figures can be identified. The 'opulent' mother goddess on a gold plaque, from

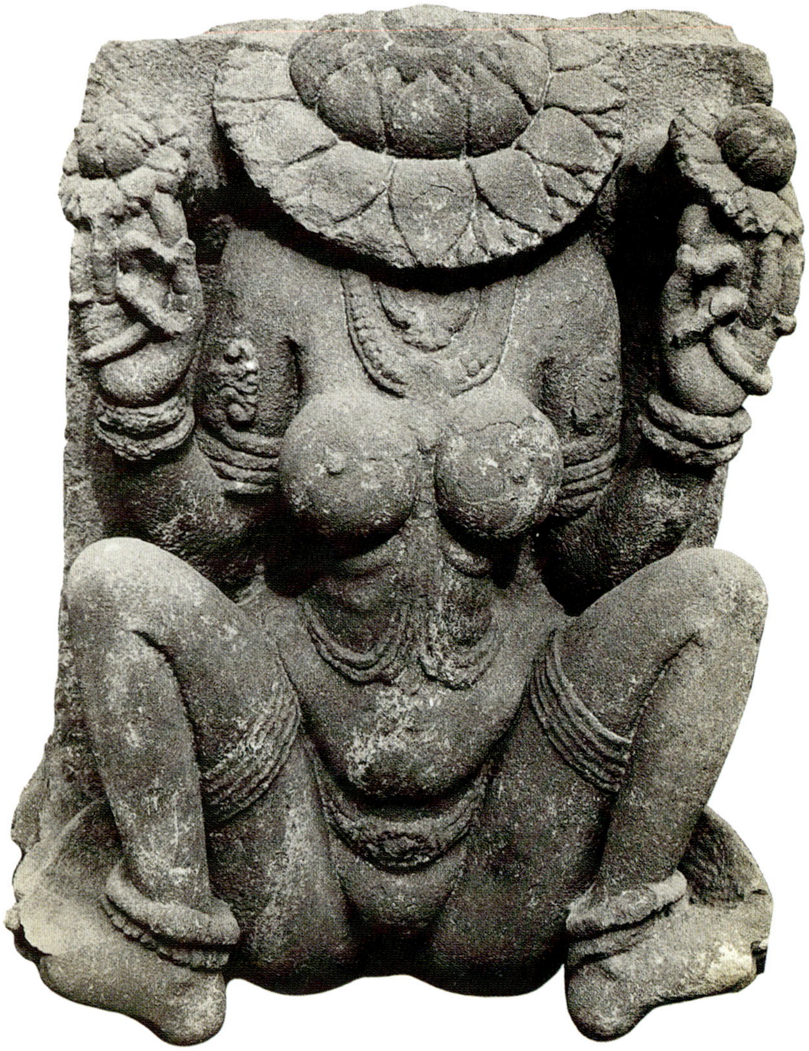

Lauriya; the 'personified yoni' type; and the goddess wearing five kinds of head ornaments known as the *panchachuda*. These goddesses, whether belonging to the *yakshi* types or the *apsaras*, represent fertility, plenty and creativity.

In fact, *yakshis* and *salabhanjikas* seen in the Bharut and Sanchi monuments in central India date to the second century B.C., and are the earliest depiction of sexual motifs. These monuments are related to Buddhism but the symbols are derived from the prevailing cultural traditions of the time. In fact, the visual representations of this period had a lot to do with widely followed cultic religions and much of the Buddhist imagery was derived from popular animistic art. 'The art of the early stone monuments of Sanchi and Bharhut represents the revival of the primitive and popular traditions which were inhibited in the court of Asoka Maurya,' says Ray Niharanjan, an art historian.

A reading of the proper names of the donors, as etched in the monuments, shows that they came from all walks of life. They were monks, nuns, merchants, scribes, householders, artisans, scribes, weavers, masons, potters, bankers and merchants. More importantly, we come to know of their religious affiliations. Apparently, they followed the cults of

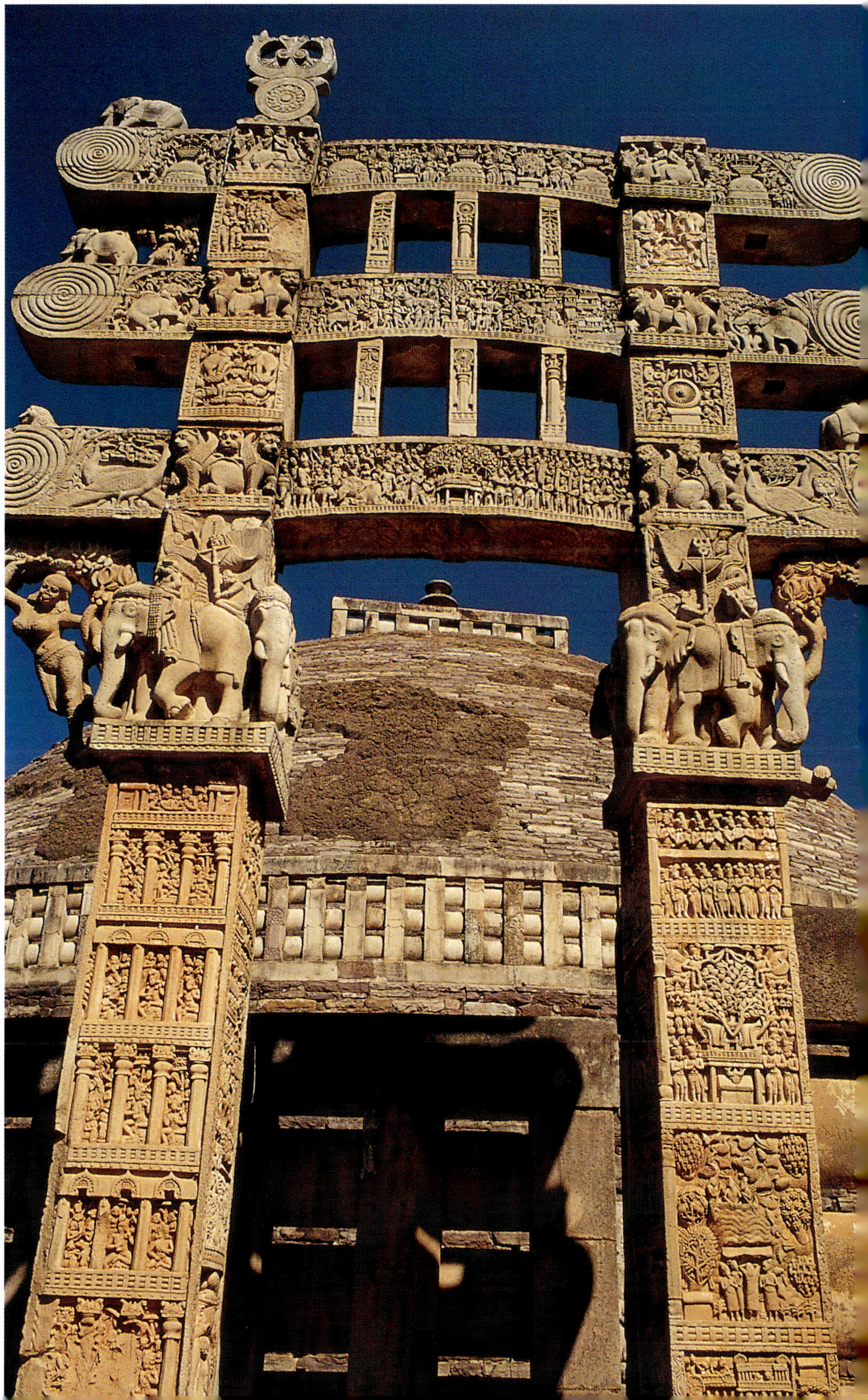

The eastern gateway to the Sanchi stupa is rich in motifs. It shows the *yakshi* known for her luscious form. *Facing page:* Lajja Gauri from the Chalukyan period. A representation of the fertility goddess, one of the four forms the mother goddess symbolised. *Previous page:* An eighteenth-century, yoni-shaped ritual vessel.

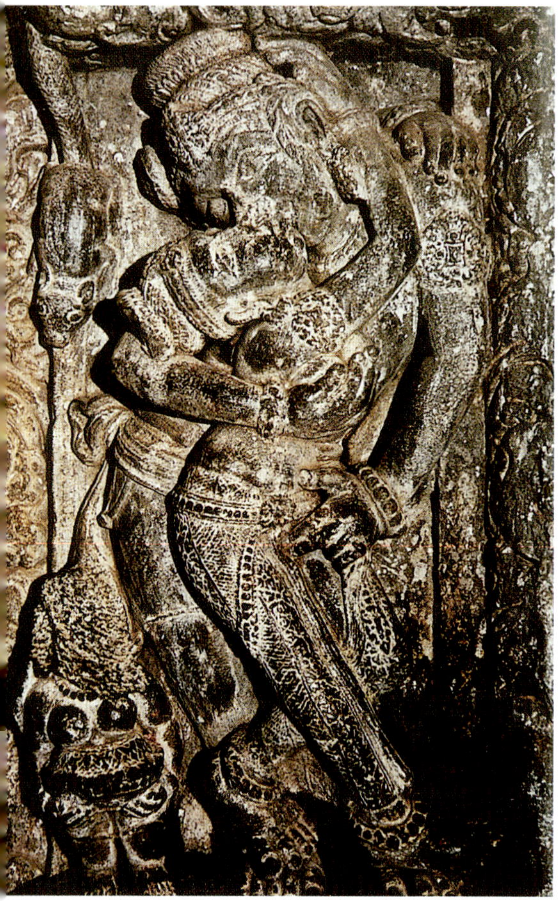

Yaksha, goddess Sri, or the Nagas, all of which were well established.

Since the Vedic period, Sri has been the goddess of abundance, fertility, bliss, prosperity, luck and beauty. In the Sri-Sukta of the *Rig Veda*, she is known as *ardra* or a green plant, full of life, a guardian deity of agriculturalists. Sri is mentioned in the Sutra literature of the pre-Christian era and also mentioned in Buddhist literature. She is a compatriot of Lakshmi, Prithvi, Sasthi, Sinivali, Raka and Jaya Sachi. Ananda Coomaraswamy refers to her as the goddess of fertility and love, basing his idea on the *Sankhyana Grihyasutra* of the fifth century which mentions offerings made to Sri at the head of the bed.

The erotic images of the goddess are symbolic of abundance and creation. They are taken from nature and are representative of its importance in fixing the idea of auspicious creativity and prosperity. One image has Sri accompanied by two elephants that are shown pouring water on her *ardra*, keeping it constantly wet. This connects the fertilisation of the female to the earth, which needs to be watered in order to sustain life. It is also representative of the clouds that rain down on the earth converting bareness into bloom.

Some images are non-erotic and indirect in their representations of the act of love and of fertility. Devangana Desai in her book, *Erotic Sculpture of India*, notes one such image on the Sanchi Stupa. It shows a man holding a lotus and a woman holding a cup. Below them are pots and symbols of luck, followed by an entire frame with a lion and a deer that is placed on a lotus plant. The plant rests on the shell of a tortoise (symbolising water, which sustains all life forms). On the northern face of the same pillar, a female sits, legs spread, with a lotus blooming from her navel. The image is, again, a metaphor for fertility and plenty.

Other images not only describe loving couples in pre-coital postures but also the happiness involved in such an act. A typical depiction shows a man and woman in blissful union, oblivious to the world, while another woman, often the *sakhi* (friend) of the female, stands near the bedchamber, looking at the couple with a serene, content and happy smile.

As mentioned earlier, the metaphors continue into the medieval period, up to modern times. Representations found on pillars can also be seen in the poetry of literary trendsetters such as Kalidas. One unique symbol links Kalidas to these depictions – that of a woman performing a vegetation rite with the aid of her male partner. Visually, one of her legs is on his and the other on a tree. Kalidas' writings term this as *upabhagaksama*, literally implying that which is fit to be enjoyed. This statement applies both to the tree and the male, and once again links nature with issues of fertility. The dual representation in this image does not disregard the human union. In fact, it connects the two and probably suggests that the coming together of a man and woman is a principle of nature, and every living object contributes to the process of creation.

Bodies fuse together in this erotic pose. Indian artists were not shy of showing couples in close and frank intimacy.

Facing page: An ivory sculpture in which the kiss represents not only the striving to be together but also the fluid langour and complementarity of body postures. *Madurai Temple Museum, Tamil Nadu.*

These erotic images did not remain the same as the ruling dynasties of India changed. They adapted themselves to the social norms of various periods. But the belief that they were auspicious and pure remained intact.

The Gandhara and Mathura schools were two important art rejuvenators of the ancient period. The Gandhara School of Art included erotic symbols indirectly in Buddhist monuments, primarily depicting them through couples holding the lotus and the cup. The art of Mathura, on the other hand, was influenced by the Kushana royal court. In this period, erotic images gained a certain romantic twist to them. Polygamous men, pre-coital scenes and Bacchanalia are common in the art of the times. Isolated examples of *maithuna* couples are also seen in the narrative Jataka panel of the Buddhist pillars of Mathura.

After the eighth century A.D., couples in coitus became an integral part of motifs in religious buildings, where they were regarded as auspicious. This was especially so for door jambs in the Kushana period. *Maithuna* motifs are also mentioned in the astronomer Varahamihira's *Brihatsamhita*. *Yakshas* and *yakshis* are deities of fertility which vegetation cults worshipped for progeny, wealth and prosperity.

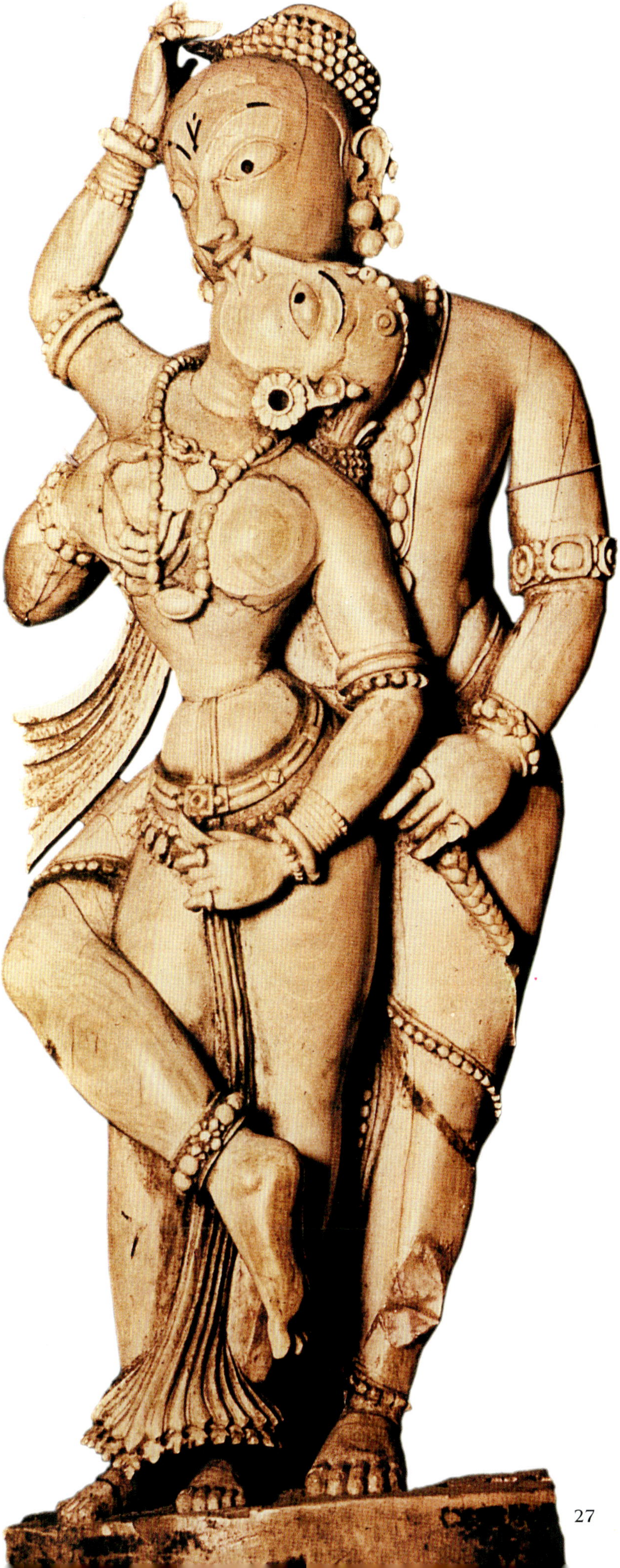

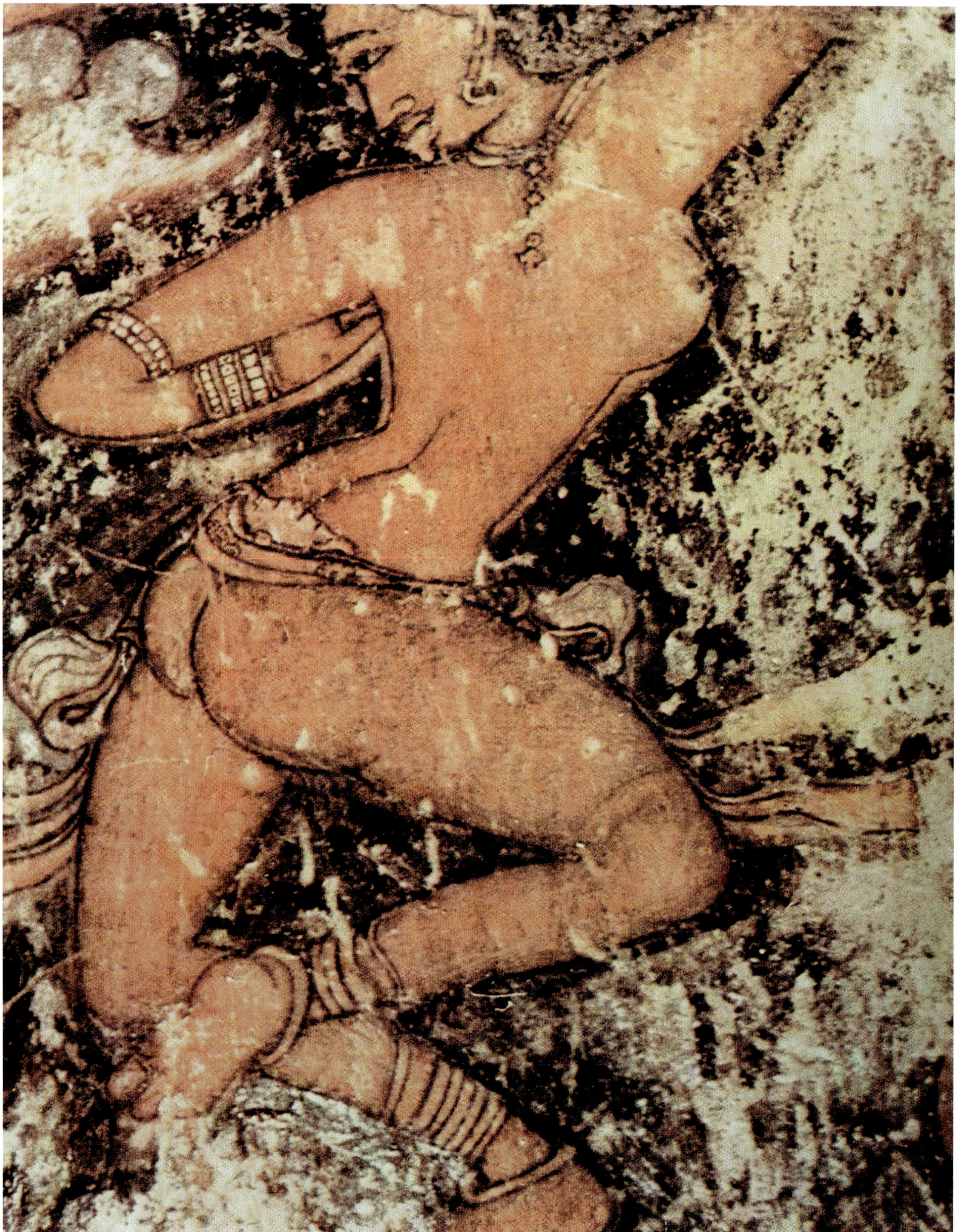

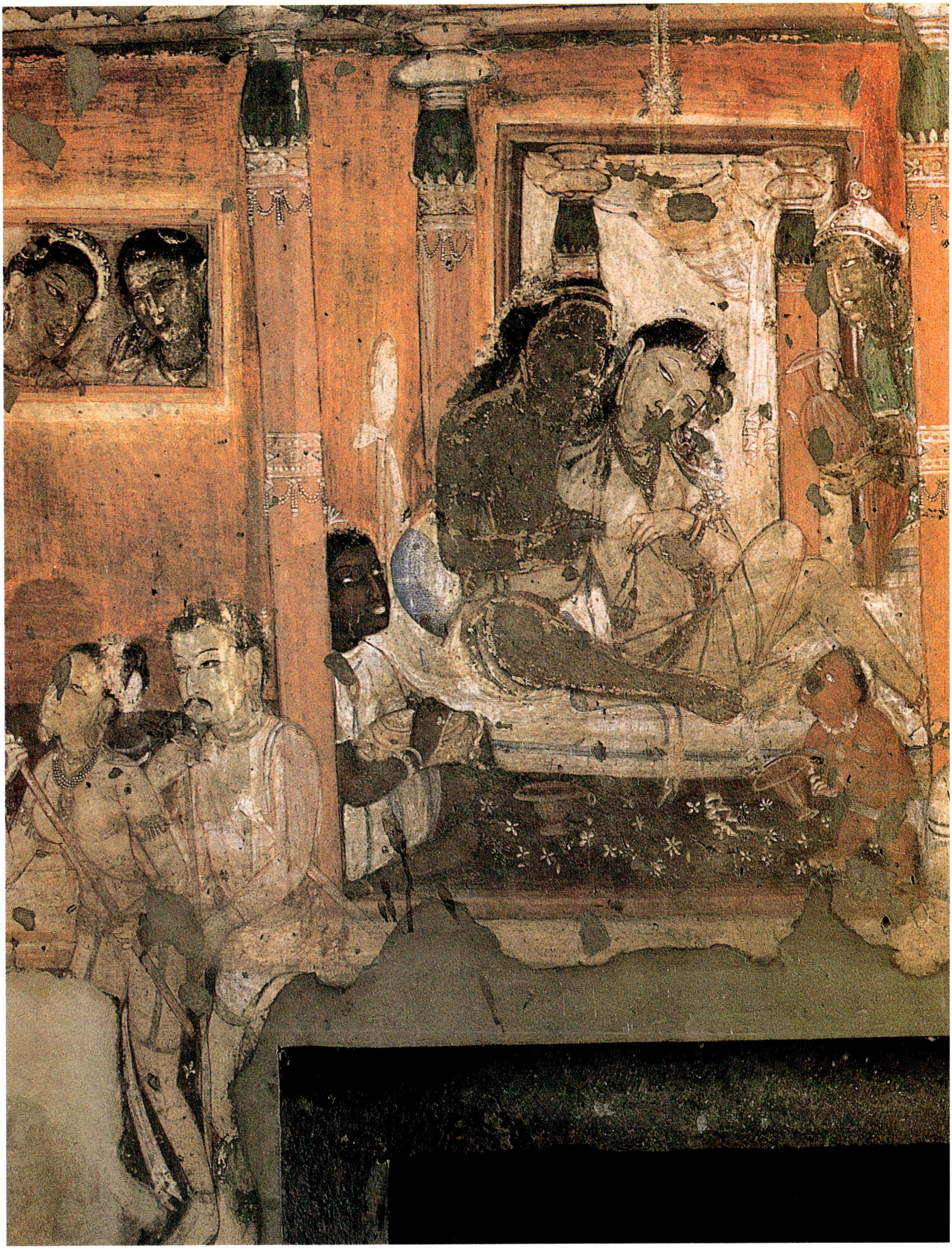

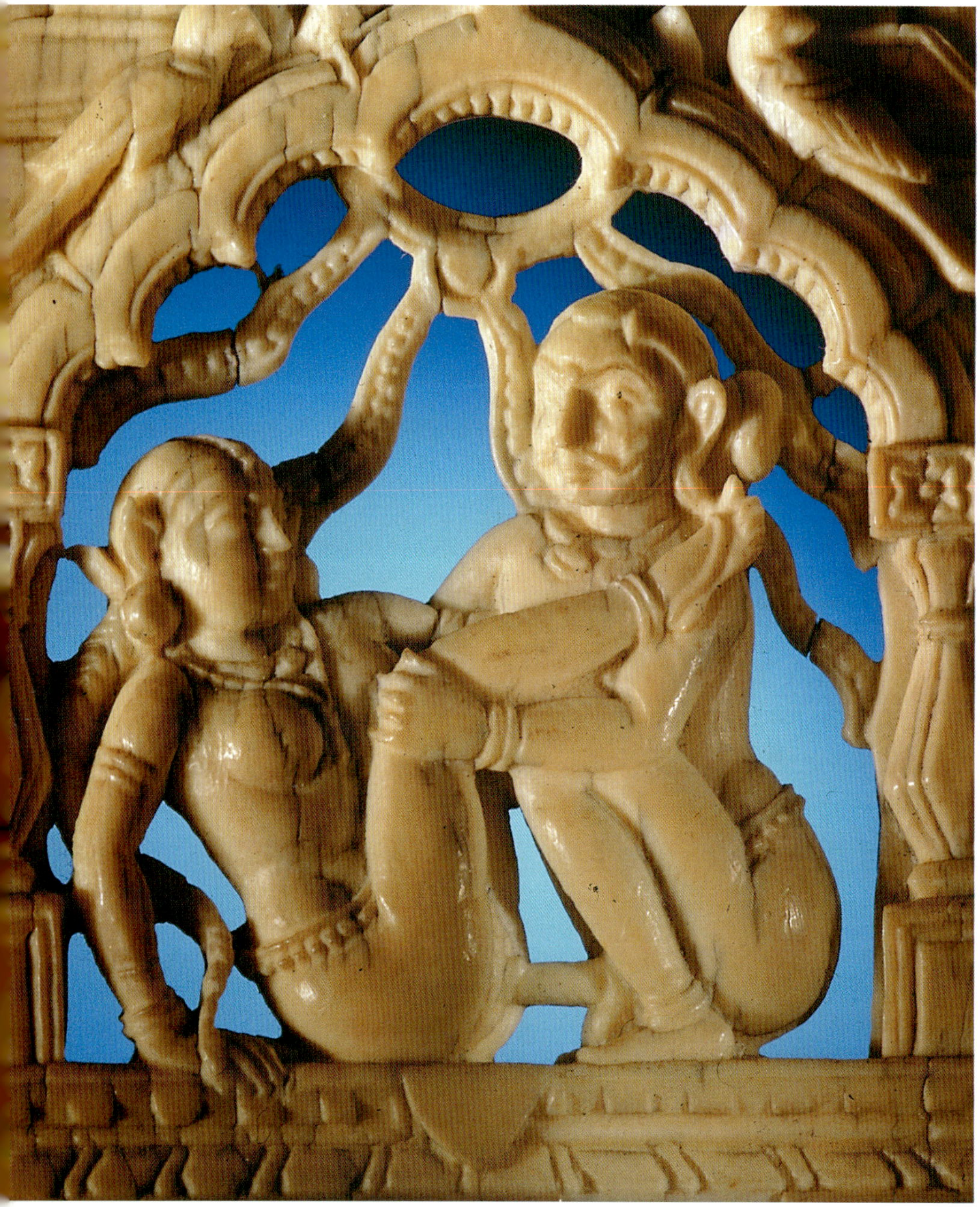

An ivory panel showing a couple in the sexual act – *maithuna*. Coitus is a metaphor for divine union in this Chola fresco from the Brihadesvara temple. *Facing page:* A Rajasthani handicraft made like a toy. The object was to teach young people the art of love. *Previous pages:* Wall paintings are suffused with the beauty, grace and elegance of the female form.

Buddhist monuments showcase *maithuna* as central motifs. These were considered auspicious and were usually placed at the entrances of caves, probably to coax good omens to dominate and enter these places. Besides the *maithunas,* there were passionate couples and threesomes shown on pillars or on entrances. Buddhist art had another flourishing school, the Chaitaka School, which included more sensuous sculptures and engravings, such as those found in Amravati and Nagarjunakonda.

The fact that most Buddhists were from the commercial class, which had its fair share of those who indulged in passion, was reflected in its art.

This view of Buddhism – of one that encourages sex – seems extremely crude and contrary to what we have been taught about Buddhists. The reason their art takes this direction is because it concentrates on the life of Siddhartha before he attained enlightenment and became the great Buddha. It shows him in courts and scenes dominated by the harem, and the depictions are correspondingly luscious and seductive. Here too the *maithuna* plays an important role. In many cases, the *maithuna* is also replaced by the *salabhanjikas*.

Besides being sensuous, Buddhist art, especially in Andhra, is highly poetic. It often reminds us of Kalidasa's *Meghaduta*. The plastic art at Nagarjunakonda portrays the miniature verses of Amaru. One of these is on how a young bride feeds a parrot her earring when it attempts to repeat to the elders what the couple said to each other on their first night.

A question often asked is – How did art progress to what we call erotic? There were three primary steps in this progression. It started from couples holding hands at puja ceremonies. Then, with the upper classes redefining what was culturally acceptable, the *maithuna* became a central motif and couples were shown kissing, embracing and in various love plays. Finally, artists went deeper into conceiving the human figure. This art obviously would not have sustained itself had it not been socially acceptable. Scholars believe that the fact that *maithuna* monuments mention names of donors, proves that the erotic in art was accepted widely in society. They point out that the names could only have been included after seeking the permission of those who were involved.

The next development came with the *nagarika* (the cultured citizen) interacting with the outside world in the form of trade. The *mahari* or the *devadasi* tradition was a living reality. The Sun Temple at Konarak has a band of sexual motifs that runs around the exterior wall of the temple, relating to the *bhakti* and the *smarta tantric*

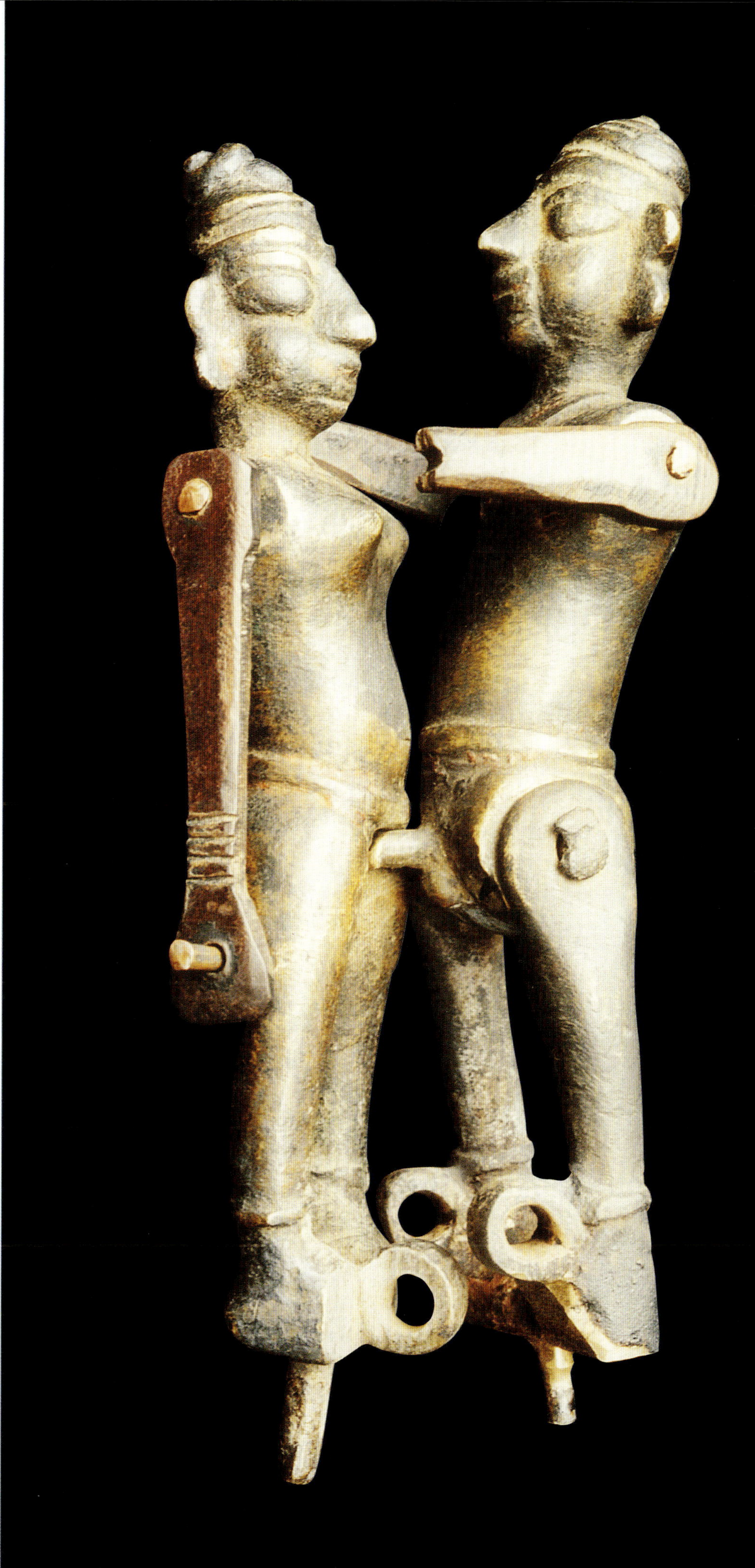

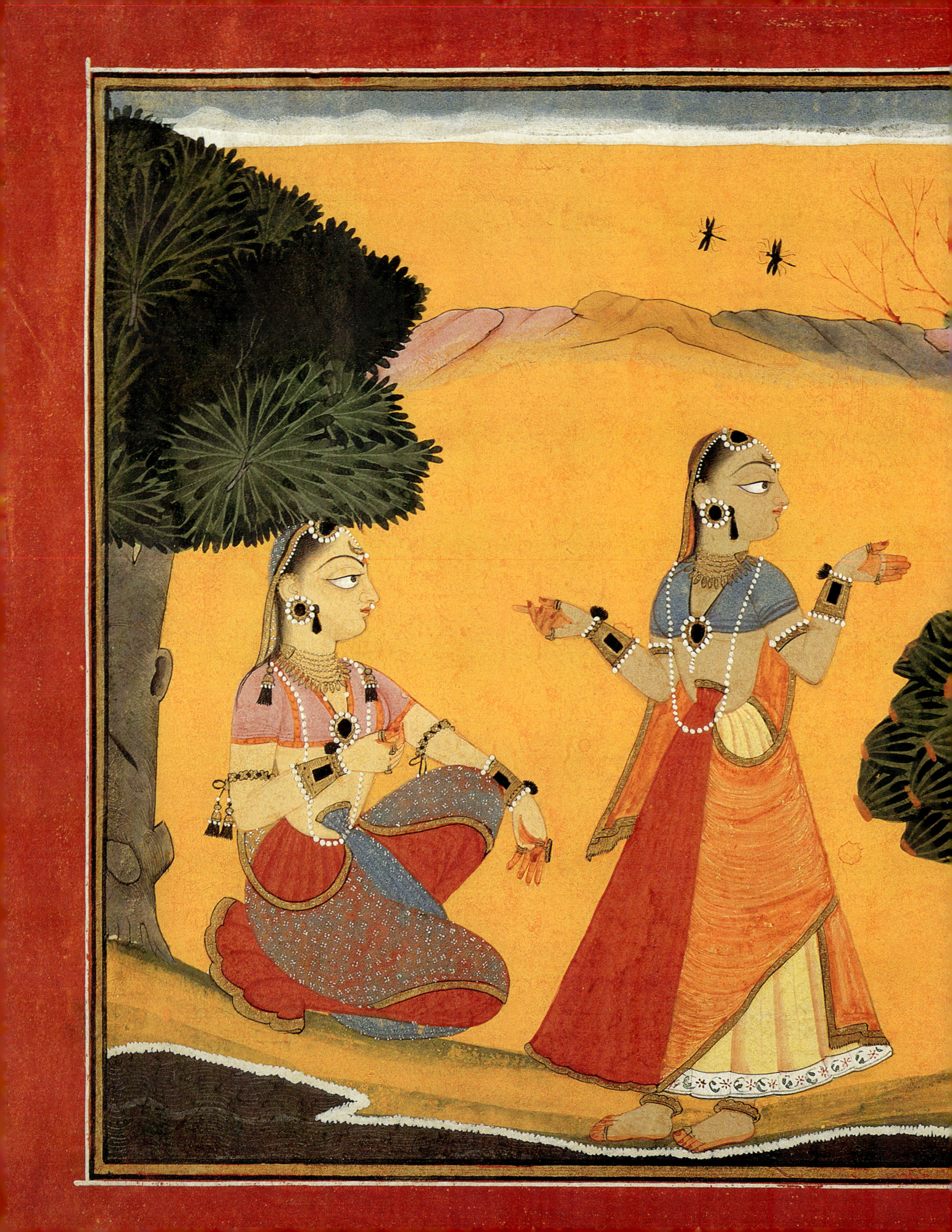

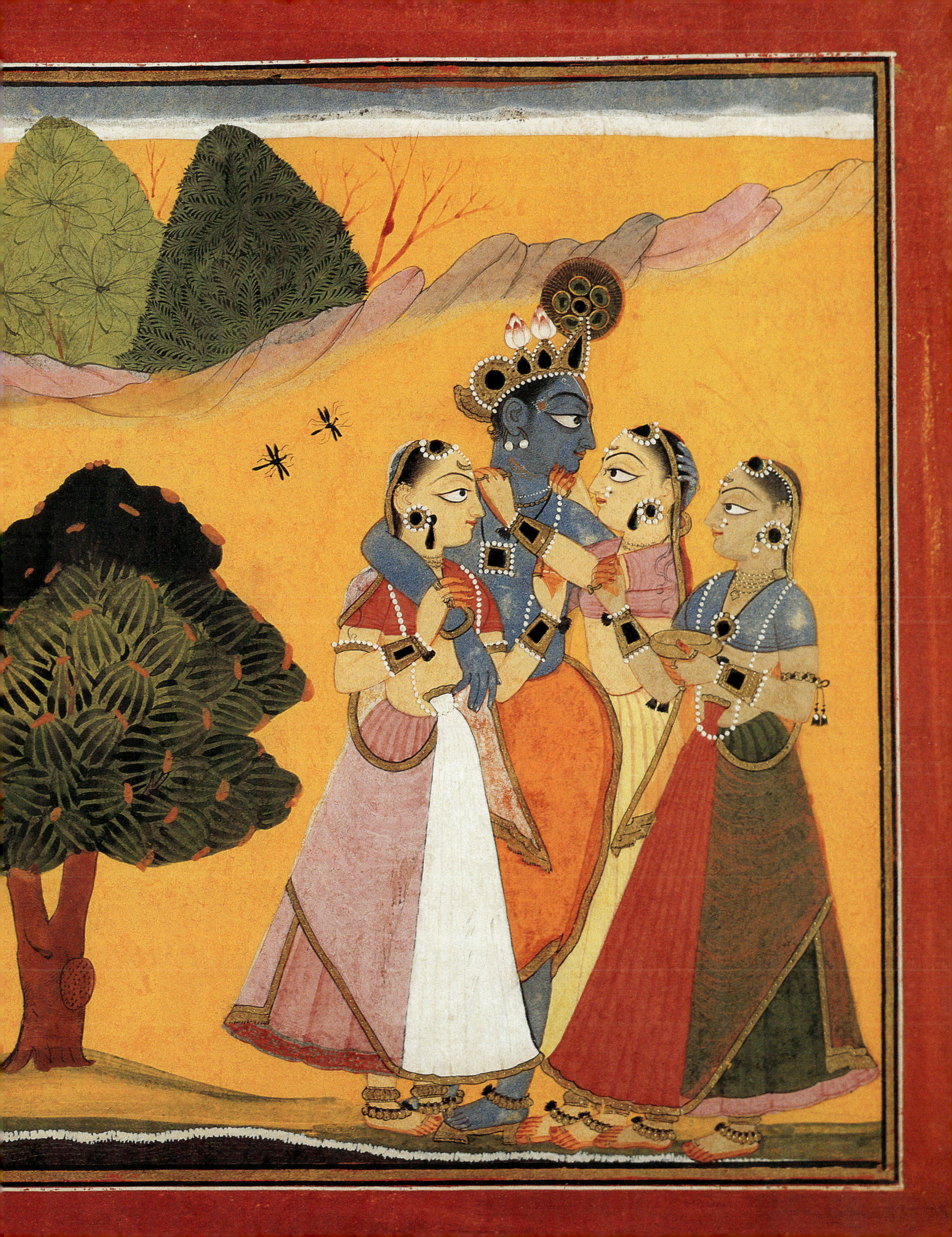

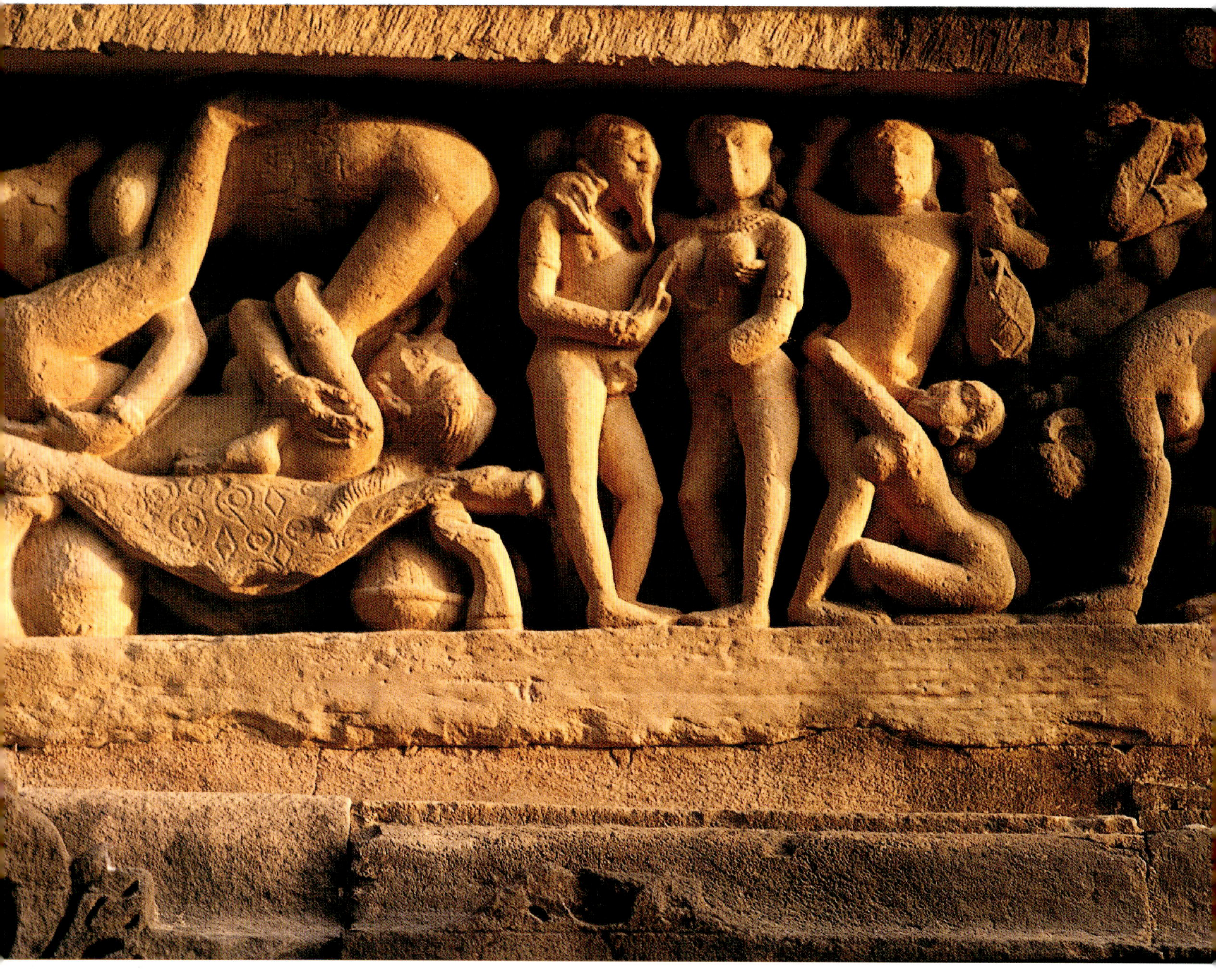

tradition. The band encompasses every erotic motif, from single copulating couples to frontal postures; oral sex in standing, sitting and seated attitudes. A striking image shows nude males and females standing with their legs apart over a phallus-like object. Then there are the *naga maithunas* that represent the fertility principle.

The Khajuraho group of temples is the epicentre of the Central Indian style of temples and is a site of erotic sensibility. Devi Jagadamba, Vishwanath, Pasvanath, Chitragupta and the Kandariya Mahadeva temples of the Chandela dynasty have a plethora of erotica. The erotic representations continue in Madhya Pradesh and in Gujarat. The temples in the Deccan plateau, be they in Maharashtra or the Hoysala temples of Karnataka in Belur and Halebid, portray sexual motifs in the basement rows and panels of the *Kakshasana* (sloping seat back of stone). Coital couples in the *kamasastriya* poses, including asectics with women; couples in mouth congress, or *kakila*, where the woman is held upside down by the man, are also seen. It is not as if all the panels of the *kakshasana* have such motifs. There are panels that represent deities and dancing women. While the Hoysala artists show cased erotica in the *kakshasana* in the temples at Belur, erotica was restricted to diminutive scrolls on the plinth.

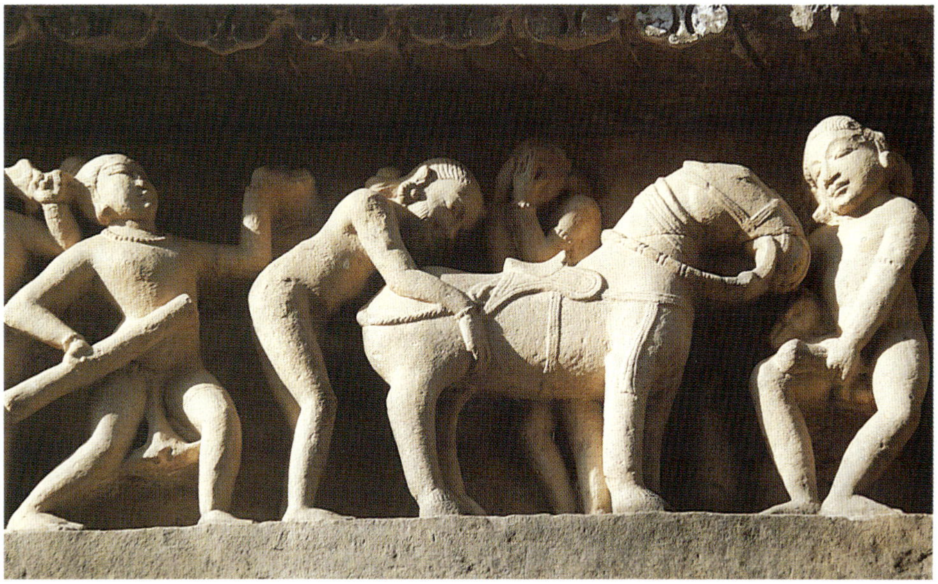

During the thirteenth century, the rulers of Vijayanagars who held sway over Mysore, saw new inventions of the erotic motif: Sugriva and his wife from the epic *Ramayana* came into play, Krishna and the *gopi* theme became popular. Female nudes associated with fertility also came into being.

The social norms of the period were in correlation with erotic visual imagery. While the Chandela temples had erotic motifs near the figures of deities on the external façade of the temple, they could also be seen on the sanctum sanctorum wall in the interiors. The Padhavali temples in Madhya Pradesh depicted orgies near divine images.

But erotic motifs in large groups are not seen in the temples of Gujarat, Deccan and Mysore, since art conventions had become inviolable. Erotica was displayed in temple recesses.

In the earliest representation of art, *maithuna* was not seen in religious buildings, but only in drawings and terracotta. After the fifth century A.D., the obvious depiction of sexual poses came about in stone sculptures, but they still did not graduate to forming a central part of temple architecture.

It was after the ninth century A.D., that a variety of cruder sexual scenes ranging from oral congress, bestiality, orgies, scenes from the *kamasastra*, were incorporated in the temple building, reflecting the social norms of the time.

The Lakshman Temple in the Khajuraho complex depicts animal passions in humans in the form of bestiality.
Facing page: A panel from the outer side of the platform of the Lakshman Temple is part of a running frieze showing a host of sexual positions.
Previous pages: Basholi Geeta Govinda from the *Chandigarh museum.*

Treatises of love

Treatises of love

Sanskrit has been the language of erotic texts in India. These textbooks on the art of love form a continuous sequence from the third century to the sixteenth century, and in contemporary India, these texts are found in vernacular versions and imitations.

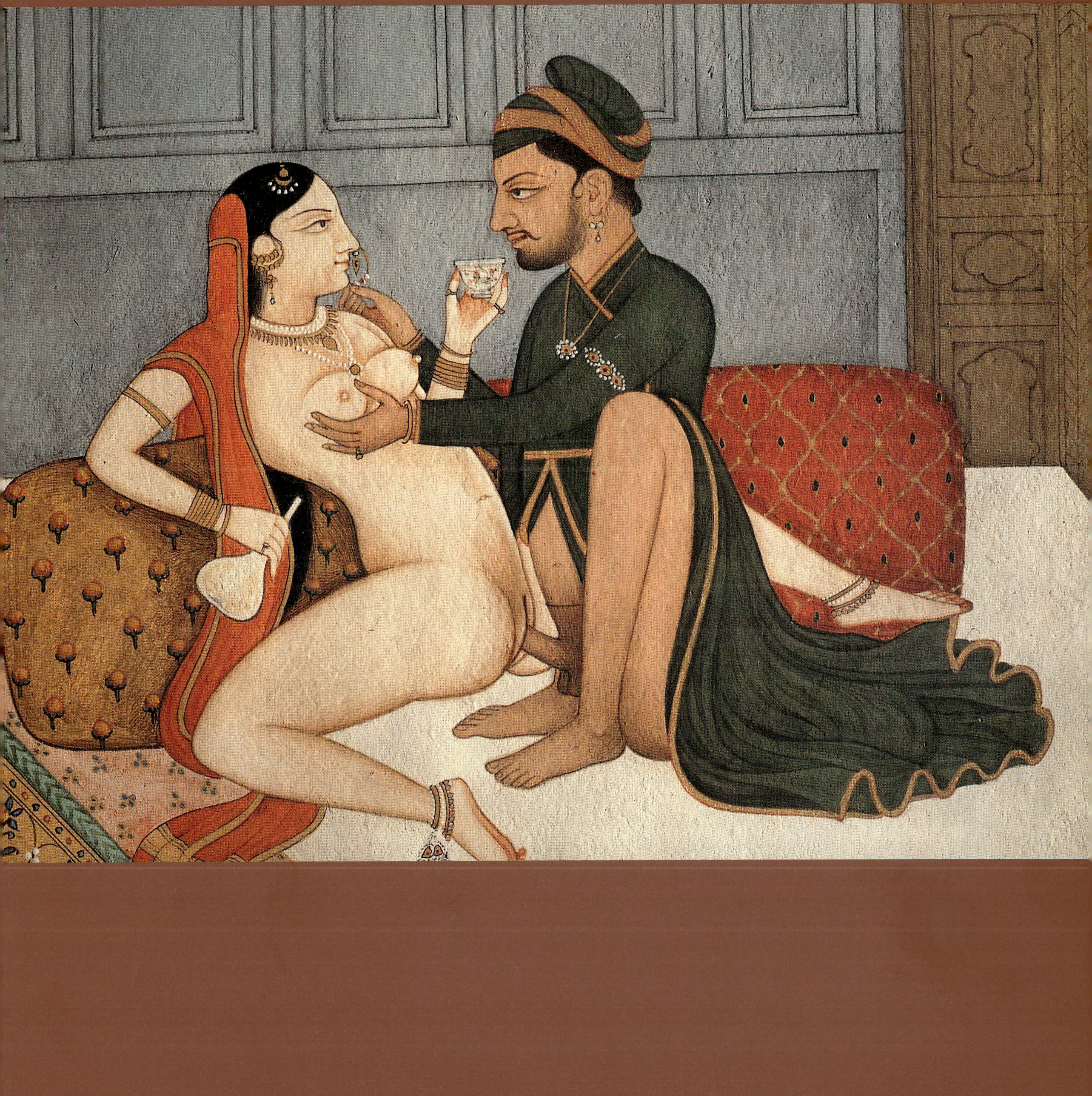

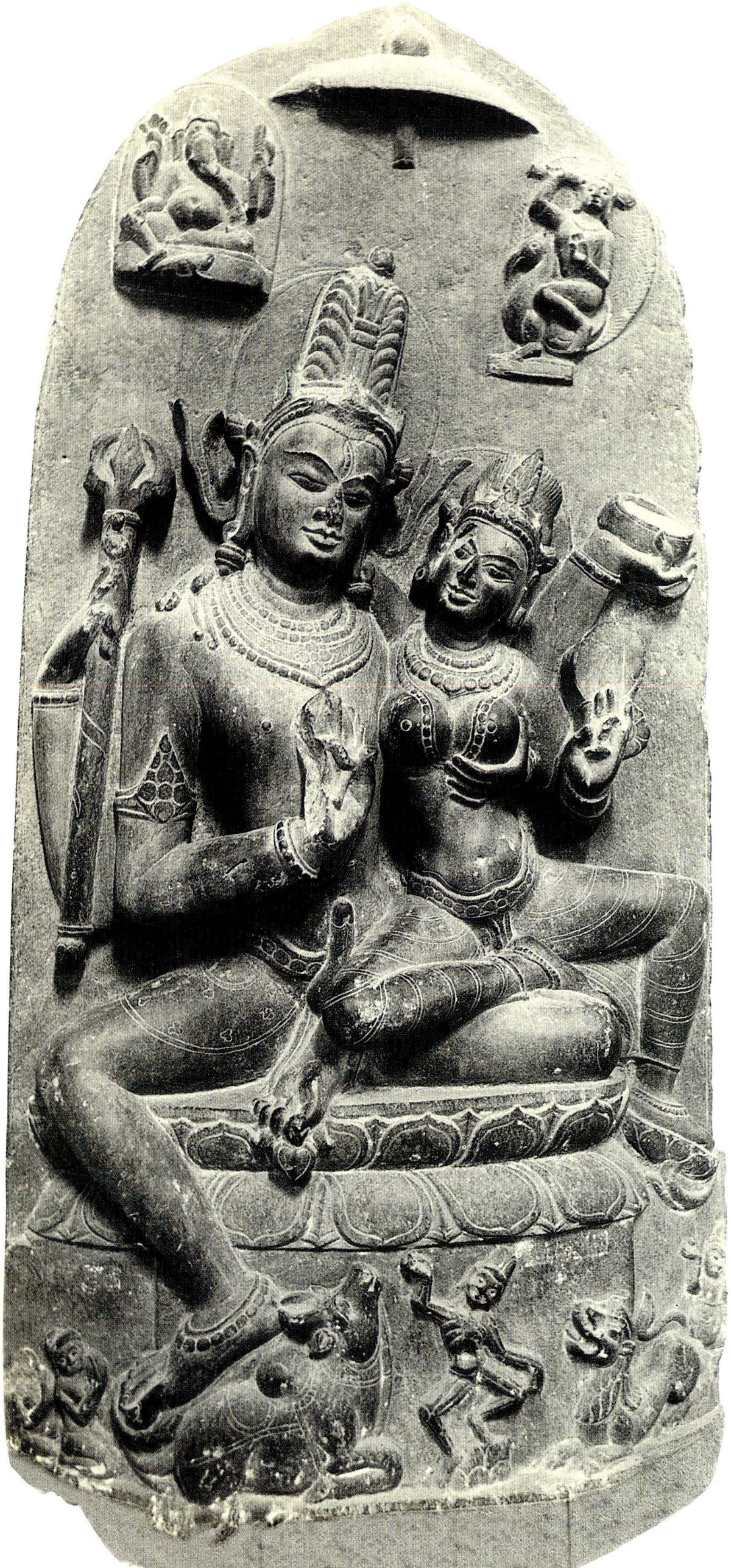

Most cultures, except the Judeo-Christian culture, produced erotologies in Persian, Chinese and Arabic, almost as extensive as those brought out in Sanskrit. But they have not retained their position in the way erotic texts have maintained their status in India. Why these love books are still considered 'classical' is due to the fact that sexual imagery plays a crucial role in Indian art, thought, literature and religion. Even where and when people were not literate, visual aids such as sculpture, painting, palm leaf books, erotic designs, posture-sheets, from the finest productions of religious art to peddler's wares and bazaar ornaments, emerged from the great erotic tradition of Sanskrit texts.

The first authors

One of the stories in the *kamasastras* associated with the origin of such texts emerges from a now-lost work. It refers to the legend of Lord Shiva falling in love with his own female emanation, thereby discovering sexuality and celebrating the pleasures of carnal copulation in an amazing 10,000 or even an incredulous 100,000 books. These treatises, it is said, were reduced by Lord Shiva's devotee Nandin to 1,000, and further curtailed by many sages, including one Dattaka. He, however, polluted a rite of Lord Shiva and was turned into a woman. When he regained his original form, he found himself equally conversant with the sexual habits of males and females. Honouring Lord Shiva, Dattaka proceeded to set down this knowledge in numerous treatises.

There are also accounts of a certain Babhravya Pancala who became editor-in-chief of a sexual encyclopaedia. Pancala entrusted the general introduction to one Carayana, the section on coitus to a Suvarnaabha, the courting of virgins to someone called Ghtakamukha, the duties of wives to a person called Gonardiya, the seduction to one Gonikaputra, that on whores to Dattaka, and that on the *materia medica* to Akucumara. It was this encyclopaedia which sage Vatsyayana probably reduced to portable size as the famous *Kamasutra*.

The earliest known text, as well as the most recognisable name in sexual literature, the *Kamasutra,* was put together by sage Vatsyayana in the third century. For a thousand years, the *Kamasutra* had no competitor. It was the only known text on love and sex. In the twelfth century, Pandit Kokkoka, seeing the changing social scene of the time, thought a new approach was required and wrote *Ritarahasya*. The *Ananda Ranga* was the other major medieval text. But both looked with nostalgic reverence at the *Kamasutra*, which was still a title to reckon with.

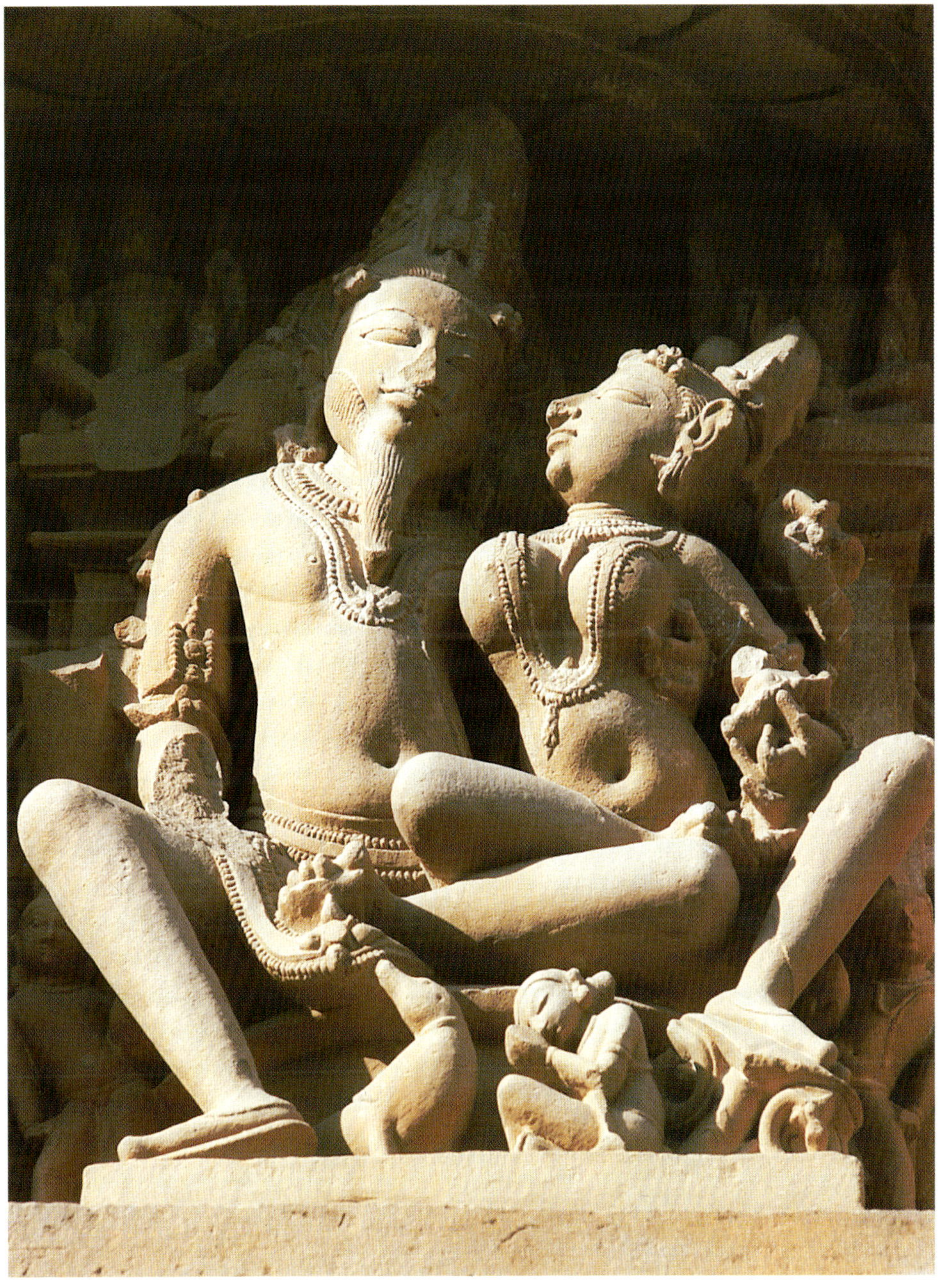

The Indian erotic tradition in texts was robustly represented visually. *Facing page:* Shiva and Parvati, a Pala sculpture. *Dacca museum, Bangladesh.* *Previous pages:* In courtly love, inhibition was not practised.

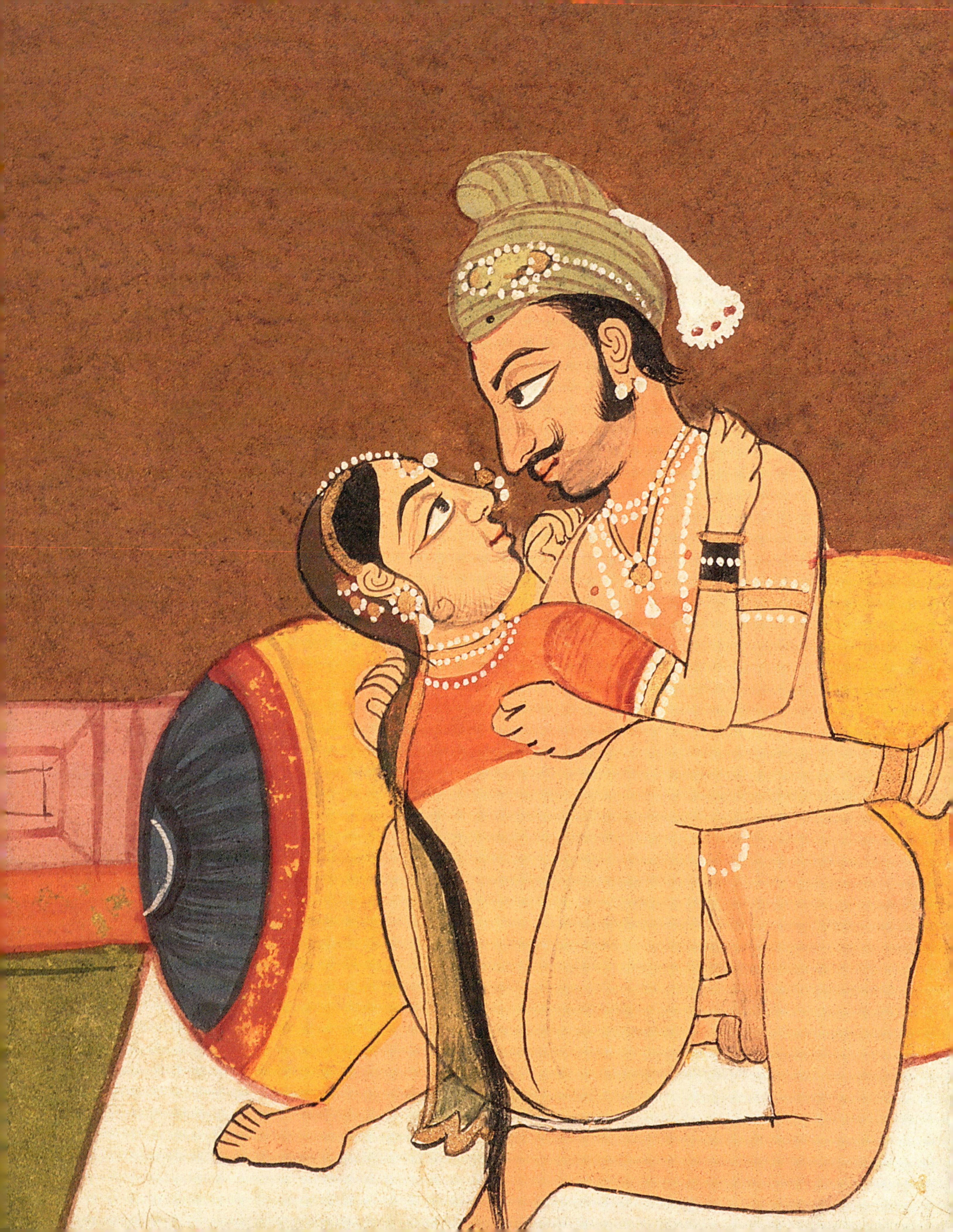

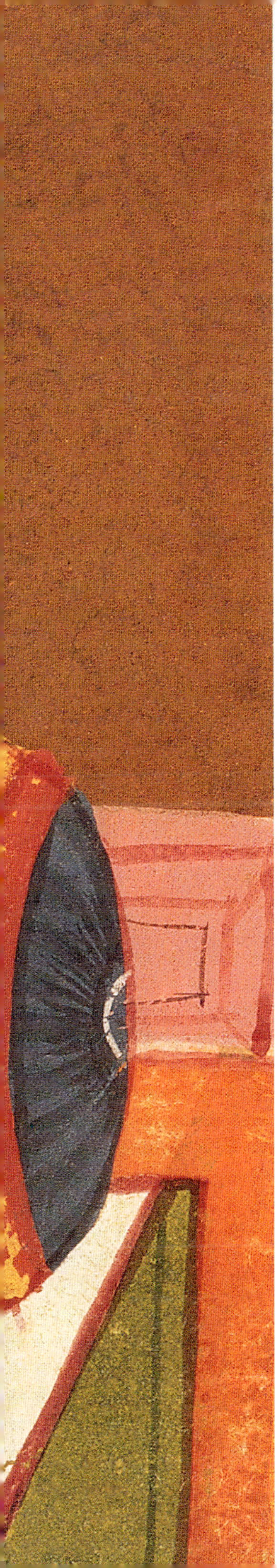

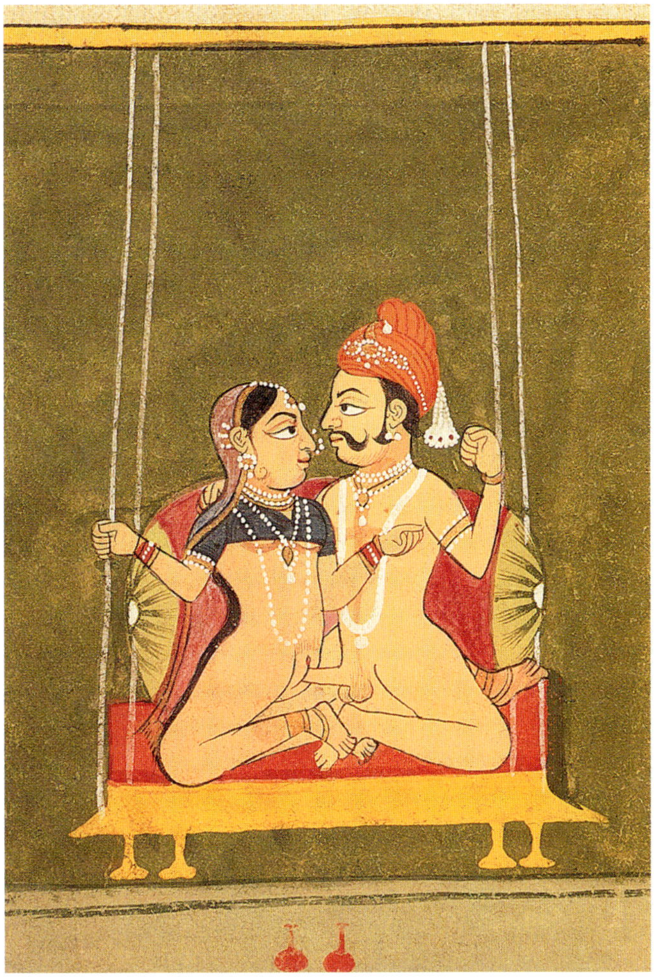

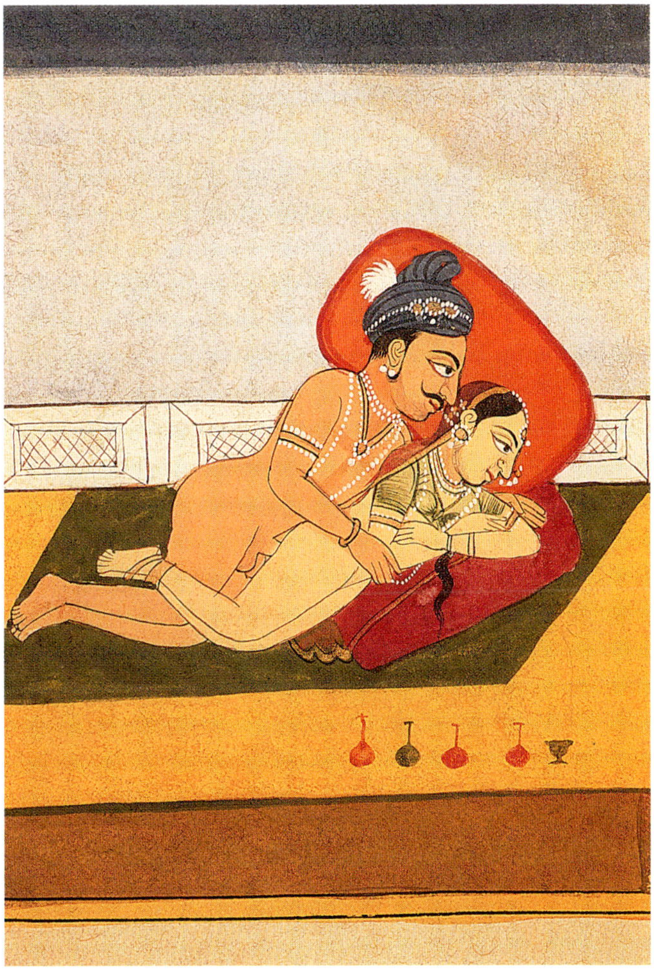

The *Kamasutra* was possible in an ancient Indian society that was liberated, happy and candid when it came to sexual affairs. Moreover, society was still more or less tribal. Women moved freely in public and young men courted girls without eyebrows being raised. Marriage as an institution had been established, but sometimes functioned on a plural basis. Both pre-marital and extra-marital sex were common. Most notably, courtesans were admired and socially accepted, and not looked down upon as is the case today.

Kamasutra: Philosophy and practice

Since the *Kamasutra* is the oldest text and a source from which all erotic imagery in art, thought and literature emerges, it is important to discuss in detail exactly what it emphasises. First of all, let us get this clear: the *Kamasutra* is a treatise not just on lovemaking, or merely a sexual manual, but also a reflection on the social and cultural practices of the period. It goes beyond sex – towards making a more complete and holistic society.

Yet, unfortunately, the book is one of the most exoticised of Indian texts carted abroad in all manner of forms and meanings. 'Do you actually do that?' is the typical reaction of a white Anglo-Saxon male who has gone through one of the many

Top: Rajasthani paintings show that society was liberated and frank, revelling in sensuality.
Bottom: The *Kamasutra* theme: man, woman, togetherness.
Facing page: How best to make love and remain in love is the *Kamasutra's* leitmotif.

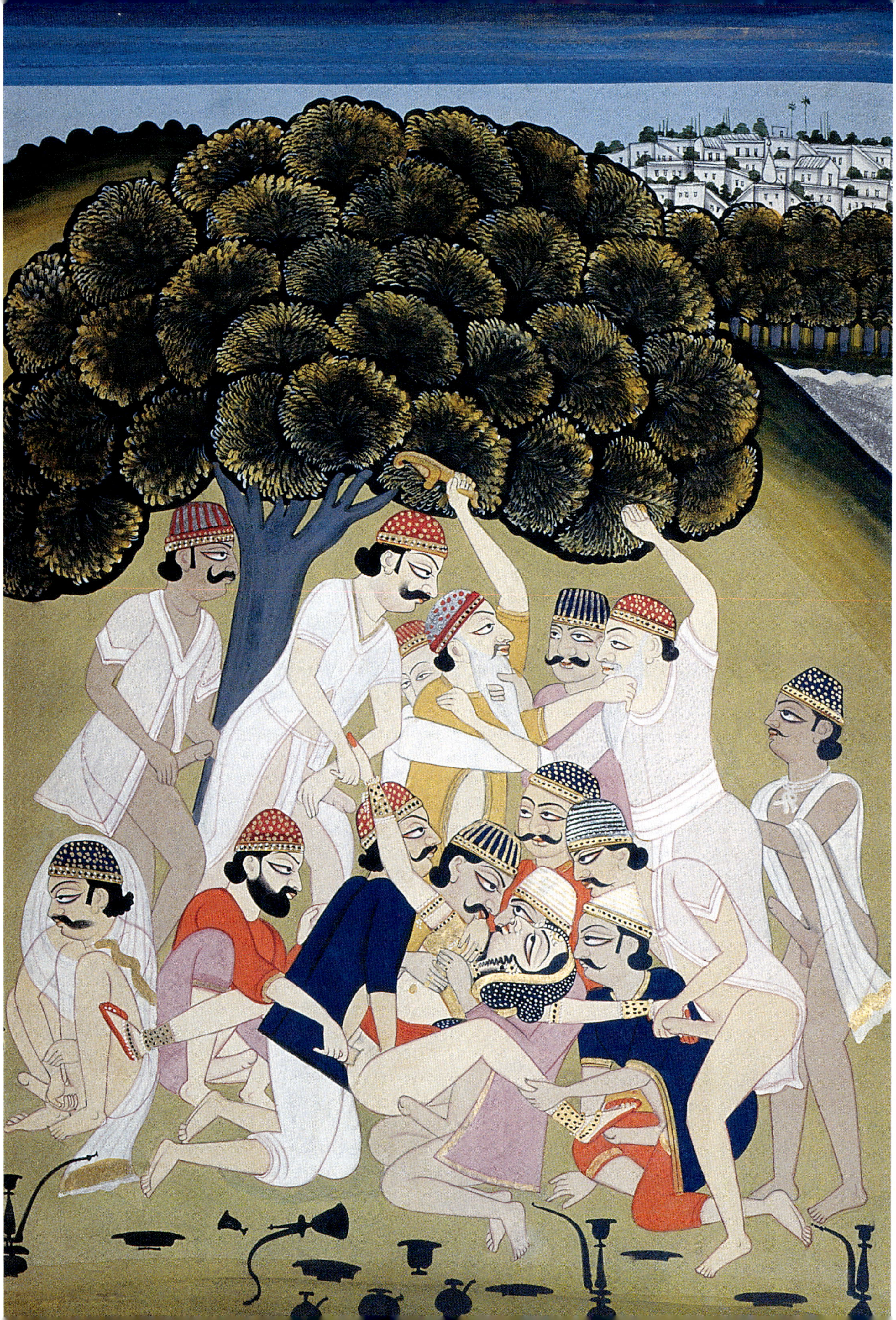

glossy *Kamasutra* productions. Often misread as a text bordering on pornography, the treatise is, in fact, a systematic study of the emotional and sensual nature of human impulses. However, it is often viewed merely as a source of titillation by many.

This glorious treatise on love and sex started in a meditative and reflective manner. Sage Vatsyayana undertook strict celibacy as a prelude to writing it. The text itself is seen today by scholars such as Chaturvedi Badrinath as an 'understanding of human life in all its expressions.'

It can be inferred from the *Kamasutra* that in the urban culture of the times, the *nagaraka* (cultured citizen) was deeply concerned with his sexual impulses. From the time a man attained puberty, the need for him to be well versed in the sixty-four arts became an intrinsic part of his all-round education. In this context, courtesans who were teachers of the art of love to the city's young men, and also doubled up as spies for the monarch, played an important role. Sex itself oscillated between the procreational and the recreational. Fertility festivals took place with citizens or the *nagarikas* treating the occasions as *kridas* or sports. Against such a backdrop, *kama* or sexual activity entered the portals of 'high' art.

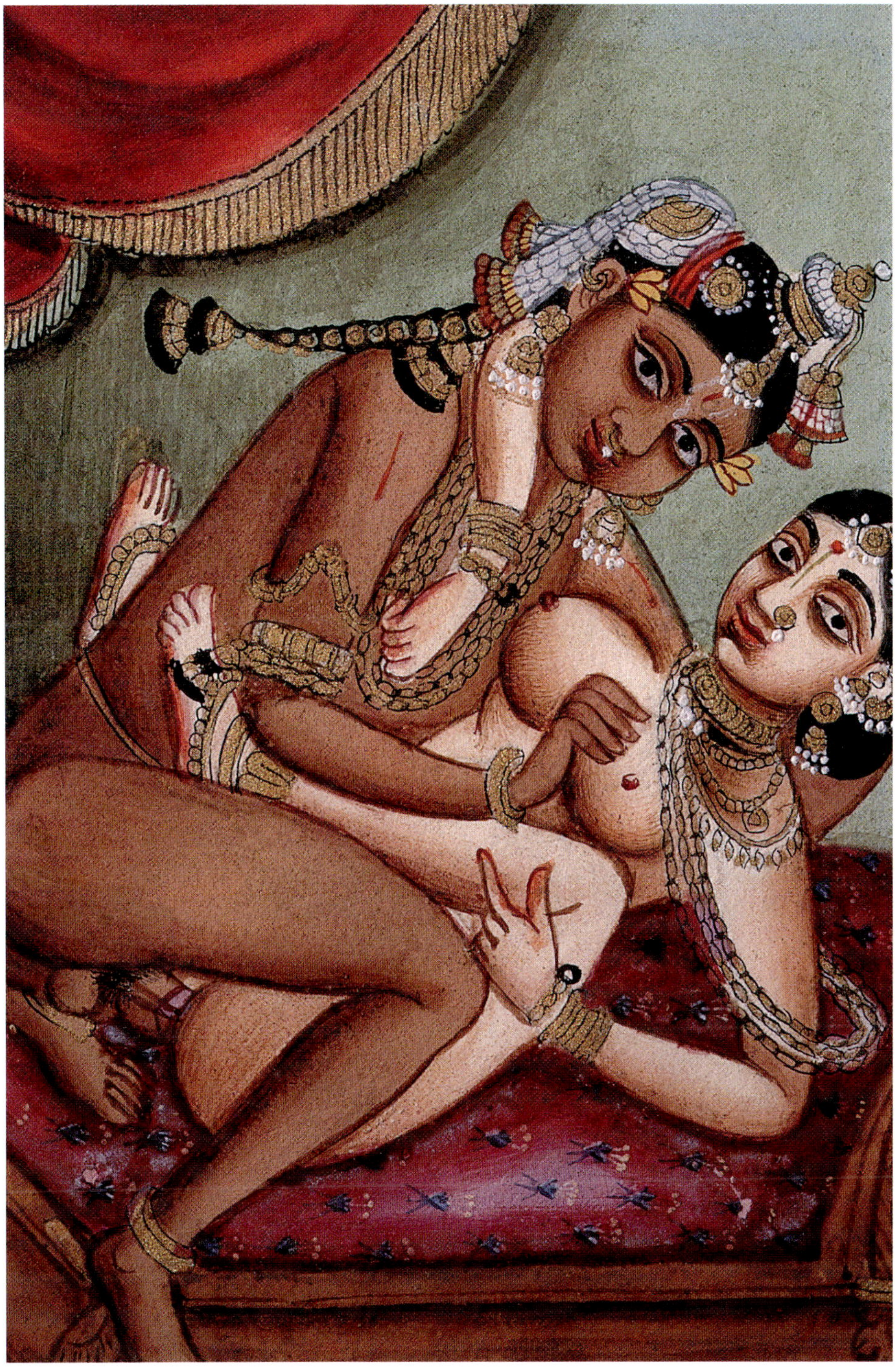

This Tanjore painting from Tamil Nadu leaves nothing to the imagination.
Facing page, right: Rajasthani painting with a fantasy theme: one woman with many lovers.

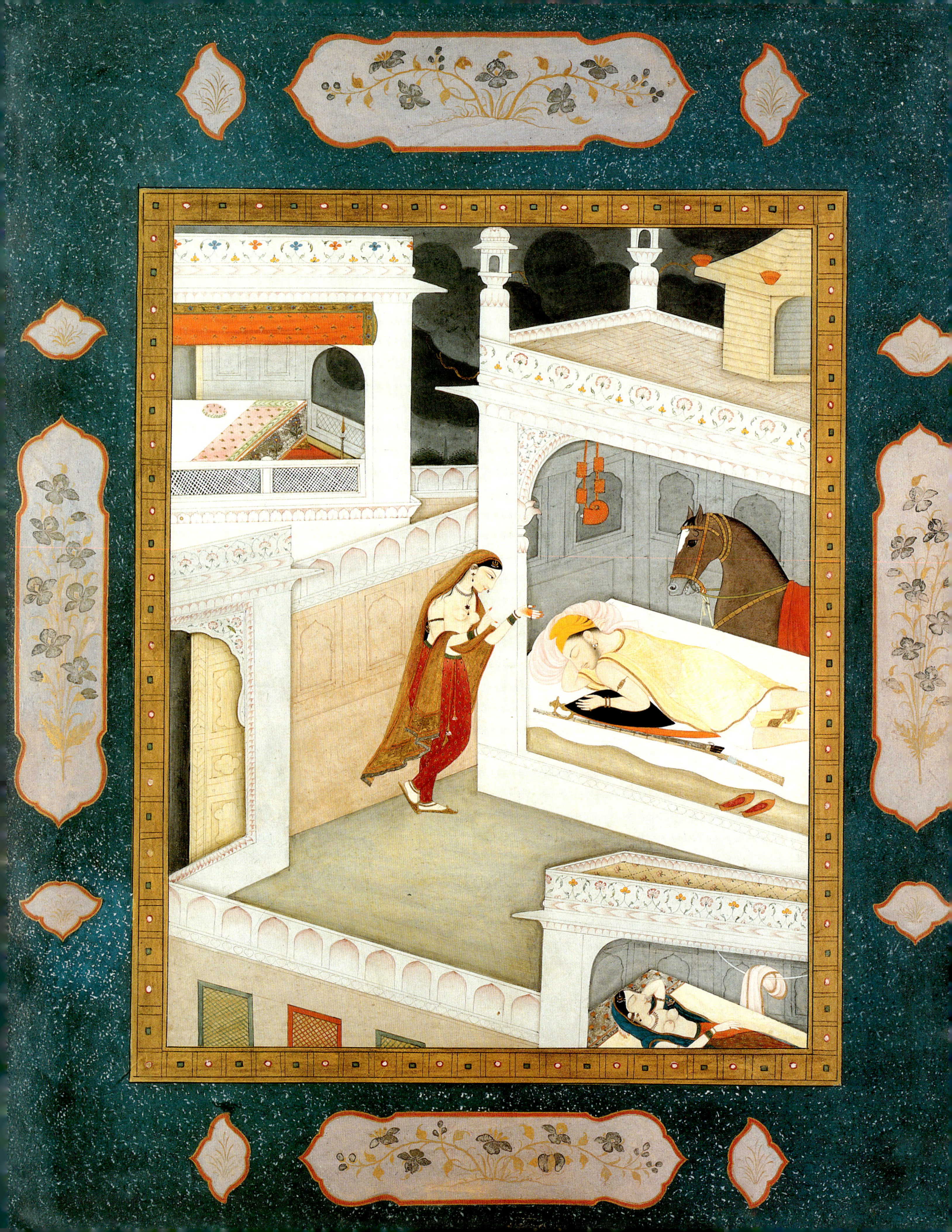

Singular emphasis was placed on the fine art of sexual intimacy as a book like the *Kamasutra* shows. Much time was spent on the preparation of love activities, with different yardsticks laid out for providing the right ambience. For example, the *Kamasutra* advises men to have a house near a lake or a river and have rooms marked off for different activities. It discusses interior decoration and goes into the details of what your bed should be like (large, comfortable, neat, with an artistic canopy and two pillows).

There is a set of codes to be followed by the participating couples – men and men, men and women, women and women, more than one partner at a time . . . . It is apparent that working men and women could not really have been part of the *Kamasutra* pantheon: they would not have had the time for the elaborate, pre-sexual preparations.

The inferences we can draw from the *Kamasutra* lead us to conclude that ancient Indian society was liberated; that sex was an integral and healthy part of its norms; homosexuality, lesbianism and orgies were known and accepted. Moreover, women were seen as equal partners in sexual activity and had equitable rights of pleasure. However, the *Kamasutra* is punctilious about the kind of woman it holds up as a desirable and winning ideal. She must be a master of the sixty-four arts and learn everything from cooking and gardening to word play, gemmology and the martial arts. Also, the underlying strain in the text implies that the woman has to be more 'untouched' than her male counterpart.

As for marriage, the *Kamasutra* believes in the idea of compatibility. This should not just be physical but extend to social and economic equality between families and partners as well. Values, beliefs and living standards should be common and shared. Understanding each others' hearts and minds is essential before enjoying intimacy. Adjustments are also deemed essential as they are the glue that hold a relationship together. A man needs to be gentle and considerate with his wife. A woman needs to reciprocate by showing equal respect, interest in his family and friends, and not broadcasting his secrets. Happy married life rests, says the *Kamasutra,* on a substratum of love, respect and trust.

The *Kamasutra* also conforms to the notion of *dharma* (the moral code practised in righteous life). There were three essential parts of the *dharmic* act – one that nurtured, cherished and

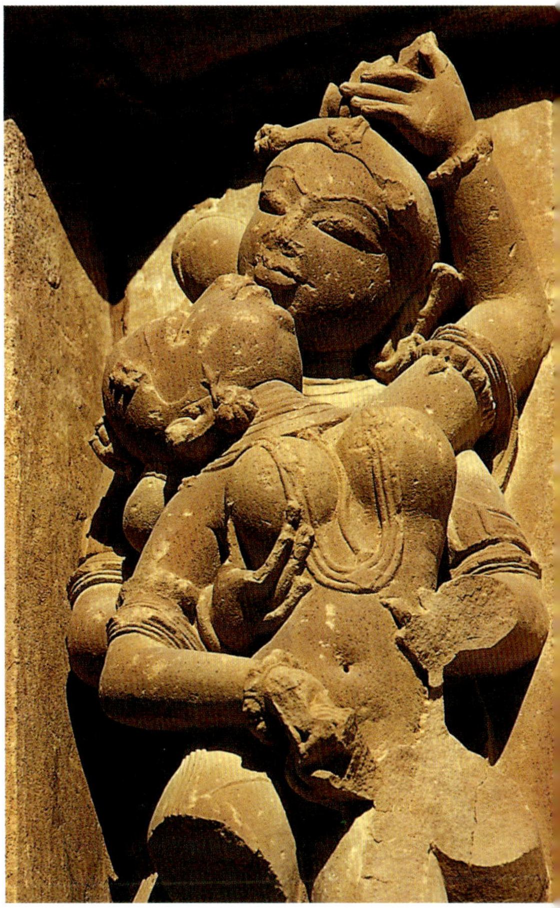

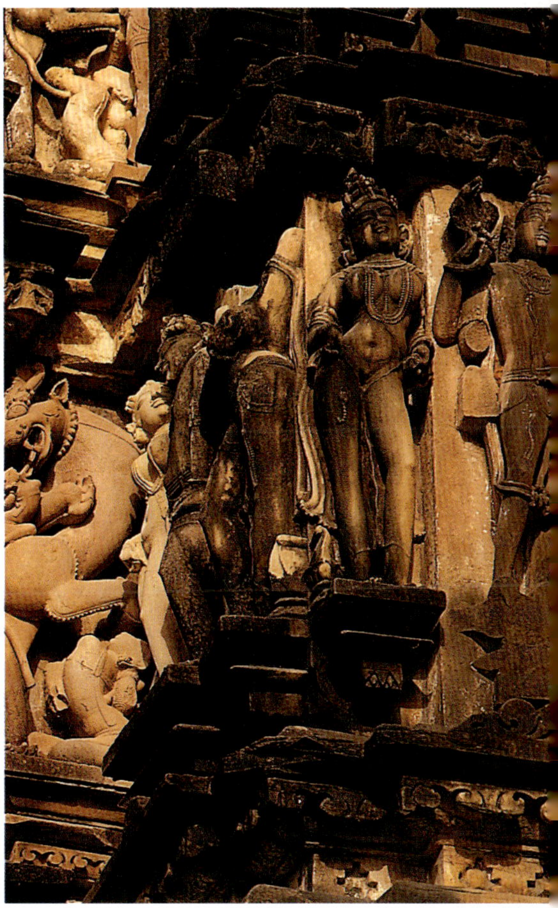

Top: The kiss is exhaustively categorised and described in the *Kamasutra.*
Bottom: Sculptures of passion throb in stone.
Facing page: A lady watches tenderly over her lover.

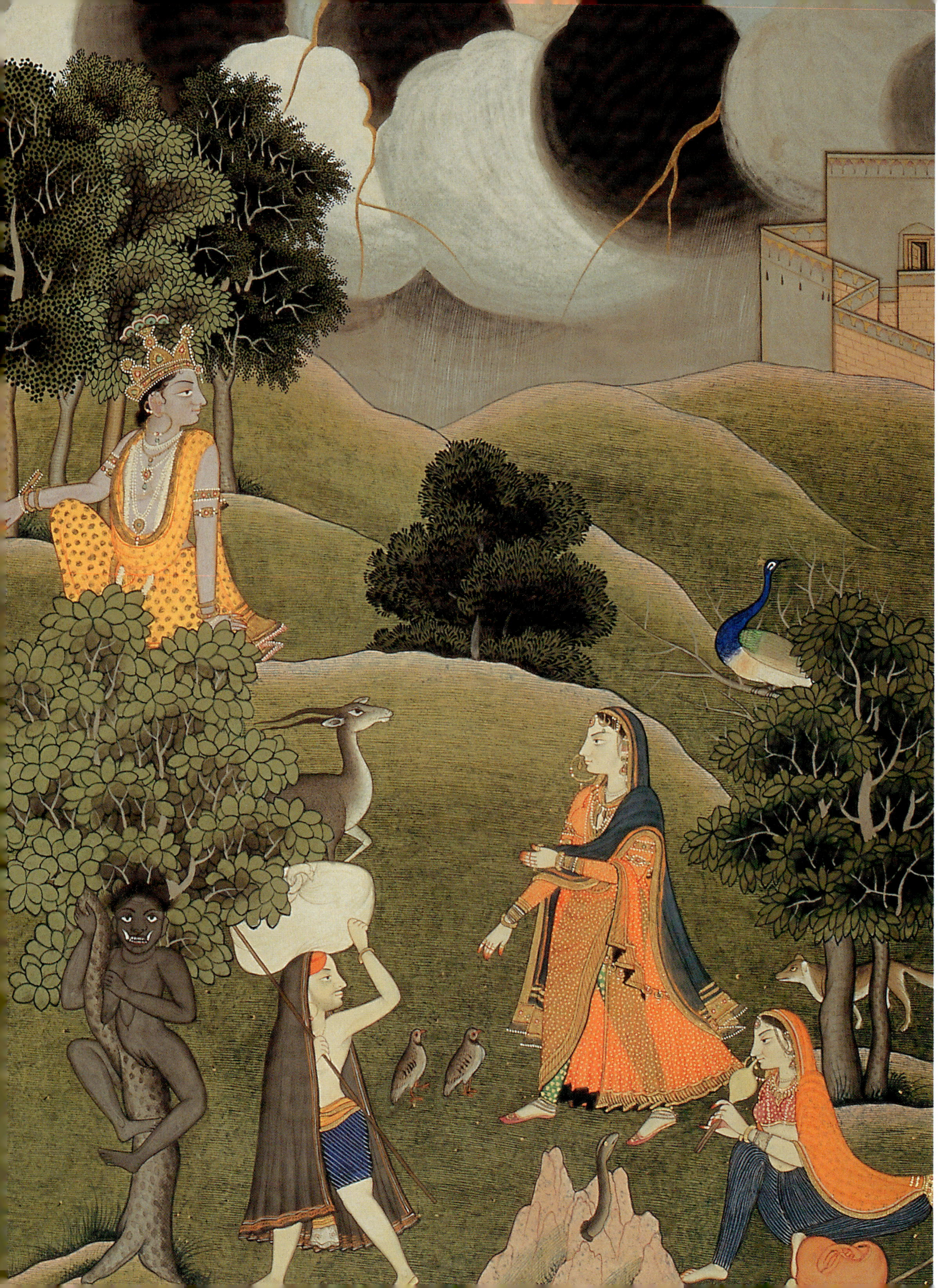

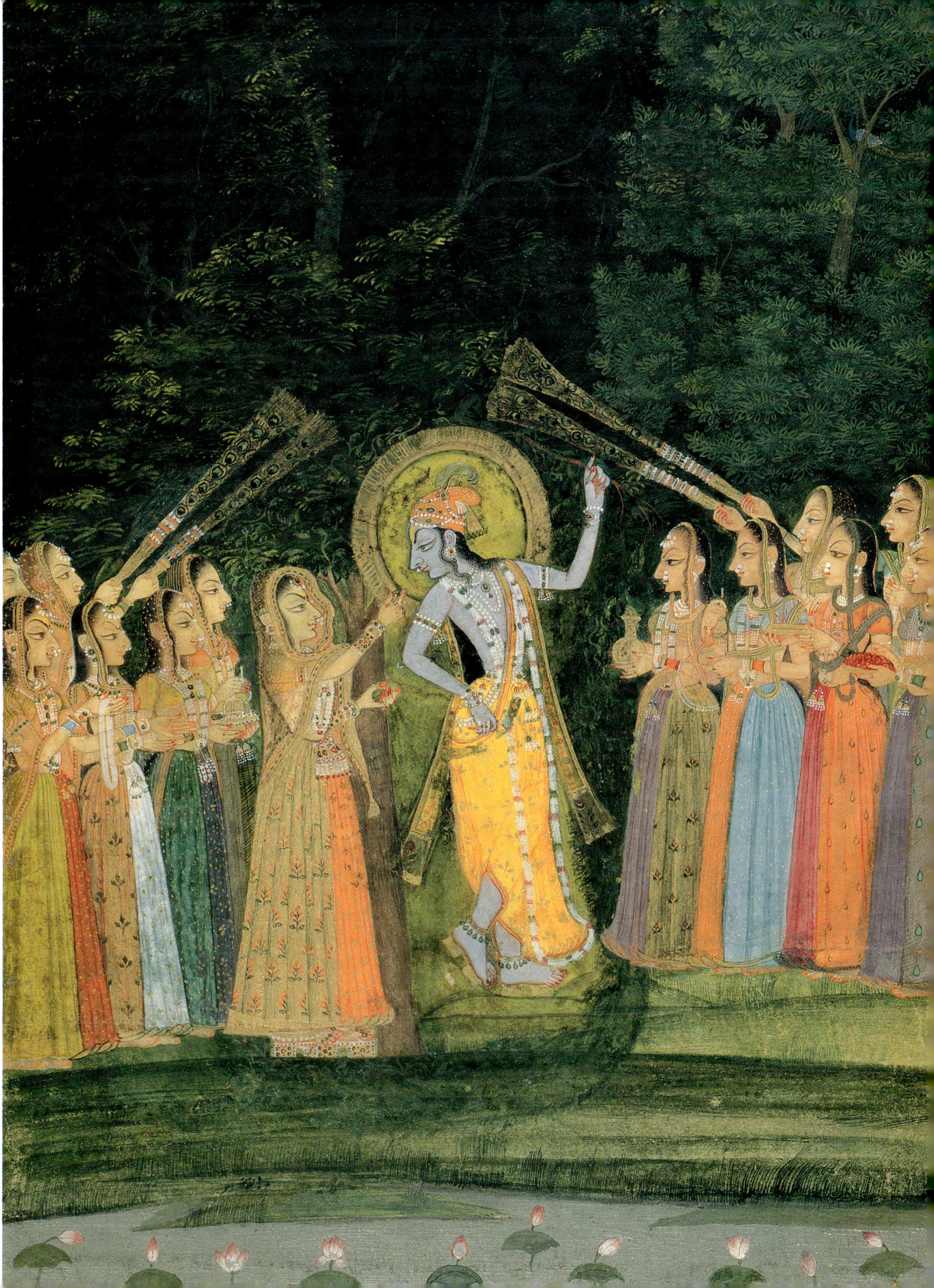

provided; that which supported the togetherness of two individuals; and that which did not infringe upon the right to another's being.

The book also has a physical philosophy. It sees sexual desires as being in direct relation to the senses of the body which are experienced as emotions and emphasise the urge to be at peace with oneself and the inner unity of the Body and mind. Vatsyayana relates physicality to the erotic, without which, he claimes, sex is meaningless. Also, since a holistic approach to recreational activities and art forms like dance, music, poetry and literature helps to develop self-realisation, and furthermore since sex is a part of such activities, it is vital. According to sage Vatsyayana, the indispensable parts of the erotic are knowledge of houses and architecture, jewels, metals and precious stones. These elements get much weight probably because the *Kamasutra* gives prominence to the place where sensual intercourse is practised, and also has men and women dress in ornaments and sensual clothes for their encounters.

The recommended pre-coital activities make the persons involved in the act more relaxed – a point the *Kamasutra* is well aware of. These recreational measures to ensure ecstatic sexual union are described in the *Kamasutra,* which contains recipes for secret love potions and tonics and lays down the activities an individual should perform during the day.

After rising in the morning, the sage advises that the man must brush his teeth, apply perfume, adorn himself with ornaments and colour his lips. Bathing daily is a must, and applying oil to the body every other day, essential. He should also shave his head and facial hair every four to five days, and all other parts of the body at intervals of five to 10 days. In the evening, there should be merriment, and then the man should wait in his room, with friends, for the woman to arrive. He and his friends should indulge in amiable conversation with her, thus putting an end to the duties of the day. The female, on the other hand, should be well versed in the 64 positions and should excel in a host of arts.

This alone is not important. Often the sexual act is related to the *ananda* of the *grihastya ashram* (house and family), though nowhere in the reading of the *Kamasutra* are the two related. For the first-time reader, the *Kamasutra* appears to be an extremely liberated treatise on various facets of orgiastic pleasure. From numerous positions, love potions, magical fantasy to dreamlike reality, from courtship to even providing the right ambience and atmosphere for indulging in sex, everything is there in the *Kamasutra*. There are even prescriptions for increasing physical beauty and for attaining sexual bliss. For instance, a man can regain virility by using the powder of dried lotus, blue lotus and *nagakesara,* in combination with *ghee* (clarified butter) and honey. The result is seen, promises the treatise, within a month. Another recipe suggests using pieces of *vacha* smeared with mango juice and preserved for six months in a crack of the *shinshapa* tree trunk. Then, the fragrance of the pieces has to be extracted. This is said to attract and win women. Besides these, as mentioned earlier, the woman and man should have a thorough and intimate knowledge of the 64 arts.

The much talked about 64 arts contain the following, as identified by Chaturvedi Badrinath in his book, *Kamasutra* (1999): vocal music; instrumental music; dancing; painting; cutting different designs on the *bhurja* leaf for display on the forehead; making designs using rice grains and flowers; arrangement of flowers in temples and homes; colouring teeth, garments, hair, nails and the body; fixing decorative tiles on the floor; laying the bed, the settee and divan; creating musical sounds with water – *jaltaranga*; playing with water – *jalkrida*; the knowledge of *mantras*, secret formulae and their use; making garlands of various kinds; making adornments for the head; dressing and decorating the body; designing decorative accessories for the body; the preparation and appropriate use of perfumes and fragrances; making ornaments; knowledge of magic; preparing ointments; deftness in manual work; cooking and other culinary arts; preparing sherbets and drinks; needlework; creating patterns from yarns or threads; playing the *veena* (stringed instrument) and the drum called *damaruka*; composing and solving riddles and rhymes; *antakshri*, a game in which one party recites a verse and the opposite party recites another that begins with the last letter of the earlier verse; reciting verses difficult to repeat, for example, tongue-twisters; recitation from books; knowledge of drama and stories; the poetical ability to compose lines of verse from a line or word one is given; woodwork – frames for cots, chairs and so forth; fabrication of mechanical arts in lovemaking; carpentry; knowledge of architecture and house construction; knowledge of precious metals and precious stones; knowledge of metals; knowledge of jewels; gardening; art of cock fighting, ram-fighting and quail-fighting; teaching parrots and mynahs to speak and sing; proficiency in shampooing and dressing hair; the art of deciphering writing in cipher;

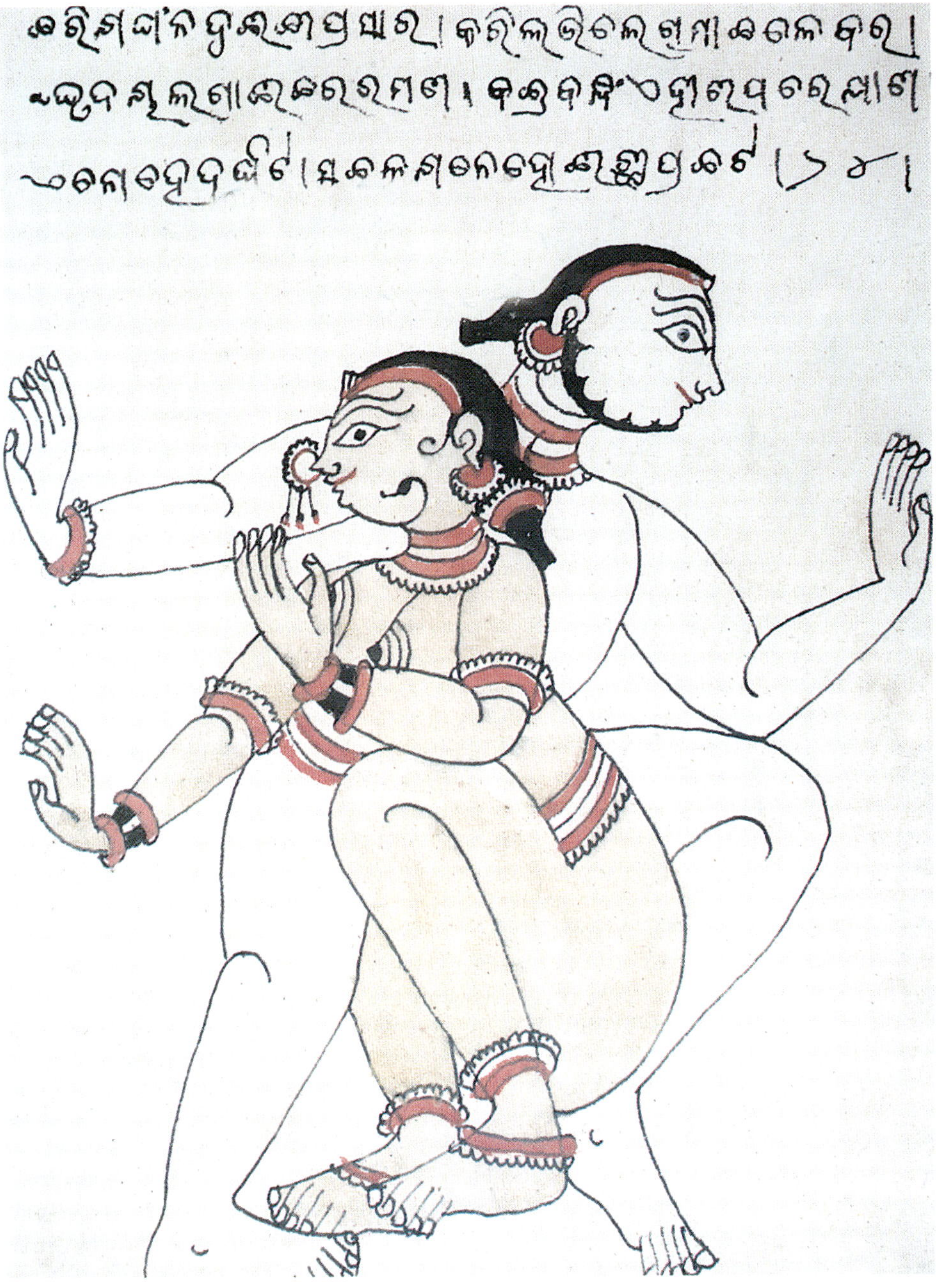

Pen and ink drawings on paper from Orissa, eastern India.
Previous page: Rajasthani paintings on the Radha-Krishna motif of divine love and union.

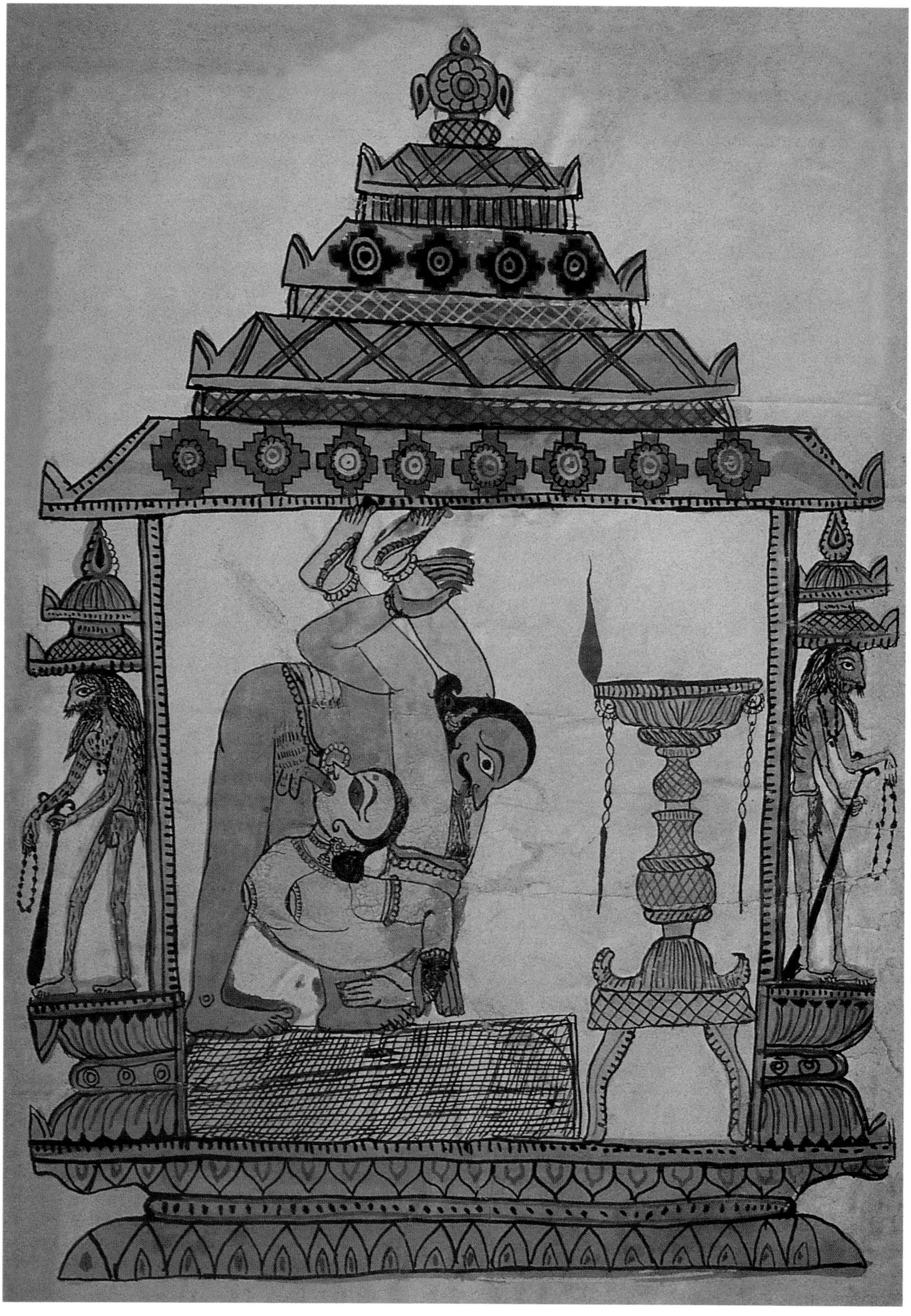

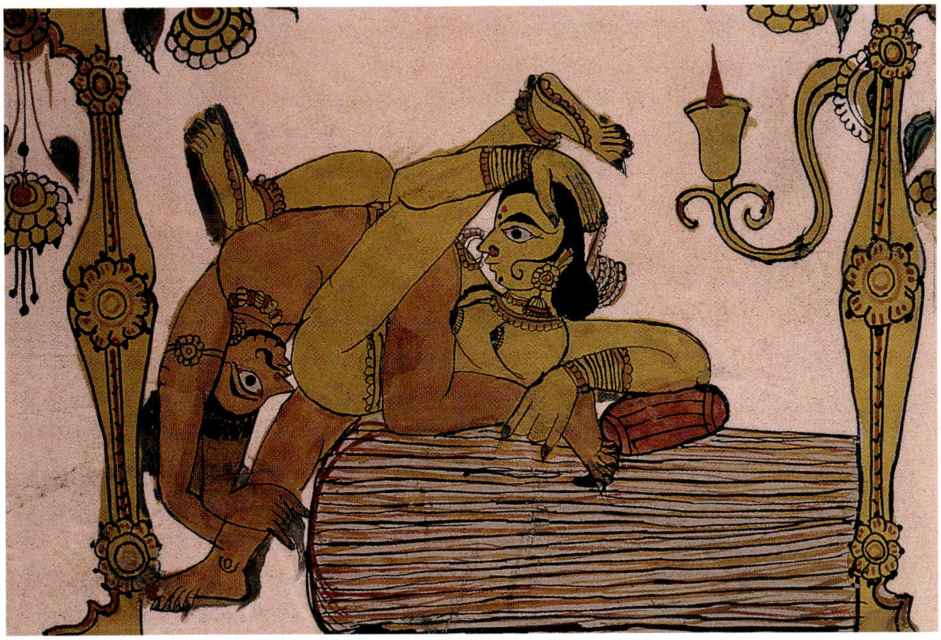

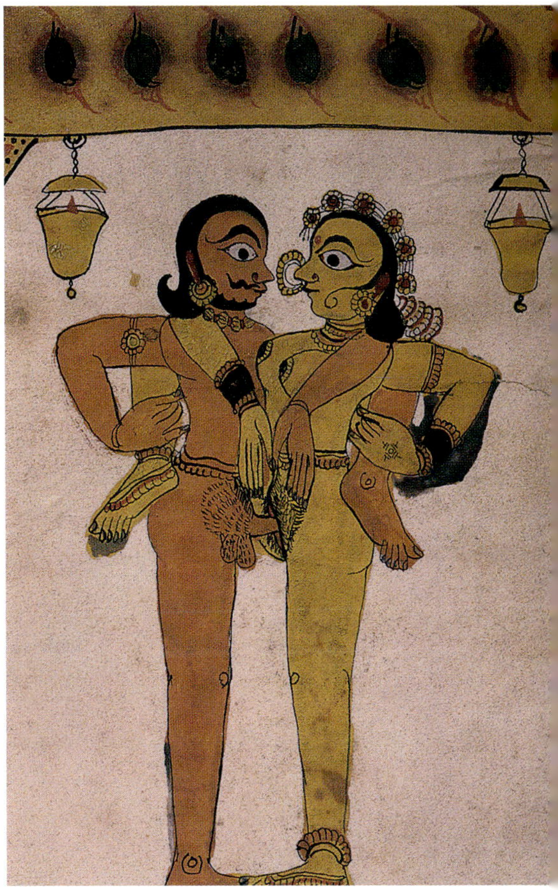

speaking in a language with deliberate transposition of words and letters; knowledge of languages of other provinces and of various dialects; art of making flower-carriages, art of chanting spells, charms and auspicious omens; constructing mechanical aids; memory-training; recitation of verse; deciphering secret codes; knowledge of etymology; knowledge of lexicography; prosody and rhetoric; art of impersonation; wearing garments artfully; various dice games; the game of dice called *akarsha*; making dolls and playthings for children; knowledge of etiquette, of the science of victory, and physical nature.

Going through and imbibing the broad spectrum of essential attributes that makes a 'perfect' individual is almost suprahuman.

Besides these, the *Kamasutra* also specifies techniques to approach and arouse the desired mate. The primary way to do this is by embracing the person. There are embraces specified for the time of actual union, and also when one limb of each individual is pressed against the other's. The former includes those called *lataveshtitaka, vrkshadhirudhaka, tilatandulaka,* and *kshiranira*. The latter involves four other types of embraces: *urupaguhana, jaghanopaguana, stanalingana* and

Pen and ink sketches with colour from Orissa
Top left: In the throes of passion, juxtaposed limbs and contorted bodies reach for each other.
Facing page: The position is definitely not for those not equal to gymnastics.

latatika. Similarly, there are four types of embraces for a man and woman who don't know each other: *sprishtaka, viddaka, udghrishataka* and *piditaka*.

Some of these embraces would not fall in the category of embraces, as we perceive them today. At the most basic level, there is a quartet of embraces: touching, piercing, rubbing and pressing. The *touching* embrace occurs when a male gets close to the female and brushes his body lightly against hers. Or a woman may, on the pretext of reaching out for something, touch the male with her breasts. This is known as the *piercing* embrace. Even if a couple walk very close to each other, their bodies *rubbing* against each other, Vatsayana classifies it as an embrace.

In the *Kamasutra*, sexual intercourse between couples not known to each other, or whose marriages are arranged, is not considered rape. It suggests ways to give the couple a chance to get acquainted and woo each other over a period of time before they indulge in lovemaking. Such a newly-wed couple, should sleep on the floor for three nights, observe celibacy, and share food at night. They should not break the oath of celibacy for a whole week, but should indulge in bathing and merriment. They should dress well and eat together. After the man has gained his wife's confidence, he should make an advance in a secluded chamber. He should approach the woman delicately so as to overcome her fears, mistrust and suspicion. This is more important in the case of a bride who has not reached puberty and is unknown to her husband. If the bride is old enough and the man has known her earlier, he can caress her in lamplight. However, if the man does not know the woman, these sensual acts should be performed in the dark.

These are ways, the *Kamasutra* suggests, to win a woman and coax her into voluntary sex. The text says no man needs to force sexual relations upon a woman. Hence, it frowns upon what would be considered marital rape in Western societies.

The *Kamasutra* emphasises equality, which does not necessarily mean being alike in any way. What is emphasised is the fact that both men and women have similar desires; therefore, the pleasures they gain should also be equal. However, the experience and intensity of satisfaction differs. The ideal manner of attaining this state of supreme bliss comes about when each partner reciprocates with equal ardour. It reinforces the fact that intimate togetherness leads to complete erotic pleasure. In fact, the *Kamasutra* – though it does not use the word – is aware that woman have orgasms. It even stresses that the man, if he is to be the ideal partner, put his pleasure second to hers.

Moreover, there is nothing patriarchal about desire in the *Kamasutra*. It sees the woman as a delicate flower to be treated with sensitivity and gentle affection. The inclusion of the woman as an equal partner and equal facilitator of sexual pleasure also establishes the fact that she is an equal, with rights, demands, desires and needs.

Books for a sedate society

After the *Kamasutra* a number of erotic texts in Sanskrit followed. Almost six centuries later, Pandit Kokokka carried the legacy of the first treatise on love further. He authored the *Ratirahasya* – 'the secrets of Rati, spouse of Kama'. The *Ratirahasya* was composed in the twelfth or tenth century and is similar to another classic text on love, the *Ananga Ranga*.

These two erotic books of medieval India, the *Ratirahasya* and the *Ananga Ranga* were written for a society which had changed from one of gay abandon to a more sedate one. Romance had taken a back seat, the woman's place was rooted to the house, men and women no longer met socially, and pre-marital courtship was unheard of. The woman was married even before she attained puberty and was under constant vigil. 'The men for whom these books were written were not lovers but husbands,' says Comfort Alex.

In *Ananga Ranga*, the *raison d'être* behind the text is stated with forceful clarity. 'No one yet has written a book to prevent the separation of the married pair and to show them how they may pass through life in union. Seeing this, I felt compassion and composed the treatise.'

Thus the *Ananga Ranga* is a marriage manual, not a lover's handbook. Sex is curtailed within marriage. That, however, does not relegate the *Ananga Ranga* into a boring manual. What sex in marriage loses in passion, it gains in spiritual mystery.

Let us examine the books that the *Kamasutra* laid the foundations for:

1. The *Ratirahasya*, known popularly as the *Koka Shastra*, between the tenth and twelfth centuries.
2. The *Panchasayaka* (Five Arrows) of Jyotirisvara Kavisekhara in the thirteenth or early fourteenth century.
3. The *Smaradipika* (Light of Love), a name for a number of different works. The earliest probably originated in the fourteenth century; the works may have undergone a partial interchange of material.
4. The very short *Ratimanjari* of Jayadeva (the Posy of Love), ascribable to the fifteenth century. In elegant verse, it corresponds word-for-word in places with some versions of the *Smaradipika*.
5. The *Kandarpacudamani* (Tiara of the Love God) by Virabhadradeva, an almost verbatim transposition of the *Kamasutra*.
6. The *Dinalapanika Sukasaptati*, or Seventy Discourses of the Parrot. In one version of this book, the learned bird employed by a king to educate his son, dilates on sexual physiology. Not to be outdone, the young prince himself delivers a discourse on erotica. In the course of this, he gives an extant list of 'advanced' coital postures.
7. The *Srngaradipika* (Lamp of Affection) of Harihara lists the same names, but without the details.
8. The *Ananga Ranga* (Stage of the Love God) of Kalyanamalla is yet another celebrated text of the sixth century, only second to *Ratirahasya* and *Kamasutra* in terms of popularity.
9. *Madanatilaka* by Chandra Raja, written around the eleventh century.
10. *Madanamandira Kamakothala.*

Some other minor and derivative texts are the *Nagarasarvasva* (The Complete Playboy) of Padmasri, the *Kamaprabodha* of Vyasya Janardana, the *Ratiratnapradipika* (Jewel Lamp of Rati) by Maharaja Devaraja, and the *Ratisastraratnavali* of Nagarjuna Siddha. There are thousands of texts in the vernacular which deal with erotology. There are certain authors who are known to have written texts which deal with erotic imagery, such as Annamacharya Kshetrayya, a Telegu poet. It is from these erotic texts, ancient and medieval, that Indian visual and performing artists have taken their inspiration.

'By you this universe is borne,
by you this world is created.
By you it is protected, O Devi.
By you it is consumed at the end.
You who are eternally the form of the whole world,
at the time of creation
You are the form of the creative force,
at the time of preservation
You are the form of the protective power,
and at the time of dissolution of the world
You are the form of the destructive power.
You are the Supreme Knowledge,
as well as ignorance, intellect and contemplation.'

—Devi-Mahatmya
(*a section of the Markandeya Purana*)

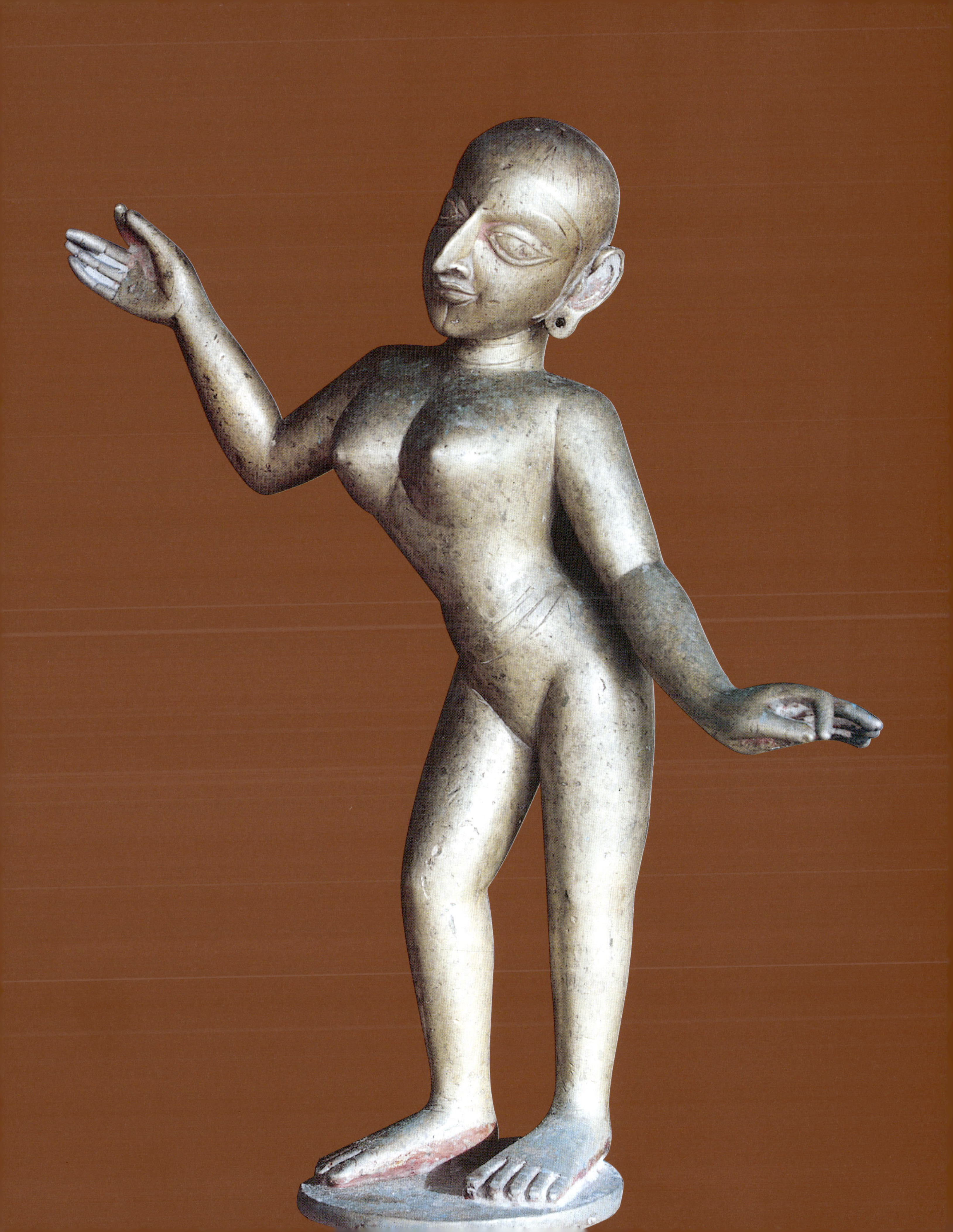

The Devi has been a part of the Indian religious pantheon since the very beginning. All the attitudes and attributes of the mother flow from her, and each of these has given her a multitude of forms. At one level, the earth, standing as a visible representative of fecundity and fertility, denotes her. On a more mundane plane, she is known as *Yakshi*, the guardian of treasure, and as *Sri*, the goddess of wealth and abundance. Finally, she is also seen to evoke nature or *prakriti*, and the virtues that reside in nature, as *Salabhanjika* or goddess of the tree.

The underlying thread of theory behind these faces of the Goddess is that she is the Divine Reality. Therefore, Hinduism views the feminine as pre-eminent. According to the Vedas, there is one supreme female goddess and she is *Aditi*. *Aditi* is said to hold the god of fire and creation, *Agni*, in her womb and thus, is the mother of the universe. Since *Aditi* nurtures, she is associated with the cow. She is that cosmic cow who feeds us and helps us evolve.

Yet, Hindu mythology also exhibits a duality when it comes to depicting the sole, powerful divinity. Then again, at times, it can be strictly monist. Over the centuries, however, the feminine force has been considered at par with Shiva, the foremost father. So, the

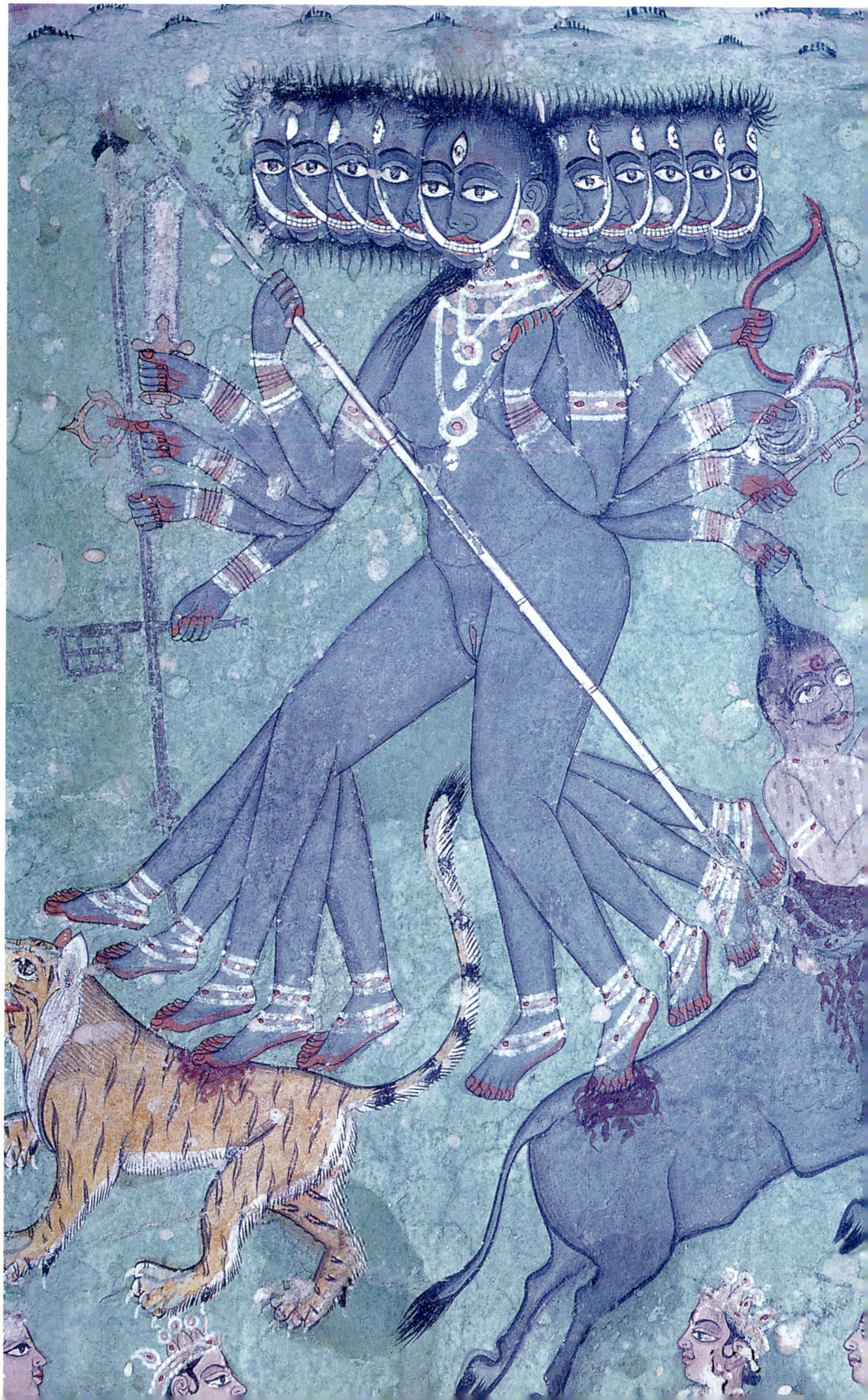

Devi–Mahatmya proclaims the Goddess to be the creator, preserver and the destroyer of the universe – virtues synonymous with Shiva. It also says that every individual, whether male or female, is an incarnation of Shiva and Shakti. However, Shakti predominates in all that is female.

The symbols of *Shakti*

Shakti means power, force, feminine energy. *Shakti* is the energy of the cosmos, the life of everything that lives. The followers of *shakti* are *shaktas* and they have been around, as far as we know, since the Indus Valley civilisation. *Shakti* was the Mother Goddess of the fertility cults during this period. Prehistoric excavations show terracotta dolls and megaliths which were devoted to the worship of the Goddess. One such megalith, built in capstone and seven-feet long, has been found in Madhya Pradesh. Bells are often rung there,or it is struck with sandstone, probably to evoke the Mother. Neither metal nor any man-made material has been used on the sculpture, which just goes to show that the Goddess of the earth, that is, pure Nature.

In other parts of India, there are domes built for the Goddess in the shape of a woman or like a *garbagriha* (womb chamber). The entrances are representative of the *yoni,* being small, narrow passages that lead to a dark

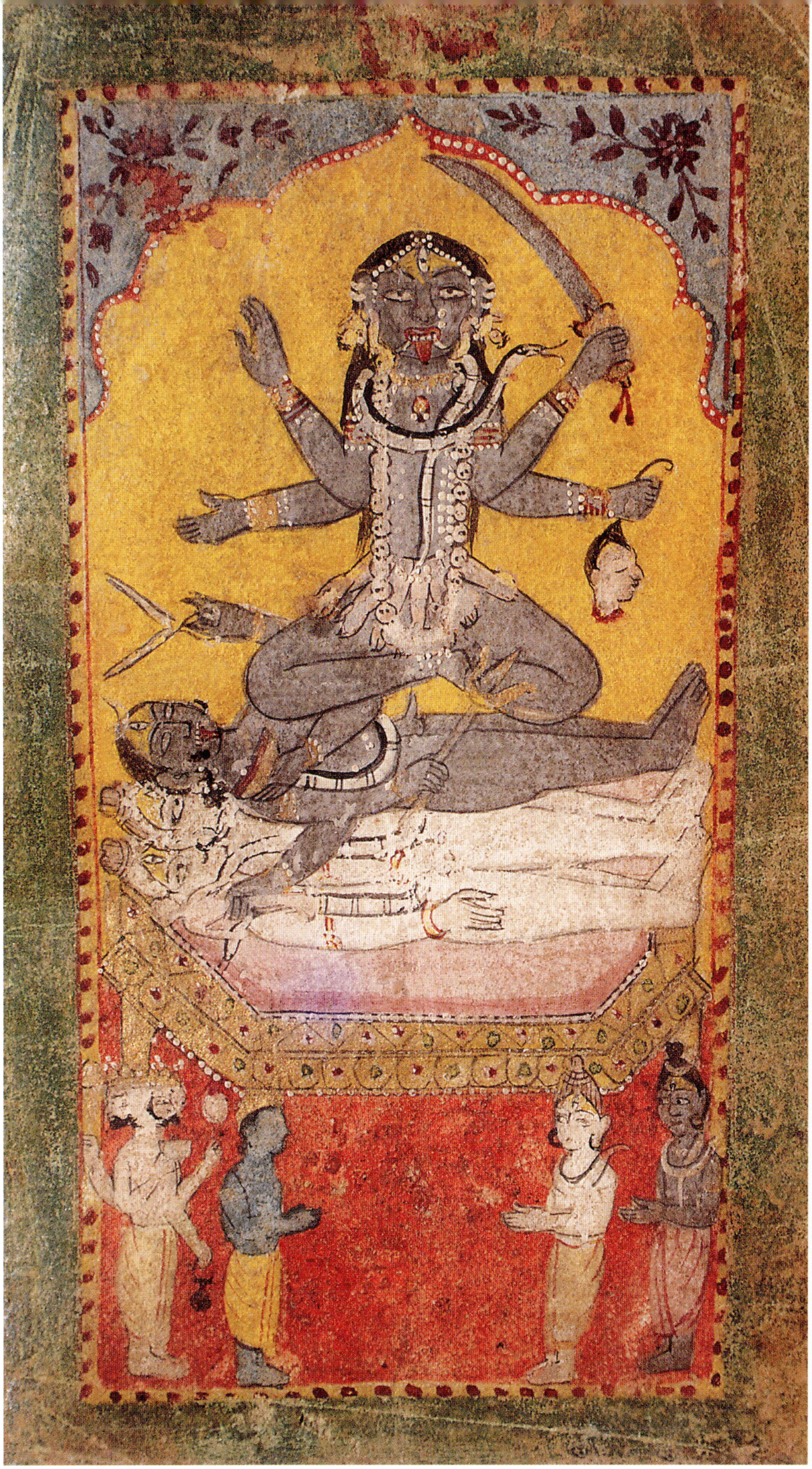

Kali seated on a supine Shiva in a Pahari painting. *Shakti,* the female principle, has been variously represented as Kali or Durga.
Facing page: Nude, multiple-formed Durga from Rajasthan, western India.
Previous page: Bronze sculpture from Orissa.

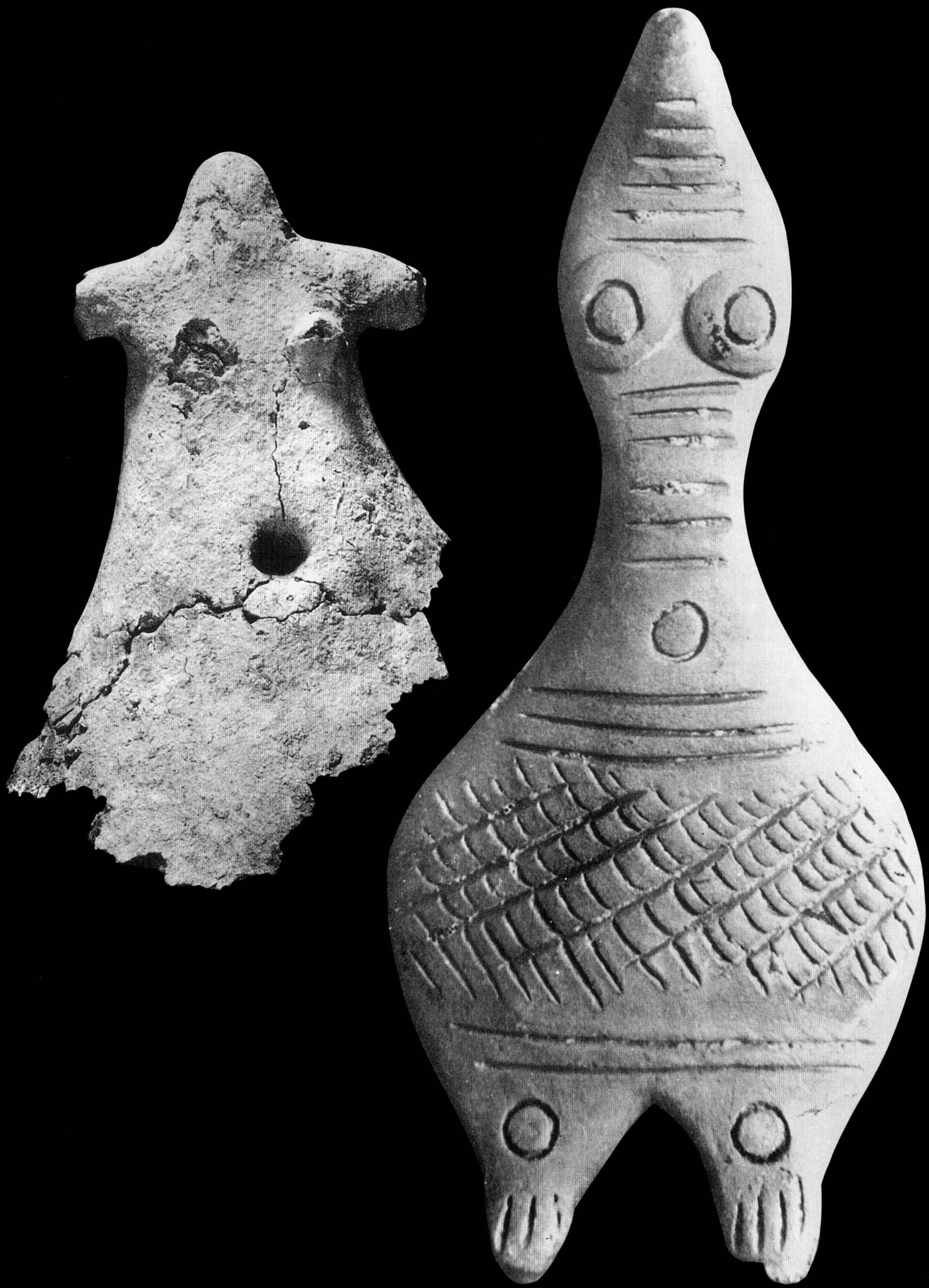

chamber, emblematic of the womb. This exaggerates their importance and lends sacredness to fertility and procreation. Cave sanctuaries also symbolise the natural womb of Mother Earth.

Man-made sculptures too pay homage to the feminine power. They often accentuate the genital areas, the *yoni* and the breasts, to enhance the poise of the female sculpture.

Divine unions

In the Shaivite tradition, Shiva and Parvati is the divine couple from whom erotic imagery flows. The eroticism in their sacred relationship is clearly represented in the story of the birth of Kartikeya, central to Kalidasa's *Kumarasambhava*. Once while Shiva and Parvati were lost in lovemaking, the gods were troubled by the demon, Taraka. They went to Brahma who took them to Vishnu, who, in turn, took the group to the abode of Shiva and waited outside for years.

At last, he spoke in a shrill voice and Shiva came out. But the latter ignored the problem totally. Then the gods sent Agni disguised as a pigeon into the couple's bedchamber. Parvati sensed the intrusion, and Shiva withdrew, a drop of his semen falling on the ground. Agni ate it and an enraged Parvati cursed all the wives of the gods with barrenness. But Agni was unable to contain the fiery seed and

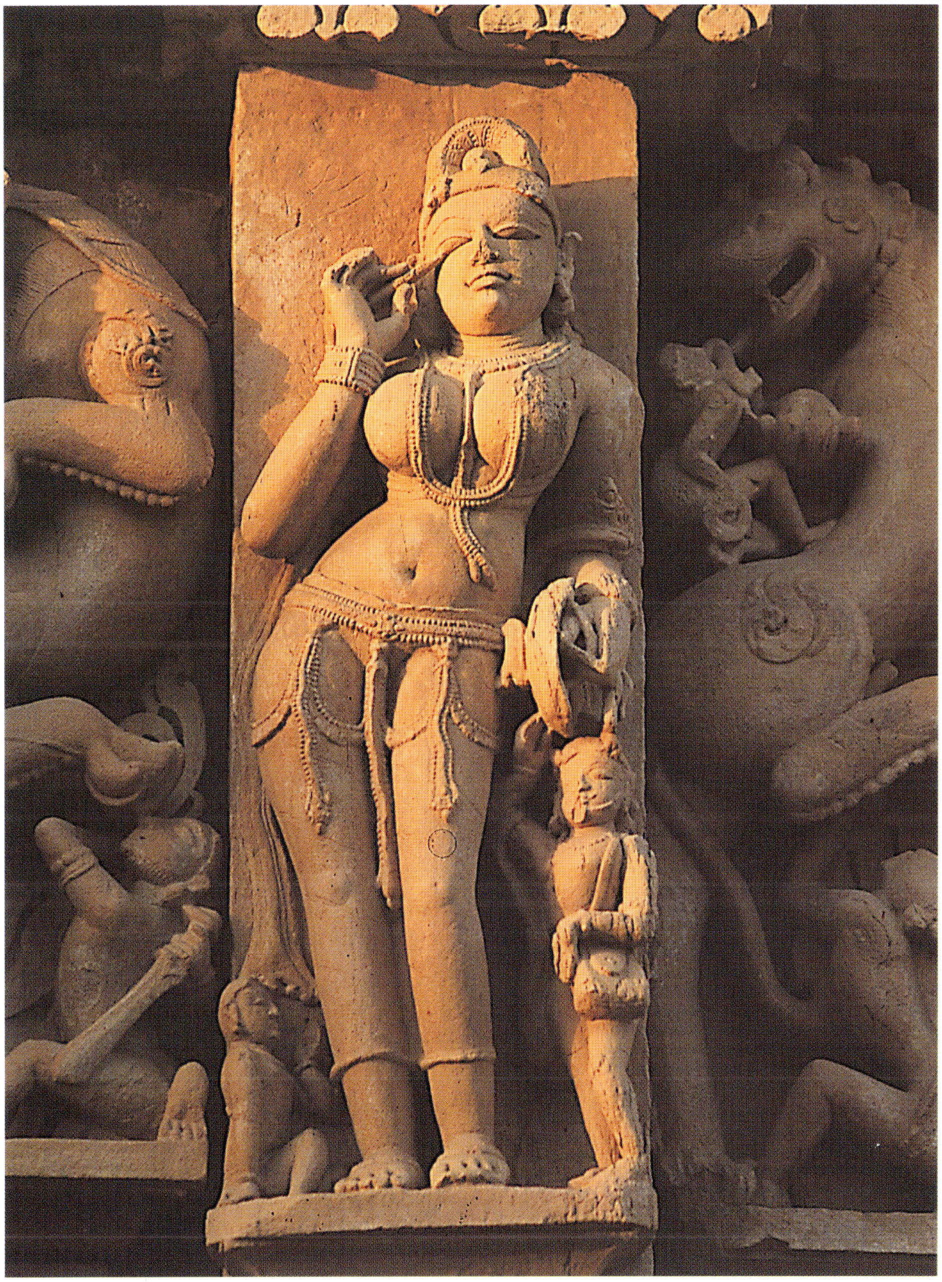

The Khajuraho temple complex is replete with *apsaras*. The nymphs are engrossed in tasks. Here, the *apsara* from the Parsvanath temple applies *kohl* to her eyes. This is only one of three or four sculptures on the subject and is probably the best among them.

Facing page: Earth goddess from Newasa, Maharashtra, belonging to the Chalcolithic period, along with a Naga-headed, semi-female figurine, symbolising fertility. (From Kausambi, the Patna Museum.)

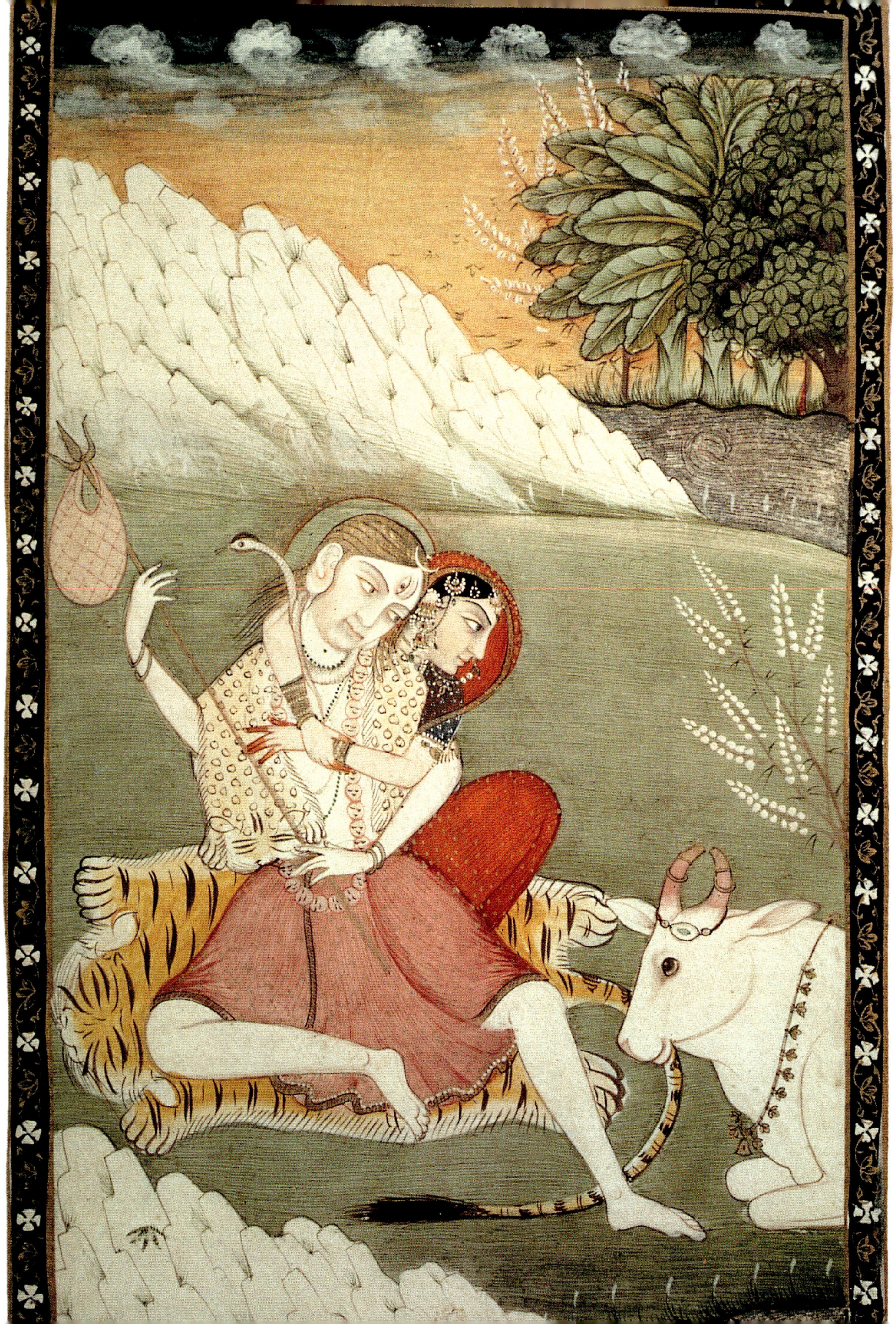

dropped it on the banks of the Ganga at a time when the wives of the seven sages (the *saptarishis*) were bathing. Six of them were feeling cold and went towards Agni, and at this point, the semen drop went through their hair, impregnating them. Thus was born Kartikeya, a child with six heads.

In the Vaishnav tradition, Radha and Krishna are portrayed both in literary texts and in visual art as two passionate lovers. They are shown indulging in love play, with Krishna, the divine lover, desired by every *gopi*.

However, the relationship between Shiva and Parvati is the more erotic one, with the *kama* aspect being more overt; that between Krishna, Radha and the *gopis* is on a more metaphysical level. In these images, Krishna is representative of consciousness – *purusha* – and Radha is synonymous with *prakriti* or nature. The primordial couple is one who is supreme in sustaining the universe through these dual forces – pure consciousness and nature.

The marriage of Shiva and Parvati, the ultimate couple, illustrates the significance of the union between *purusha* and *prakriti*. When Shiva went to Aushadhiprastha (near Mount Kailash in the Himalaya) to meditate with Nandi and his attendants, Parvati and two of her *sakhis* approached him with flowers and fruit. Though Shiva had noticed Parvati's unparalleled beauty, he persevered in his meditation. He ordered that Parvati not be brought into his presence because any contact with a woman destroyed penance. Hearing this, Parvati proclaimed she was *prakriti*, which sustains and destroys everything that is incarnate, though Shiva might be pure consciousness. Shiva, unaffected, continued his meditation. And Parvati, serene, continued to serve Shiva.

Finally the god of love, Kama, sent by the gods to break Shiva's reverie and inspire love for Parvati in his heart, shot five arrows at him. Shiva, furious with Kama, opened his third eye and burnt him down. But Shiva was attracted to Parvati. The couple were married and celebrated their

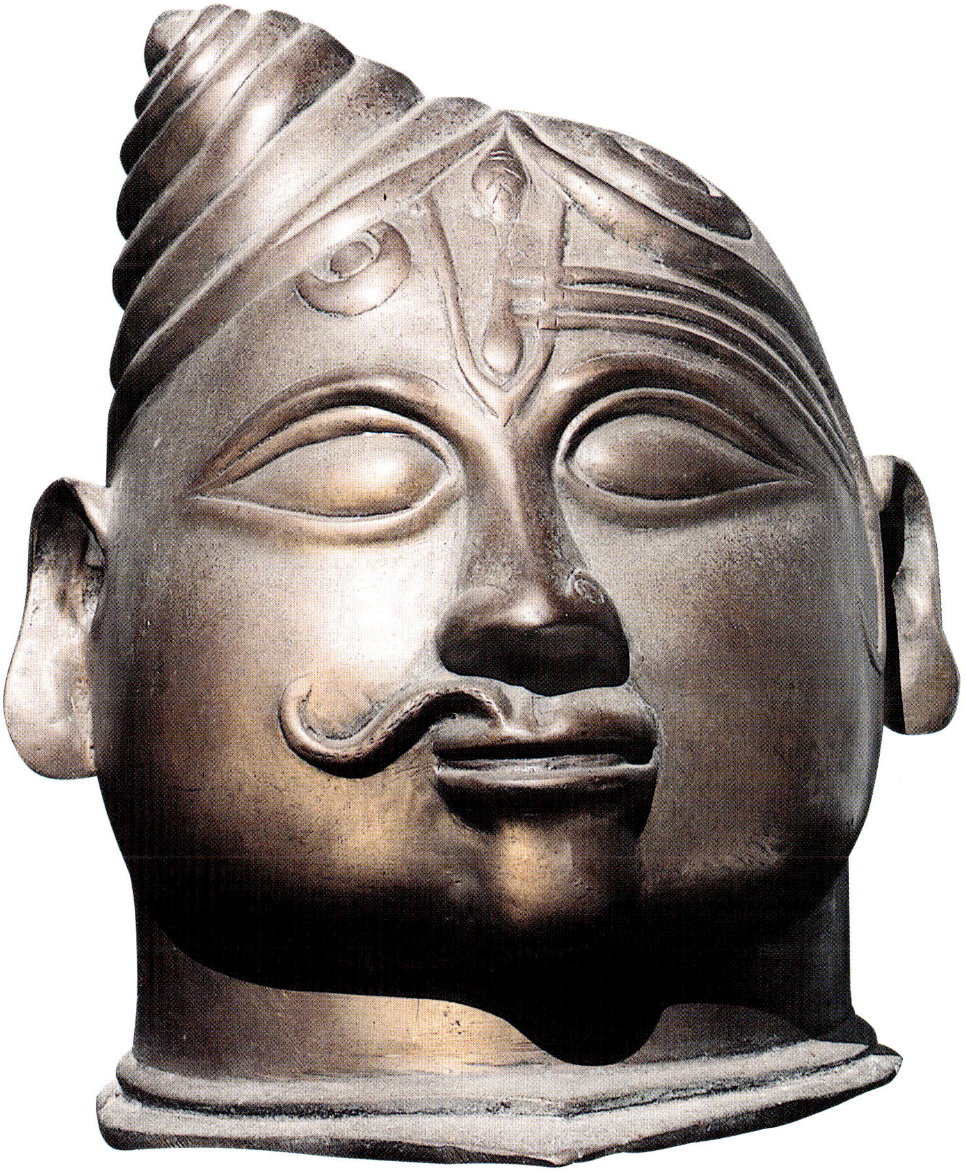

Mohini merged with Shiva – Maharashtra, western India.
Facing page: A Pahari miniature has the eternal couple, Shiva and Shakti, sitting on the tiger mat. Shiva's mount, Nandi, the bull, sits nearby.

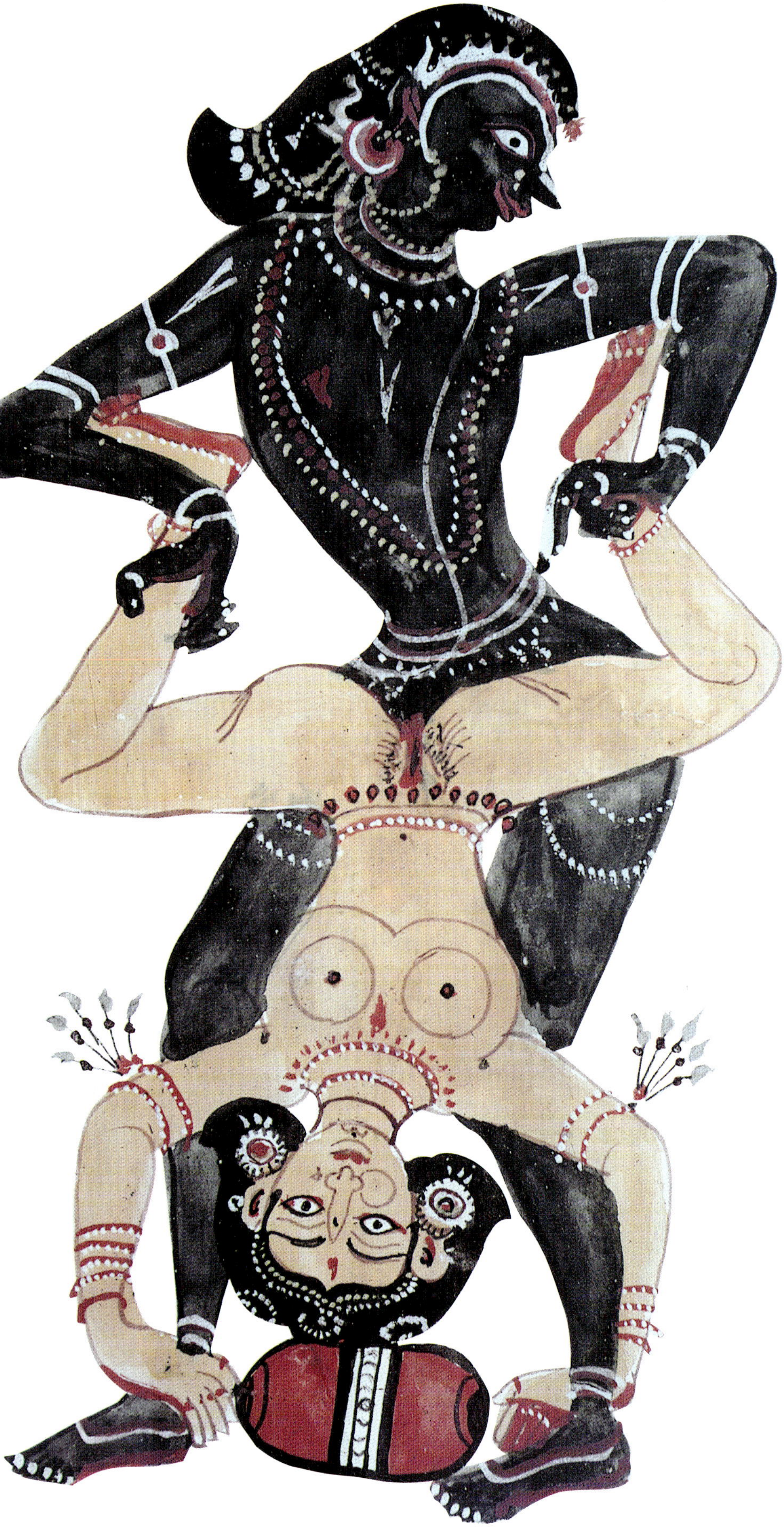

honeymoon on Mount Kailash, where they indulged in lovemaking and lovers' quarrels.

Southern interpretations

The Shiva-Parvati wedding is a central theme of religious practice in South India, especially in Tamil Nadu. The story is narrated by the dwarf sage, Agastya. The sage had been sent to the South to maintain physical equilibrium in the world when all its denizens were attending the wedding of Shiva and Parvati. Agastya dug up a *lingam* under a tree and worshipped Shiva. Pleased, the Lord blessed him and the sage had a vision of Parvati attired in her wedding sari.

In Tamil culture, the story begins with a flood. It is said that Parvati descended upon the earth from Kailash to atone for the sin of closing Shiva's third eye. She worshipped Shiva in the form of a *linga* and he flooded the town of Kanchi to put her through a test. Parvati clutched the *linga* to prevent it from being destroyed in the flood. She embraced it so tightly that, even today, the *lingam* is said to be marked with the impressions of her breasts and bracelets. This Tamil myth is erotic but the eroticism is used to indicate the unmatched love and intense devotion Parvati had for Shiva.

Tamilian myths have drawn copiously from Sanskrit writings.

However, they are essentially different in one aspect. The Sanskrit myths perceive Shiva's dual personality: one, erotic; the other, ascetic. The Tamilian legends concentrate their theories on Parvati and suggest her dual persona: one where she is dark, violent, erotic and dangerous; the other where she is bright, quiet, compassionate and romantic. The first of her characteristics is that which resides in the Southern Goddess who has risen from the dark womb of the earth. The second of her traits belongs to the Northern Goddess, who resides in the pleasant abode of Kailash. The Southern Goddess bears little resemblance to the Goddess from the Sanskrit tradition, but is closer to the one worshipped in folk and tribal traditions. Tribal traditions seem to touch base with reality, hence, the Goddess projects both the dark and the compassionate side as a part of her divine self. Another significant difference in the Sanskrit and Tamilian legends is regarding the marriage tale. In the Sanskrit tradition, Parvati is encouraged to marry Shiva so that their offspring can destroy the demon *Taraka*. However, in the Tamilian tales, Parvati is a virgin, and gods and men alike believe the Southern Goddess should remain so to retain all her energy and defeat *Taraka*. Hence in the Tamilian tradition, the eroticism comes about whenever it refers to the love of Parvati with Shiva – a single-minded devotion that is ardent, nearly crazy, and incomparable.

In Tamil culture, Parvati becomes the consort of Shiva much later. Initially, Shiva's companion was Kotravai, later affiliated with Kali, who keeps the rhythm when Shiva dances. As *ardhanari*, she resides in one half of Shiva. Ilango, in his epic, *Silappadikaram*, refers to the Goddess of Madurai as the consort of Shiva.

Sculptures of *Shakti*

In all forms of worship, the divine female is one who embraces the form of force, *shakti*. This concept dominates tantric practices. Tantric customs consider the cosmic woman to be a balanced combination of the powers of Shiva, Brahma and Vishnu. It is said that at the woman's *yoni* sits Brahma, the Creator, since the *yoni* is associated with the place where every life realises its uniqueness and from where there is procreation. At her breasts, a source of nourishment, resides Vishnu, as he is the preserver. On her head, or *shish*, there is Shiva or pure consciousness, which exemplifies the decomposition and re-absorption of the cosmos.

Shakti worshippers also claim that men and women are not at war but can together realise the feminine aspect of the entire universe. If they were to be in conflict, then they would disturb

A cultic image which depicts the overt feminity of form in an Orissan painting.
Facing page: A sexo-yogic pose from Orissa shows the male and the female mirroring each other in the positions they take up.

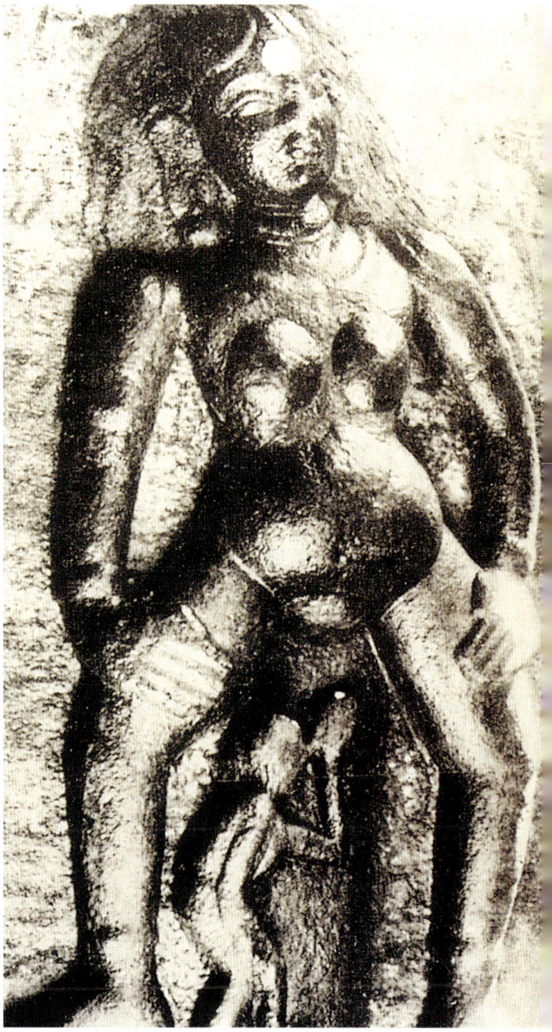

equilibrium. Therefore, for humanity to progress and grow spiritually, the two must be in harmony with each other. An illustration of this concept is probably best realised in the sculpture of *Kamakalavilasa* (of love or pleasure), where the male and female duality of a single human being is shown. The sculpture has one breast, and the other side of the chest is flat. It also has an erect penis. Another similar sculpture from the eleventh century shows the figure touching that one breast, thus symbolising the concept of fertility and feminine force.

This sculpture is one of many that shows female strength by exaggerating the reproductive organs. There are others which are more overt in showing female supremacy as regards procreation. In these, the *yoni* assumes various manifestations. The triangle, *yoniyantra*, represents the Mother Goddess who is the source of all life. Many sculptures show the goddess with spread legs with a devotee crouching under her *yoni* and drinking the *yoni tattva* or the 'sublime essence'. In the *yoniyantra*, the *yoni* is said to have ten parts, each a manifestation of the Devi. For *yoni* puja, a representation of the *yoni* is painted to symbolise the Devi and then worshipped.

Though these are man-made manifestations of the *yoni*, just as there were natural reproductions of the phallus, such as the one in Amarnath, the *yoni* too has been seen to emerge naturally in Kamakhya, in the state of Assam. It is said Shiva was destroyed by the death of his wife, Sati, and he roamed the earth in a state of insanity with her body on his back. Vishnu, who followed him, cut up Sati's body piece by piece to relieve Shiva of his burden. Pilgrimage centres came up where her body parts fell. Today, there are 51 such *shaktipithas* (seats of shakti). The place where Sati's *yoni* fell was Kamakhya, and a temple was built on the hill top. The temple does not have any idol, but within the temple there is a rock in the shape of a *yoni*. A natural spring in the cave keeps the cleft moist. During July through August after the first burst of the monsoons, *ambuvachi*, the water through this cleft turns red due to the presence of iron-oxide. This is symbolic of her menstrual blood and is a ritual drink.

Forms of force

In tantric rituals, menstrual blood is considered sacred, and a menstruating woman is placed in a specific category during rituals. It is believed she possesses energy unlike any other and her body functioning is related to the processes carried out by nature. In a certain ritual worship called the *chakra* puja, the menstrual fluid forms a sacred drink and is usually taken with wine. The *yoni* is worshipped and is to be touched with one's lips and anointed with sandalwood. Participants also indulge in offering oblations from a *yoni*-shaped vessel called the *arghya*.

The *yoni* forms such a significant part of religious practices and is considered so sacred, that not just religious shrines but various aspects of life are related to it. The *yoni, kunda* is placed right in front of the altar of a *yagna*. This is the erect *yoni,* and the triangle symbolising it points upwards. But, the *yoni* in nature is believed to resemble a lotus in the early stage of its opening, as well as when it is in full bloom. It is said that like the lotus, which neither gets saturated with water, nor gets dirty in the mud, the *yoni* remains pure forever, and its purity is not destroyed by its actions. The lotus has been represented in many ways as it is a symbol of creation. An image from the Kangra School shows Rati and Kama making love, lying on a lotus with Kali standing on Rati. What is interesting in this depiction is that Rati is in the dominant position. The union of the two characterises completeness, while the lotus symbolises creation. The figure of Kali, representing the creator, preserver and finally destroyer, presides over this act. Such a union brings a great deal of energy to the surroundings.

The *Koka Shastra* theorises that there are 18 focal points which are

Facing page, top: Kali stands astride Shiva in a Pahari painting, being energised by his erect phallus.
Facing page, bottom left: The two principles, Shiva (male) and Shakti (embodied by the female), converge together in Tantric rituals in a Rajasthani painting.
Facing page, bottom right: In this powerful Pahari image of Chinamastama, the headless goddess, regeneration and death go hand in hand.

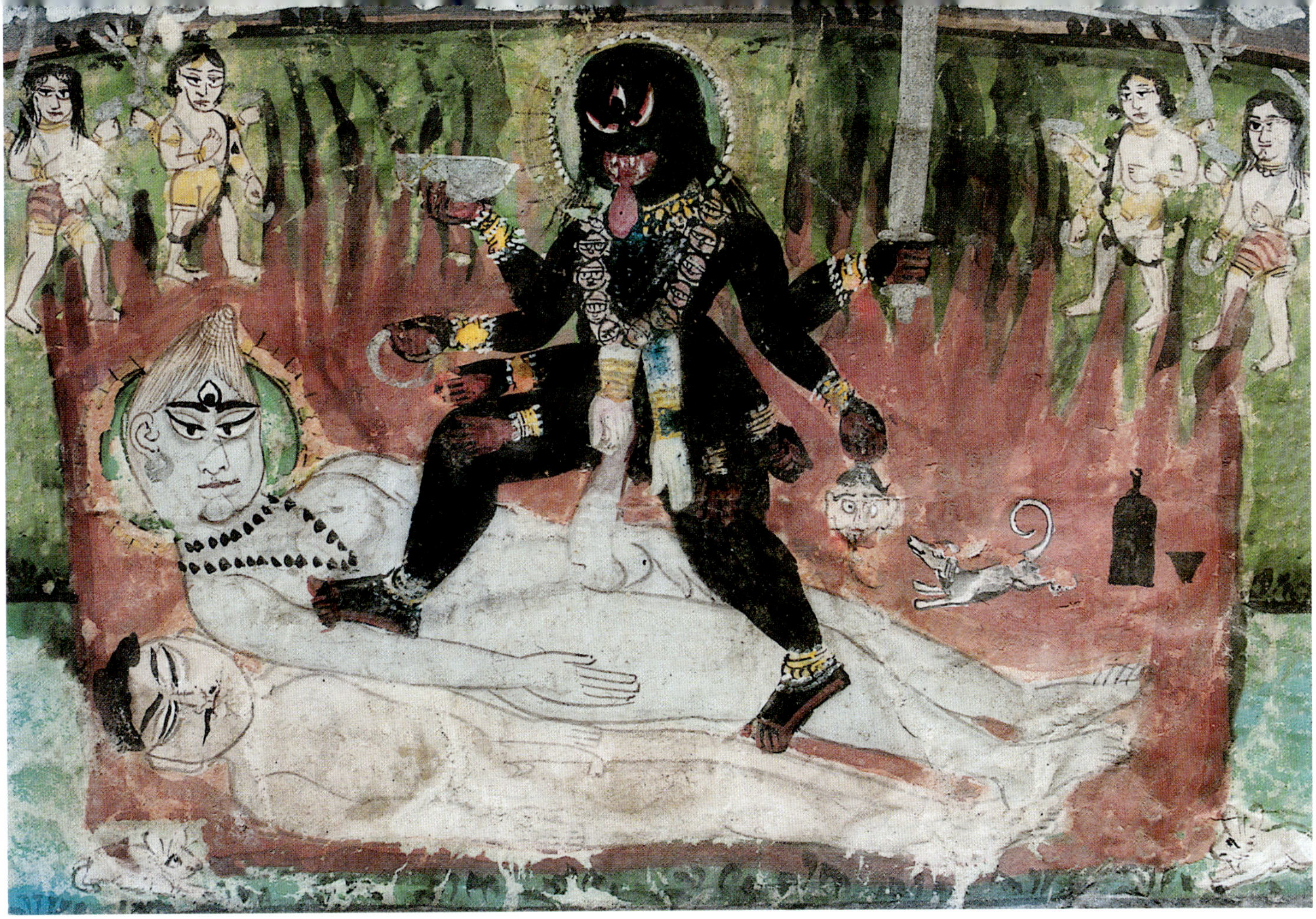

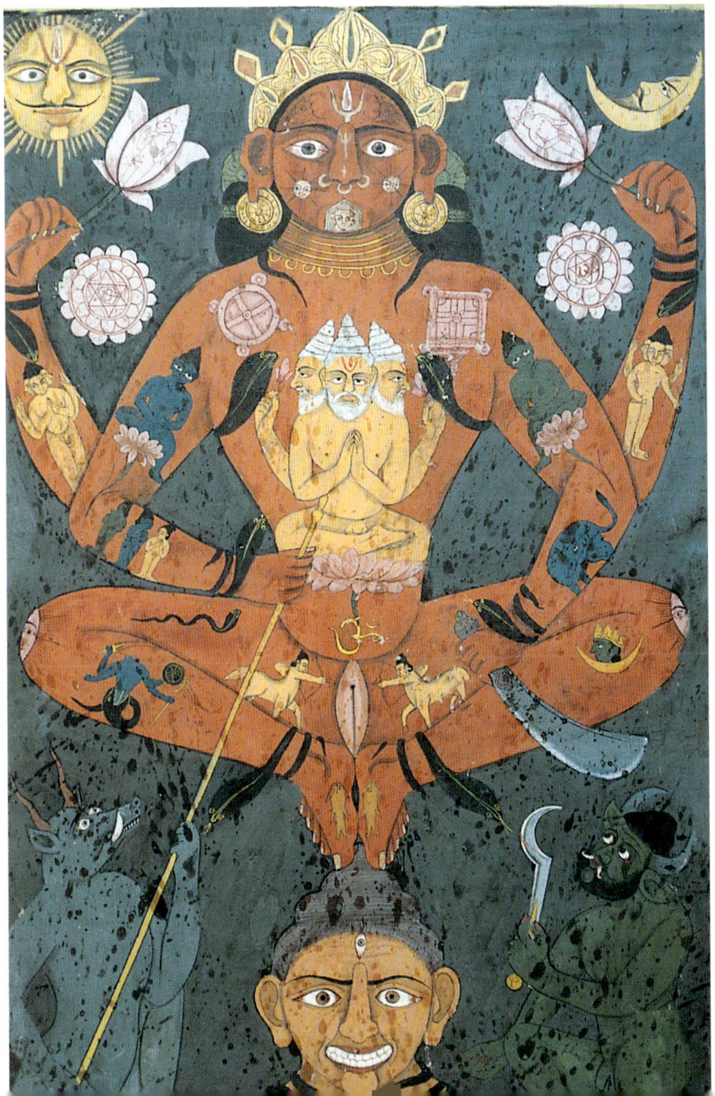

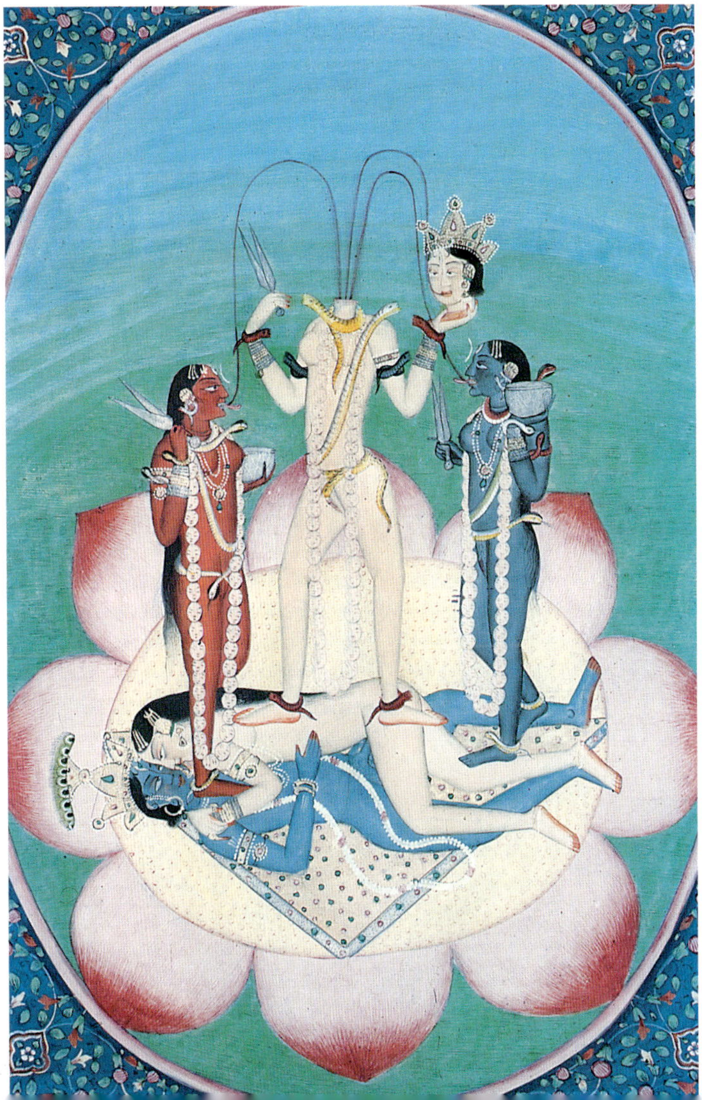

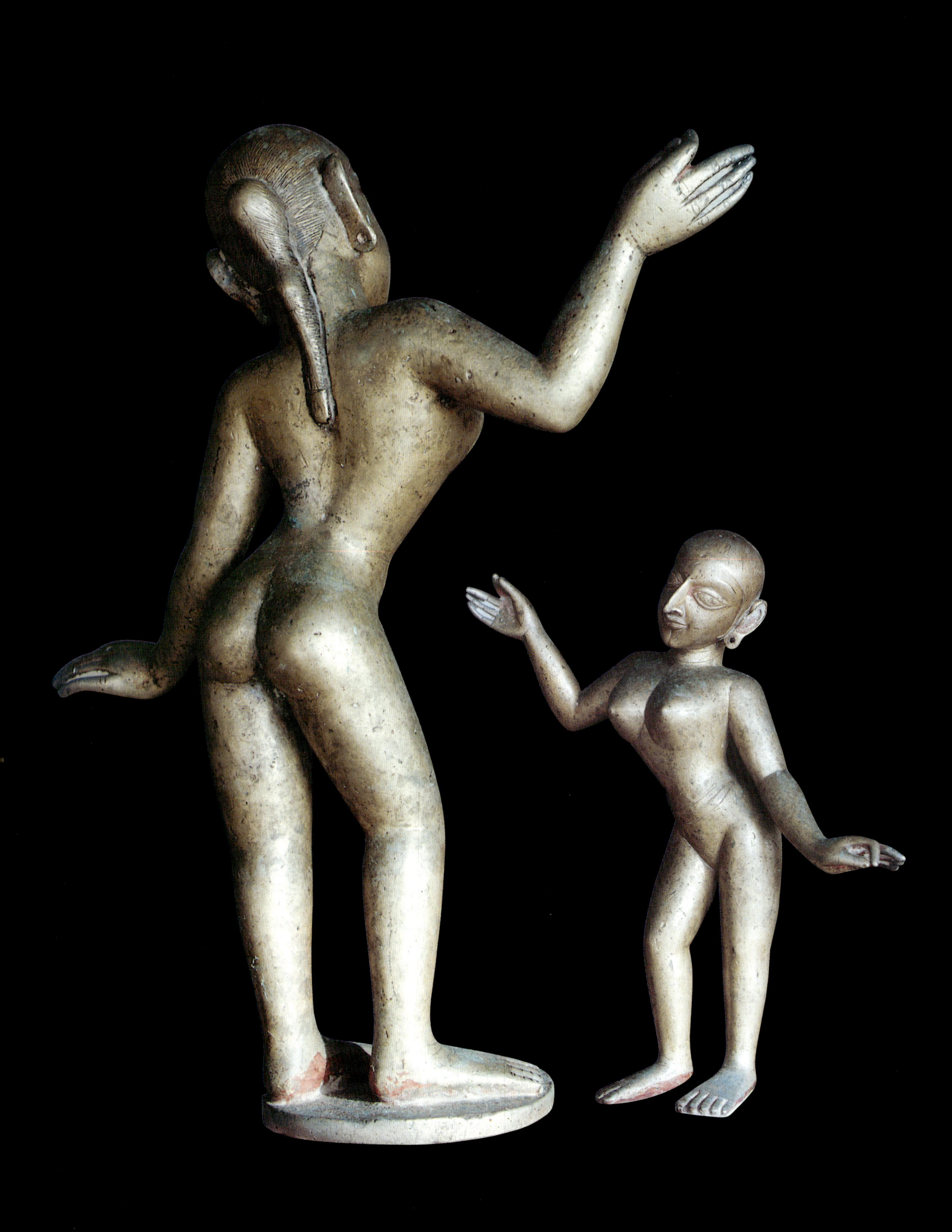

energy centres and they are in synchronisation with the lunar cycle. The tantric scriptures mention extensive body language, the science of *amritkala* which charts the energy, foci in the female body.

The energy in the female body is considered to be intense. The goddesses in Indian mythology are representative of this extraordinary power. Even Durga was born when a plethora of male divinities became powerless fighting the demons. The overt and bold sculpture of *Dakshinakali* presents Kali standing over Shiva and energising the inert form under her feet. Shiva is seen lying with an erect penis, which stands up like a *linga*. This sculpture points out that the woman has energy to pass to the man and her eroticism lies in the ways she can transfer it. Kali's energy here is seen in the superior position she takes up, standing atop Shiva. The nakedness of the goddess in this sculpture, as in many others, is considered to be natural and makes any naked woman a symbol of nature.

Nakedness is attributed to the *yogini* who, in her *tapas* (meditation towards excellence which aims to be to one with the Godhead), is closest to *prakriti* or nature. The ritual nudity of the *yogini* thus has an intrinsic value, with Nature in all its limitless bounty, displaying its boundless capacity to create.

Mircea Eliade in his study of yoga says: 'Every naked woman incarnates *prakriti*.' Hence she is to be looked upon with the same adoration and the same detachment that one exercises in pondering the unfathomable secrets of nature. Nudity was not meant to titillate or excite the senses; it was part of the deeply reflective and meditative stance of Indian philosophy. Innumerable images of women in the Ajanta caves which are primarily devoted to Buddhism, are seen in a state of dishabille. Many of the main female characters of the Jataka stories are dressed in transparent drapery. The upper torso is bare. The responses these cajole are not erotic. Instead they convey a deep loveliness which stretches towards reverence.

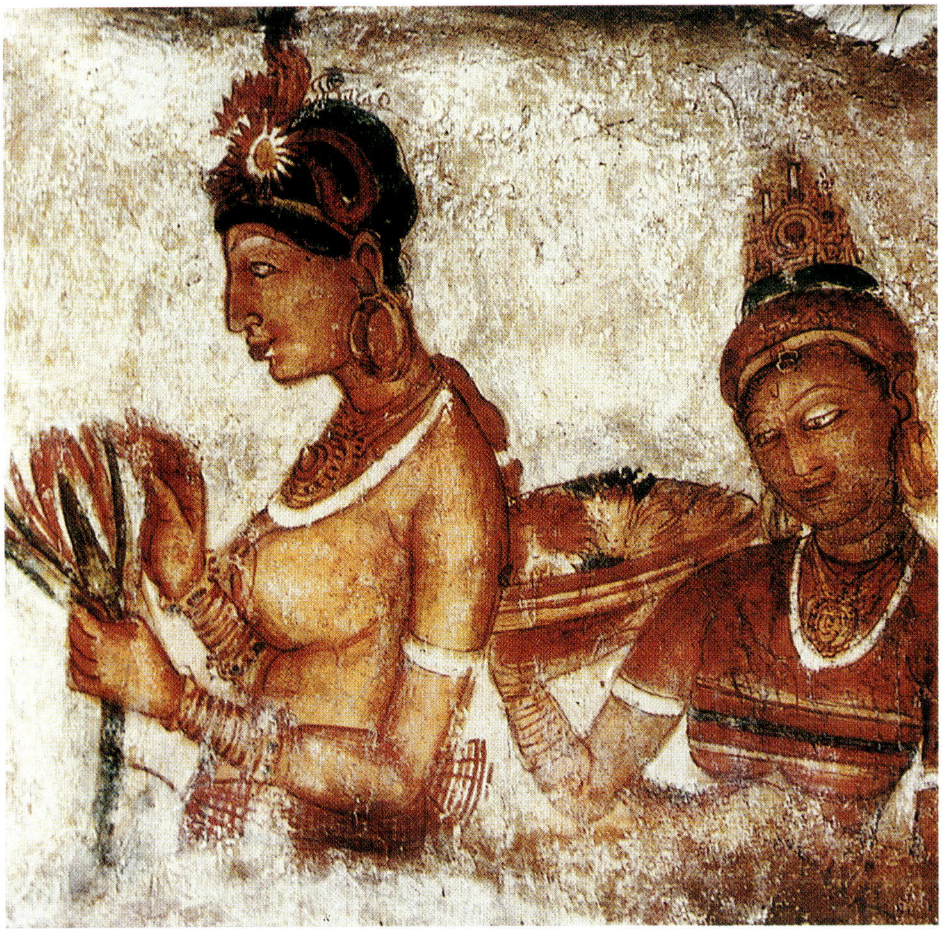

A female image from the frescoes in Sigiriya, Sri Lanka.
Facing page: Bronze image of Radha from Orissa. Every maked women, it is believed, incarnates *prakriti.*

Worshipping the father

Worshipping the father

For over 2,000 years, a feat of faith has been reclaiming the hearts of devotees in this land: the worship of Lord Shiva, the creator, preserver and destroyer of the Universe. Never mind that he presents a dual picture at every turn. The lord of the yogis and ascetics is also the object of affection and lawful husband of Goddess Parvati. He is said to be the Formless, one whose sole garment is the sky; but to the mind of the *bhakta,* he assumes a divine shape and lustre. He has three faces; three eyes, two of them closed, the third gazing at all of Eternity. He has a trident in his hands and the sickle-shaped moon perches atop the mountain of his hair, from where the river Ganga flows down with her promise of redemption and message of purity.

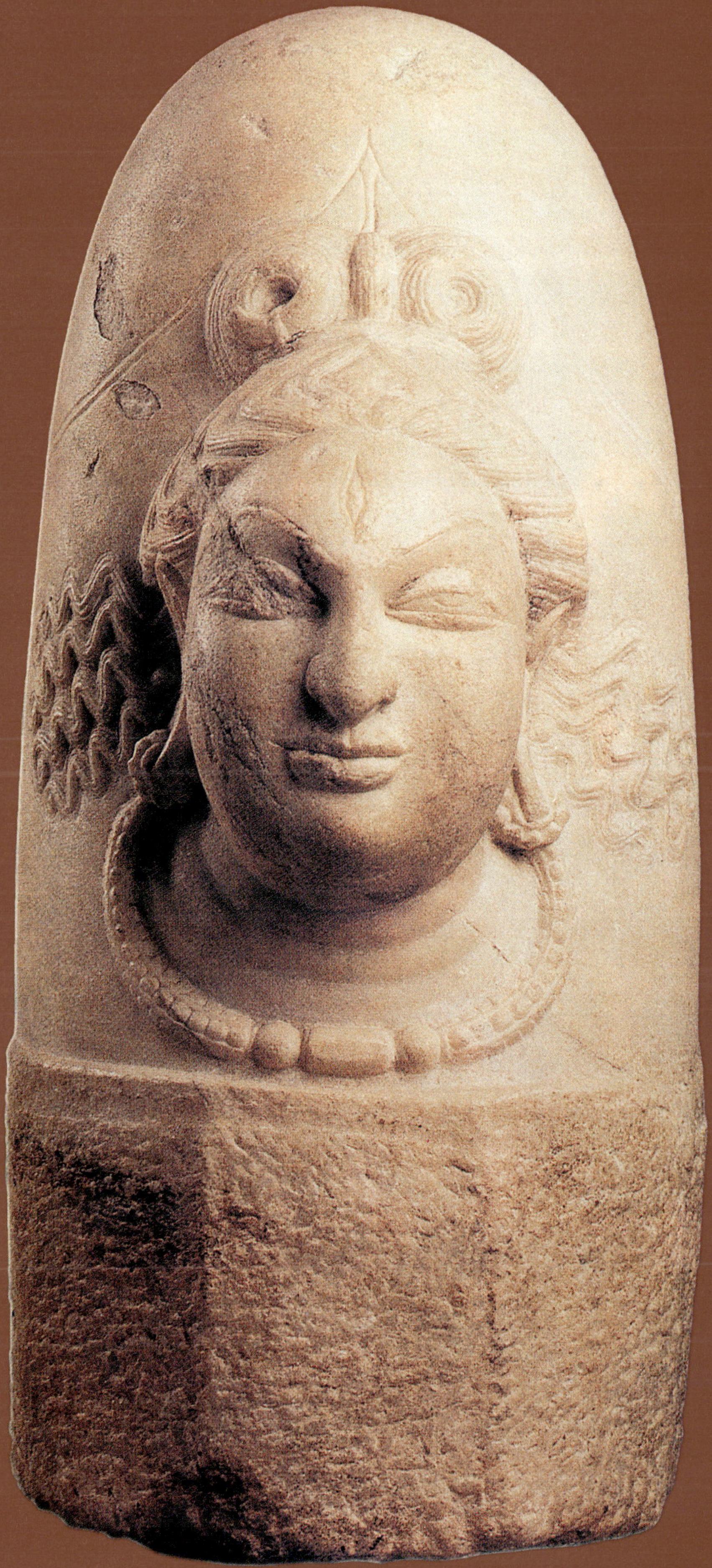

Lord Shiva, father of all creation, is depicted sitting in a cross-legged yoga posture over a tiger mat, snakes coiled around his body, his skin smeared with sacred ash. A figure who would surely inspire awe and open-mouthed astonishment were he to appear (in a flash, we presume) on the streets. In the scriptures (the *Rig Veda*, the *Vajasaneyi Samhita* of the *White Yajurveda*), the word Shiva appears as an epithet of Rudra and means The Auspicious. The early scriptures mention only Rudra and not Shiva in their hymns. He is described as a tawny or exceptionally fair youth with braided hair, decked in gold ornaments. During the Vedic period (3000-1500 B.C.), Rudra was identified with Agni and his contact with Prithvi or earth is said to have given birth to the Maruts or the winds. His other synonyms are Ugra and Isana. Yet, by the period of the Puranas (edited around the third to fourth centuries), Rudra emerges as one of the supreme deities and even gains superiority over Vishnu and Brahma. With Shiva's admission into the fold of the higher gods, there seemed to have come over the followers of the Vedic cult and Shaivism (Shaivism is one of the oldest and most widely spread cults in India), a strong desire for reconciliation.

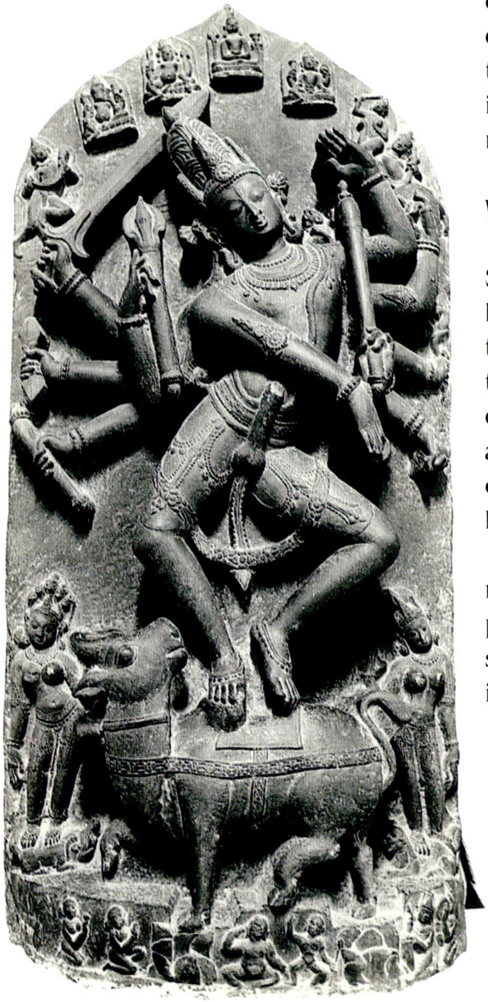

Who is He?

But the surprising fact is that Lord Shiva is rarely worshipped in his human form. In the innumerable temples scattered over the towns and the countryside, a simple round, cylindrical object (the *linga*) resting on a spoon-shaped base (*yoni*), is enough to make the *bhakta* bow in loving veneration.

Together, the *linga* and the *yoni* represent the male and the female principle, energy or essence. This dual symbolism makes for a host of interpretations, each adding meaning

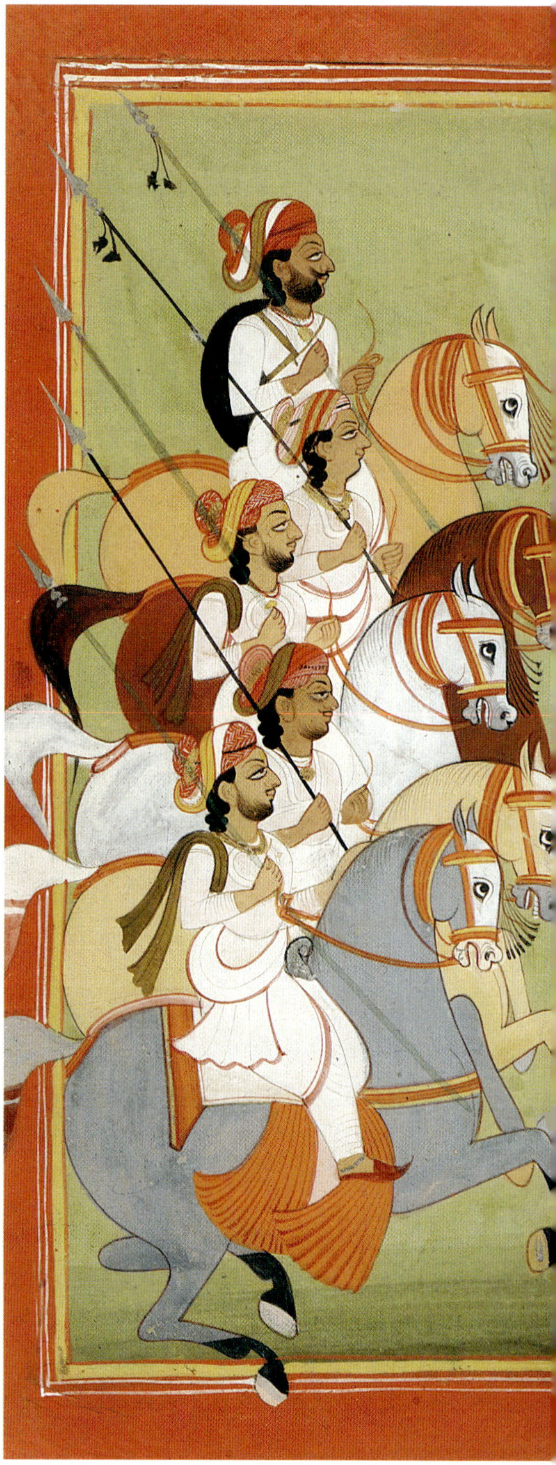

to the object of worship. But it is clear that the two are interlinked. 'When Shiva is united with Shakti, he is able to create, otherwise he is unable even to move,' says a verse in the *Saundaryalahari* (a treatise in praise of the primordial female power or Devi that is attributed to Shankaracharya). In the *Anandanubhava*, it is stated that *Shakti* 'is of the form of the pleasure derivable from *Guhya* (the female organ) and that Shiva is the *linga*; the union of these two is the cause of the joy that is found in the universe.'

The earliest reference to phallic worship is found in the *Rig Veda* where the phallus is called *shishnadeva*. The *Markandeya Purana* alludes to the *haryardha* form of Shiva, where the female generative principle is identified with Vishnu. In the *Linga Purana*, the *pradhana* (nature) is called the *linga* and the Paramesvara is called the *lingin* –the sustainer of the *linga*. The pedestal of the *linga* is the Mahadevi or Uma and the *linga* is the visible Maheshvara. At a later period, this non-Aryan emblem was identified with a god, Skambha, mentioned in the Vedas. Skambha was 'conceived as co-extensive with the universe and comprehends [sic] in him the various parts of the material universe, as also the abstract qualities of *tapas*, faith, truth and divisions of time,' says Gopinath Rao.

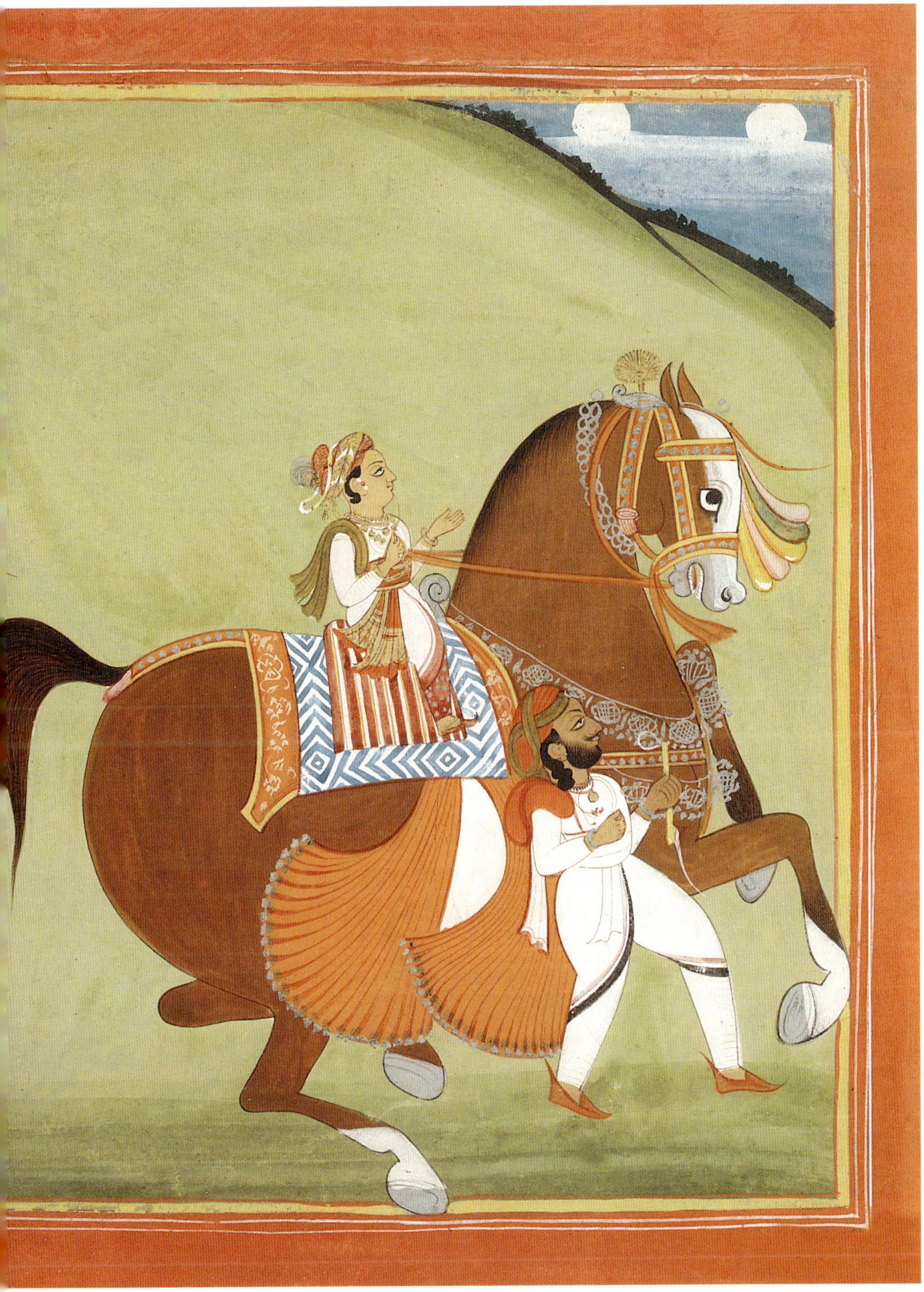

Warriors going off to battle. Valour was seen in some cultures as an essential part of virility.
Facing page: *Natraja*, Shiva as Lord of the Dance, with an erect phallus. *Dacca Museum, Bangladesh.*
Previous page: A *mukhalingam* from North India. Exquisitely shaped phallic symbols have the face of Shiva protruding from them.

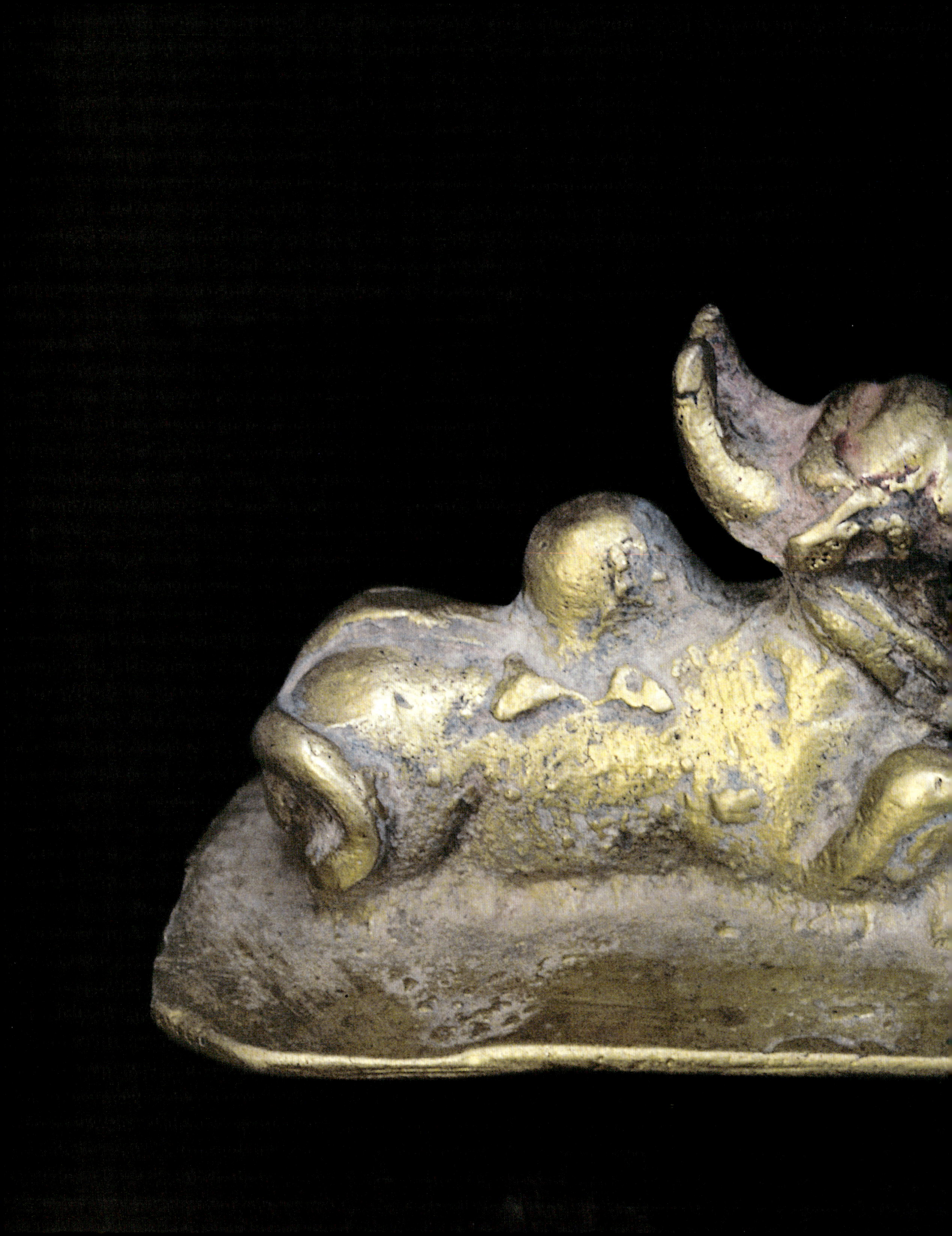

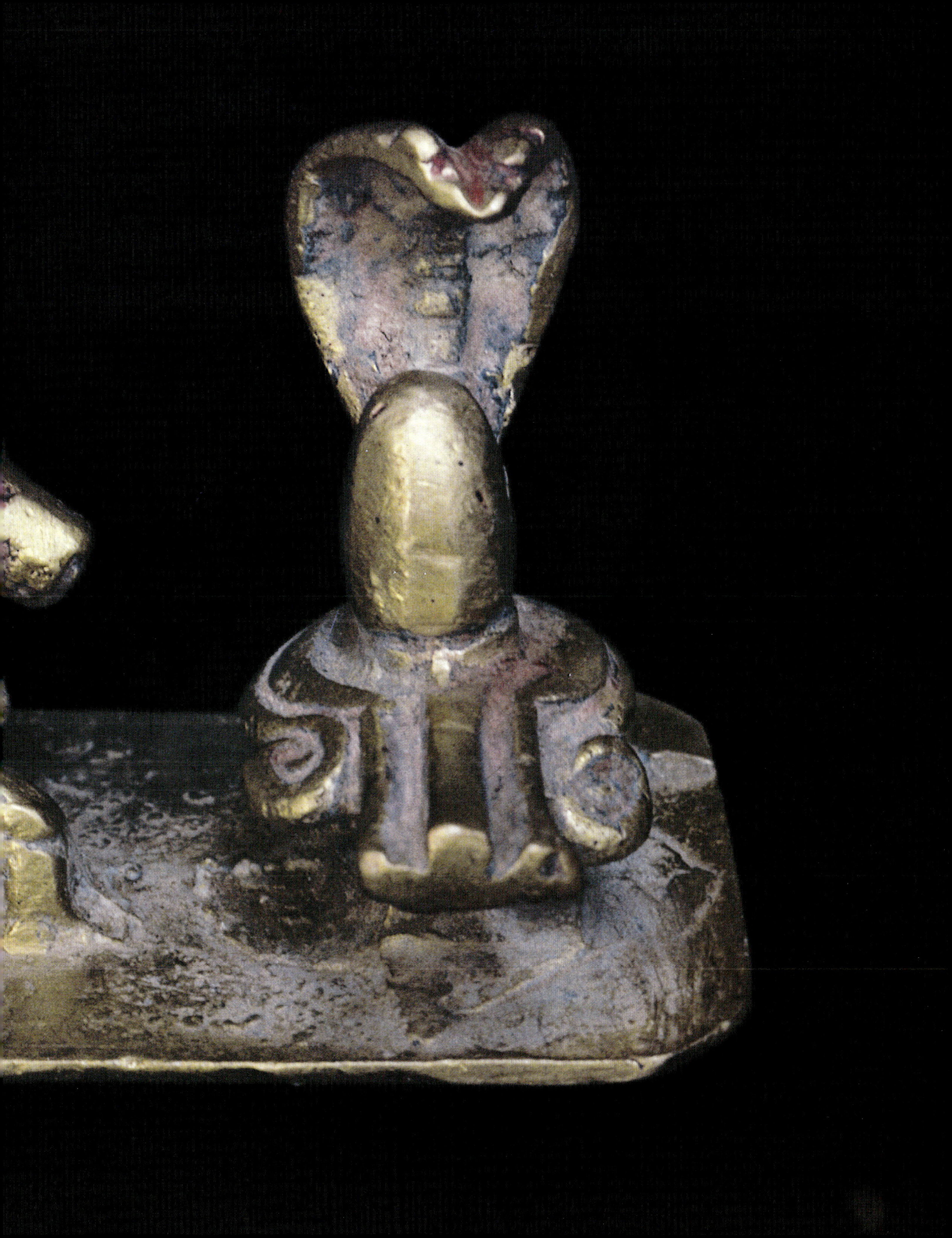

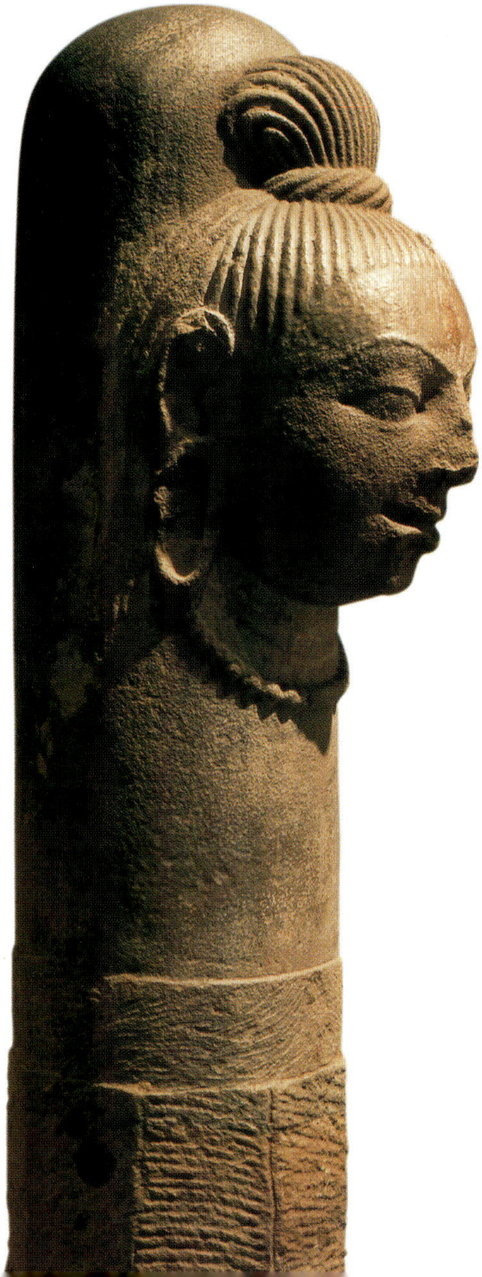

Below: A *mukhalingam* from Madhya Pradesh.
Facing page (top): A seal from the Indus Valley civilisation shows Shiva in the form of Pashupatinath or Lord of animals. He sits in the traditional yogic posture. *National Museum, New Delhi.*
Facing page (bottom): A *mukhalingam* from Maharashtra.
Previous page: Shivalinga under the canopy of a serpent, watched over by Nandi.

Phallus: Type, meaning and myth

Once Brahma and Vishnu were fighting over who was supreme. Brahma said he was supreme because he was the creator; Vishnu claimed his superiority by proclaiming that he was the creator and destroyer. Just then a blazing pillar of coherent light appeared and Shiva's voice sounded from within it, proclaiming that he was pre-eminent as he was the creator, the preserver and the destroyer. The two gods were stunned into silence. Forgetting their fight, they set out in opposite directions to determine the size of the *lingam* but were unable to measure it even though they journeyed for thousands of years.

The *Linga Purana* provides a perspective in which the tale can be understood. It says the *linga* has its roots in the formless and in the non-manifested. Shiva is, therefore, himself without the *linga*. Further, the *linga* belongs to Shiva and he who possesses it is the Supreme Being. Indeed, the the phallus is the foundation of the entire world and all is issued from the *linga*. He who desires perfection of the soul, recommends the *Purana*, must worship the *linga*.

The *Shiva Purana* contains Lord Shiva's own categorical statement: 'I am not distinct from the phallus. The phallus is identical to me. It draws my faithful close to me; therefore it must be worshipped. My beloveds! Everywhere an erect penis is to be found, I am present, even if it is no more than another of my representations.'

But the word *linga* is not something coined for the erect organ. What it essentially means in Sanskrit is 'sign'. It refers to the characteristic that distinguishes male from female at birth, the reproductive organ.

The fact that the phallus alone should be worshipped seems chauvinistic but that is not so. For one, the phallus is the bearer of the semen, which is the seed of life. Hence it is the 'creator in mankind' says author A. Danielou in his study. It is not a symbol, therefore, it has been picked at random, but is worshipped because it denotes a universal truth. The phallic symbol has been in existence the world over since the Paleolithic (Old Stone Age) period, but it is only in India that it has been a consistent motif in art, literature and religion from prehistoric to modern times.

References to the phallic cult are found through the length and breadth of the country, particularly in south India. The first ithyphallic symbol was seen in the Indus Valley civilisation. Danielou speaks of how the 'rough and courageous Aryans discovered a marvellous civilisation in India – cities of gold and silver with splendid palaces

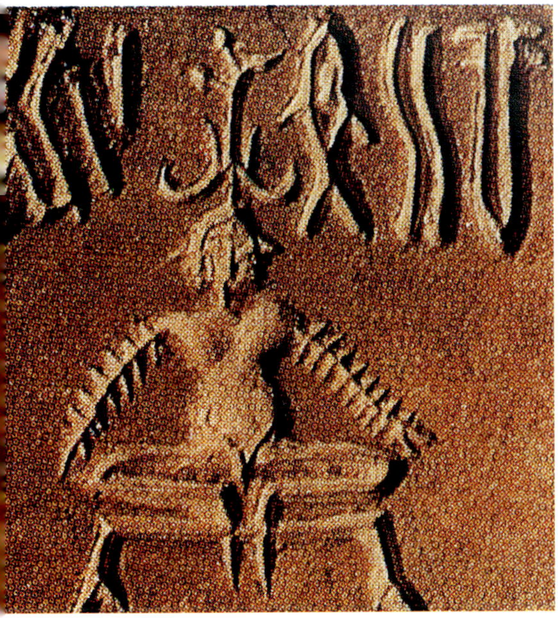

and incalculable riches, offering every pleasure. These cities were inhabited by a dark-skinned people, who worshipped the phallus and the snake, and who fought bravely against the invader.' Thus, the phallus was not known to the Aryans and was also not part of Vedic writings. But there is mention of Shishnadeva, the phallic god, in the *Rig Veda*. However, his worship was banned due to the socio-cultural norms of the period. This probably had much to do with the phallus being associated with pagan cults that included black magic and sorcery in their rituals of worship. But the revival of Shaivism in the second century B.C. redefined attitudes towards the phallus in Vedic texts.

As an organ, the phallus plays a dual role. It is the tool of procreation and also the giver of divine ecstasy or *ananda*, which emerges from the union of the phallus and the *yoni*. *Ananda* ultimately leads to detachment and enlightenment.

Pleasure and desire are also manifested through the phallus. Agni, the lord of fire, has in fact been represented as drinking the sperm which gushes out from Shiva's phallus. Desire leads to physical union from which procreation takes place. The sperm or *bija* which is produced from the phallus contains the entire heritage, race and characteristics of a person. The *bija* is venerated and is found in both the mortal and immortal. It is part of the crescent moon adorning Shiva's head and it is in the Ganges which Shiva carries in his locks.

The icon of Shiva, the phallus, is usually shown vertical and called the *Urdhvalinga*. Here, the erect phallus is divided into three sections. The lowest is square and concealed within the pedestal – representative of Brahma, the creator and the gravitational power that holds and shapes the world. The second portion is the octagonal central section symbolic of Vishnu – the main force which gives birth to matter. Finally, comes the uppermost section which is cylindrical and an emblem of Shiva, who is the potent

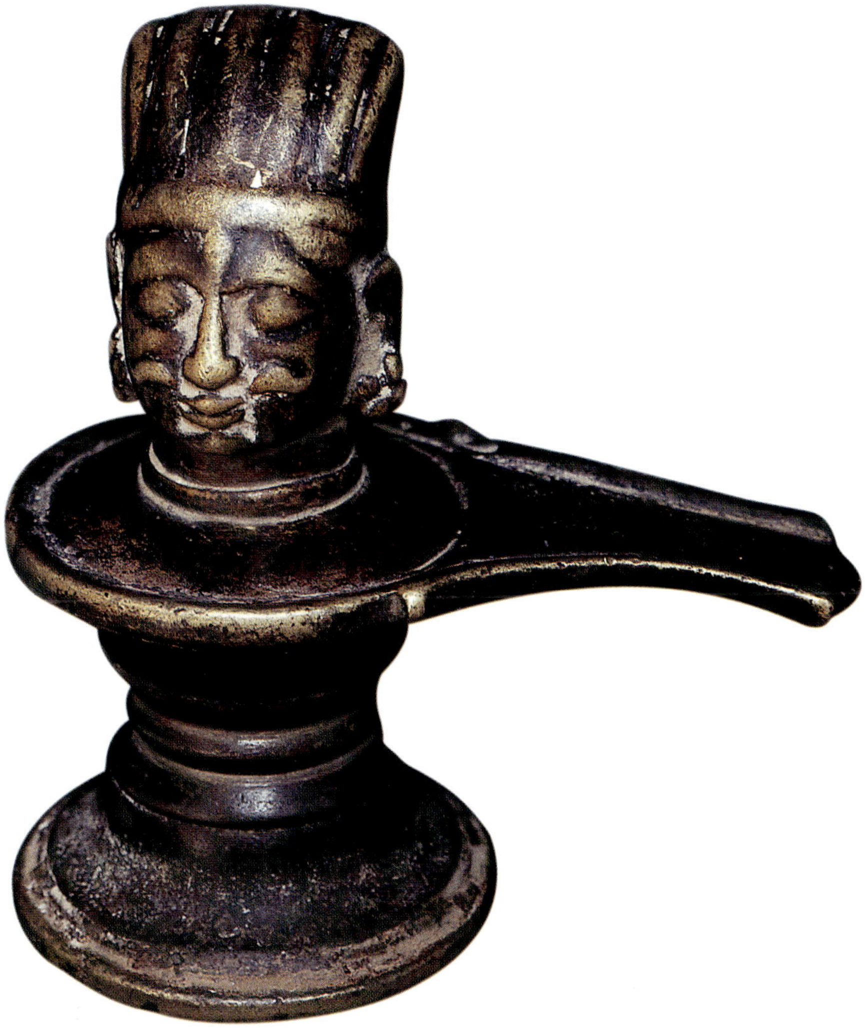

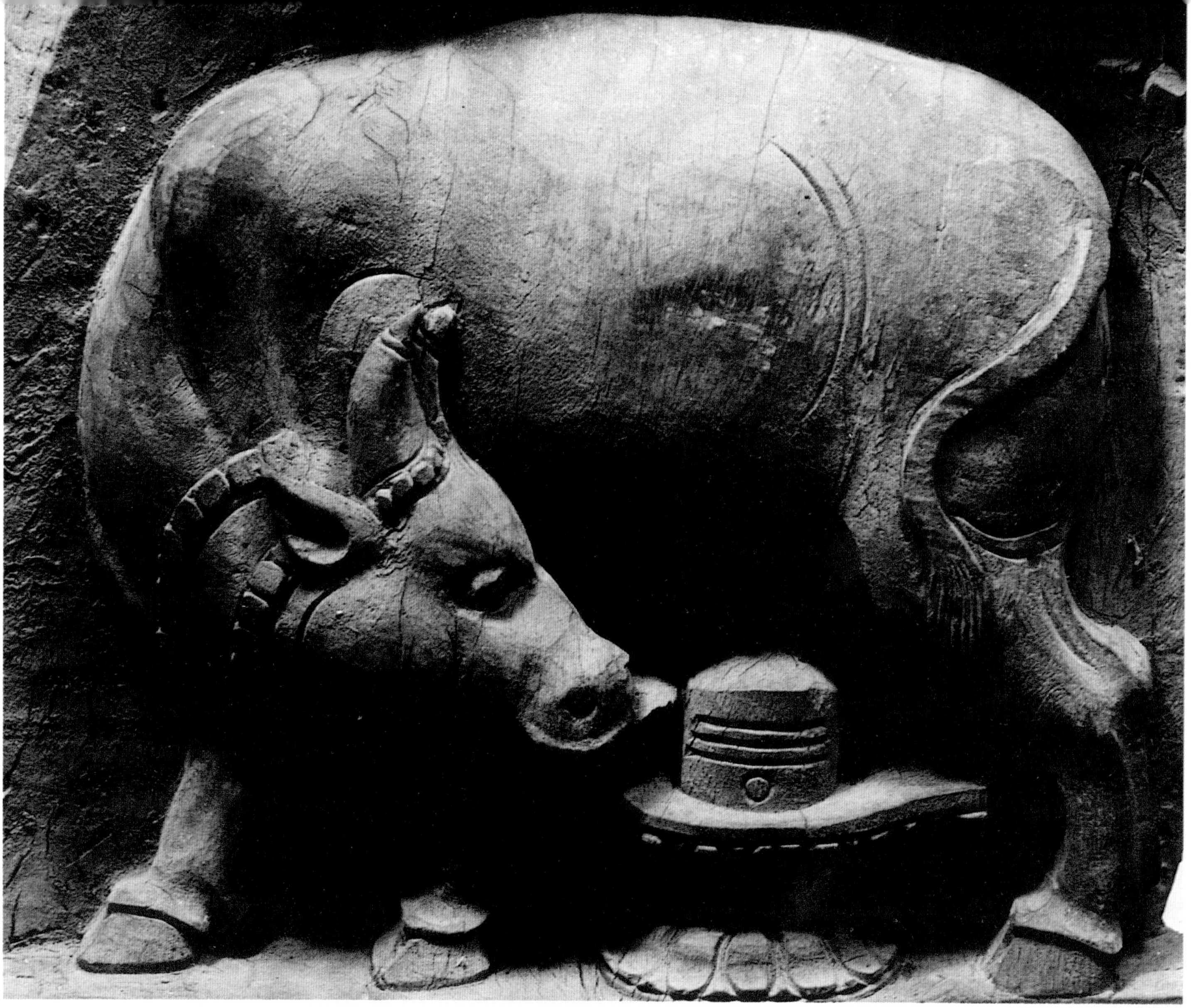

force of expansion. The base of the *linga* is, of course, nothing else but the *yoni* or the womb in which all matter realises its individuality.

The *bindu* concept of Shiva (*bindu* being point limit, that is, the short moment between being and non-being) emphasises departure from the universe. As a concept, *bindu* (literally, dot or point) neither negates nor posits but emphasises acceptance of all. It also stands for the *sarvanandamaya chakra* (centre or energy node of bliss). It is light itself, beyond all colours, and is generally represented without colour.

The world's axis is represented as a pillar of light, as a *lingam* of light that traverses the universe from one side to the other and is visible to those who have attained the transcendental level of perception.

Another interpretation sees the merging of the *linga* with the *yoni* as the first point of contact with what is natural. But, mark you, the *linga* is still not wholly submerged with the *yoni*. Therefore, the *linga* is thought to be away from nature's reach. The part of it that touches the *yoni*, approximately one-fourth, is symbolic of the mortal universe and all that it contains. The three-fourths that is withdrawn from the *yoni* exemplifies the immortal or the divine.

Yet another factor that shows the paramountcy of the *linga* is its placement in the temple. It is usually placed in the centre of a dark room. The room itself is symbolic of the *yoni* and is the *garbagriha* (sanctum sanctorum) of the temple. The axis of

Nandi shown licking the *lingam* in a stone sculpture from north India. Nandi is the mount of Lord Shiva. *Facing page:* One of the most complex representations of the *shivalingas* from south India. It shows a number of themes associated with Lord Shiva: the *mukhalingam*, at its periphery Ganesha, and the cobra that covers the *linga* in an unusual form. *Crafts Museum, New Delhi.*

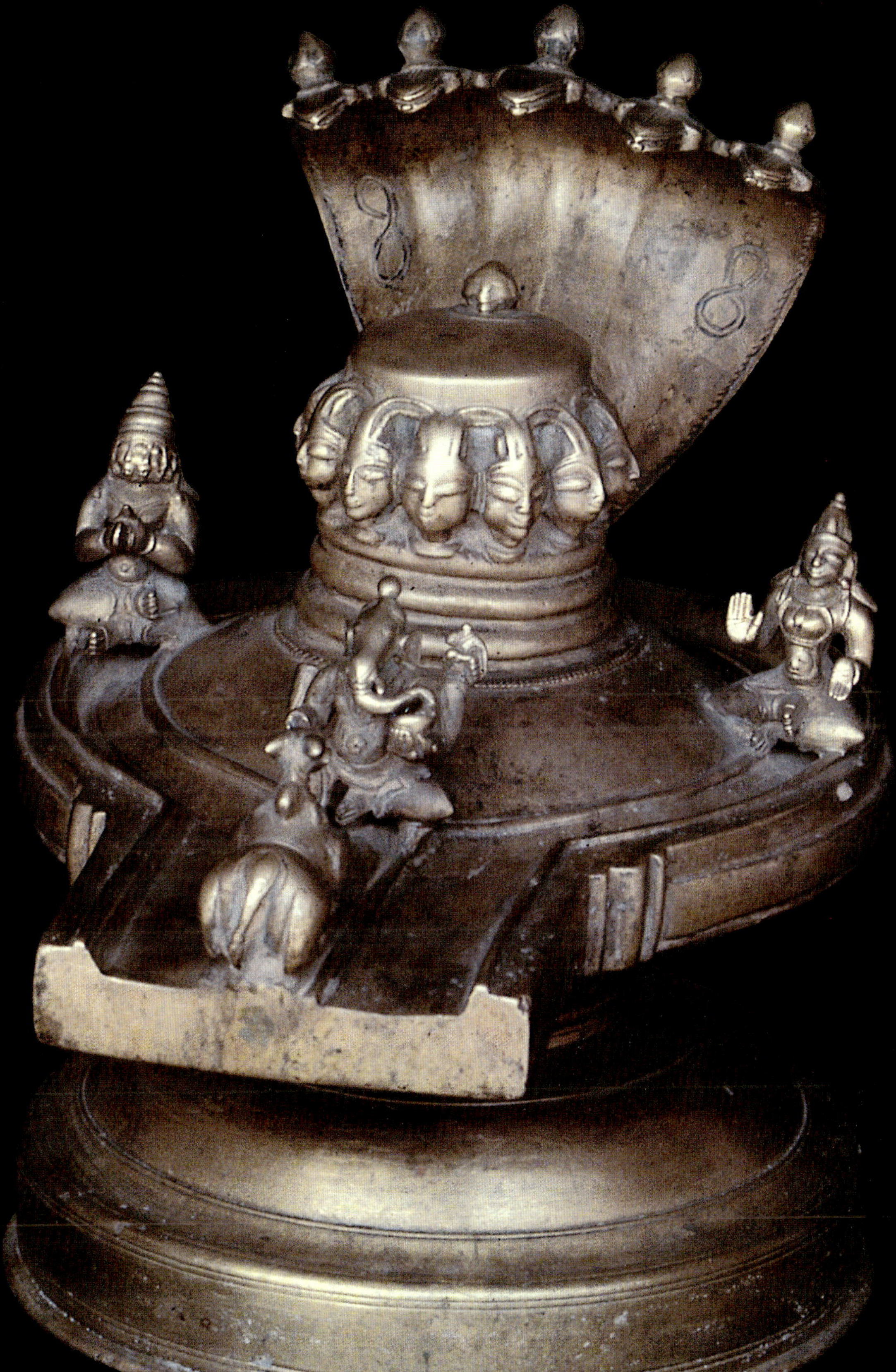

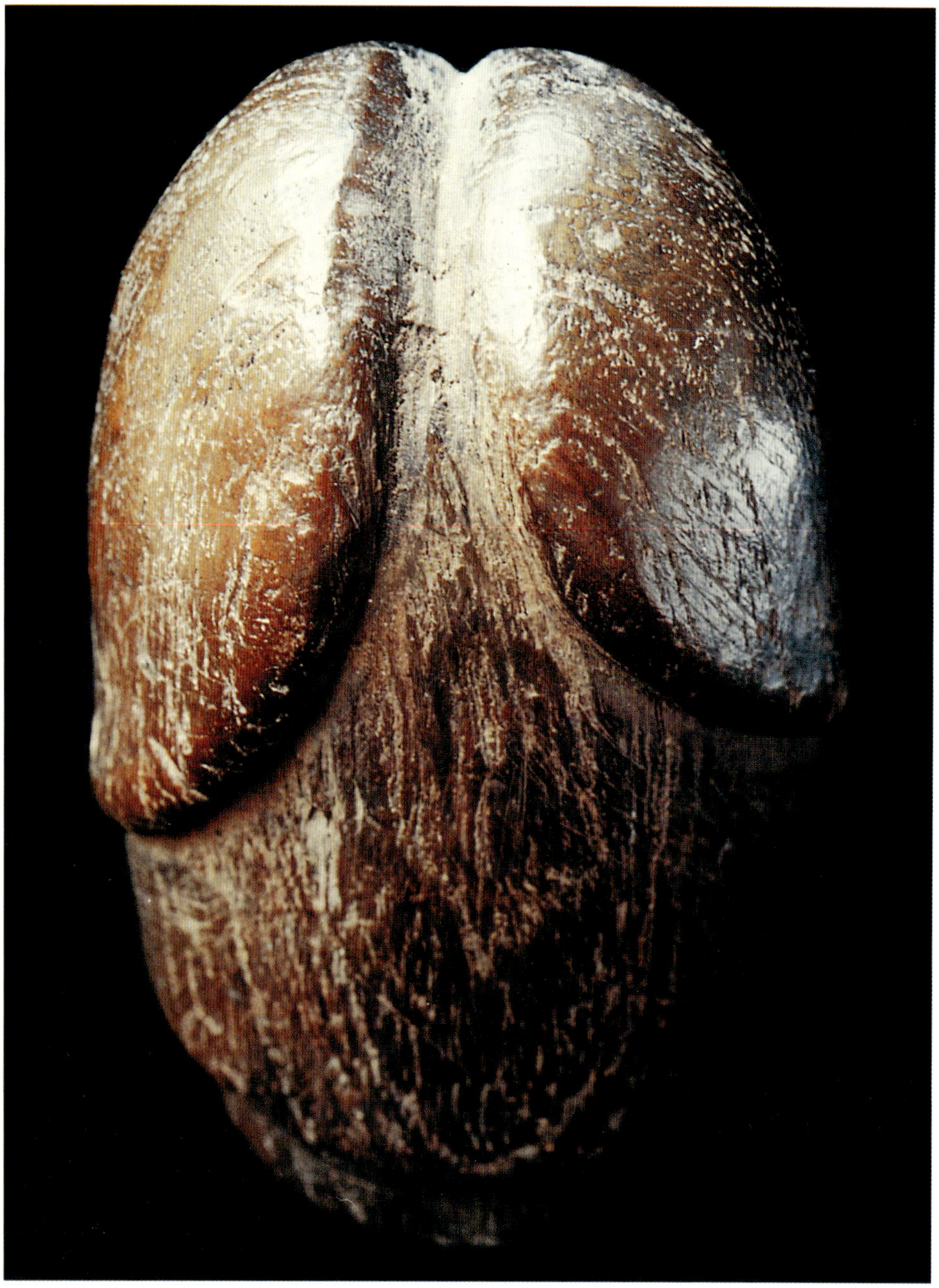

the *linga* is in a direct line with the central peak of the temple roof. This is said to elicit and represent the *lingam* of light.

The *lingam* has many forms in the Hindu religion. One theory of the *akasha lingam* suggests that the *lingam* is nature itself, where space is characterised by the phallus and the earth by the *yoni*. The sky appears to be a gigantic arch rising above the feminine earth just as the phallus rises above the *yoni* in many sculptures. All the openings in the earth are considered wombs. In these wombs, rituals which ensure procreation are performed.

The *lingam* is not only recreated by man with stone in temples, but some believe it comes into being naturally when Lord Shiva's semen falls on the earth and creates what is around us. A *linga* that materialises by itself is called the *svayambhu linga*. One such natural *linga* is the ice *lingam* seen at Amarnath in Kashmir. 'The *linga* . . . has been the centre of the innermost sanctuary of every Shiva temple over the last two thousand years,' says Stella Kramrisch in her study of *lingas*. There are, in fact, sixty-eight *svayambhu lingas* and all are major pilgrimage spots.

Another natural form of the *linga* is found in the stones of the Narmada river. These stones are popularly called *shalagrama*.

The *lingam* not only exists in nature; it has a face to it as well and is called the *mukha lingam*. Stella Kramrisch mentions that the vertical *lingam* in the cross-legged position has the capacity to retain the seed and canalise it upwards towards the brain, thus converting sexual energy into mental power. This transforming of the procreative into the creative faculty is symbolised in the *mukhalinga*.

The *mukhalinga* is a variety of the *manusha lingas* and is distinct from all other *lingas* in that it bears one or more sculptures of a human face on its surface. Sometimes it has five faces corresponding to the Isana, Tatpurusha, Aghora, Vamadeva and the Sadyojata aspects of Shiva.

The details of making a *mukhalinga* are given in both the *agama* and tantric texts. The *agama* texts (the *agamas* are special revelations of knowledge in contrast to the Vedas, which are general revelations of knowledge and are said to have been handed down by Lord Shiva himself) hold forth in an elaborate dissertation on the male, female and neuter nature of stones, timber and all other objects involved in the making of the *lingas*.

They broadly divide the *lingas* into two classes – the *chala lingas* or the moveable, and the *achala lingas* or the immoveable. Various *agama* texts give details about the composition and the making of the *chala lingas*. The *Kamikagama* (an *agama* text) classifies the different *lingas*: *mrinmaya* (those made of earth), *lohaja* (those made of metals), *ratnja* (those made of precious stones), *daruja* (those made of wood), *sailaja* (those made of stones) and *kshanika lingas* (those made for the occasion and then disposed of). The *Suprabhedagama* classifies the *achala* or *sthavara lingas* into nine different heads. In fact, a *svayambhu linga* is considered the most sacred: that is, even above all the rules laid down in the *agama* texts. The largest number of the *achala* or the *sthavara lingas* are the *manusha lingas,* which belong to that class of *lingas* which has been set up by human hands. The *manusha lingas* are made up of three parts: the lowest is known as the *Brahmabhaga*, the middle section as the *Vishnubhaga,* the top section as the *Rudrabhaga*. The lengths of the *lingas* vary according to the different classes of the *lingas*.

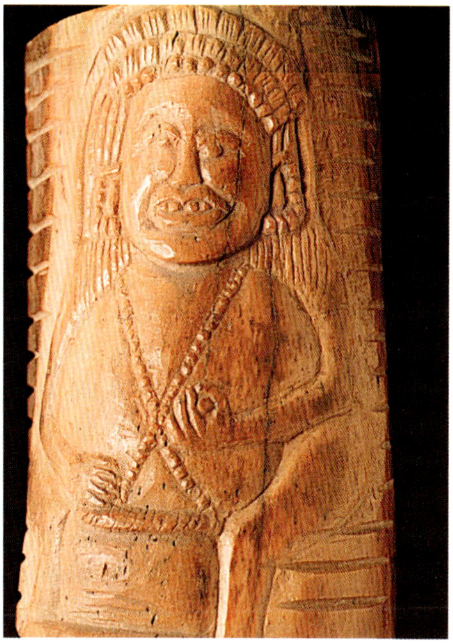

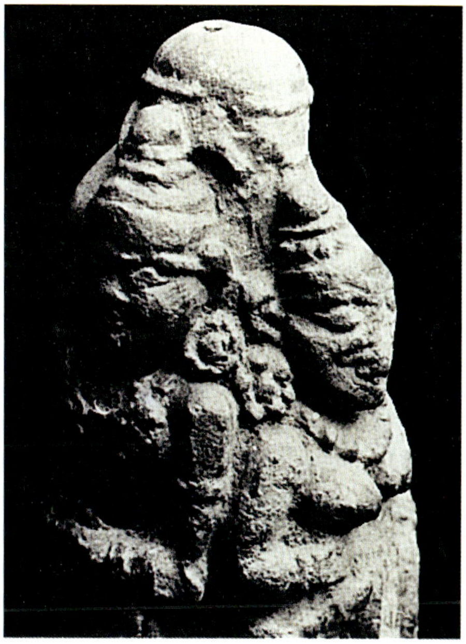

Top: A Shungha period buffalo horn with a demonical figure from Chandraketugarh, West Bengal.
Bottom: A penis in terracotta from Chandraketugarh.
Facing page: A penis head that is attached to a bamboo pole in a fertility dance for unmarried males who challenge each other in an erotic ritual dance, Karnataka.

Tantra: Universe of union

Tantra: Universe of union

Tantra predates all texts in India. Lord Shiva and the Devi are considered the authors of the tantras themselves. Rather than espouse a withdrawal from life, Tantra encourages the fullest acceptance of human desires and feelings. For the tantrika, it is the via media between the physical world and the inner reality. 'His aim (the tantrika's) is not the discovery of the unknown but the realisation of the known, for "what is here, is elsewhere; what is not here, is nowhere" (*Visvasara Tantra*). The result is an experience that is even more real than the experience of the objective world,' says Ajit Mookerjee.

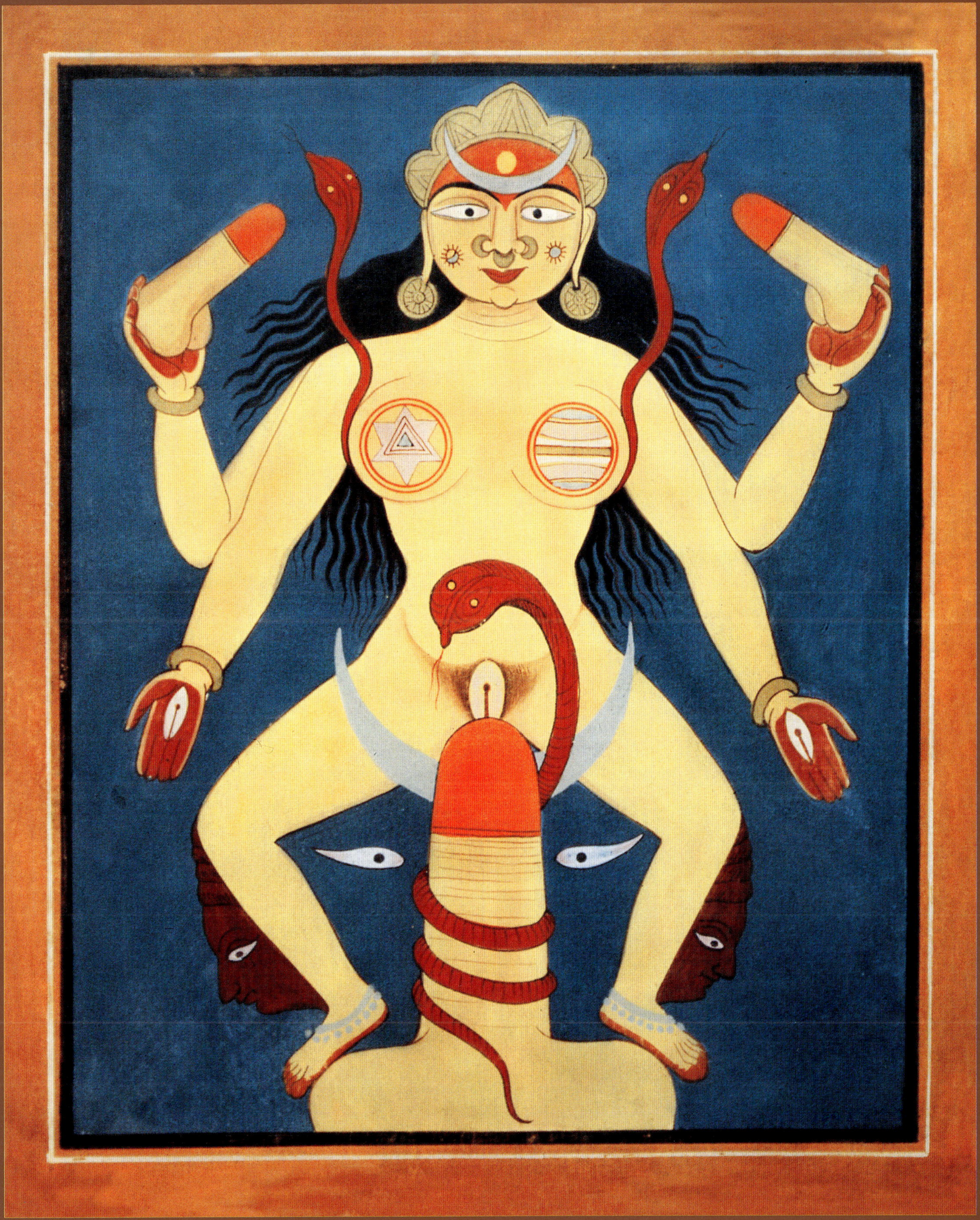

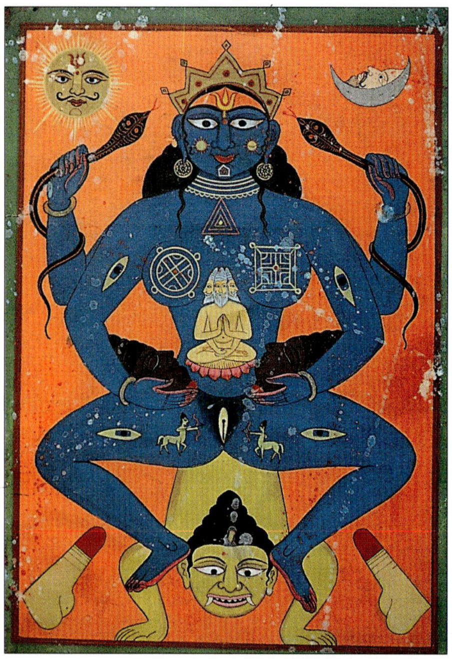

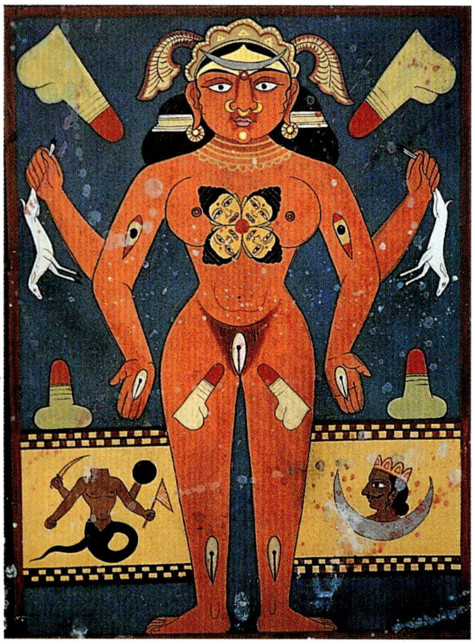

The term tantra has been subject to considerable misinterpretation owing to its interchangeability. The shadow of the black arts has often fallen on it and it has easily fallen into disrepute. But the power of tantra is undeniable. Its negative use, believed adepts, can be counter-balanced by the power of the mantra.

There is also confusion about tantra being a religion or a mystic cult. Woodruffe defines it as 'an encyclopaedic science. It is practical and has no concern with wordy warfare. It lights the torch and shows the way step by step until the sojourner comes to the end of his journey.'

Woman as the primal force

According to tantra, everything is based on the duality of the male (*purusha* — pure consciousness) and the female (*prakriti* — cosmic force of nature). The male or *purusha* is static, it is only through union with the female *prakriti* or *shakti*, the kinetic energy, that everything is created and obliterated. *Purusha* and *prakriti* are the cosmic manifestations of the human male and female. In tantra, the two poles come together to form the whole in an experience of supreme bliss or *ananda*.

The same philosophy runs through the Buddhist tantric texts, the differentiating factor being that there the female, *prajna*, is static, and the male, *upaya*, is the kinetic force.

In tantric practices, the woman assumes a dynamic and dominant role. The rituals concentrate on female worship and elevate the woman to the level of the cosmic force. The woman is the repository of dark and light aspects: she is creative as well as dissolute, sensual and sublime, benign and horrific. She is *shakti* herself, the mother womb of the universe's recurring cycles.

The tantrics view the universe as being one with themselves. The psychological and biological functions of the human body are a tool through which the ultimate energy, the *kundalini shakti*, can be awakened to unite with the supreme being, Lord Shiva. The *kundalini shakti* lies coiled up in our being in spinal psychic energy centres, called *chakras*. When the *kundalini* awakens, all the kinetic forces that charge various centres focus to perceive the higher, cosmic level above the individual level. The *kundalini shakti* opens the numerous torpid areas of the brain – a limitless store of unfathomable amounts of energy. The opening of the *kundalini*, that is, *jagriti*, releases this energy and raises the individual to the plane of cosmic consciousness, opening the lotus with a thousand petals, on the top of the head or *sahasrara*.

Top:. All three rare paintings on paper are probably from a small cultic sect. Here, the male Purusha and the female Shakti are shown.
Above left: Shakti, the mother womb of the universe's recurring cycles.
Facing page: The tantrics view the universe as one with themselves. The psychological and biological functions of the body are used to awaken the *kundalini*.
Previous page: Tantric painting from Rajasthan of the mother goddess dancing before the *shivalinga*.

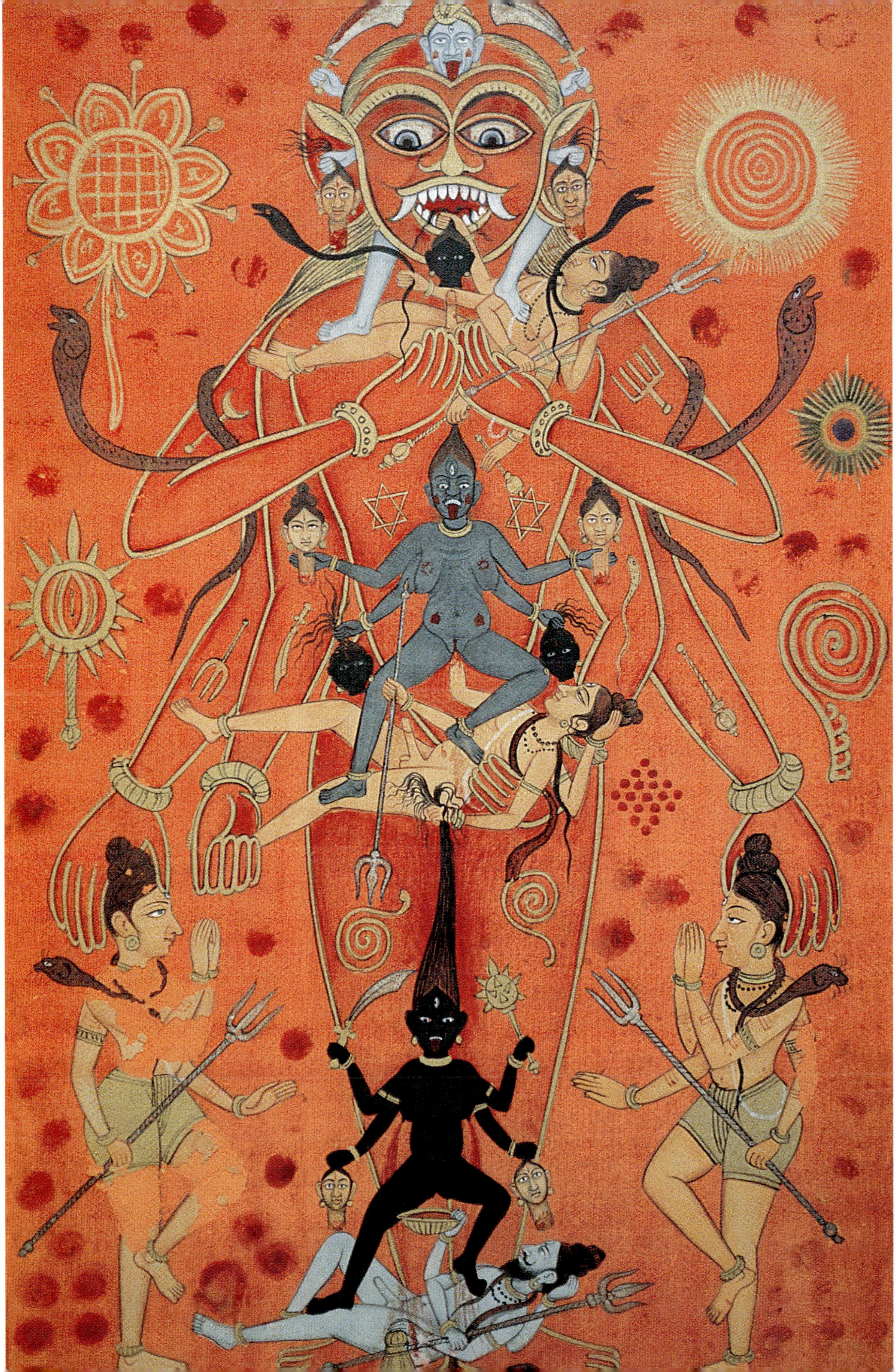

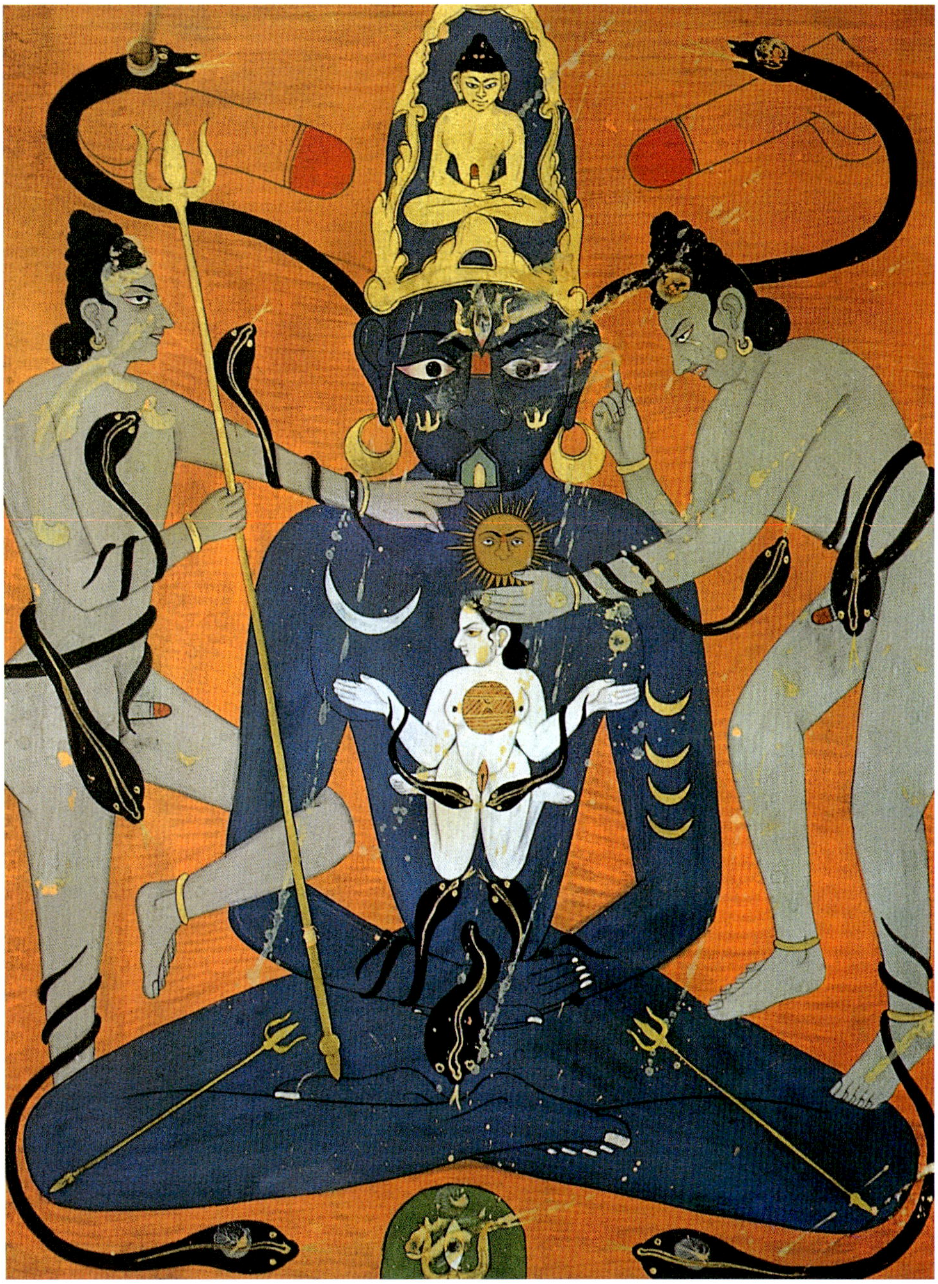

Shakti can be aroused through systematic control of breathing or *pranayama,* a part of the science of yoga. Meditation requires rhythmic breathing to get all the atoms to flow in one direction and towards one central point in the body. Once all the atoms are concentrated there, the *kundalini* is awakened. Very often this leads to possession of supernatural powers or *siddhis*. India's ancient *rishis* or sages classified them (as they did the various stages of awakening or spiritual progress) into eight categories. Among these the best known are *anima*, the power to reduce oneself to the minutest size; its reverse, *mahima*; and *laghima* or the attainment of weightlessness.

Tantric philosophy underlines that practising yogic *asanas* can arouse the *kundalini*. This means that everything that fastens us to the world becomes a starting point towards liberation. The philosophy goes so far as to include sexual interaction and to see sexual intercourse as leading to that bliss which is associated with the Divine. There is such intense sexual energy in the body, says tantra, that it can liberate the psyche of an individual. However, tantricism does not advocate uncontrolled hedonism. Tantrics express sex in the form of *yab – yum* or the the male and female in love-play. The basic function of tantric rituals is to attain a non-dual *sahaja* (union) through *upasana* and *sadhana*. The tools that aid the tantrics in their *sadhana* and *upasana* are mystic circles or *mandalas*, mystic diagrams or *yantras*.

The right sexual practice in tantricism is one driven by right intentions and is carried out only after sufficient induction.

Also, sex is neither immoral nor moral; it is amoral. One story emphasises the non-ethical nature of sex. Once Chandidas, a high priest and rebel-poet of the fifteenth century in Bengal, fell in love with a lower caste washerwoman, Rami. To him this woman was an incarnation of the primordial woman. But the class difference put him in an awkward position: should he uphold social values or do as his heart commanded? Chandidas then approached his temple deity who told him to love the washerwoman like none other, as no God could give him what she could.

Such love that surpassed the boundaries of what was socially acceptable became a theme in tantric practices. Soon, only he who could unfold the strength of love could see the Supreme Being.

The woman too was not sidelined; indeed she has the most important role to play in the union. She is seen as the arbitrator between the ultimate and that which is earthy. She is the mover of all creation and deified into a

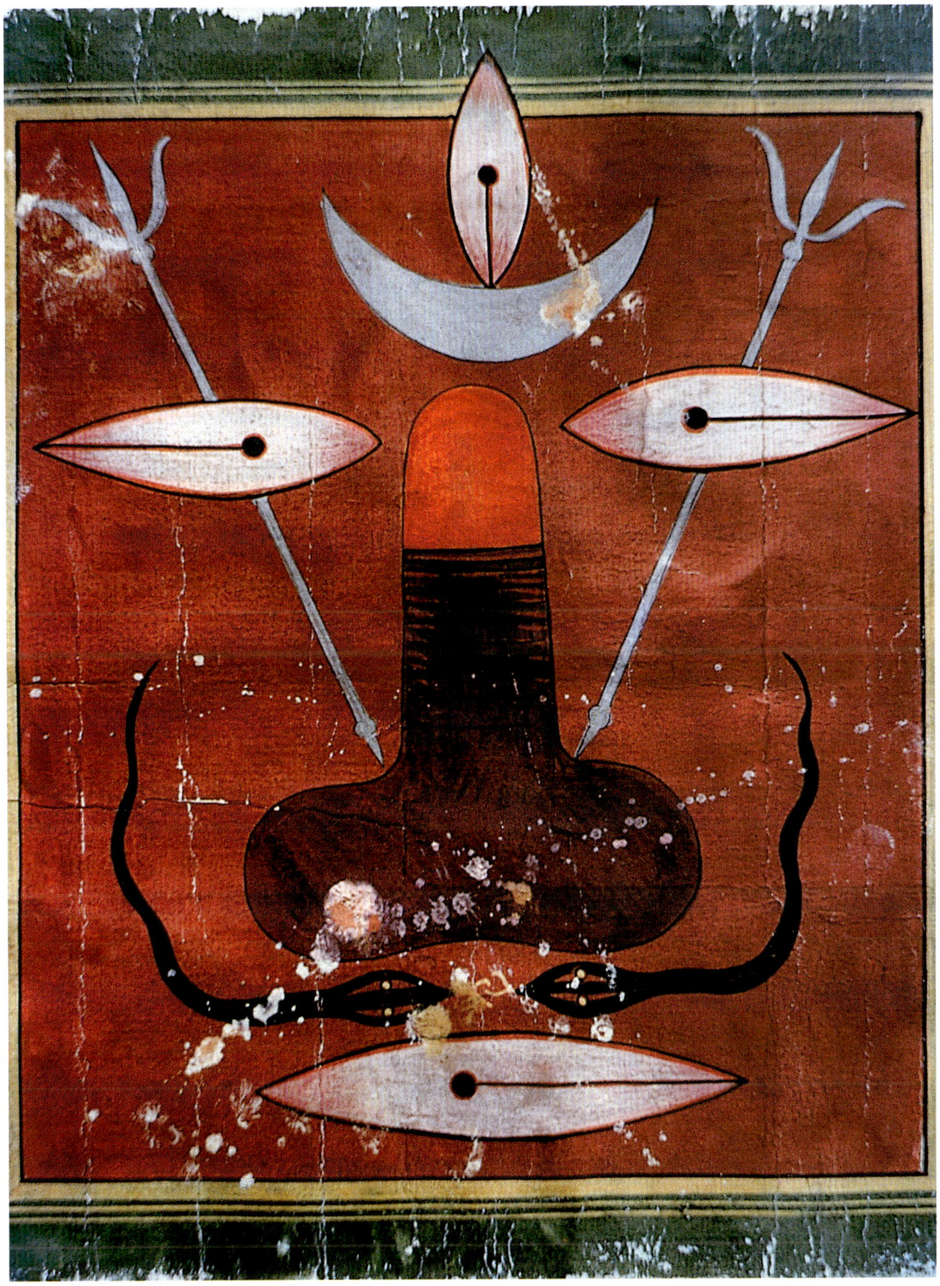

In this Rajasthani painting, the eyes of Lord Shiva are seen in the form of the female *yoni*, with his *linga*. *Facing page:* A Rajasthani tantric painting shows a yogic devotee who personifies within his own form, the male and female aspects of creation.

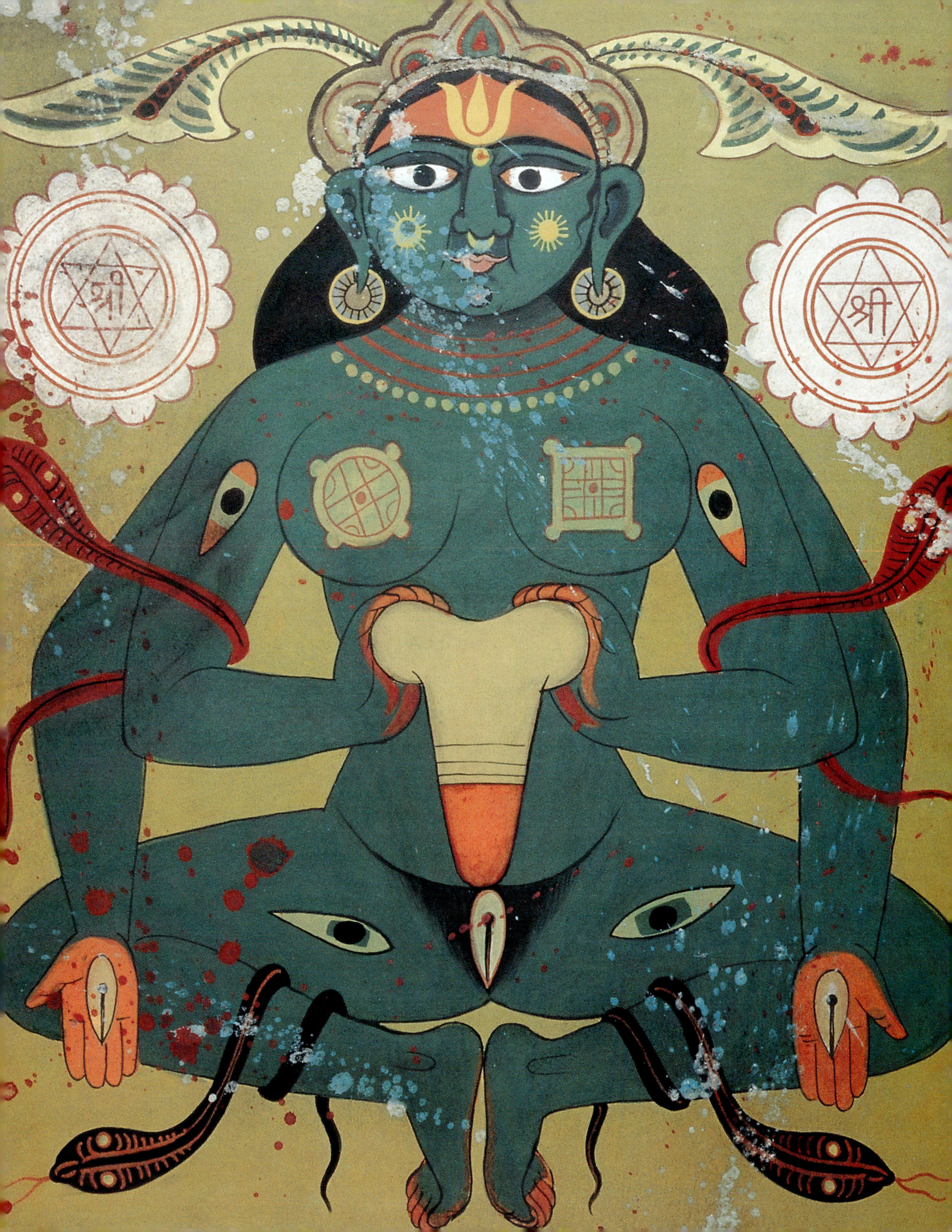
श्री
श्री

goddess worshipped in two forms: as a *kumari* (virgin) and as *shakti* (female). *Shakti* is known as *Tripura Sundairi* in her form as the goddess of desire.

Tantric practices are, in fact, incomplete without the recognition of female divinity and form. The *Ardhanarisvara* (Lord Shiva in half-male and half-female form) image also clearly defines the dual forces that are required to sustain the universe. The worship of the female principle is believed to be the most innocent form of tantric worship. The extreme forms of trantricism begin with drinking. The orgies begin with worshipping the woman from head to toe and then pouring wine over her body, and finally drinking the wine which is then considered highly consecrated.

Tantra pegs spiritual experience at various levels, based on the devotee's state of mind and disposition. There are three types of dispositions: *pasu*, that is subject to the common customs; *vira*, one which is capable of an experience of a stronger nature and has the strength to 'play with fire'; and finally, *divya*, the most developed of all three. A man in this state can experience supreme joy eternally and is in touch with the 'inner woman' and 'wine' constantly. Here the 'inner-woman' is the *kundalini* and 'wine' refers to the knowledge gained through excellence in yogic practices.

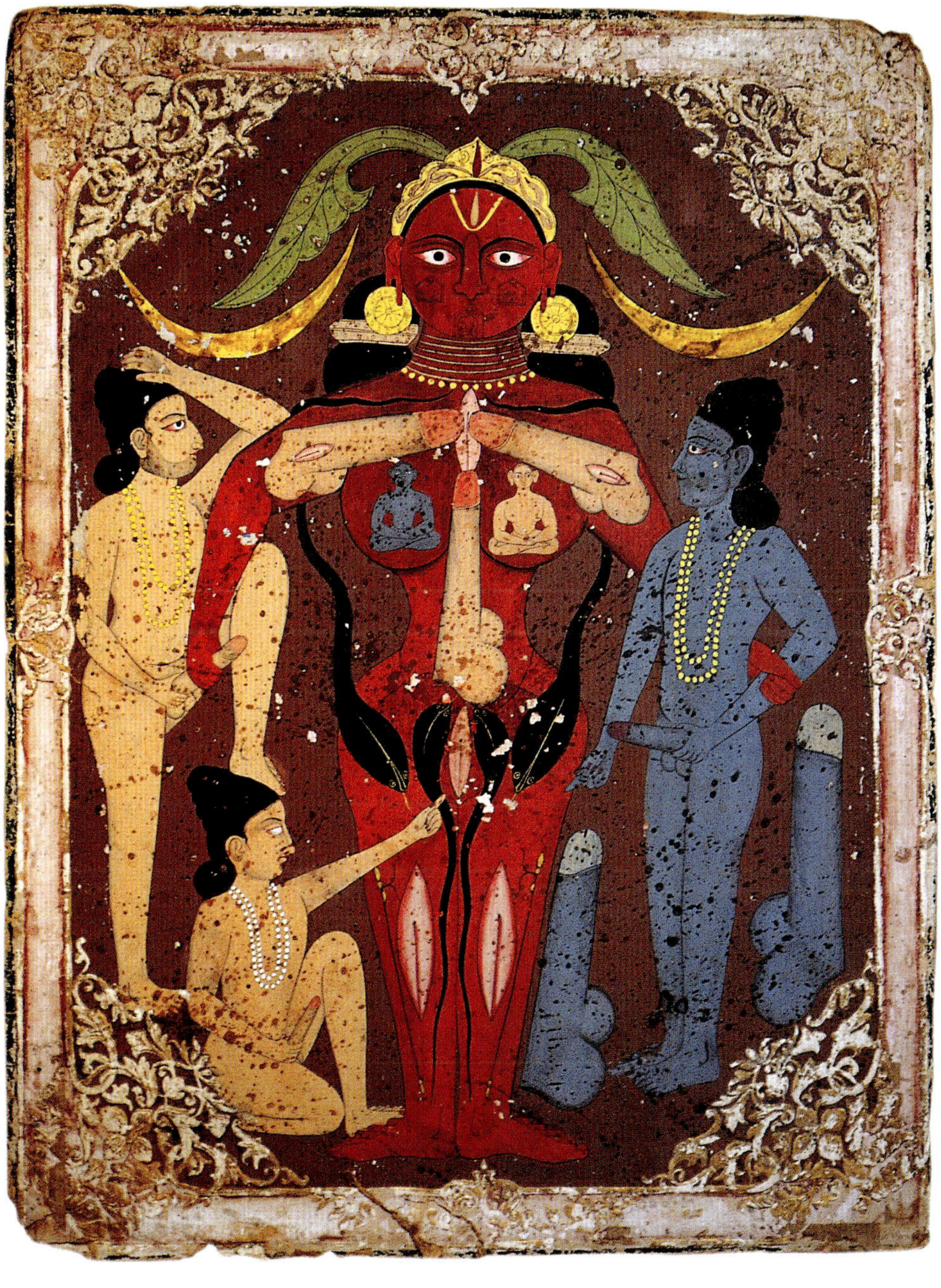

A Rajasthani image portraying nude male devotees surrounding the personification of the female principle in the form of the goddess.
Facing page: A Rajasthani Tantric cult image showing a female in a yogic posture displaying her *yoni*, her body embellished with numerous phalluses.

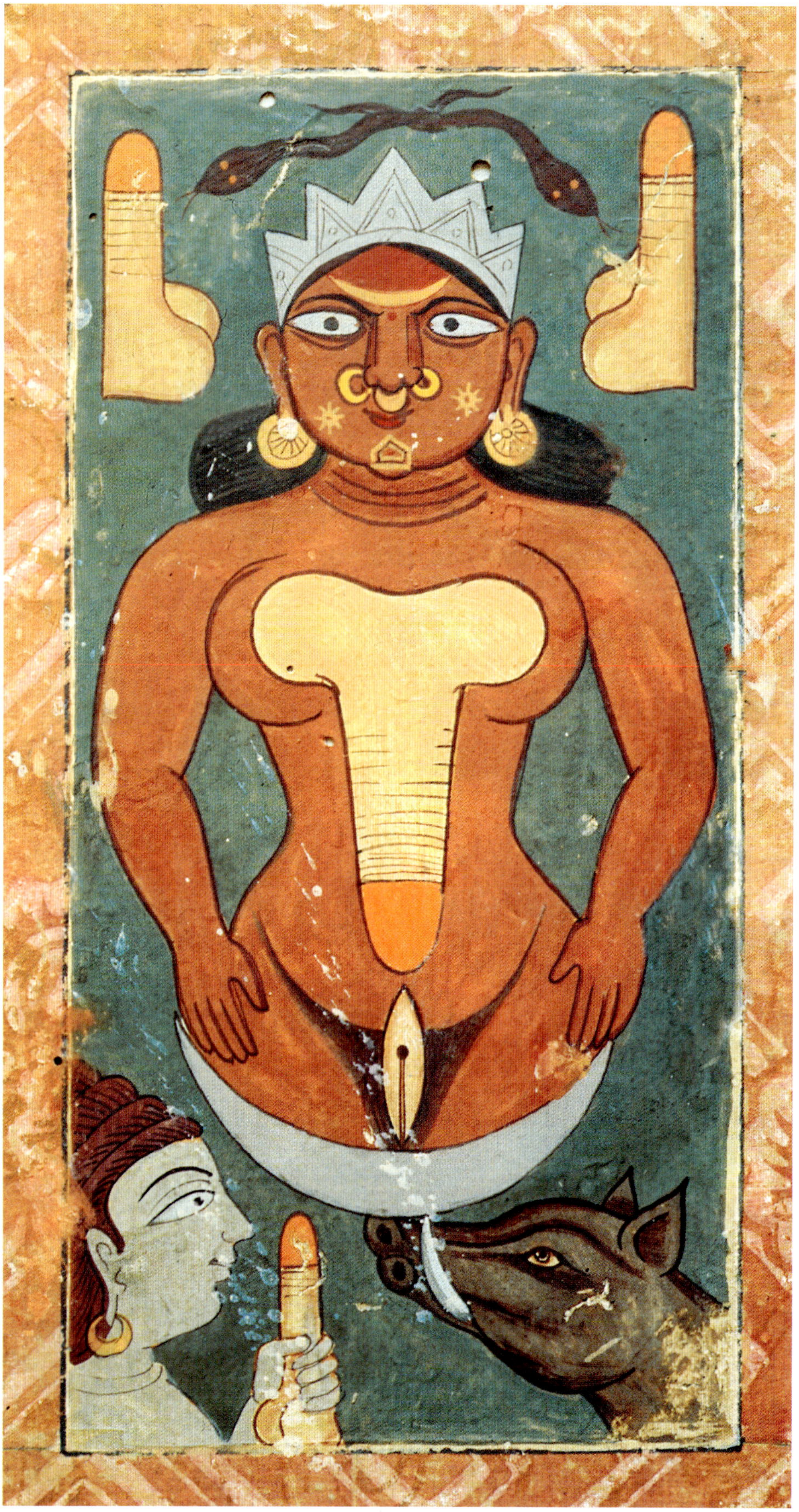

There are numerous and varied practices which arouse the *kundalini*: the *dakshinachara* (right-hand path), and the *vamachara* (left-hand path, where the woman is involved); and the *kulachara* (a combination of both). In addition to these, there are mixed practices such as the *Vedic*, *Shivas* and *Vaishnavas*. The practitioners of the left-hand path exercise the panchmakara, union of the five Ms: *madya* or wine, mamsa or meat, *matsya* or fish, *mudra* or parched cereal, and *maithuna* or sexual union. But those who are unable to detach themselves from shame, hate and fear are not deserving of this path. The most important part of the ritual is the *chakra puja* or circle worship, performed under cover of night. It takes place around a *yantra* drawn on the floor, while the devotees sit around it in a circle, and the host and his *shakti* are placed at the focal point.

The twilight zone or *sandhya* has a special significance for tantrics. *Sandhya bhasha* or *sandha bhasha* is the language of this time period, filled with erotic meanings. What is said may not be what is actually put into action. So, 'inserting his organ into the mother's womb', 'pressing his sister's breasts', and 'placing his foot upon the guru's head' are symbolic references. In *sandha* terminology, the 'organ' is a symbol of the contemplating mind. The 'mother's womb' is representative of the *muladhara chakra* or energy centre at the base of the spine. The 'sister's breasts' mean the heart centre or the *anahata chakra*. The 'guru's head' is metaphorical of the *sahasrara*. But why are these rituals written in a code? Perhaps, only to preserve and protect the rituals from prying eyes. It also gives a common language to its practitioners. It must be noted that in tantric texts and rituals, abusive language has a duality to its meaning, one that is concrete and the other which is symbolic. The central essence nonetheless is to transform experience into awareness.

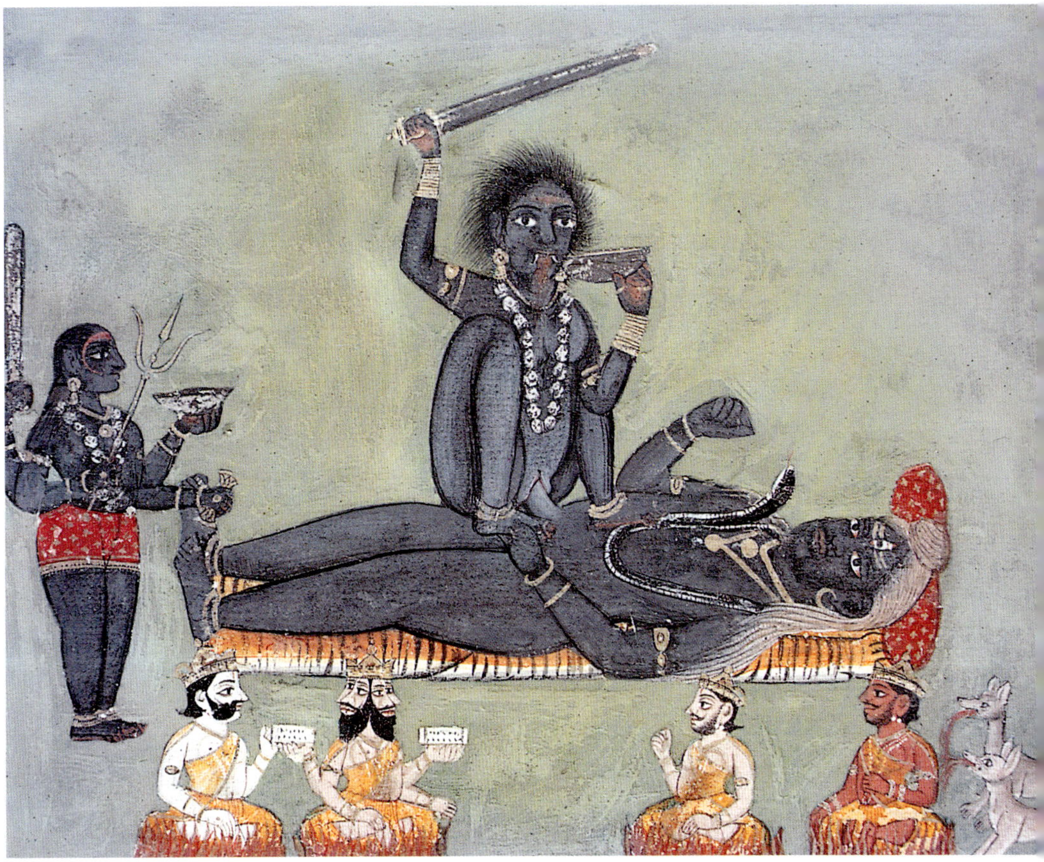

Worship in tantra

Tantra is an old art. We find evidence of tantra in the Indus Valley civilisation. Excavation of symbols of yogic postures and of fertility cults point to the existence of tantra. Moreover, there are significant chunks where tantric rituals draw content from the Vedic tradition. The *Brihadranyaka Upanishad* mentions the woman as being the centre of a Vedic ritual:

'Her lap is a sacrificial altar; her hair the sacrificial grass; her skin the *soma* press; the two lips of the vulva the fire in the middle (this is a reference to the fire generated in the slot by the rubbing-stick used in ancient times, for the sacrificial fire so generated is holy). Verily, the world of him who practises sexual intercourse knowing this is as great as the world of him who performs the *vajapaya* (strength libation).

Eventually, tantra was mentioned in the *Upanishads* and the *Puranas* and reached its zenith in the medieval period.

Sadhana is the essential aspect of tantra. It is not mere worship but is the union of *purusha* and *prakriti*. As Woodroffe says: 'Tantra repeatedly says that one is to adore the deity by becoming a deity (the *devata*) himself. The *Ista-devata* is the very self of *atman*, and not separate from it. He is the receptacle of all, yet He is not contained in anything for He is the great witness, the eternal *purusha*. True tantric worship is in and by the mind.'

The less subtle form of tantric worship is that of the *yantra*. The *yantra* is the form of female creative

Kali squats beside an inert Shiva. The image depicts the transfer of energy between the male and the female. *Facing page:* A Rajasthani tantric image depicting the goddess personified with the phallus and the *yoni*..

energy. Form is born of *yantra* itself, is manifested by *japa,* and awakened by mantra power. A *yantra* is a tool generally drawn on paper or engraved in metal, a tangible form of the deity, that aids meditation. Mantra is the sound equivalent of the deity; the *yantra* is the diagrammatic equivalent. The primordial sound is the monosyllabic *Om* (or amen), the basis of cosmic evolution. All other mantras originate from this sound. Sound and form are interrelated. Every sound has a visual counterpart, just as every visual image has a sound frequency contained within it.

There are three broad divisions or sects into which the tantrics organise themselves: the *Saivas*, those who worship Shiva; the *Vaishnavas*, those who believe in Vishnu; and the *Saktas*, those who focus their beliefs in *Shakti*. Tantricism is not restricted to a place but centres around specific areas known as *pithasthanas*.

These energy centres, dedicated to the worship of feminine power and the *lingam*, are said to be the places where the body parts of Sati, eternal wife of Lord Shiva, fell. She had plunged into the sacrificial fire at her father's *yagna* when she found out that her husband's portion of the sacred offerings had not been set apart. Shiva, her ever-devoted husband, carried her body on his back. To relieve this burden of sorrow, Vishnu cut it piece by piece. The story symbolises incomparable love and immortal union.

Concepts of completeness

Brahmanda is another concept that denotes wholeness. *Brahmanda* comes from the union of two words: *Brahman* which means the Absolute, and *anda* or egg. *Brahmanda*, thus, means cosmic egg. Completeness or union in tantra is realised with the combination of *Brahmanda,* the circular *shalagrama,* and the *Shiva linga*. The *Shiva linga* is akin to the phallus, though according to the *Skanda Purana*, the *linga* means the space in which the entire universe was created and destroyed. The *linga* rests on the *yoni*, the womb of nature or *prakriti*, represented by a circle. Instead of the circle, sometimes there is a triangle. The *bindu* within the circle/ triangle means acceptance of all. The triangle, *bindu* and circle are essential figurations in tantric practices.

There are various grades in which different rituals are practised and linked with art forms. The tantrikas have developed a methodological way where 'cosmic crosspoints' are created where an individual encounters a noumena. There are two ways to get to these crosspoints: by going through the human body, which means conducting rites and rituals or using *yantras*, *mandalas* and deities;

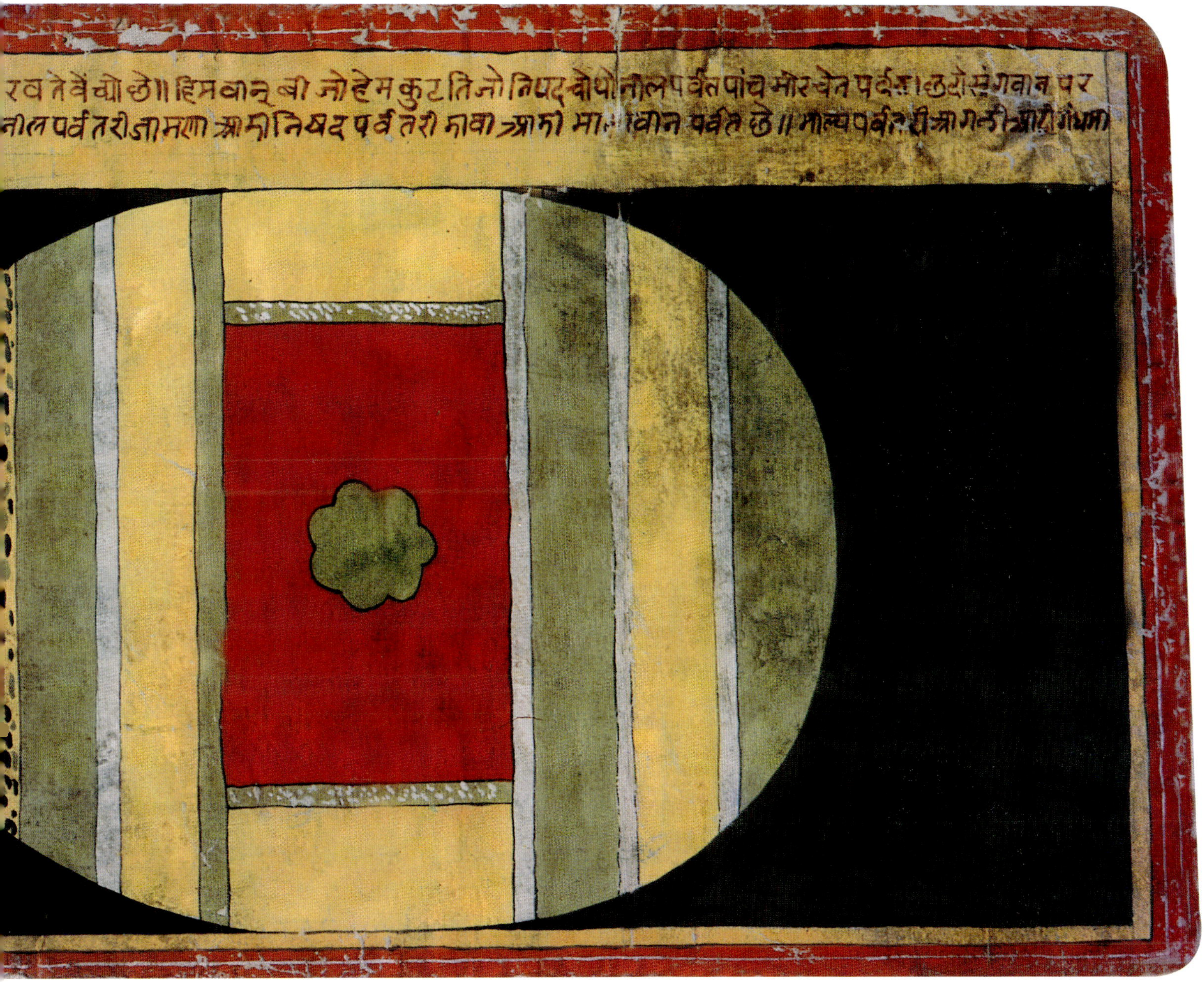

A rare miniature painting symbolises the universe.

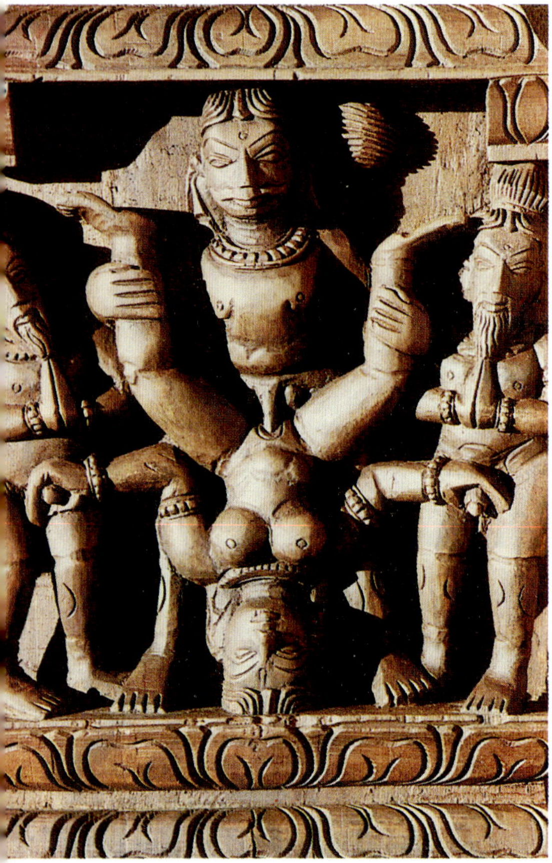

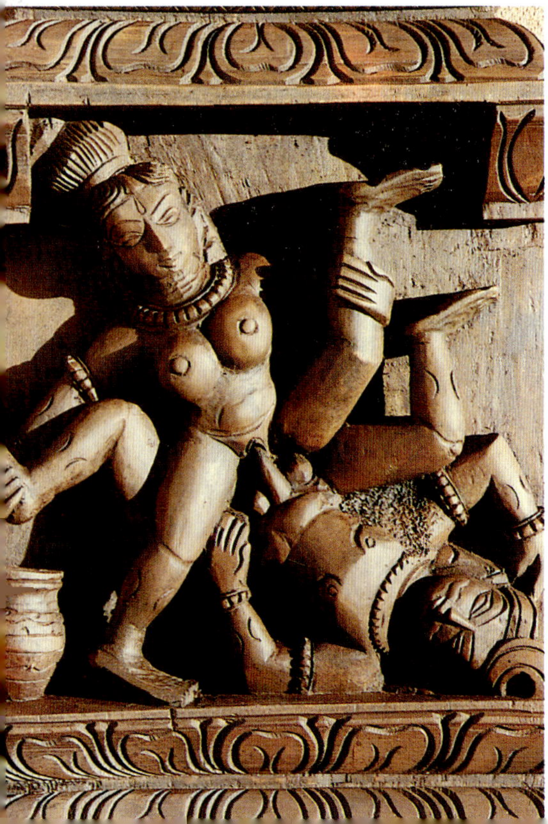

or by repeating *mantras*. Both systems involve all the senses at different levels, and all lead to the central goal of self-enlightenment.

Images of union

Symbols and images that emerge from tantric philosophy are widespread. They cannot be understood at the simple level of art criticism, based on form, style, colour, theme and figuration. They transcend into a higher form: for the tantrics, the art itself is an icon, or a part of the process of worship.

Sexo-yogic postures so widely manifested in the embellishments of temple facades and interiors are part of tantric practices. Two bands full of *maithuna* couples run parallel to each other in the Khajuraho temples. The lower band at the base represents mundane life. The upper band portrays interlocked figures symbolic of a transcendental union. These figures do not coarsely represent sexual intercourse. The lower band is synonymous with earthly practice, while the upper band corresponds to a higher level. From the tantric viewpoint, the figures depict the rise of sexual energy from the ordinary plane to a higher level where the *kundalini* is awakened. But these have been misinterpreted as mysterious pagan rituals where sex is part of the ritual practices. These figures are not

Top left: Exquisite woodcarvings from Tamil Nadu as decorative art on the temple *ratha* (carriages) used during the annual procession of the divinity.
Left: A religious system based in Hindu thought, complicated in rituals, promised quick liberation.
Top and bottom right: Sexual intercourse showed the binding of the negative and positive sides of creation.
Facing page: A powerful representation of intercourse.

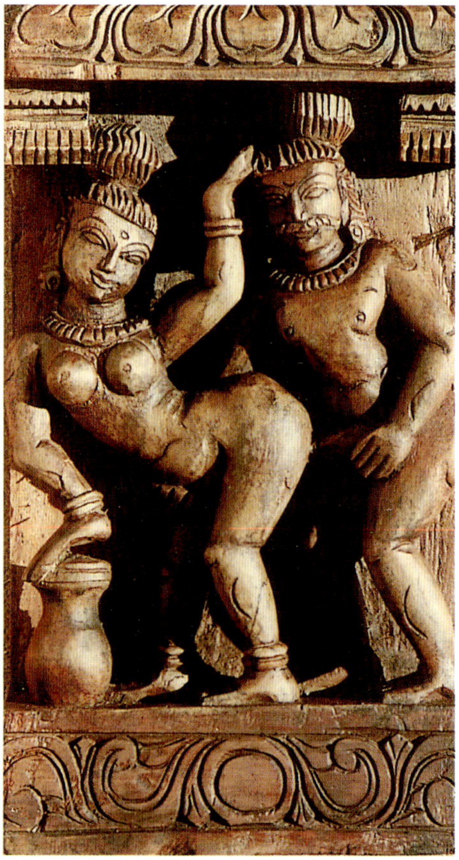

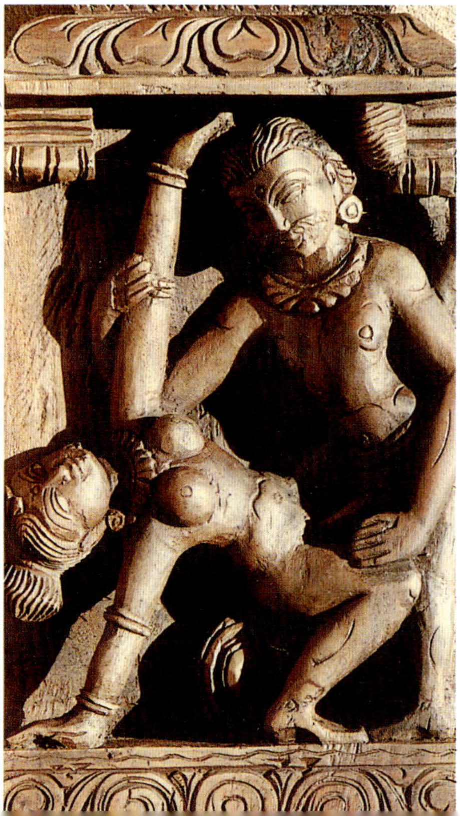

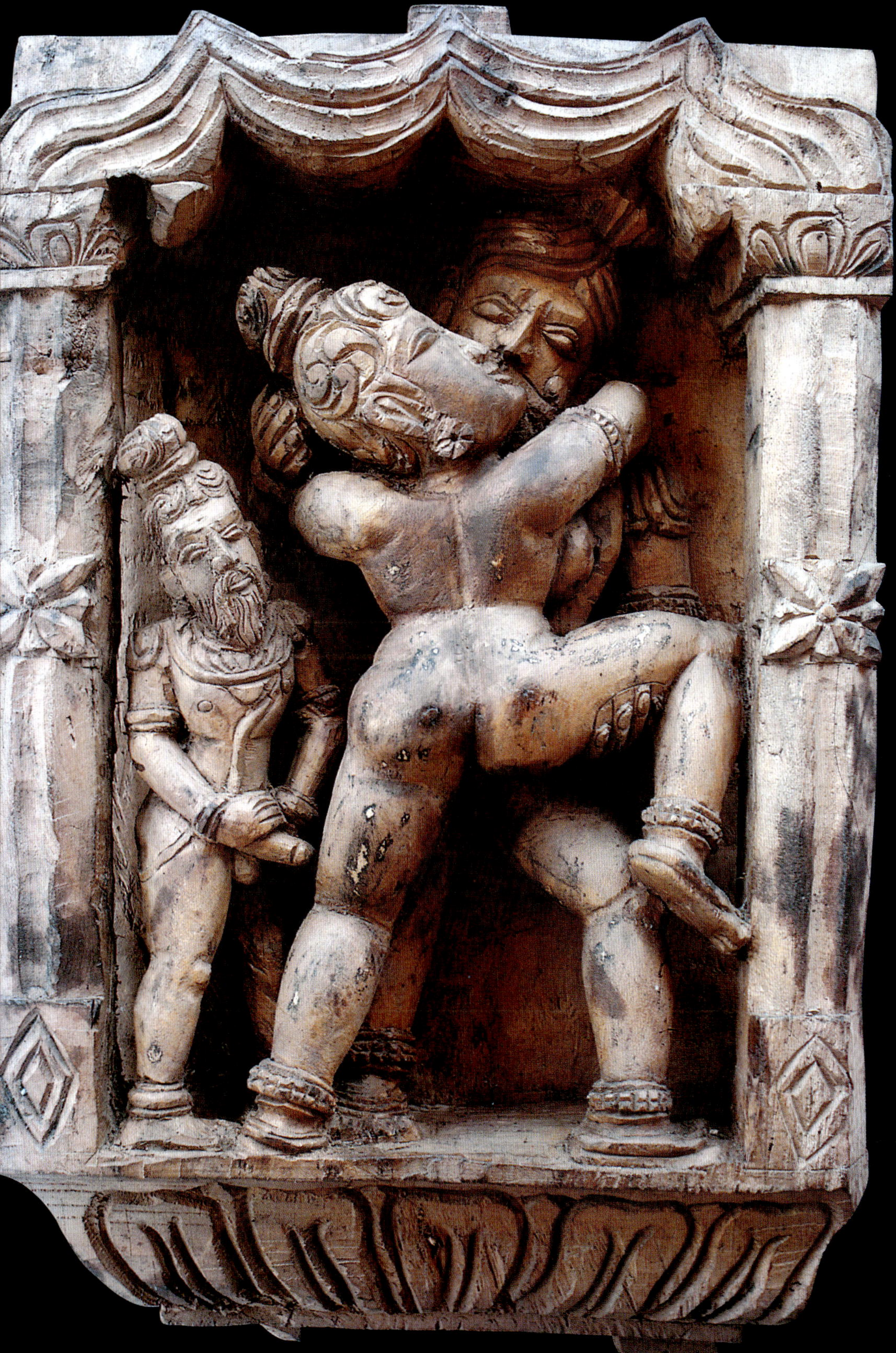

meant for sensual enjoyment. 'They clearly suggest tantric yoga *asanas* are for attaining realisation through union with a female partner,' says a scholar, 'and this is why perhaps the poses are so unconventional and intricate.'

Tantric images are, thus, a link in the journey from the earthly to the cosmic plane. Ritual and art practices in tantra are interchangeable. Both are directly related to social norms and are in existence even today.

From explicit sexo-yogic postures to abstract images, there is a whole new world of visual culture that is overtly erotic. Images of phalluses and wombs, vulvas and the cosmic egg are rampant. *Sri yantras, kali yantras* in the form of geometric patterns, *mandalas, kundalini shakti* – are found all over. Each symbol has a counterpart in the nine *chakras*. The outer plane has three concentric circles (the three corks of ignorance – bodily, astral and causal) in a square that is symbolic of the participant being infatuated through human aspirations and desires. The *bindu* is ultimate *ananda* and is part of the *sri yantra* known as the *nav chakra*.

Dualism is the base of all tantric philosophy. Astronomy deeply influences tantra, and celestial tides and the movement of planes determine the time for rites. Images and art traditions relate to the emergence of the universe from the cosmic waters – serpentine drawings based on the sevenfold divisions of the universe as a cosmic river of time and reality . . . .

A unique image, from nineteenth-century south India, portrays a five-headed serpent enclosing the *Brahmanda*.

Paper drawings, painted icons on cloth, stone sculptures, architectural patterns in religious buildings, metal sculptures, objects of everyday usage such as vessels and urns in the shape of organs, are all part of tantric art. Cosmograms from the Jaina tradition are depicted in the cosmic *purusha* (*Purushakara Yantra*). The *purusha* does not stand alone as a part of

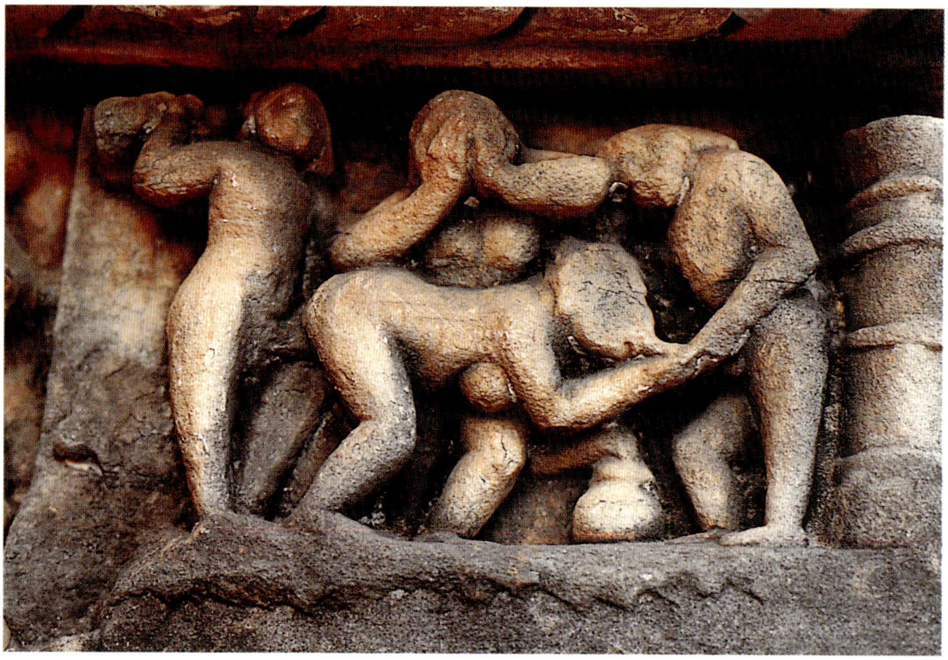

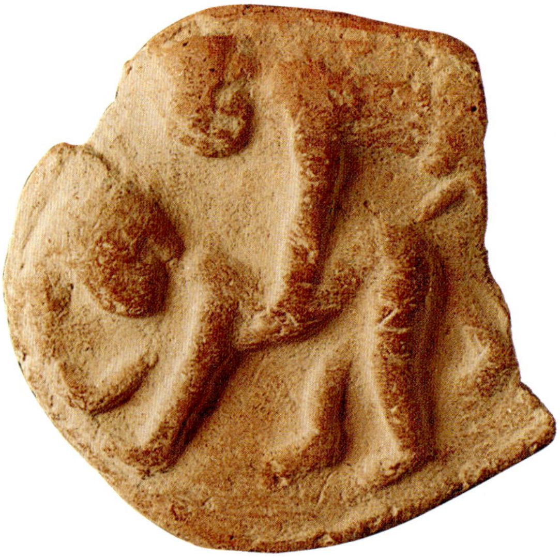

Top: A shy helper hides her face from the sexual love play between a couple.
Bottom: Small erotic terracotta, Shunga period, from Chandraketugarh, West Bengal.
Facing page: Wild abandonment in body movement, as also tenderness and arousal are part of this Khajuraho frieze.

tantric imagery. A few other common images that form popular themes are Goddesa Kali on her own and also when standing over Rati and Kama. The couple is making love, depicting the merger between kinetic energy and pure consciousness.

Images of destruction also form a theme. They blend naturalism and intuition in a single impulse. On the other hand, the ecstasy of joy is seen in tantric *asanas* in painting and sculpture. Tantric art encompasses both beatific and terrifying images which can also be interpreted though Abhinavagupta's *rasa* theory.

This just goes to show that physical love was never denigrated in India during the ancient period. It was considered natural, its acceptance increased in the medieval period, when erotic images were included in temple sculpture. When depicted in religious places, the sexual act came to be regarded as the primary means to gain deliverance.

These images are in abundance in Khajuraho, Konarak and Bhuvaneshwar. They are often reviled today as being perverted. Whatever the artist had in mind while depicting these enticing female figures, it is certain that they originated from the ancient concept of the Divine Mother. The female is symbolic of fertility and motherhood, and sex is a symbol of the divine female as a progenitor.

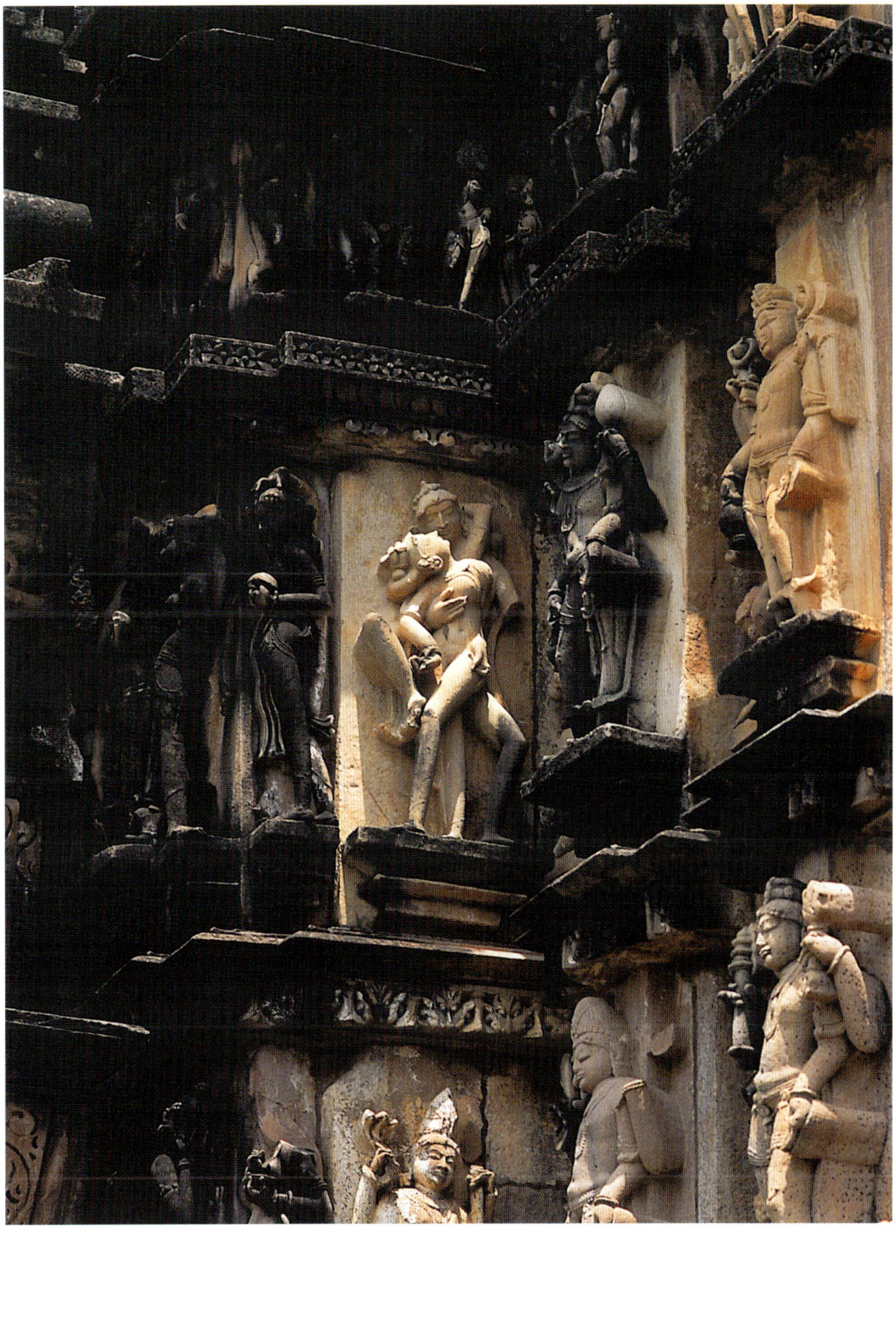

The feminine form

The feminine form

The undraped feminine form has been a constant source of inspiration for artists in ancient, medieval and present-day India. The country's art has not just painted an embellished female form; it has been careful to make a subtle distinction between loveliness, *saundarya*, and grace or *lavanya*. Perfect and harmonious proportions produce beauty, but cannot necessarily invest it with grace.

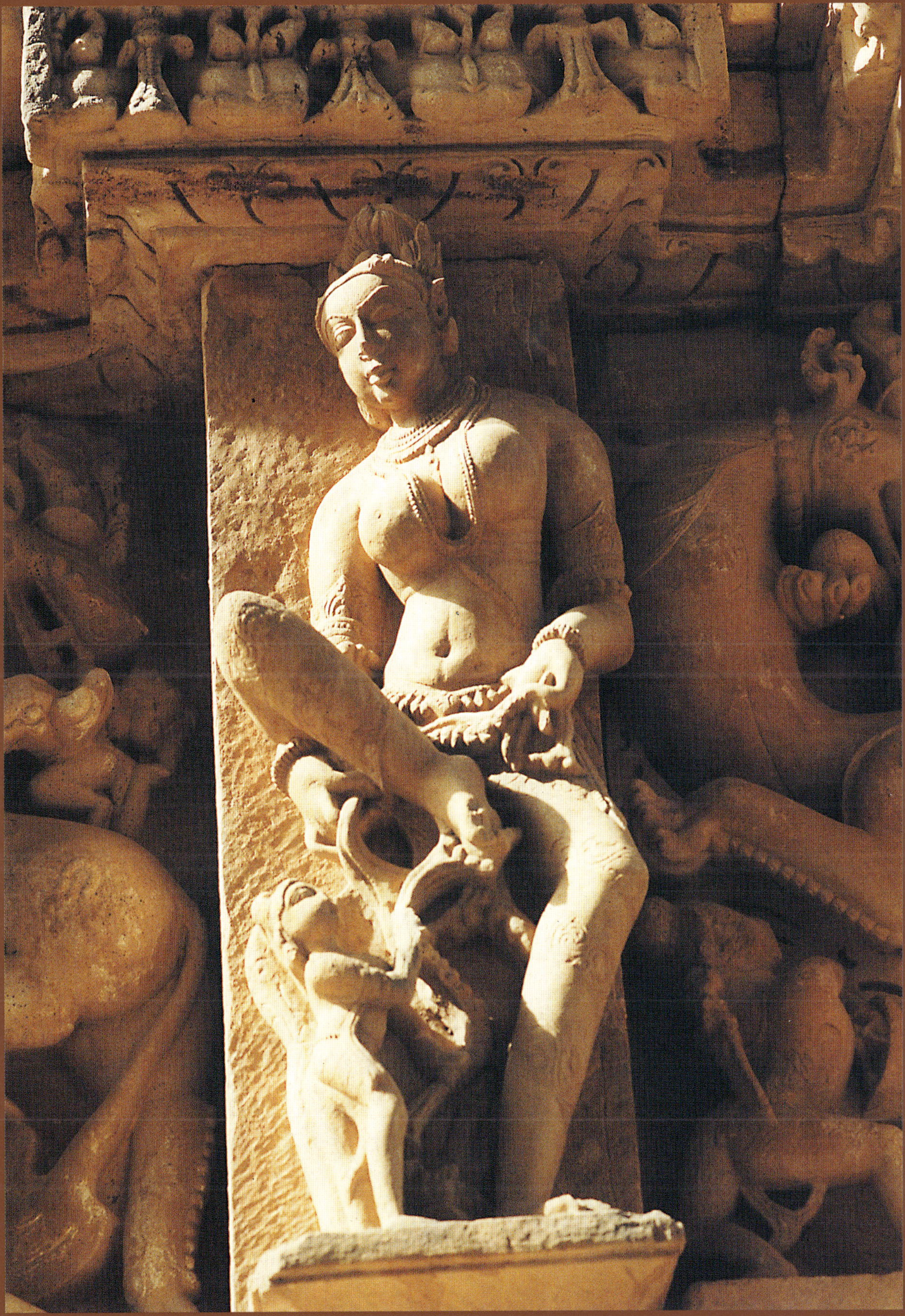

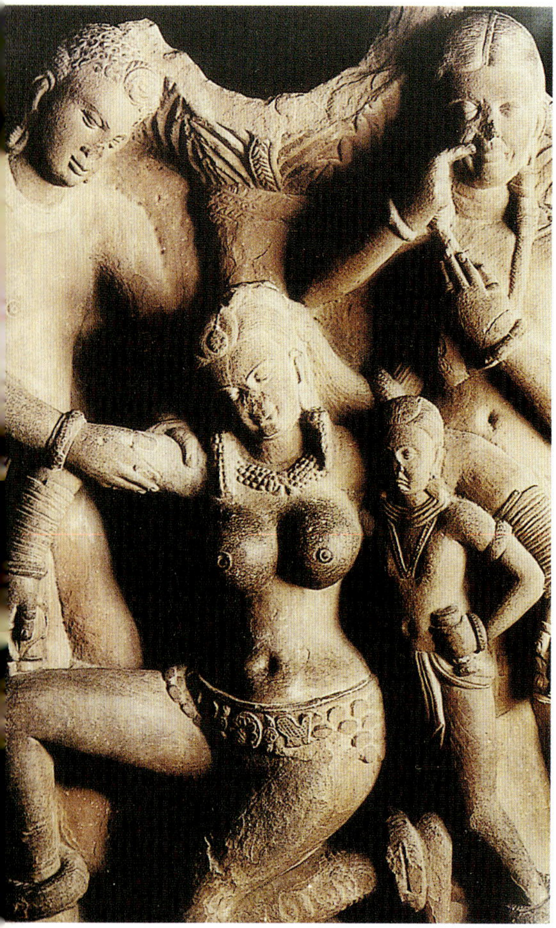

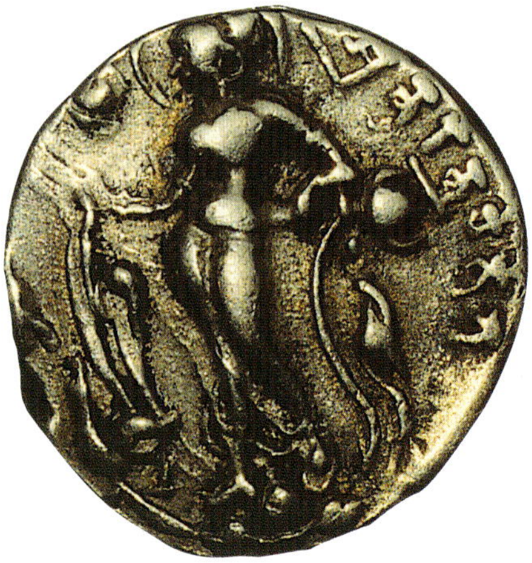

Perhaps *lavanya* may be expressed as inner beauty of the soul and not only of the body. As the *Isvara Samhita* says, it is only that which is beautiful and imbued with grace that can thrill the mind and produce within one the sensation of joy and pleasure, not transiently, but for all time. Never has the Indian artist succeeded better in conveying grace than when creating his masterpieces of the female form.

Forms of perfection

There is an interesting legend about how woman was created. The description is so Indian in spirit that it sums up the very essence of what makes a woman. 'In the beginning, when Twashtri, the Divine Artificer, came to the creation of woman, he found he had exhausted his materials in the making of man . . . . In this dilemma, after profound meditation, he did as follows: He took the rotundity of the moon, and the curves of creepers, and the clinging of tendrils, and the trembling of grass, and the slenderness of the reed, and the bloom of flowers, and the lightness of leaves, and the tapering of the elephant's trunk, and the glances of deer, and the clustering of rows of bees, and the joyous gaiety of sunbeams, and the weeping of clouds, and the fickleness of the wind, and the timidity of the hare, and the vanity of the peacock, and the softness of the parrot's bosom, and the hardness of a diamond, and the sweetness of honey, and the cruelty of the tiger, and the warm glow of fire, and the coolness of snow, and the chattering of jays, and the cooing of the *kokila*, and the hypocrisy of the crane, and the fidelity of the *chakrawaka*, and compounding all these together, he made woman, and gave her to man.'

In Indian art, the ideal of female beauty is a youthful one, but mature women and mothers with full breasts 'like a pair of gourds', and hips 'like the swell of a riverbank' are typical forms of beauty. Divine beauty transcends all ideals of human perfection, although the sense of the sensual is never quite absent. Endowed with all the gifts of youth, grace, and bodily allure, the voluptuous *apsaras*, the celestial *surasundaris* and the worldly *nayikas*, not only charmed and enticed the males of the earth, but even disturbed devotees and marred their sacrifices.

The unabashed tenets of the quintessentially Indian feminine form were: a swelling and curvaceous bosom, a harmonious swell of wide and rounded hips, a slim waist and the serpentine grace of slender limbs – graces which the Indian sculptor rendered with admirable perfection, and which were often nude. The young maidens of Sanchi and Mathura were sculpted with the lower region uncovered except for narrow

Top: The feminine form is celebrated with mature women, full breasted and heavy hipped.
Bottom: Female form is a glorious recurring motif.
Facing page: Feminity in all her glory. The Gyaraspur Devi in Madhya Pradesh, Gwalior Museum.
Previous page: A major highlight of the sculptures at Khajuraho is the depiction of *apsaras* engrossed in different tasks.

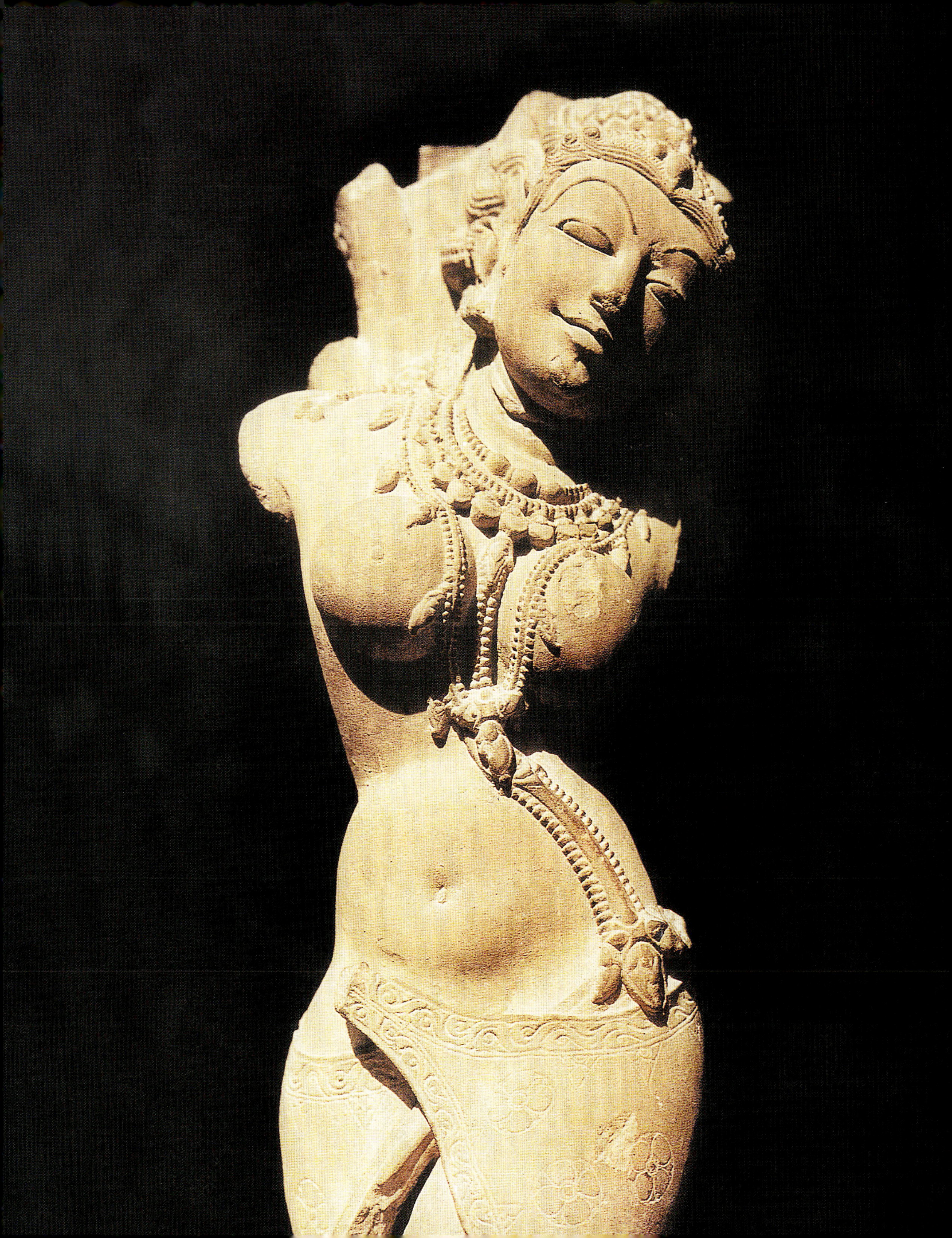

ornamental girdles. Complete nudity was not the common idiom of art even in later times.

Yet, however bare the female form, nudity of the flesh alone could not have had much meaning for the Indian sculptor. He has always striven for spiritual essence. Since the highest type of divine beauty is the *spirit*, the male principle, the divinity of the female was a counterpart of the male's. In the medieval period, with the rise of tantra, the emphasis shifted to the female, though the cult remained limited to a handful of devotees.

The Indian sculptor then created the ideal superwoman by prominently characterising the secondary sexual features and adding them on to the original divine ideal. The poets of the ancient world, and also the scriptures, listed, the characteristics of such beauty. Some of the prominent pointers were the mark of the navel set low in the body, a face like the full moon, eyes resembling the petals of the lotus, lines on the neck like those on a conch-shell. The parameters of womanly charm are set out forthrightly in a *Mahabharata* passage. Draupadi appears before Queen Sudeshna in disguise during the long exile of the Pandavas and offers her services, surprising the queen with her beauty: 'Your heels are not prominent, and your thighs touch each other. You have great intelligence, your navel is deep, and your words are well

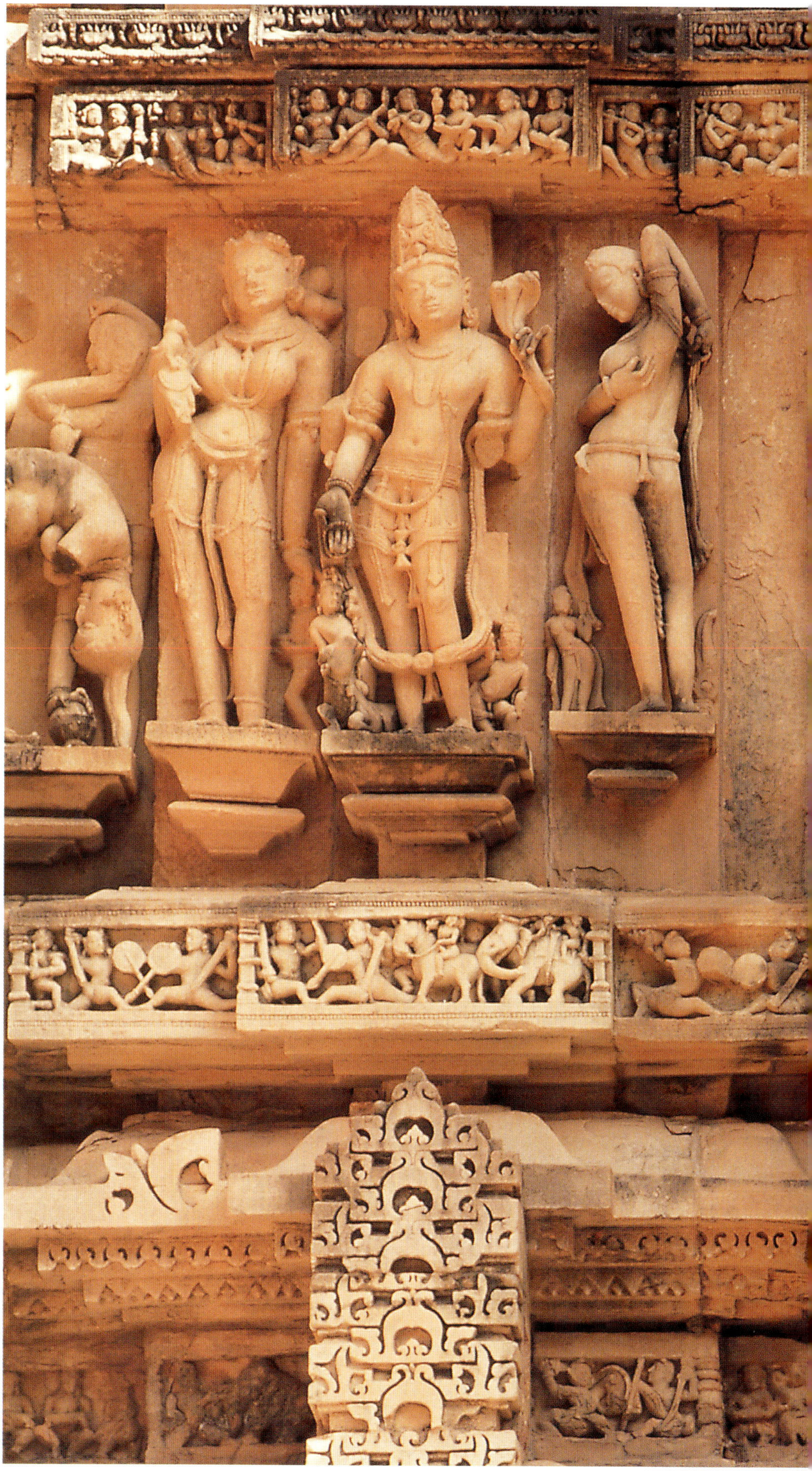

A band of sculptures from the south wall of the Laxman temple. The central figure depicts an erotic couple.

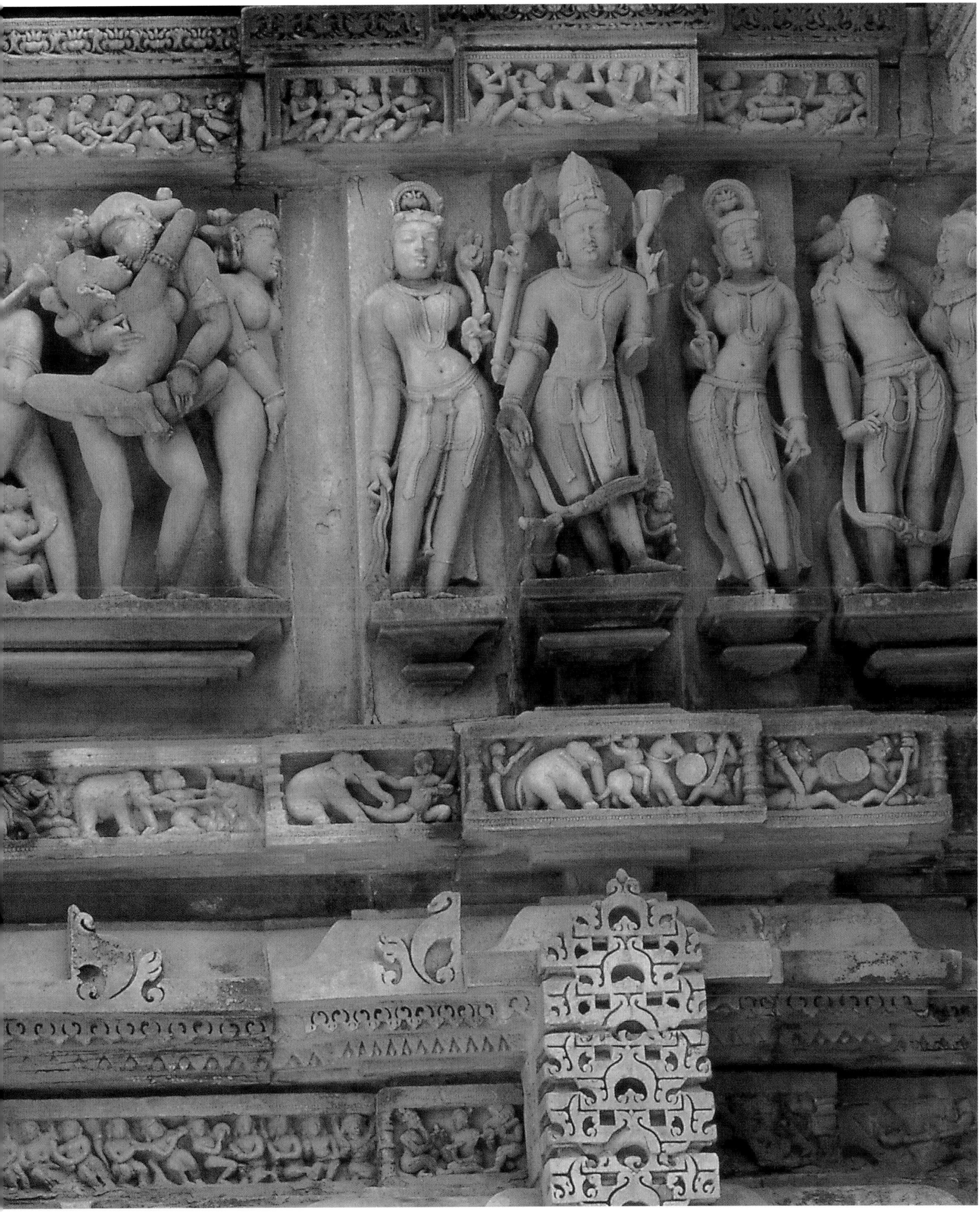

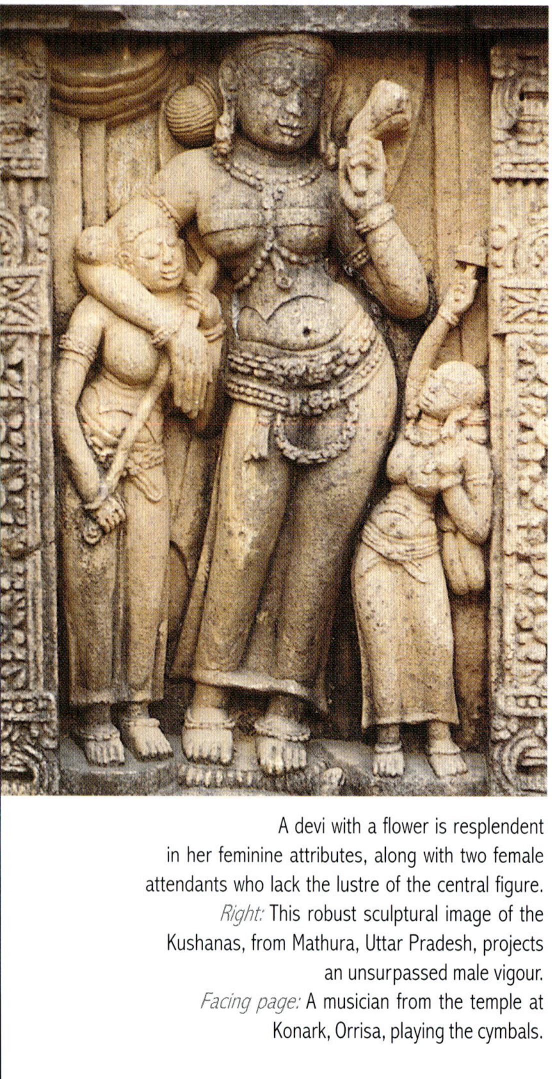

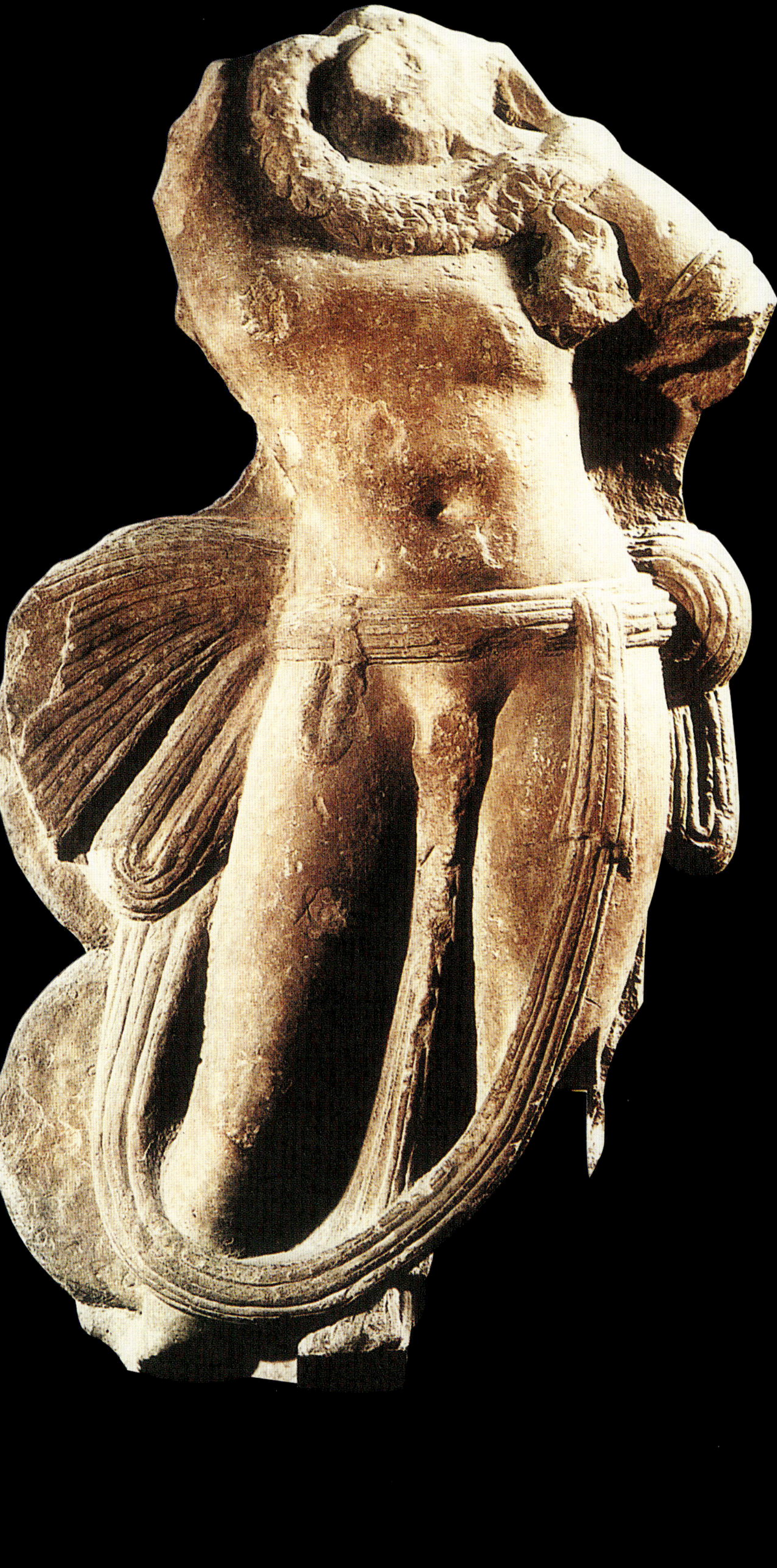

A devi with a flower is resplendent in her feminine attributes, along with two female attendants who lack the lustre of the central figure. *Right:* This robust sculptural image of the Kushanas, from Mathura, Uttar Pradesh, projects an unsurpassed male vigour. *Facing page:* A musician from the temple at Konark, Orrisa, playing the cymbals.

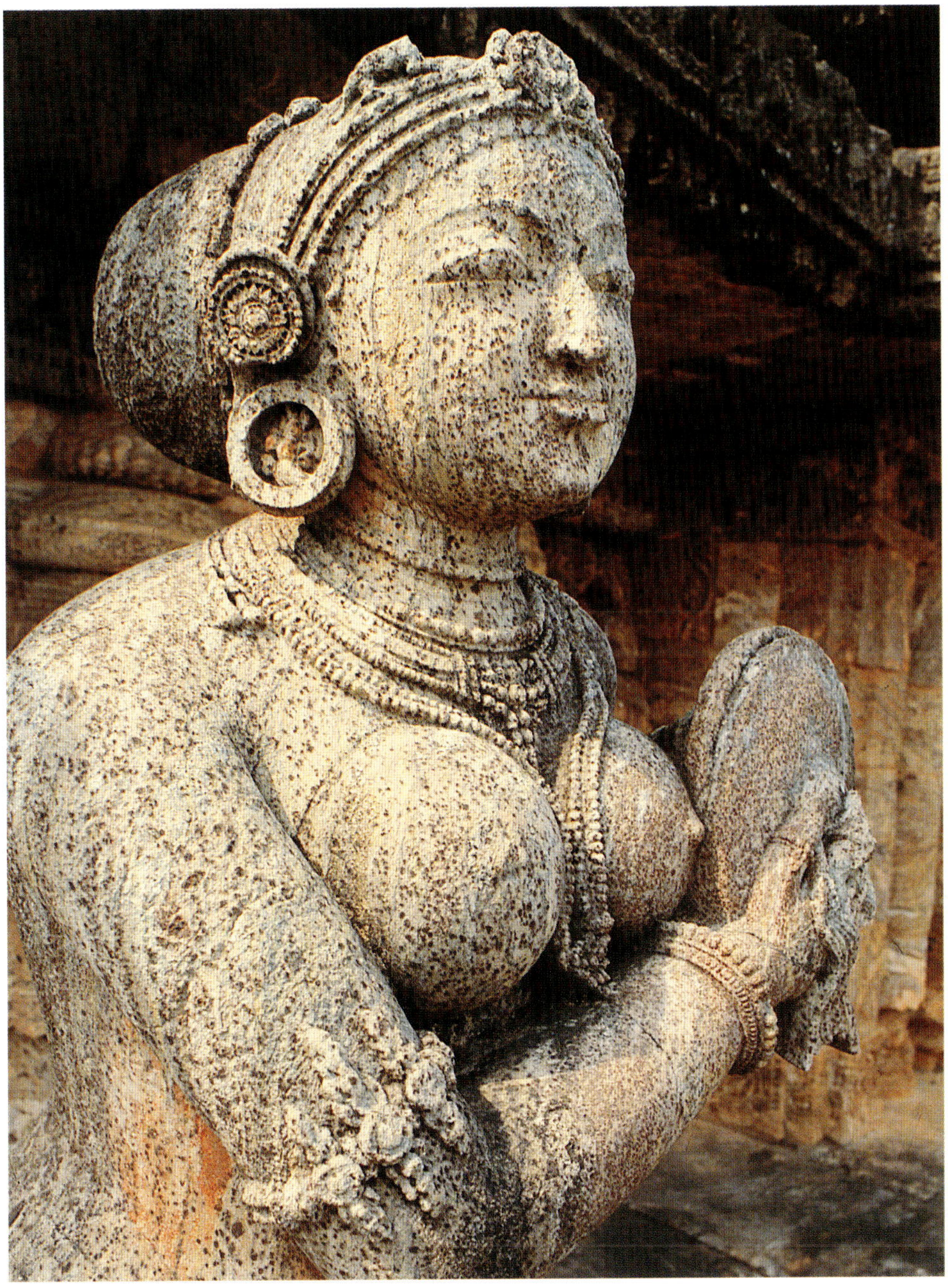

chosen. And your great toes, bosom and hips and dorsa, the toenails and palms of your hands are all well developed. The palms of your hands and the soles of your feet and your face are ruddy. And your speech is sweet, even as the voice of the swan. Your hair is beautiful, your bosom shapely, and you are possessed of the highest grace; like a Kashmir mare, you are furnished with every auspicious mark . . . . Tell me beautiful damsel, who thou art?' (Rustam J. Mehta.)

Numerous mentions of scantily dressed women are found in the works of poets and artists. In the *Markandeya Purana*, the Great Goddess *is* Absolute Beauty. 'You are more enchanting than enchantment itself. You are more beauteous than all the beautiful things of the earth. You are the ultimate, the transcendent. You are the supreme beauty.' (Rustam J Mehta). The beautiful *apsaras* and the women of this earth all radiate sensuous loveliness. They also symbolise *Mahamaya*, the Supreme Enchantress, who at the same time is *Mahavidya*, the Supreme Deliveress. She is also *shakti*, the female energy that leads man to salvation, freedom from *samskara* – the fetters of the cycle of life and death. The semi-divine damsels of heaven carry this message to humanity through their sensual charms and alluring devices. Perhaps that is why the Indian artist refrained from investing the faces of his feminine

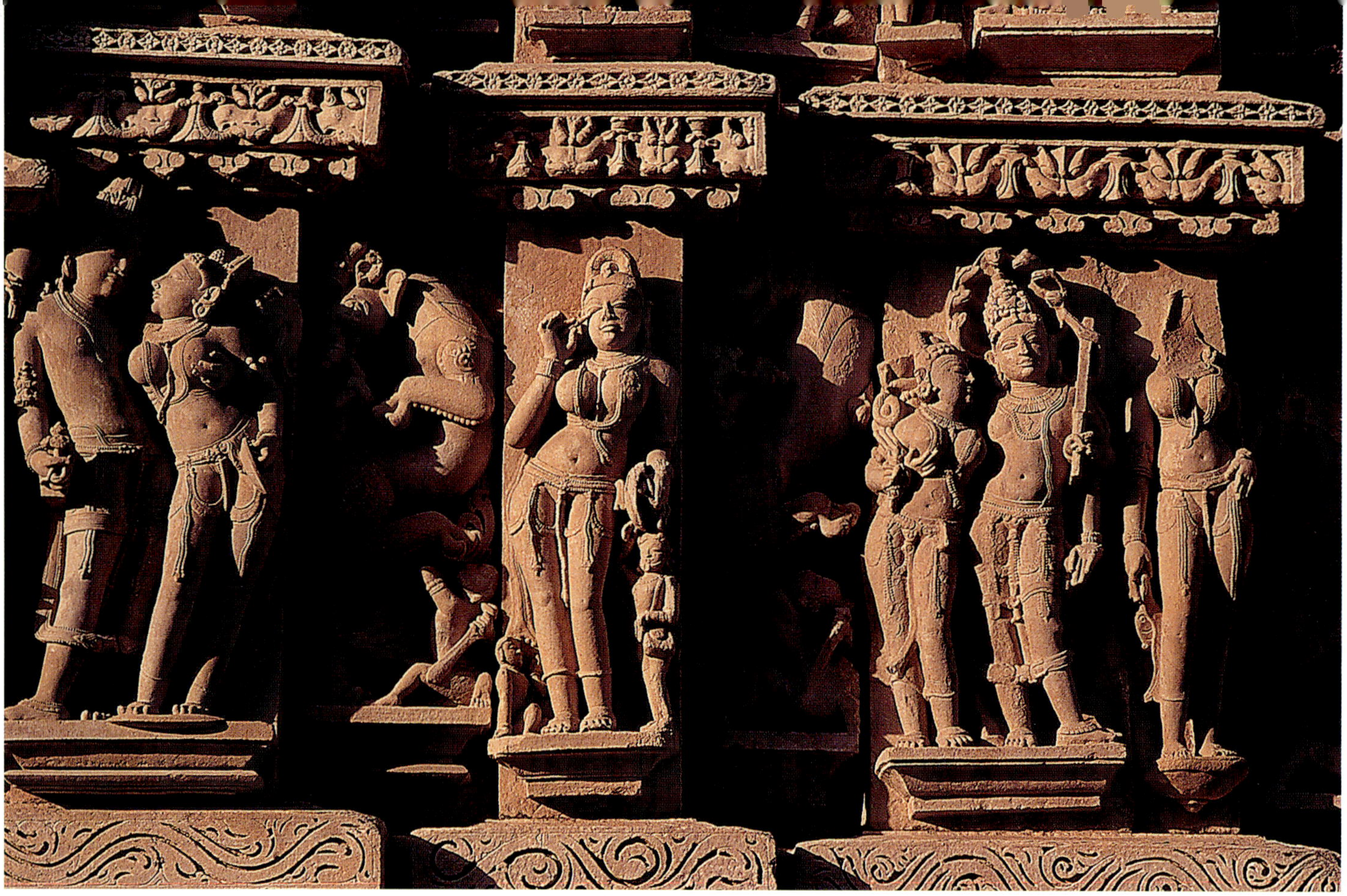

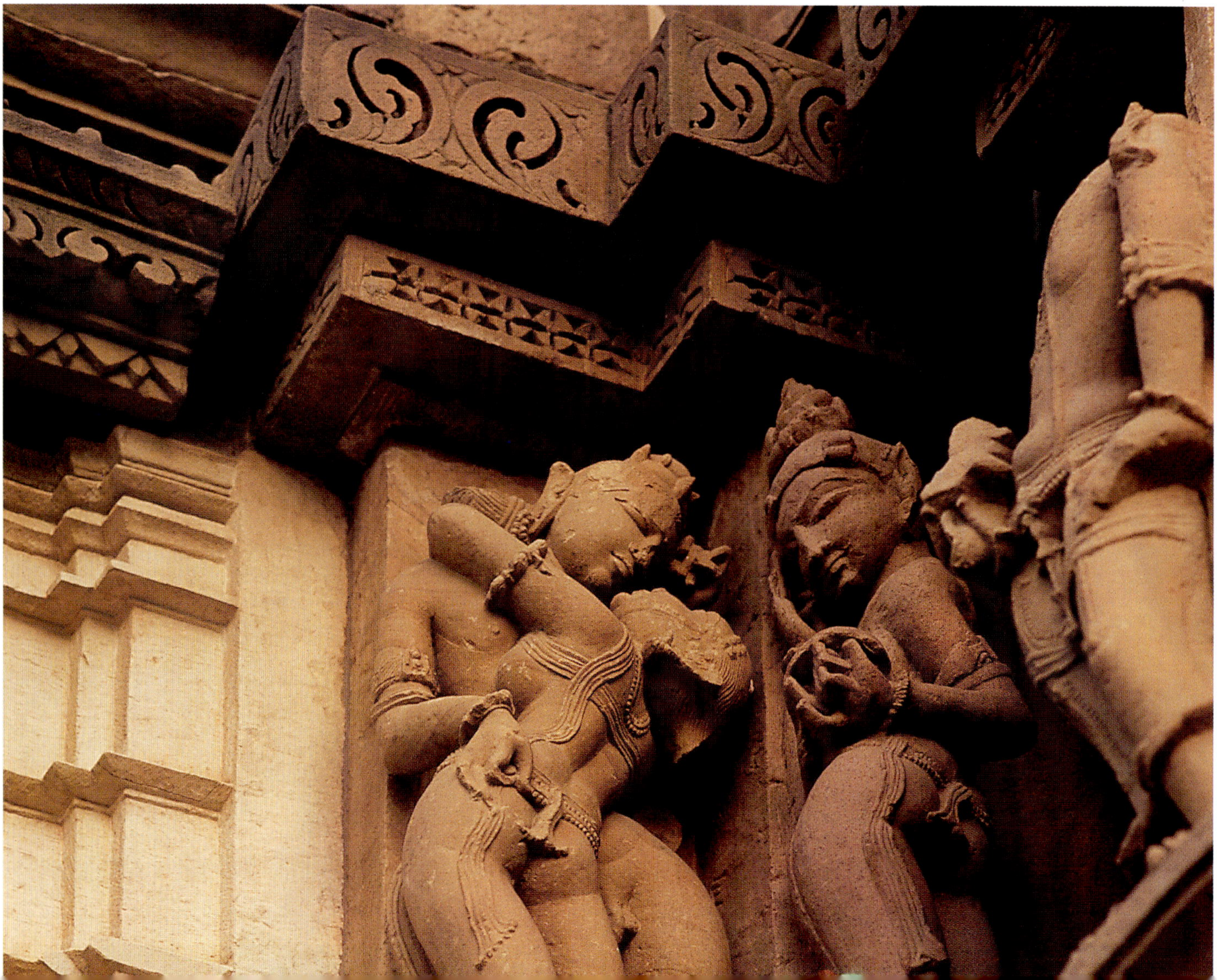

creations with much expression, emphasising instead their inward consciousness and latent potentialities.

In the court of beauty

Beautiful women have always played an important part in early Indian life. King Suddhodana of the Sakyas surrounded his son Siddhartha, the Buddha to be, with beautiful dancers and damsels in the palace grounds, so that enamoured of their charms, he might not forsake all to be the Universal Deliverer as foretold. Ravana's harem and his life therein, as described in the *Ramayana*, are well known. The *devadasis* – dancers and women of free love, the slave-girls of the temple gods, thronged the sacred precincts. The dancing *apsaras*, ever beguiling and seductive, inhabited Indra's heavenly court. The *maithuna* couples – the male and female embracing form – so replete in Indian arts, are emblematic of creation.

The patterns of beauty at Mathura, for instance, were so crafted that the image was a synthesis of desirability formalised in one body, sometimes rather artificially. It innocently contrived to touch the mainspring of man's inherent instincts, even if it lost naturalness and a free artistic sweep. The Gupta age saw a refinement of the erotic sentiment in its figural art in an era graced by the great Kalidasa, and poets and dramatists who produced a

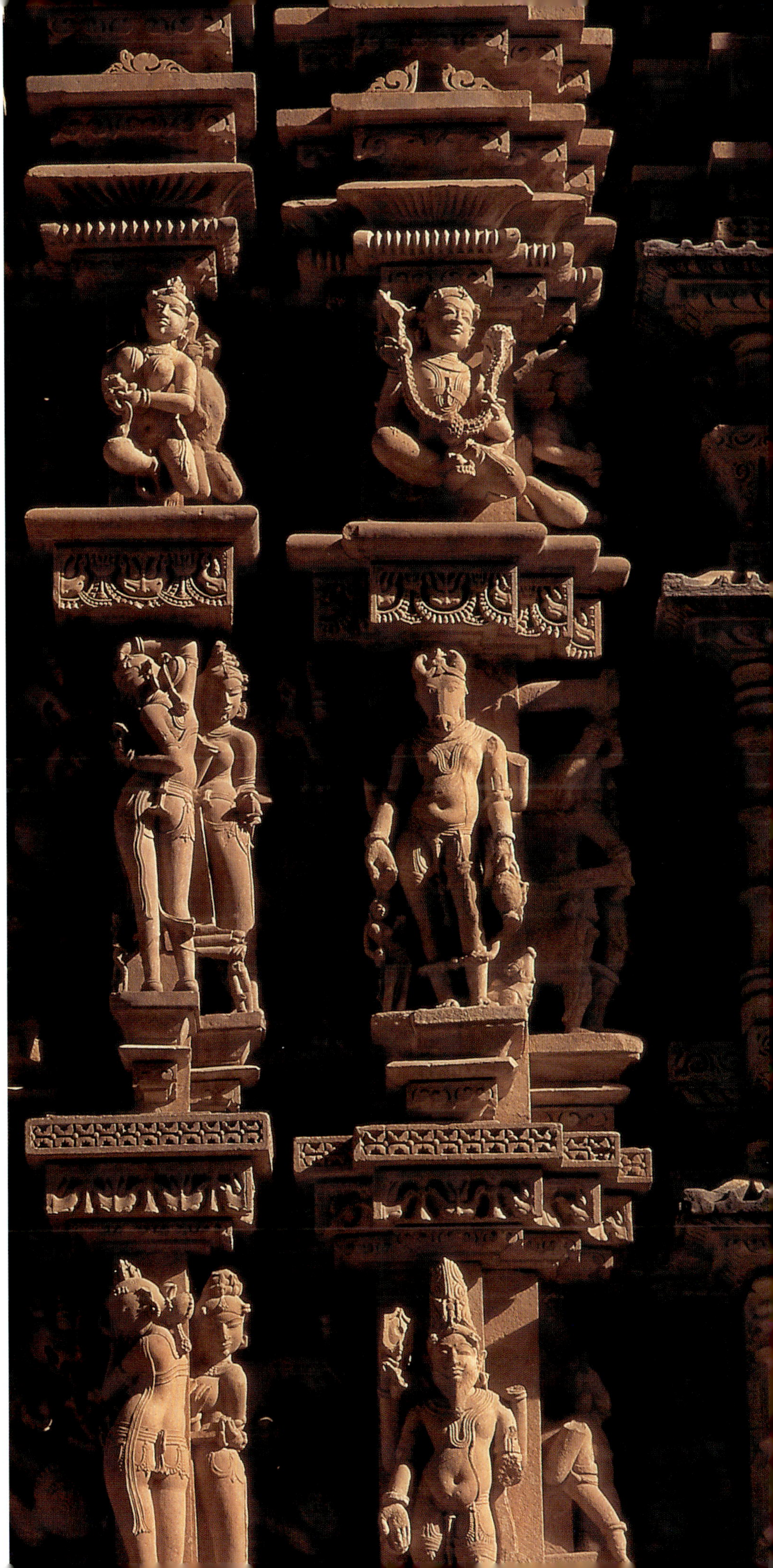

The sculptures that adorn the Khajuraho facades focus on earthly sensuality and divine love.
Facing page, top: The south-facing lower band from the Parsvanath temple at Khajuraho has as the central figure, a statue of a popular subject – an *apsara* painting her eyes with *kohl*.
Facing page, bottom: Couples in erotic positions belong to the secular theme at Khajuraho – the artisans gave full vent to their imagination, going further than the *kamashastras'* prescriptions.

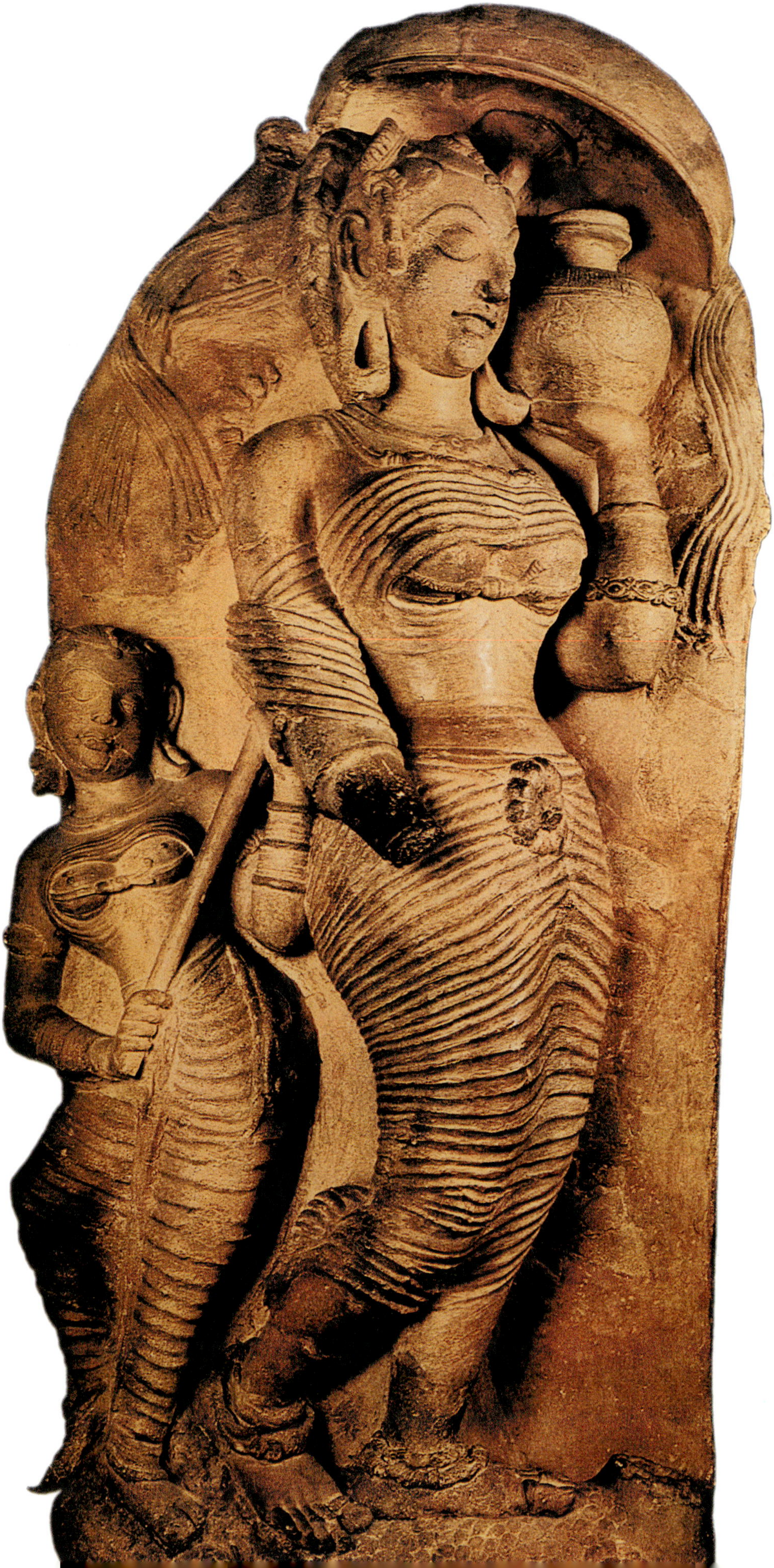

rich literature teeming with lyrical but rather frank descriptions of their heroines. Post-Gupta art, on the other hand, oozed with sexual charm, often heightened by the pose of the figures and simulated action. Their languid grace and inviting eyes spoke of promised love. The ample breasts and revealing clothing, even the tight-fitting ornamental girdle firmly clasping the slim waist over the fleshy hips, enhanced the calculated effect. The poses also showcased their sexual charms to the best effect – breasts lifted high, the body often curved slightly backward with the wide hips thrust tantalisingly forward, even if the faces are downcast and the eyes half closed. A provocative invitation underlay the assumed modesty of the figures.

There was a peculiar sensuality in the earliest representations of the female form as seen in the *yakshis* of Bharut, Sanchi and Mathura. Emblematic of the spirit of fertility, the figures were drawn to meet mortal needs. These semi-divine figures, which exude attributes of ripened fecundity, were full-breasted and lovingly contoured. The goddesses are ever-youthful, ever-exquisite in body and form. They seem to embody womanhood as it conformed to man's desires, conditioned by race and age.

While the Mother Goddess was the ultimate creator in the form of female energy, nude figurines were known in

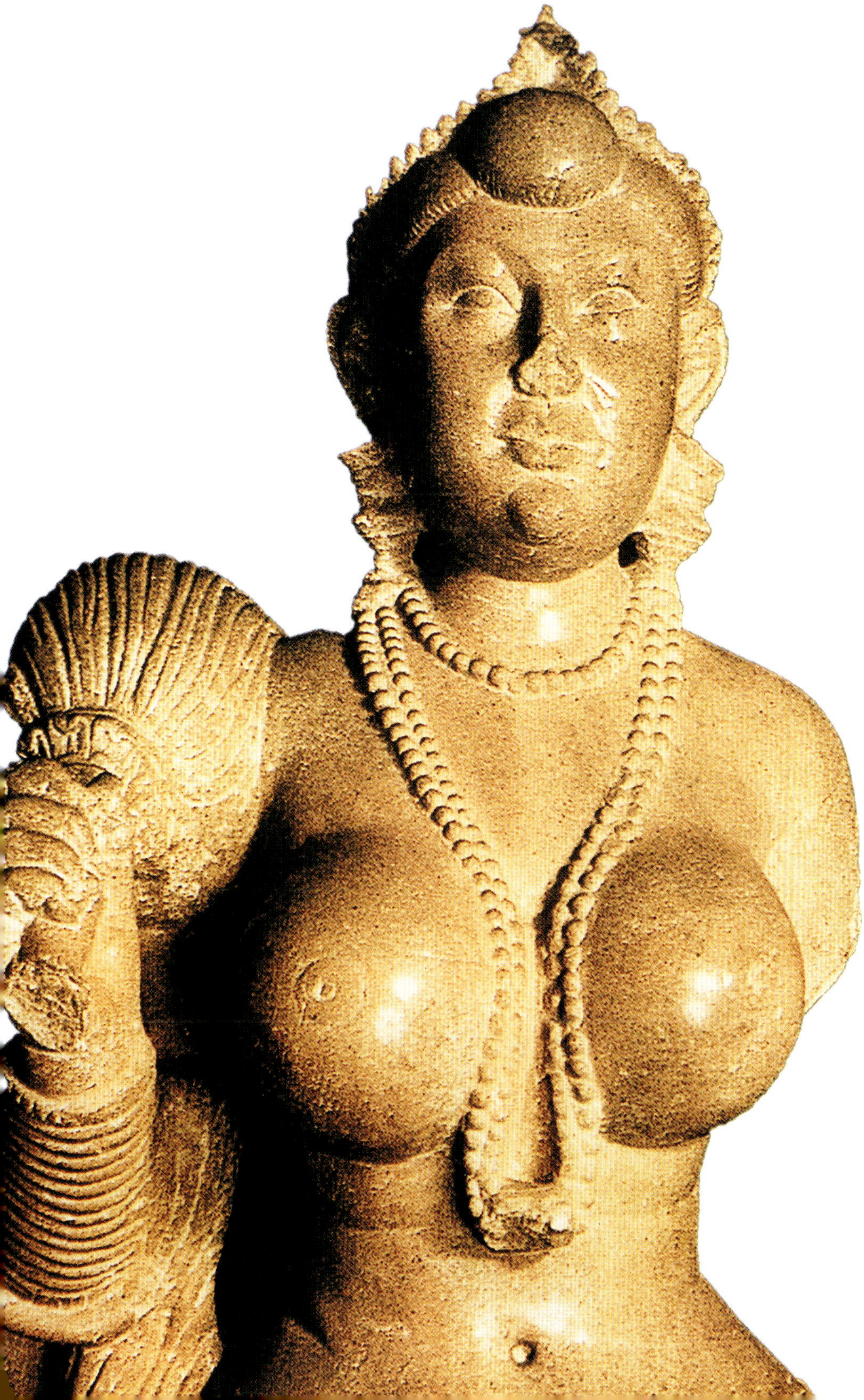

Indian art right from Harappan times. Nudity in Indian art is amoral because the goddesses who also portrayed worldly femininity are often naked and always unashamed in the realisation of bodily perfection according to the tastes and demands of the times. In Indian art, the shame of bodily exposure neither obtrudes, nor do the close relationships between men and women in the ultimate realisation of desire, as seen in the *maithuna* sculptures.

The erotic art of India is of ancient lineage. The bronze female nude figurine from the Indus Valley is full of sensuousness. This is evident in the treatment of the back, the hips, the buttocks and the legs, which are marked by overtones in movement. The figurine probably was part of a ritualistic exercise, in the way female nude figures are made today – to satisfy the 'gaze'. There is also another terracotta female figure from this period which might have lent inspiration to the images at the beginning of the historic period. Another nude image from Lauriya Nandangarh is a gold plaque, which represents a Mother Goddess. The flaring hips and the pronounced pudenda cleft stamp her unmistakably as a fertility spirit.

The Mathura period continued the theme of sesnsuality. Emphasis was laid on the full bare breasts and wide heavy

The famed *yakshi* from Didarganj epitomises the ideals of traditional Indian beauty. *Patna Museum, Bihar.*
Facing page: Garbed as a village belle from Achichhahra, Ganga Devi, beneath her parasol, glides gracefully upon her mount or *vahana,* the crocodile. Floating on the great river, she personifies purity. *National Museum, New Delhi.*

Divine or mortal, traditional Indian female figures were imbued with allure and everlasting youth. Here, a *yakshi* from Uttar Pradesh tenderly fondles her own breast.
Facing page: *Gandharvas* and *kinnars*, musicians and singers of heaven at the Kailashnath temple, Ellora.

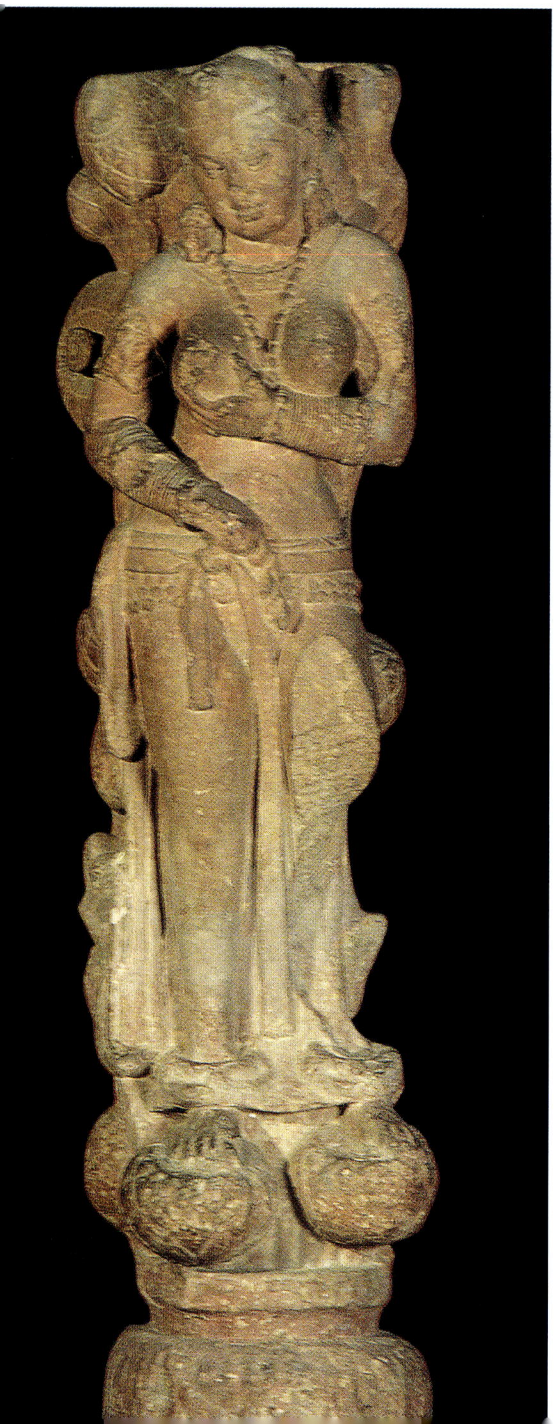

hips; they had an earthy charm, and their bodies were endowed with the eloquence of physical desire. Coomaraswamy says: 'It will, indeed, have been observed there is scarcely a single female figure represented in early Indian art without erotic suggestion of some kind, implied, or explicitly expressed and emphasised.' During the medieval period, the art of the Chandelas and the Eastern Gangas had a frankly erotic sentiment.

Whether divine or mortal, the Indian artist imbued his female figures with great beauty, lure and passion, and an aura of everlasting youthfulness. As in idealised Greek art, women in Indian art could never be old. The feminine was so glorious that even the gods on occasion took the female form for special purposes. On one occasion, Vishnu transformed himself into the astonishingly beautiful Mohini in order to captivate and beguile the *asuras*. The enchanting *apsaras* in the court of Indra lived in free love with the *gandharvas* and *kinnars* – the musicians and singers of heaven. The comely *surasundaris* came to be identified in the medieval age with the supremely desirable maidens of the heavenly courts of the gods. Originally water nymphs, they rose out of the waters during the churning of the ocean by the gods and the *asuras*. Endowed with beauty though they were, none would have them as wives, and it was finally decided that they should be the wives of all. According to legends, the *surasundaris* and *apsaras* formed a common theme in latter-day art and figures of luscious damsels began to crowd the walls of medieval temples. On temple walls, their fleshiness and marked physical characteristics almost belies their semi-divinity. Their beauty may be self-sufficient; however they were certainly not detached from the world, but very much a part of it.

Sculpting the figure

The visual artist followed the *shastric* prescriptions as laid down in the *Shilpa* texts while embarking on the making of images right till the medieval period. For the *shilpin* or artist, the glory of nature was the ideal of feminine grace. The beauty of Goddess Parvati, wrote Kalidasa, lay in the perfection of her limbs, created with the limpid charm that permeated all nature. Kalidasa compared the grace of form to the creeper, saw the ripple of silver in the sunlit waters in the eyes, the softness of the feathers of the peacock in the hair, and the flickering eyes of the startled deer in the glances of love. Ultimately the appreciation of beauty lies in the eyes of the beholder, for beauty is often an expression of the artist's internal vision.

The ancient Indian poets concentrated on specific areas of the female body, bridging the gap

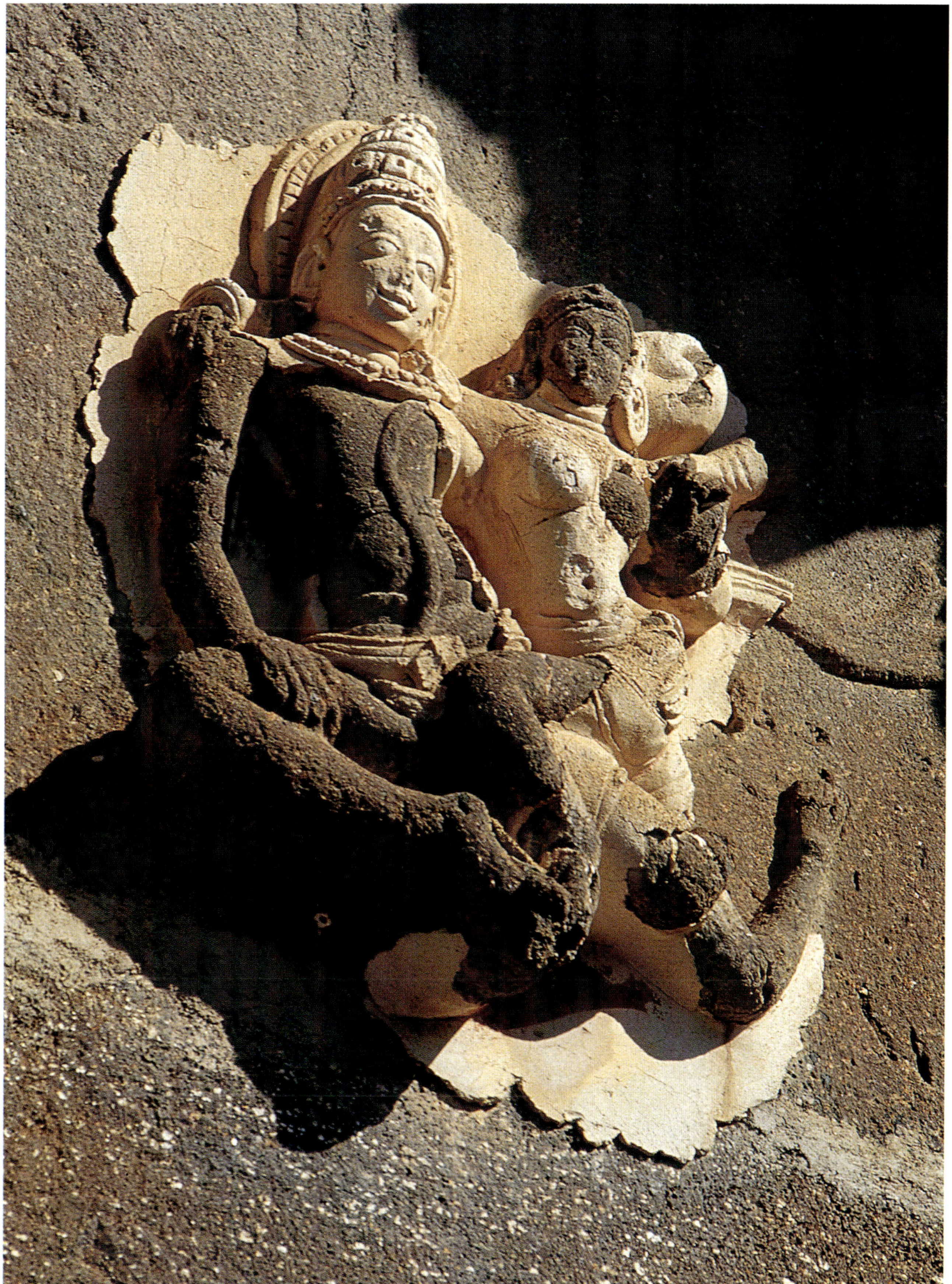

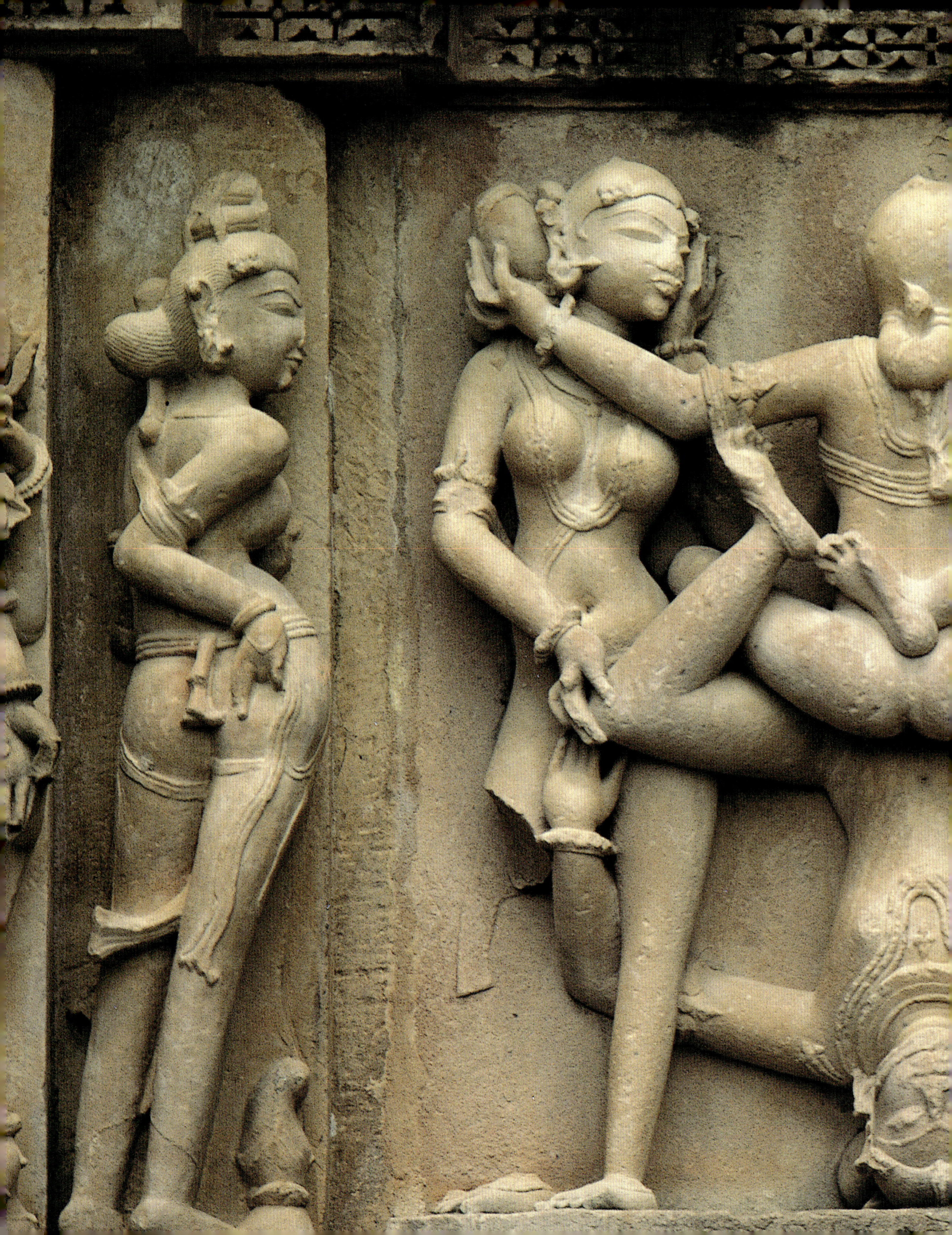

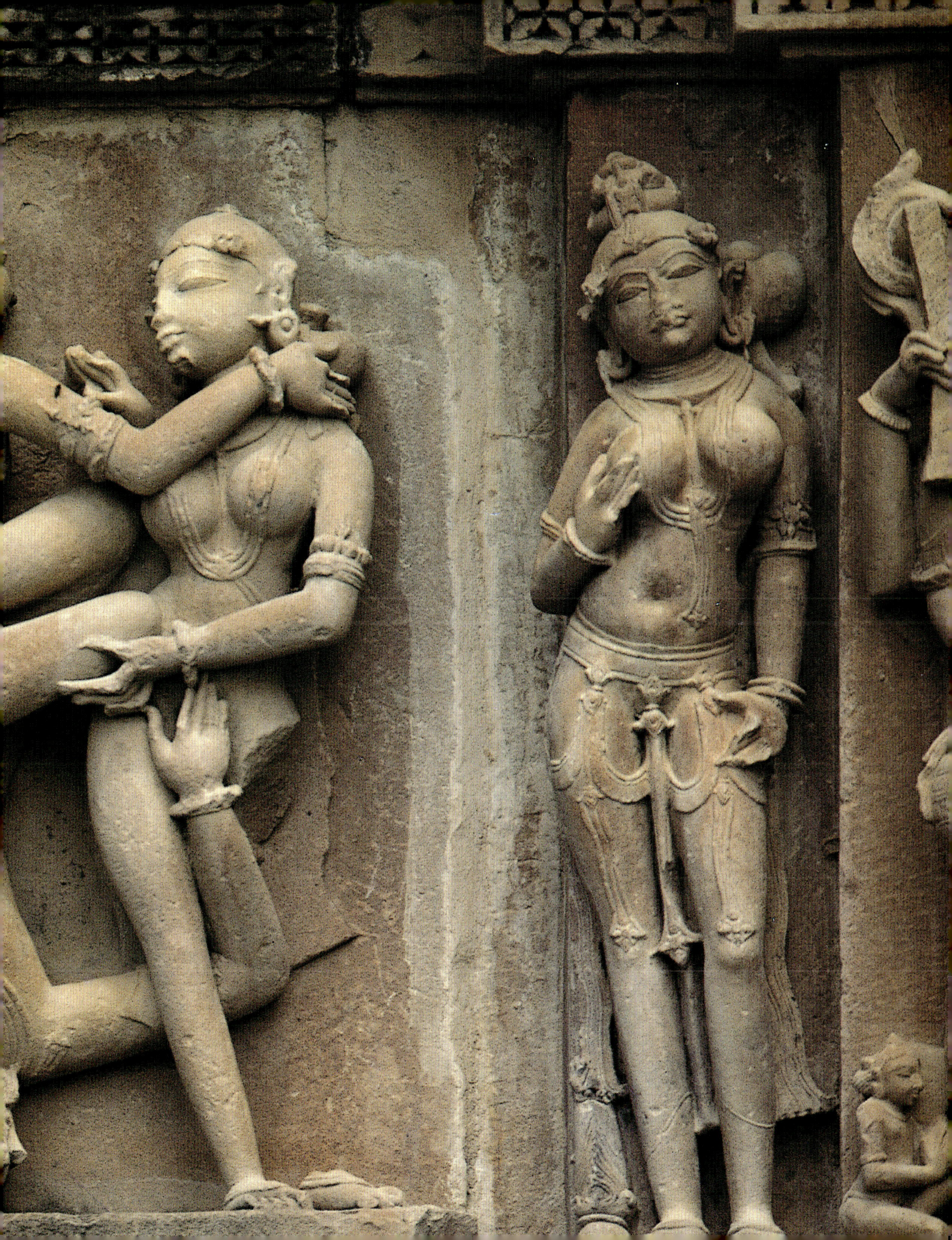

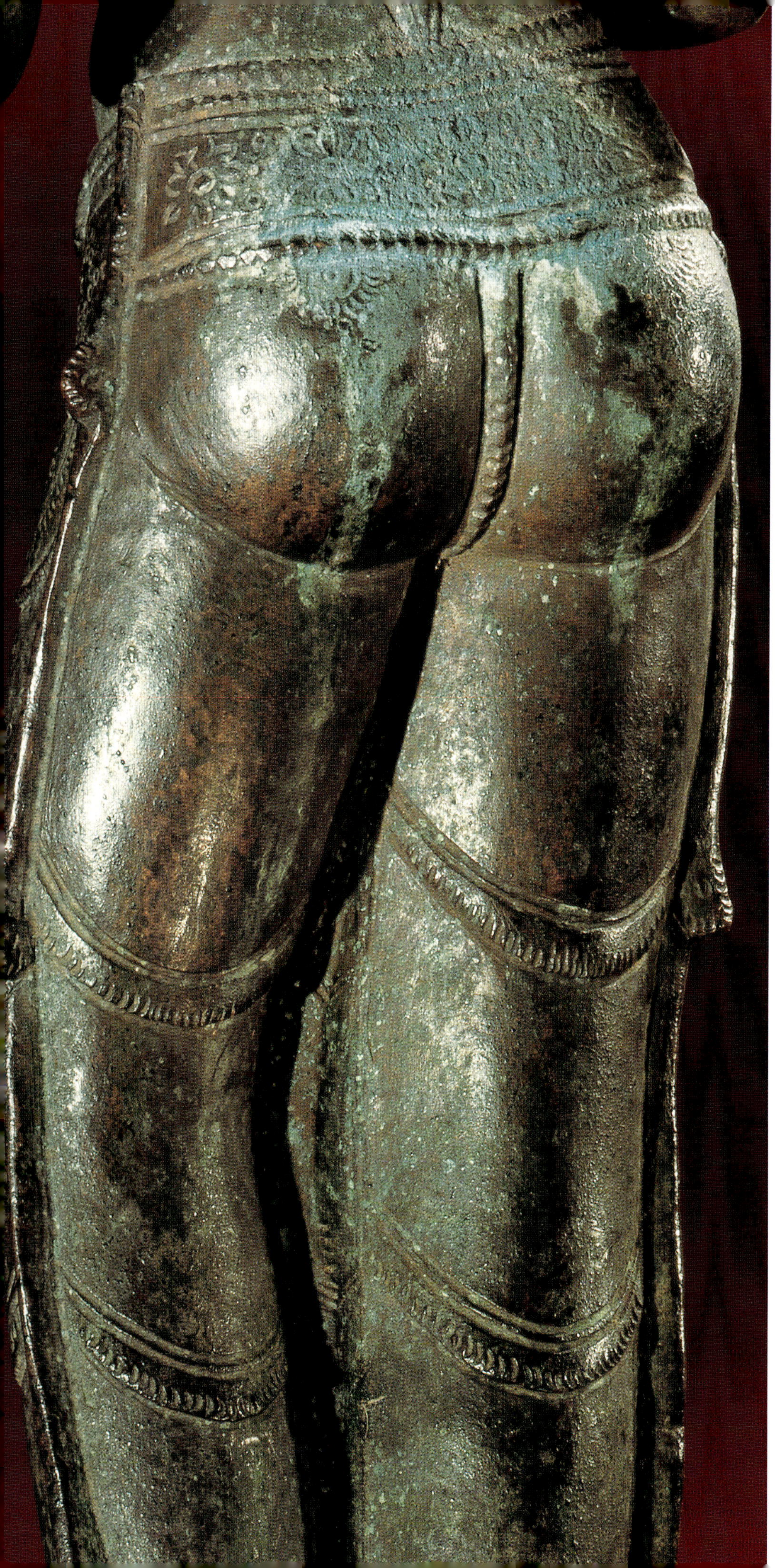

between beauty and eroticism: the female was full breasted, narrow waisted, with flaring hips, with three folds in the middle, long legs and supple thighs, slender or full – signs of femininity, sexuality, and motherhood – inviting and alluring men and gods alike. The generous breasts signify motherhood; the wide hips promise fecundity. The greatest impact is allowed to lie within the areas of the bosom and the pelvis. For they symbolise and visualise in stone or words, her sex and fertility, her dominant place in life as the only vehicle of procreation and preservation of the human race. The female body alone is the soil in which the generative is absorbed, nurtured and brought to the male seed that will ultimately lead to new life. This emphasis on breasts, hips, and thighs was evident even in prehistoric art.

Women in ancient and medieval India were undoubtedly aware of the allure of a beautiful face and an attractive body and certainly knew how to enhance their feminine graces. Many sculptural compositions at Khajuraho and Bhubaneshwar show women admiring themselves in the convex metal mirrors of the time, touching up their coiffures, painting their toenails and the soles of their feet. This is also apparent in Vatsyayana's *Kamasutra* and later works based on it, which provide many beauty tips.

Using flowers as an adornment was a specialised art. According to Yashodhara, there were two aspects of this art – the *samyojya* or making necklaces by weaving petals and other precious stones with thread, and *asamyojya*, which was the making of solid ornaments like bangles, bracelets and anklets. The women of the time included gymnastics, walking, games and sports of all kinds, physical exercises (with and without apparatus), breathing exercises, boxing, wrestling, hunting, and the art of self-defence in their repertoire of skills. The art of massage was the profession of the *samvahakas*, employed by those who could afford them.

At all times, however, it was the male gaze which was polishing and honing the form. The physical characteristics of the feminine form were altered to suit the social norms and the tastes of the patrons and the period. From the large, ripe, fecund forms of the ancient period, a more classical shape emerged in the Gupta period. It was during the medieval period that the feminine form was explored and enjoyed to its fullest potential by artists and poets, the emphasis shifting from the divine and the procreational to the recreational.

The social prescriptions of the period were also a factor in how women were represented. During the Mughal period, women were seen as consorts, rarely painted or sculpted as befitting their earlier popularity. In fact, they were the least popular as subjects. In the Pahari, Rajasthani and Deccani genre of painting they reclaimed their position as *nayikas*, with their beauty and aesthetics reaching an all-time high. As goddesses, as consorts of kings, as *gopis* and *nayikas*, they had their own story to tell.

However, nudity was glossed over during certain periods and in certain art forms. Overt nudity was a rare occurrence in Mughal and Rajasthani paintings unless the subject or the patrons demanded it. Obscenity was largely avoided. But even earlier, say, at Ajanta, where figures were semi-nude, one does not find them obscene. Neither did Buddhist art ever cater to the 'baser' instincts of man. In subsequent periods, especially in the depiction of the Radha-Krishna theme, the erotic element began to surface. Here, the tight *cholis* accentuating the shape of the breasts and their curvature were the rule. The nude bathing *gopis* in the lotus pond were often represented as begging Krishna for their clothes. The postures of their bodies with their long hair hiding the vital parts of their body ensured propriety.

The Kangra *kalam* too depicted the breasts clothed in short, tight *cholis* of see-through muslin. It may be stressed that no particular person served as the model for female beauty in these

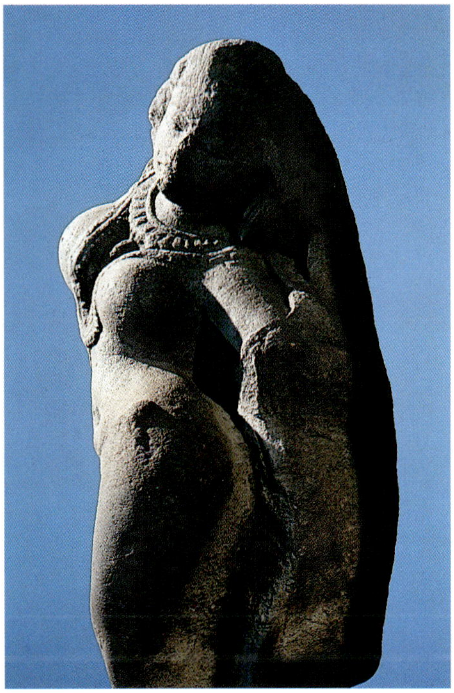

Rhythm and movement and the lyricism of line were the hallmark of traditional sculptures.
Facing page: The Indian sculptor, sensitive to the female form, imbued his figures with a great deal of sensual grace.
Previous page: From the north wall of the Vishvanath temple in Khajuraho – this posture is based on a yogic exercise, that of *shirshasana* or the headstand. Two female assistants support the couple while the male fondles their genitalia.

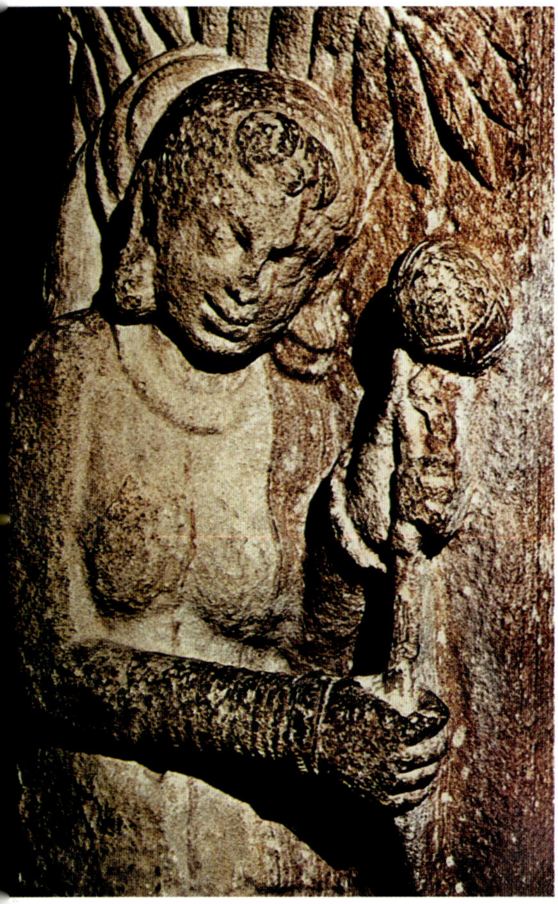

Yakshi on a Kushang pillar from Sanghol, Punjab.
Facing page: A dancing girl admiring herself in the mirror. *Halebid temple, Karnataka, south India.*

paintings. This beauty was a sum total of the best elements from various beautiful female bodies, that is, it was The Ideal Beauty. The paintings of the different miniature traditions, particularly those relating to the Geeta Govinda theme, are heavily laden with erotic sentiments in keeping with the literature that demanded such portrayal.

Often, the passionate nature of the literary text being depicted compelled the artist to depict Radha and Krishna in various stages of physical union, and yet such representations were devoid of any indication of gross obscenity or pornographic overtures.

Though in ancient India, poets and dramatists always eulogised the beauty of women, there was a certain categorisation of their types. Technical writers on the science of love have described these types, of which the best fourfold classification first appeared in the *Rati Rahasya* (tenth century) of Pandit Kokkoka. He classified women into four types according to their physical characteristics: *Padmini, Chitrini, Shankhini* and *Hastini*. While the first was held as the supreme, the last was the least desirable. The *Padmini* was soft like the lotus bud, emanating freshness and a pleasing body odour. She had eyes like those of a startled gazelle; their corners were scarlet. Her breasts resembled the *bilva (bel)* fruit in terms of their flawless rotundity; her nose was small and beautifully shaped. She had a golden-hued complexion like the *champaka* flower, and the lustre of the soft lotus petal. Second to her was the *Chitrini*. She had an attractive gait, was of medium height, slim yet well developed, with firm breasts, full lips, wide hips and fleshy symmetrical thighs. She was passionate. The *Shankhini* was neither too fat nor too thin, but had a tall body and long legs. She was fair complexioned with tiny veins showing through the skin. Her walk was undulating, and the pelvic region well formed. Having a certain superficial sexual charm, she was actually cunning and unchaste, her voice harsh and unmelodious. The *Hastini* was the least desirable because of her graceless walk, thick limbs, heavy feet, and crooked toes. With huge and pendulous breasts, like the brows of an elephant, as mentioned in *Ratimanjari*, she had a short neck; her hair was unattractive; her body corpulent, and its smell unpleasant. With thick lips and body covered with excessive hair, especially the pubic region, this *nayika* was not appreciated by the cultured mind.

Other women were classified as the Deer, the Mare and the Elephant types, each suited to certain kinds of men, who were classified into three categories: the Hare, the Bull and the Horse. Since female breasts formed such a vital part of feminine beauty, ancient Indian literature contained

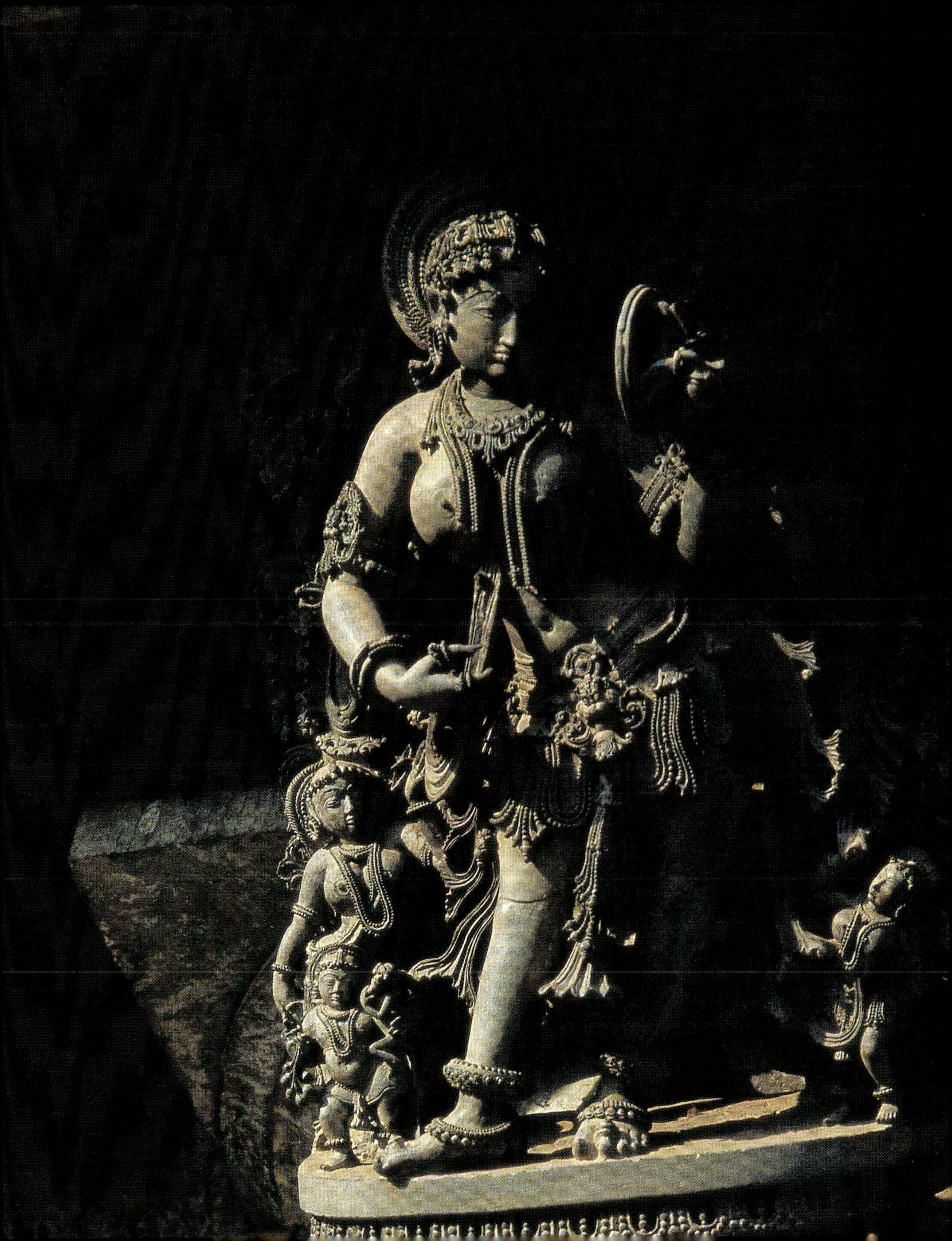

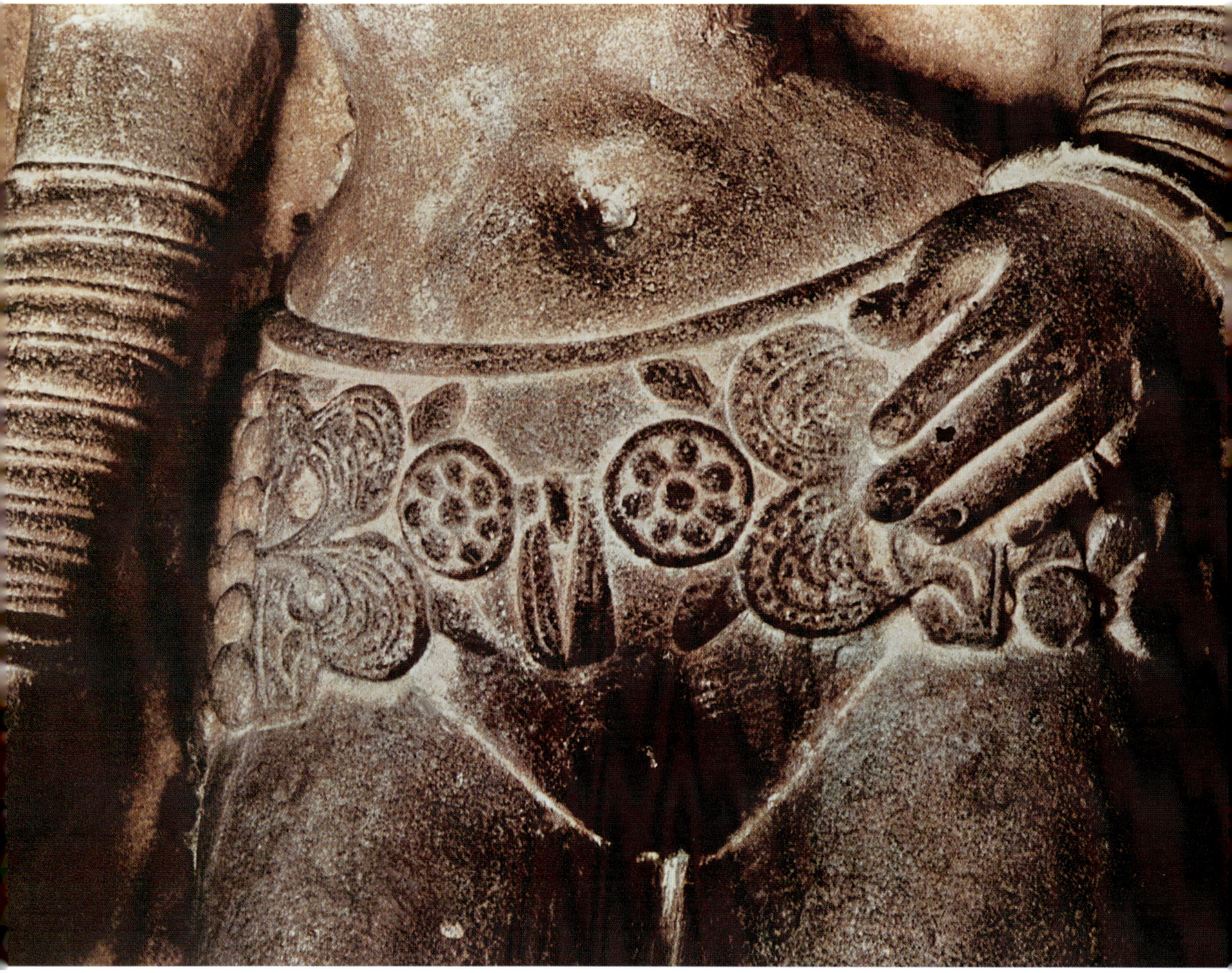

When it comes to sculptures of feminine beauty, the Kushana works are unsurpassed.

prescriptions for females to enhance the size of their breasts. For example, the *Rati Rahasya* recommended a regular massage of the breasts with a paste made of antimony and rice water.

Another classification was given by the sixteenth-century poet Keshava Das in his treatise, *Rasikapriya*. He categorised women on the basis of different states of mind caused by factors such as longing, disappointment, coyness, a natural reserve, anxiety and jealousy. Keshava Das recognised only eight kinds of *nayikas*. The *Nabodha* was a young girl who was shy of meeting her lover alone in solitude. The *Mugdha* was proud of her charms and was willing to go with her lover, any time, anywhere. The *Sambhoga Nayika* longed for union with her lover and boldly proclaimed her love. *Prostapatika* was the one who was suffering due to a long separation from her lover. The *Agata Bhartrika* was the one meeting her husband after a prolonged absence. When she waited expectantly and longingly at her doorway, she was *Nayika Vasakasajja,* who was ready with the bed prepared for the husband or lover she expected any moment. The *Khandita* was reproachful, for her lover had come home after spending the night with another woman. The *Vipralabdha* felt neglected and sorrowful for she longed in vain throughout the night. The *Pravatsvatpatika* felt into a fit of dejection on learning that her husband was going on a long journey. The *Agamapatika Nayika* was pleased to hear her lover would arrive soon. The happiest was the *Agampatika*, whose husband had just returned after a long separation, and she wanted him at once. The *Abhisarika Nayika* was represented in Rajput paintings, a heroine so stricken with love that she went out at night, unafraid of the devils and dangers in the jungle. The *Swadhinapatika* held her lover in utter subjection and knew her power over him. The *Abhisamdhita* or *Rupagarita* was given to unnecessary resentment and pretended to be easily offended.

The continuity of the representation of the female form in Indian painting was present right from the Ajanta frescoes, from the second to the sixth centuries. The half-draped female form was a common feature in the frescoes, but they were devoid of the erotic since Buddhist art never catered to the sensual. But a thousand years down the line, in the Pahari and Rajasthani miniature tradition, there was an infusion of erotica. The *nayikas* of the Rajasthani miniatures wore tight blouses ending just below their firm breasts, above the midriff. However, certain techniques were used to enforce decency. The vital parts were often covered with the woman's long hair and a hand placed over the naked bosom. 'A mood of mild flirtation, a sort of 'petting', was the limit of the usual run of Rajasthani miniature art,' says Rustum J. Mehta. The Rajasthani tradition outlined feminine beauty in terms of large eyes, flowing tresses, firm breasts, slender waist and rosy, soft hands. The Kangra School of Painting presented the female form even more subtly. Women were always clothed in tight *cholis* made of thin cloth to accentuate their breasts. The beauty portrayed in these reflected experiences and recalled faces from real life. Radha is said to have had the synthesis of many beauties and was not just a singular pretty face. In a third school, that is the Pahari miniatures belonging to the Sattriya School in Assam, the images were more overt. Their poetry is full of sensual depiction.

The continuity of the ascription and prescriptions for the female form is evident even in the works of contemporary artists. There have been innovations, fusion, reinvention of the '*original* ' female form, yet there are feminine characteristics which remain constant. The influence of the Western concepts of beauty – narrow hips, flatter breasts, leaner legs – all part of Western aesthetics – is influencing the Indian concept of beauty. It is only now that women have reached a status of objectification and commodification, and lost their independent status as individuals with meaning, content and reference.

Inside tribal territory

Inside tribal territory

Indian tribal art offers an imagery that is violently erotic and visually stimulating. Both the textual references and the visual graffiti extend an imagery which is raw, primitive and physical and related to fertility rites, cultic practices and physical interplay. It deals with everyday affairs and does not relate to the more cerebral and philosophical ideologies in which the classical arts are foregrounded.

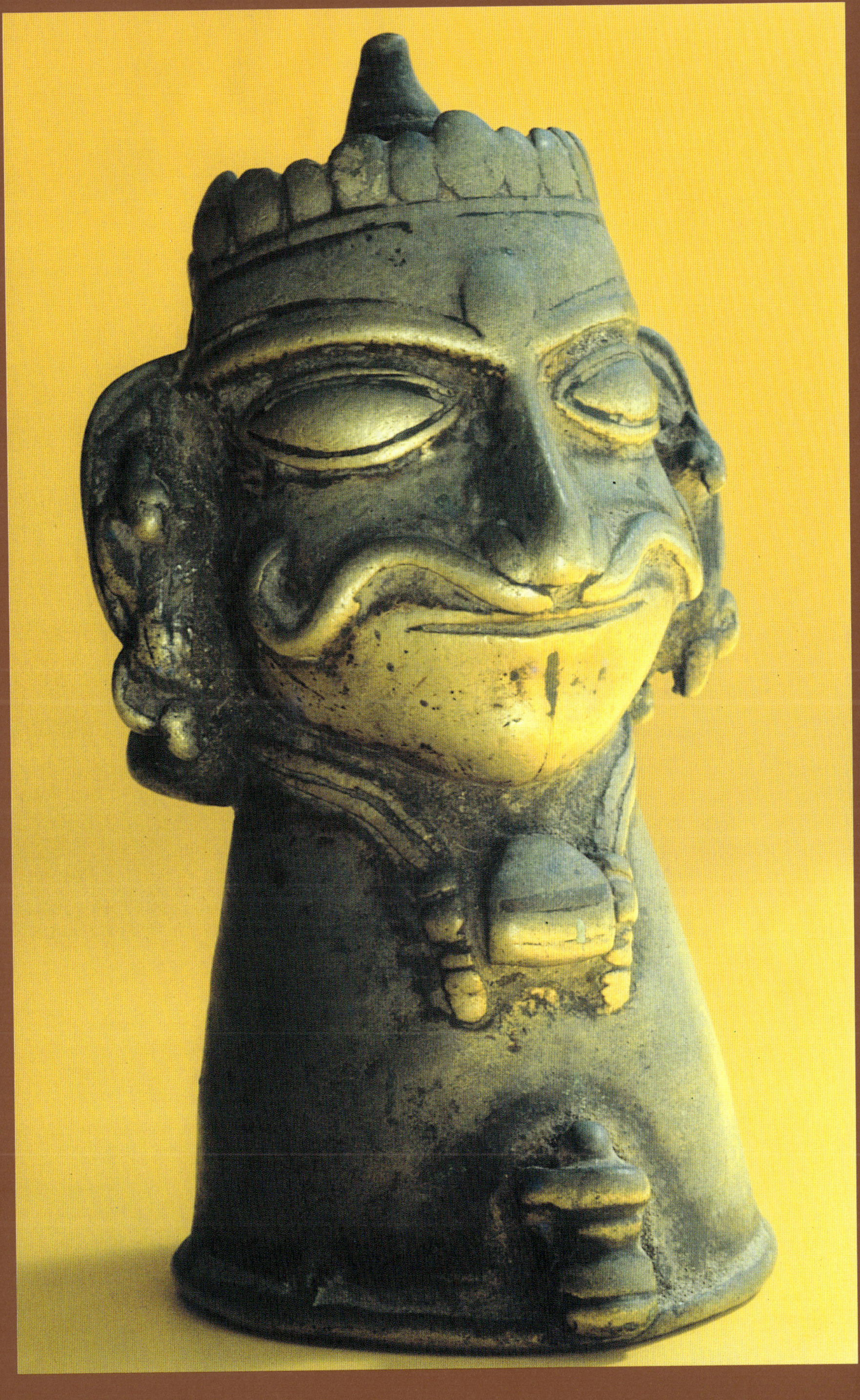

Erotic images are painted on walls, sculpted in metal and used as part of cultic practices. The text of such imagery is decoded from the songs, folk dances, folklore and forest stories of the different tribes.

One such tribe, the Santhals, which lives in central India and practises shifting agriculture, is more expressive of sexual attraction and lovemaking. The tribe accepts courting, but if a couple is caught in the act, it is fined. The middle and eastern Indian tribes, in contrast, lay great store on the physical appearance of the male and the female. It is all right for a man to be even moderately handsome, but a woman has to be a beauty.

Of forms and females

Tribes have two basic conceptions of feminine beauty. The slim, slender girl, who has an erect figure and perfect breasts, finds much favour with the tribal societies of the *Ao, Lhota Nagas* and *Murias*. The round, short female with a firm posterior is much cherished among the *Konyak Nagas*. The women of this tribe wear clothes that appear erotic to the outsider but are sign of beauty to those from the tribe. The dress comprises a narrow cloth, only four inches wide, that is slipped on the buttocks and shows off the median line as the woman walks. The way she walks adds to her elegance. If she has a smooth stride, with swaying hips, then she is considered charming. So is a girl whose walk is brisk. A girl with a wobble is not appreciated.

Songs in the Santhal tradition describe the beauty of the female form. Though the aspects of the girl's body are of great importance, her face must also have appeal. But this is a matter of secondary concern when compared to the breasts, buttocks, legs and waist. Her nose should be straight and her hair long; her eyes should neither be too large nor too small; her teeth should be regular; the cheeks round and chubby. The complexion of the body is of no consequence and a dark girl is considered as pretty as a fair one. The dress and ornaments should be simple and drape her body so as to accentuate the buttocks and her movements. This ideal then typifies grace. Moreover, a girl who is strongly desired for sex must have an amiable disposition. The personality, thus, is also of significance in a girl.

The ideal mate and marriage

In contrast to these numerous codes for a woman, the man gets away. At the most, all that is required is that he be smart, with a spring in his walk, have broad shoulders, with the torso tapering towards the waist. His

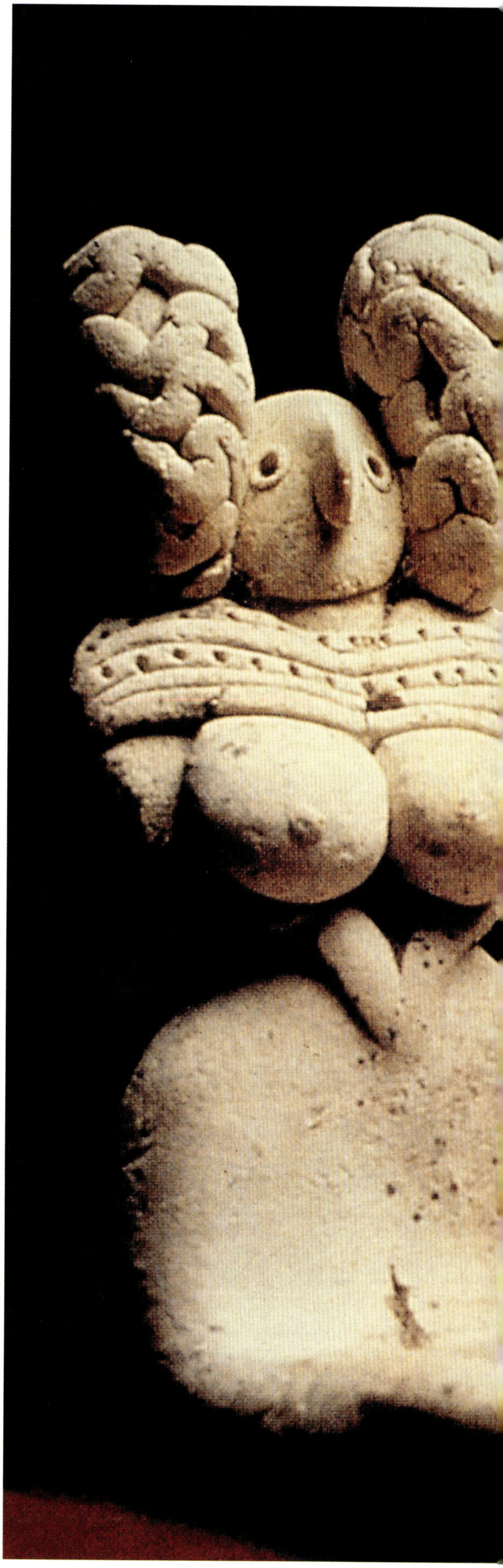

Terracotta images of fertility goddesses.
Previous page: A *mukhalinga* from Maharashtra.

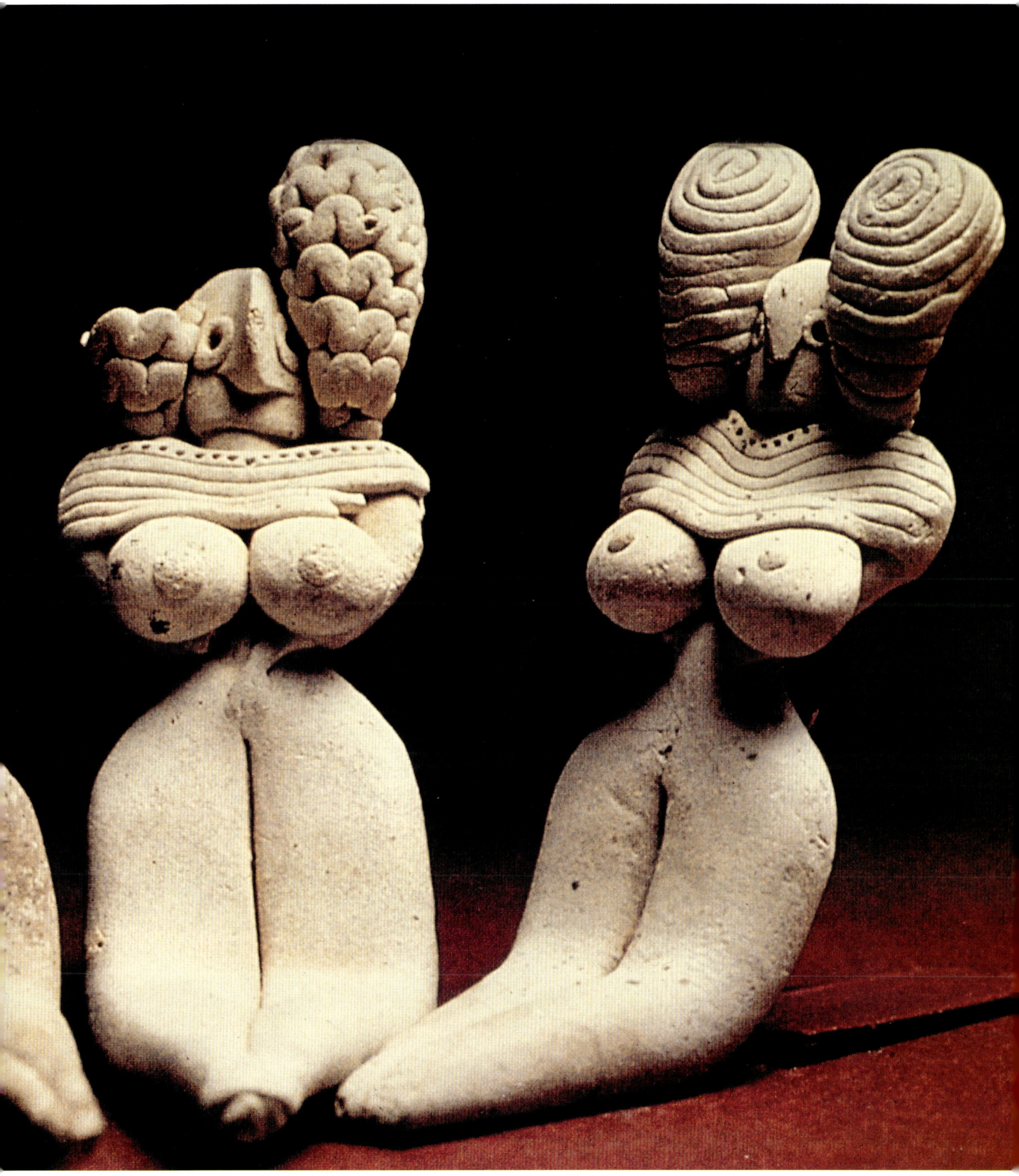

personality should be genial and his skills must involve playing the drums and the flute. It is a bonus if he has plump cheeks, curly hair and regular features, but it does not matter if he does not have them. His manner with girls and his approach is what singles him out.

Once the standards of beauty are met, the issue of attraction and seeking a lover come into focus. After the Santhal boy and girl reach puberty, they enter a period of sweet romance. They indulge in sex, though this is not merely for enjoyment, but is a need of the heart. The elders wink at this, but not if the children are caught *in flagrante delicto*.

Once a boy has fallen in love, his prime objective is to possess the girl completely. This desire is often attributed to a growing friendship and gets its sanction from an archetypal forest tale. The story goes that once a boy grazed cattle with his sister-in-law. The girl matured, and in the fields he often caught sight of her smooth thighs. One such day, the boy saw her vital organ. 'I could check myself no longer,' the story continues in W. Archer's *The Love Of Krsna*. 'I pushed her down with my hand. The girl was a virgin and I had to hurt her. Her sex was very tight and I was full of joy. After that we grazed cattle together and I took her every day.'

Often the girl is shown protesting, and there are times when the boy does not relent, coaxing her to let him take her. Sometimes the boy fails to win her over and then uses force. This does not gain him the girl's approval and leads to punishment.

Santhal boys consider their girls to be their 'property'. The girls are free to choose whichever boy they like and often take the initiative to approach the boy first. But they cannot turn down a boy, nor can their parents keep them in an ivory tower. An apocryphal story relates one such instance warningly. Apparently, a girl's parents kept their daughter segregated from boys in the proud belief that if she were to be married, her unmatched beauty would not wither away. To keep boys away, they got two guard dogs to accompany her whenever she went out. The village headman's son saw her and was determined to take her.

One day the boy's buffalo died. He cut its legs and followed the girl into the forest. When he tried to approach her, the dogs pounced on him and he threw the meat to them. The dogs went for the meat; the boy for the girl. The story underlines the fact that sooner or later a boy must have a girl.

Social fencing

There are social restrictions to such desires and relationships. The boy and girl must not be caught dating. They must not flirt overtly, and a girl must not be open about meeting a boy. Often the trysts are not long, but if they are, the girl must get ready for interrogation and endeavour to escape by means of a white lie. When the time for marriage

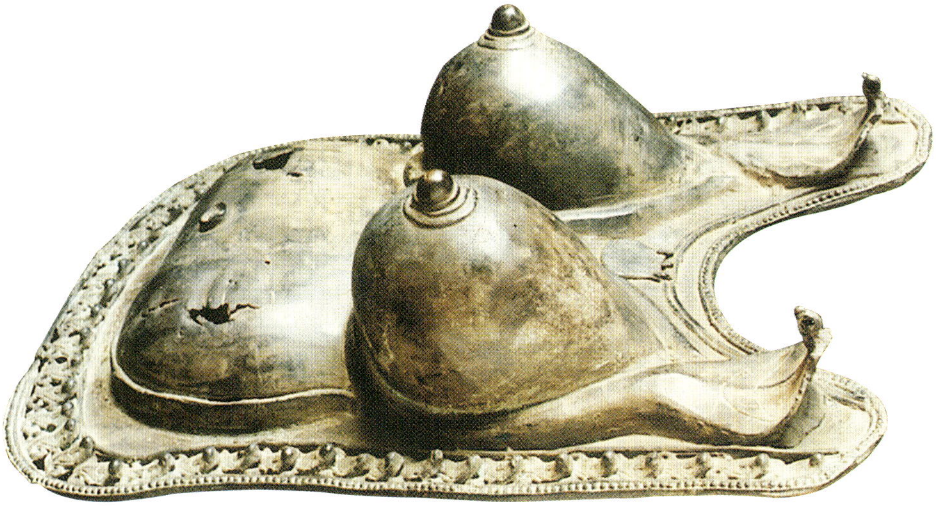

A body mask used in the ritual fertility dance of the Bhuta cult in Karnataka. *Facing page:* A wood carving from the temple *ratha* in Karnataka, depicts a *maithuna* couple.

approaches, the risks associated with a meeting increase. However, if the girl is not caught with her paramour, does not neglect housework, and her parents do not concern themselves with what she does during the day, she can meet him as often as she pleases. Often relationships last a maximum of five years. The boy then gets married to another girl and the girl is married to another boy. The respective spouses accept their premarital sexual explorations. Often when boys are attracted to girls outside their society, they ask their parents to go to the girl's family and propose marriage.

There is an element of contradiction in the way Santhal society reacts to these relationships. It is not the sexual act that matters to them. What does matter is that any interaction should be within the ambit of the rules of their society. As long as the norms are followed, the couple is free to act as it wishes. But if the laws are broken, the two are penalised with a fine.

The Warli circle of life

More complex is the cultural structure of the Warli tribes who are concentrated in the Thane region of Maharashtra. The Warlis see the world as a circle with no end. It represents the womb that is capable of endless births. They draw circles on any

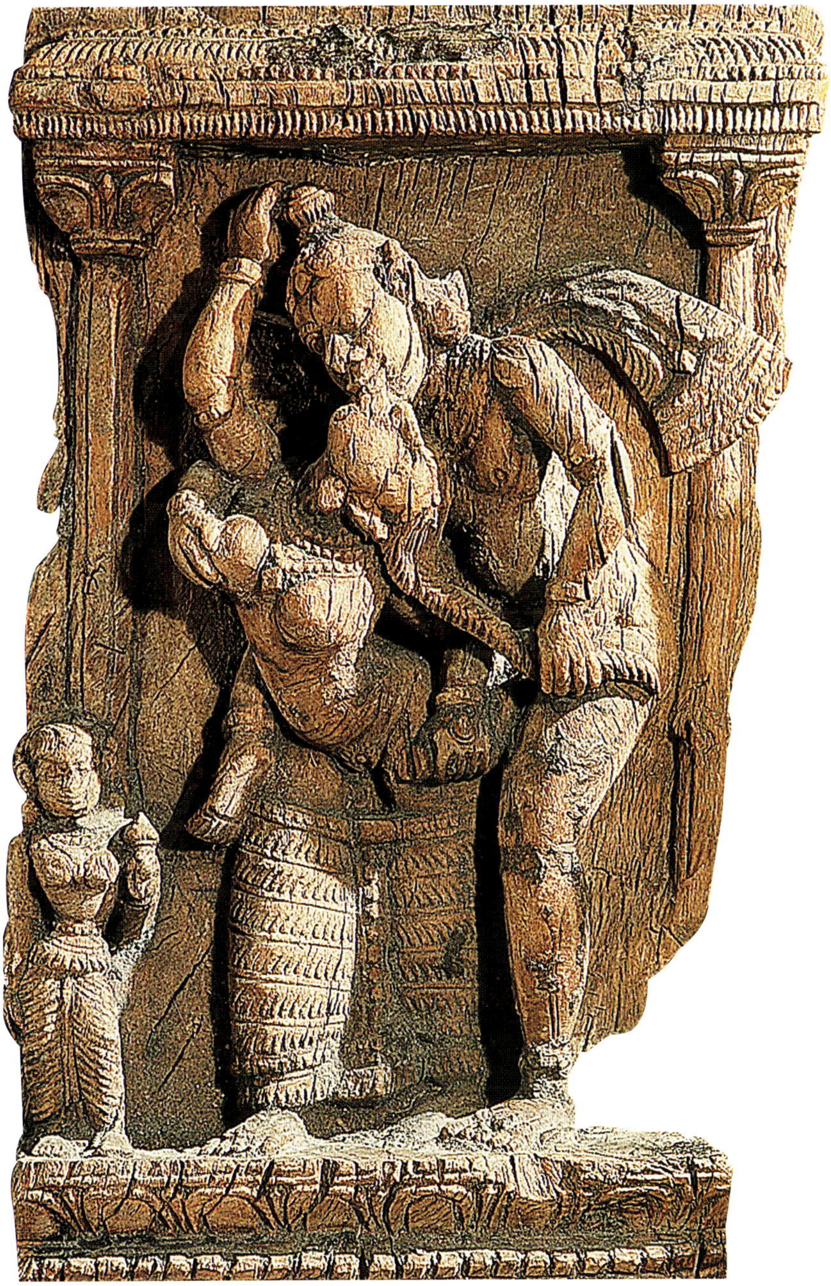

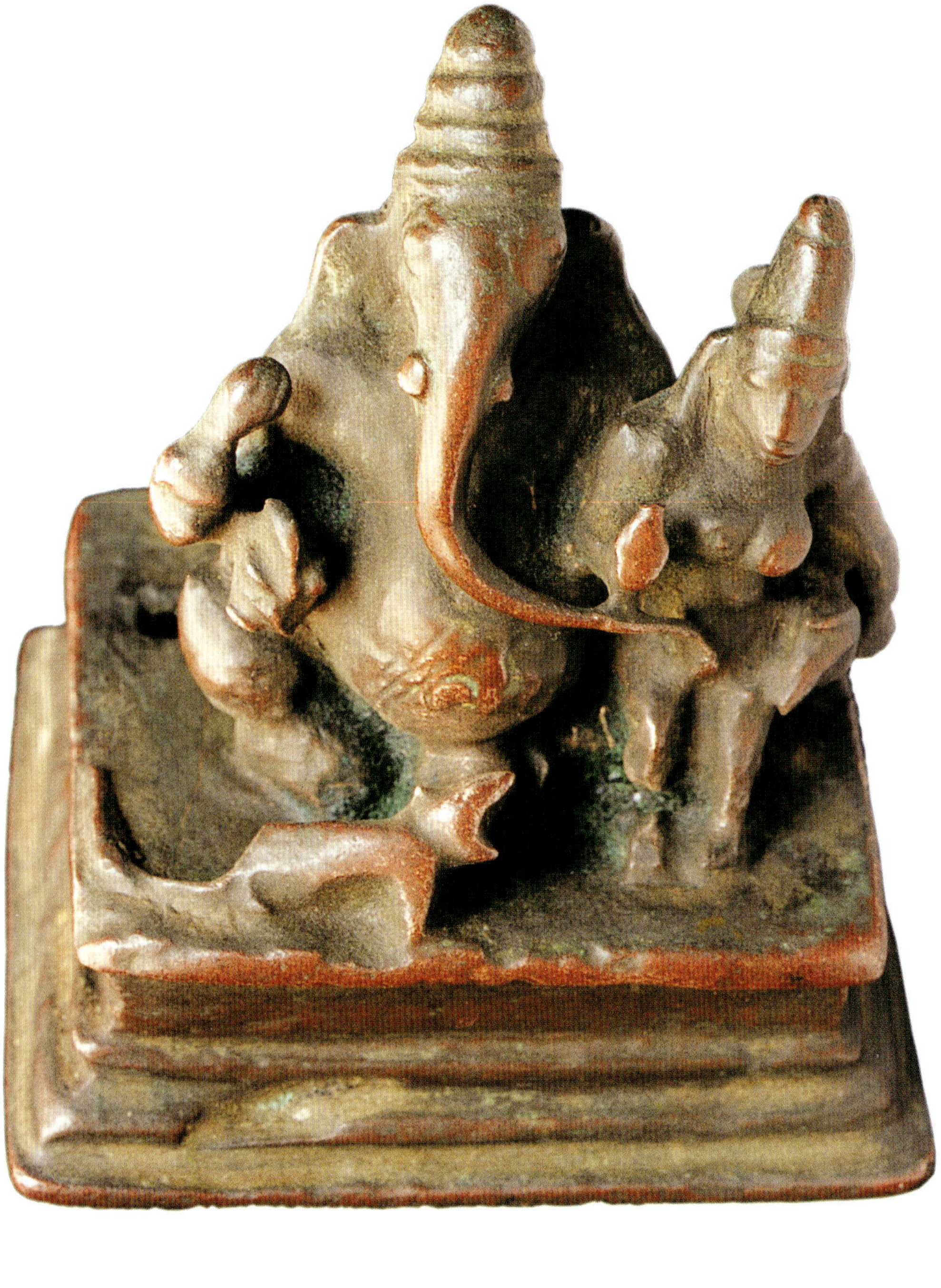

occasion – birth, marriage, or even death, because it encompasses the essence of their lives in that one perfect round.

Their fertility cult is also associated with the cyclic year. The year is born, it matures and then it dies. That is why each wedding, which usually takes place after the harvest, is seen not just as a union between a man and a woman, but as the coming together of a divine couple. The act represents and is a part of the union of the universe.

The cult of the Mother Goddess amongst the Warli tribes shows a dual attitude towards her worship: they concentrate both on her destructive and creative powers. On the one hand, they see an impure, menstruating woman, who can control her periods as a witch. One of their paintings shows a menstruating woman who 'stinks so everyone runs away from her,' says Yasodhara Dalmia in her book, *The Painted World of the Warlis.* On the other hand, the goddess is looked upon as the creative power that encompasses the universe.

Yet, surprisingly, the Warlis are a patriarchal society, and a man gets to marry as often as he wishes, whereas the woman cannot marry again. But the women frequently leave their husbands. A widow undergoes a *pata* ceremony or a secret marriage where

From Tamil Nadu, a bronze image of Ganesha with his consort. His trunk fondles her *yoni.*

she has to remain with her husband's brother. 'But customs are not hidebound and many couples live together and have children without getting married,' says Dalmia. 'The transitory nature of their society, pointing to an earlier matriarchal cult, is indicated by the fact that men still have to pay bride-price; only priestesses can perform marriages, and the role of the maternal uncle is important in many rites and rituals of the year.'

The Warlis believe that death is the same as marriage and observe the same rites. Death is also presumed to have fertile or regenerative powers as seen in the death statues of the tribe.

Painted faces of Palaghata

Another important visual preoccupation of the Warlis is marriage paintings. No marriage ceremony can be conducted without the presence of these. Marriage paintings from different geographical regions offer a variety of visual imagery. From the presence of two animals, to the bride and the groom, to two triangles merging into one (triangles are a metaphor for the female creative energy), all this can be seen in marriage paintings and refers to sexual union.

The vegetation goddess, Palaghata, and her guardian, Pancasiriya, are the central figures in these paintings. Palaghata also bears a resemblance to the Mother Goddess.

Dalmia explains the origins of the word *Palaghata* in her book. It is the combined form of *pal* meaning plants and *ghata* meaning pot. *Palaghata,* thus, is a pot overflowing with plants and is symbolic of the goddess of fertility. The goddess Palaghata is visually represented as a headless figure who sits cross-legged. This position resembles the birth-giving goddess in the Indus Valley seal, whose arms and legs are stretched apart, and a five-leafed plant springs from her womb. The Palaghata goddess can also be compared to the Almapur goddess of Andhra Pradesh. Stella Kramrisch, art historian and indologist, suggests that this position is a posture taken for sexual intercourse and for giving birth.

The cross-legged posture is assumed at the time of marriage, and the image could be a metaphor for sexual intercourse, says one line of thought. 'Palaghata may stand for an elemental energy,' says Dalmia, 'which is both sexual and intellectual, and which alone is procreative.' Palaghata then becomes the sexual energy of the universe and not just the individual. She is both the fertility goddess and the, *yogini* and her cross-legged position marks the zenith of sexuality and asceticism. Thus Palaghata, the goddess, is the creative power that encompasses the entire world. Since she means the essence of life for the Warlis, her form ranges from the abstract to the figurative. Also, as she represents reality for the Warlis, she is worshipped in the image of man and bedecked in material decorations drawn from daily Warli life.

However, the image of the Palaghata – which emerges from the central figure of the Indus Valley Mother Goddess and is adapted to suit the cultural needs of the different tribal societies, has also seen changes, turning from a square shape to a more curvaceous form. It shows the emergence of a more sensual woman, thus giving a new profile to the Mother Goddess, and suggests that the Warlis moved to a complete enjoyment of human sensuousness. The changing figure, from a rectangular form that appeared like two boulders enclosing two animals within two triangles, is related to the way the Warlis feel about their world. At first, the triangular *yoni* represents the endless creative capabilities of the woman. Over a period of time, the image decreases in size and dignity, very much in keeping with the influences of the changing world outside the community. But in spite of all influences, the Palaghata remains large enough to withstand the threats of the outside world.

Popular art

Popular art

Since the ages, the Indian subcontinent has assimilated and encouraged diversity. It has played host to many religions and cultures which coexist even as they retain their individual characteristics. The centripetal tendency of Indian culture has received another push with globalisation. With this the concept of the outsider has gone out of the window, and people are adopting and adapting views, attitudes and lifestyles.

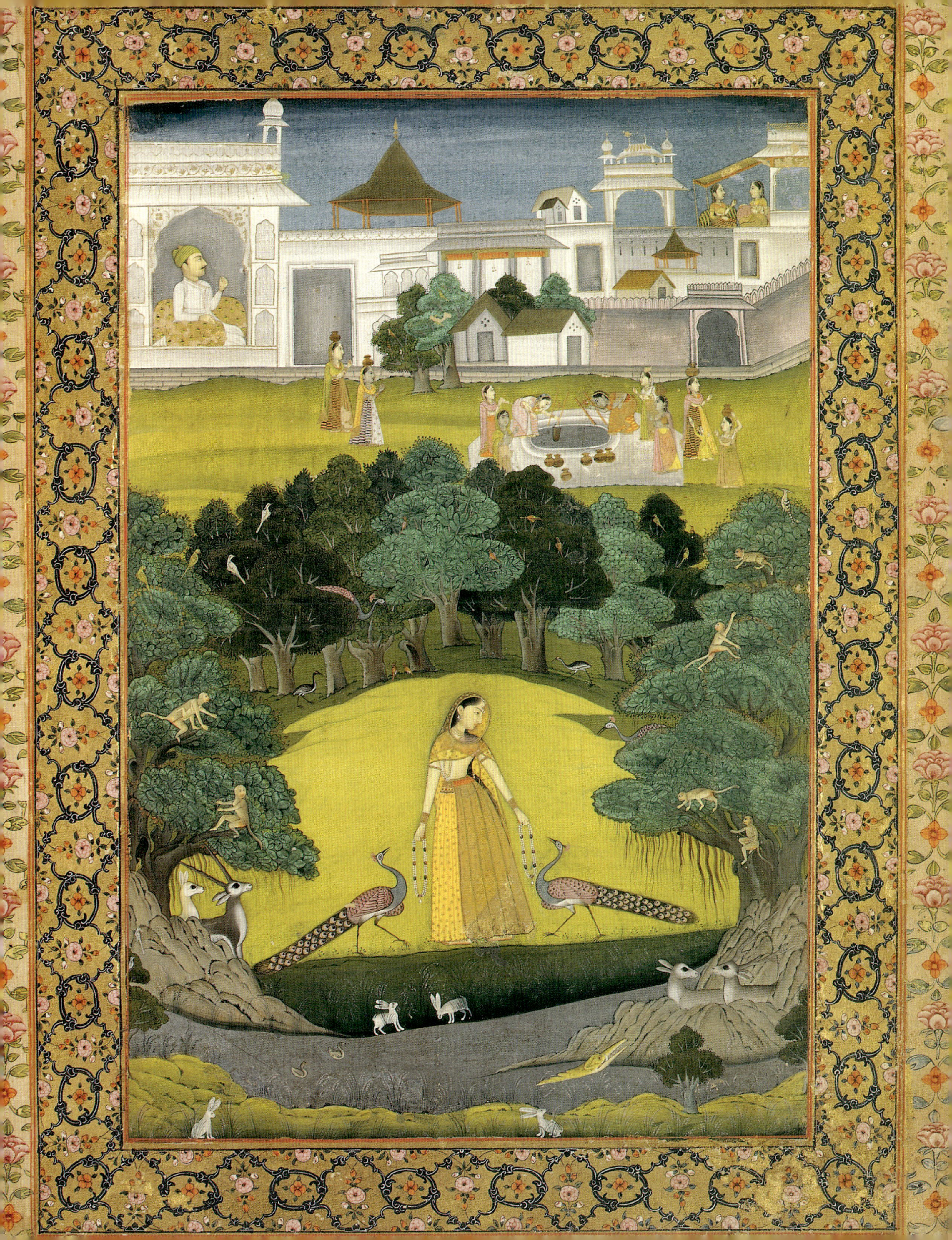

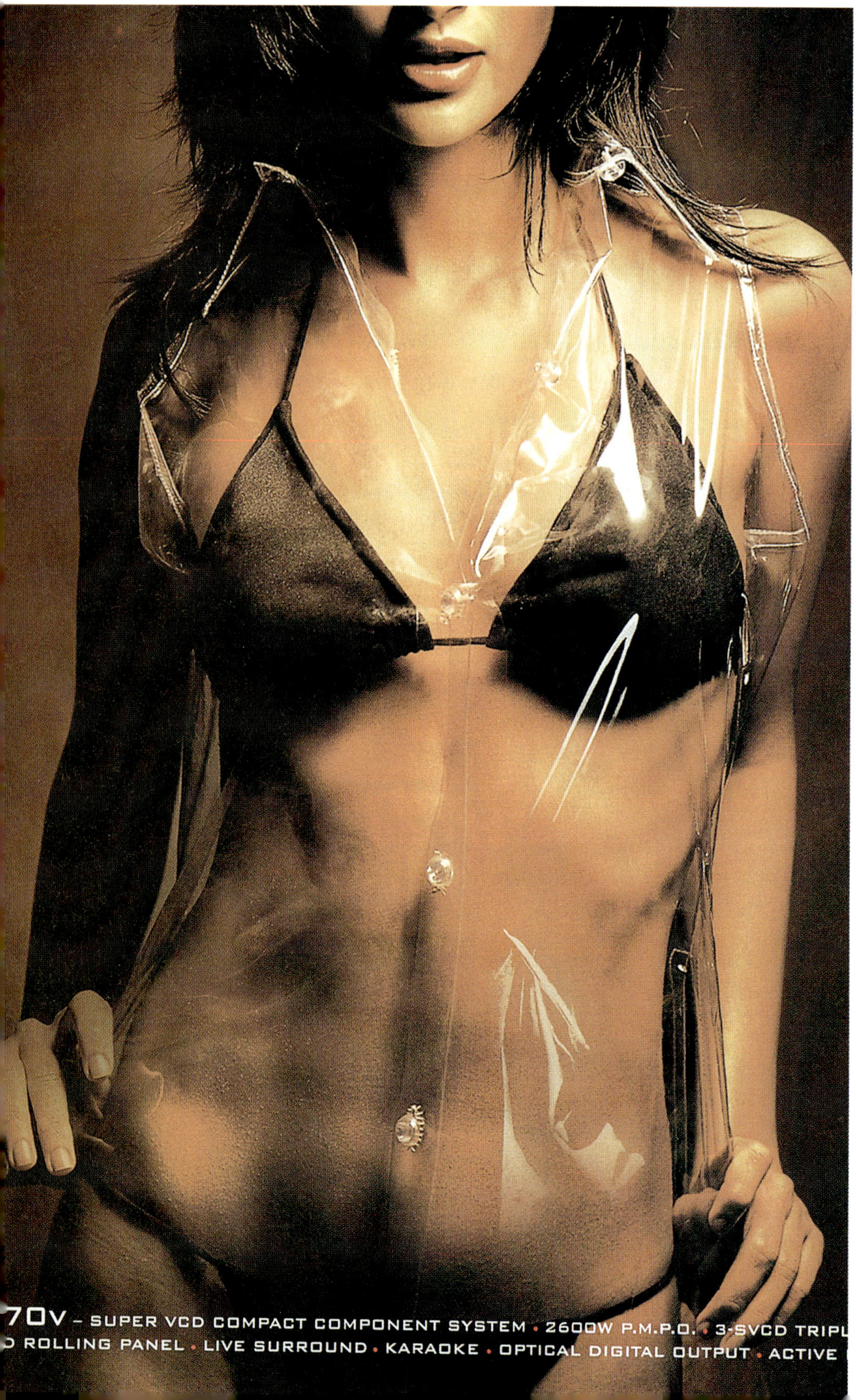

The arts – especially painting, literature and the films – are fields in which the change is most noticeable. In fact, the arts and their messiahs have gone on to form a cultural industry that consists of institutions or actions that work towards changing culture subtly. The route to transformation is through encoding. A certain attitude, belief or value is coded in a message and sent to the audience to capture the mind market. The audience is crucial as, in contrast to a decade or two ago, it is no longer passive

Advertising: This is the West

The most visible media of messaging is advertising – one indicator being that it comes in for a lot of flak. For example, the advertisement for a certain toothpaste that makes an overt reference to a kiss catches the censor's eye. But the censorious gaze is not in keeping with ancient and medieval Indian visual culture. As an eminent authority, Philip Rawson, says: 'This beautiful sexual-religious culture survives only to a small extent in India. But as a result of puritan pressures generated during the nineteenth century by an alliance between high-caste Indian prejudice and British-style Christianity, it is not publicly acknowledged. And today Indian society has become so

Advertisers are not shy and explicit imagery is used to influence the target audience.
Facing page: Exploitation is the name of the game and it makes catching your eye so much easier.
Previous page: The comely maiden draws even the animals towards her in a miniature painting.

inhibited that not even a kiss may be seen in a movie. 'Of course, the public stand is often different from private morality.

It is not as if the culture industry is beyond the influence of the messages. Advertising again offers an example. Today, the West influences it highly, and advertisers convert their ethics to suit that ethos. For various reasons advertisements often deal with imagery that is explicit. Explicit images hit the audience via what can be called a *bullet-theory effect*: the same image is repeatedly thrown at the viewer to firmly impress it on the mind and influence the decision to buy.

But the audience is not a simple, passive entity; in fact, it can be categorised into three divisions. The viewer can have a *dominant* or *preferred* reading habit, meaning that he/she is influenced and believes in the message — no questions asked. The second set comprises those who have a *negotiated* reading habit. That is, though they may be impressed by the message, they are not necessarily converted into consumers. But this set is still a good advertising target. Finally, there are those who have an *oppositional* reading habit. They look at an advertisement but choose to read it in a manner contradictory to its message.

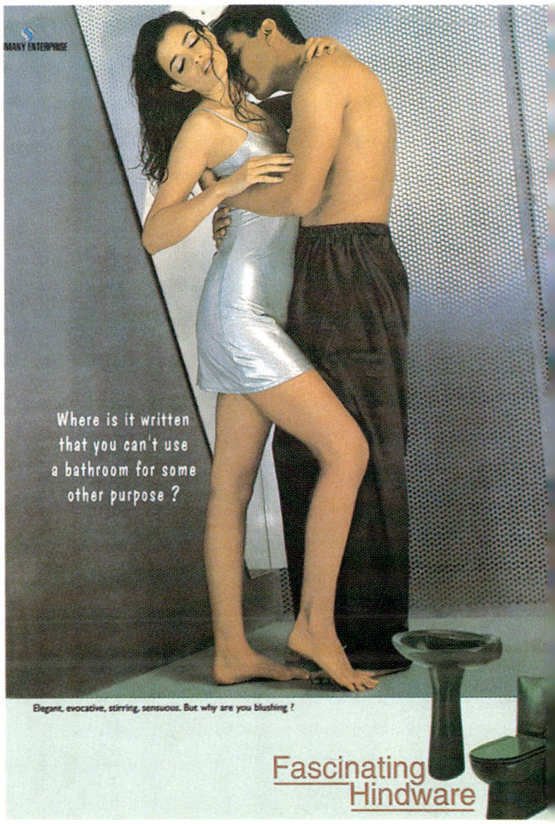

Take for example, a familiar advertisement for an undergarments brand uses the stereotyped knight-in-shining-armour theme. It has a man in a bathrobe, showing off his muscular torso and his underwear, rescuing a much harassed, mini-skirted girl from the villain prowling the street. The last shot shows the girl hugging the man while he holds her waist. A *dominant* reader here would link the underwear and male machismo. A *negotiated* reader would not accept the idea at first, but depending on the number of times the advertisement is shown, he may be tempted. An *oppositional* reader would quiz the whole idea and it would not have a positive effect on him.

Note that this image has nothing to do with the aesthetics of pleasure or *vilas* as found in Indian erotica.

Another objection that can be raised against these sort of messages is that of objectification. The advertising content gets erotic by exploiting the woman's body. It shows her bound and at the mercy of the man, both when she is attacked and when she is saved. In the first case, she is helpless because she is 'weaker' than the attacker. In the second, she is awed by her rescuer and instantly sinks into his arms. The woman is thus shown dependent. Apparently, her short, tight and sleeveless dress is what provokes the attack and, simultaneously, it enfeebles her.

By the time the advertisement is over, a human being has been turned into a provocative sexual display piece. This is *objectification*. It is alien to the concept of Indian sexuality, but is symptomatic of contemporary trends in Indian society. Today, even the Indian gazes at the feminine form with an occidental eye. The benchmark for the code of beauty now rest with the West: women who are sexy have thin

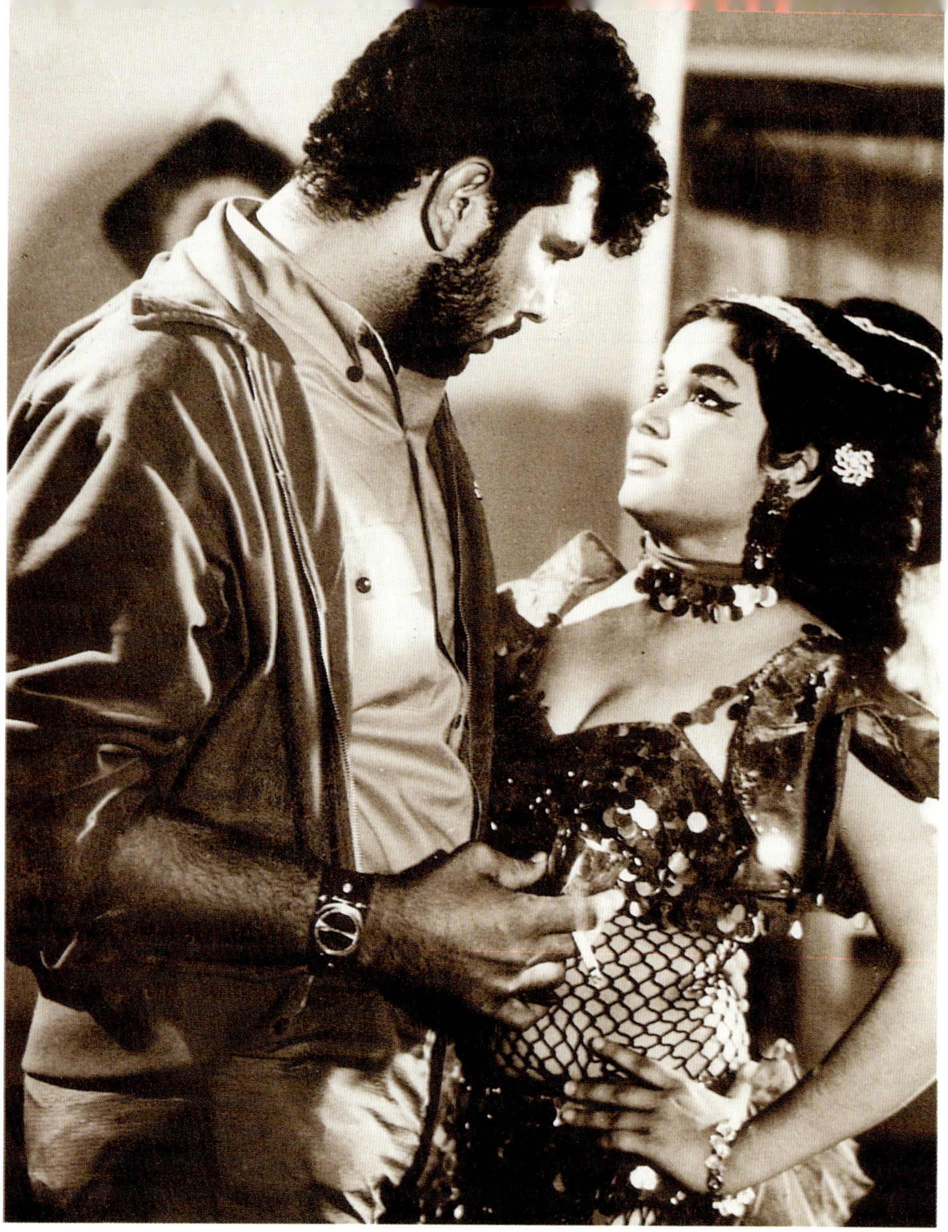

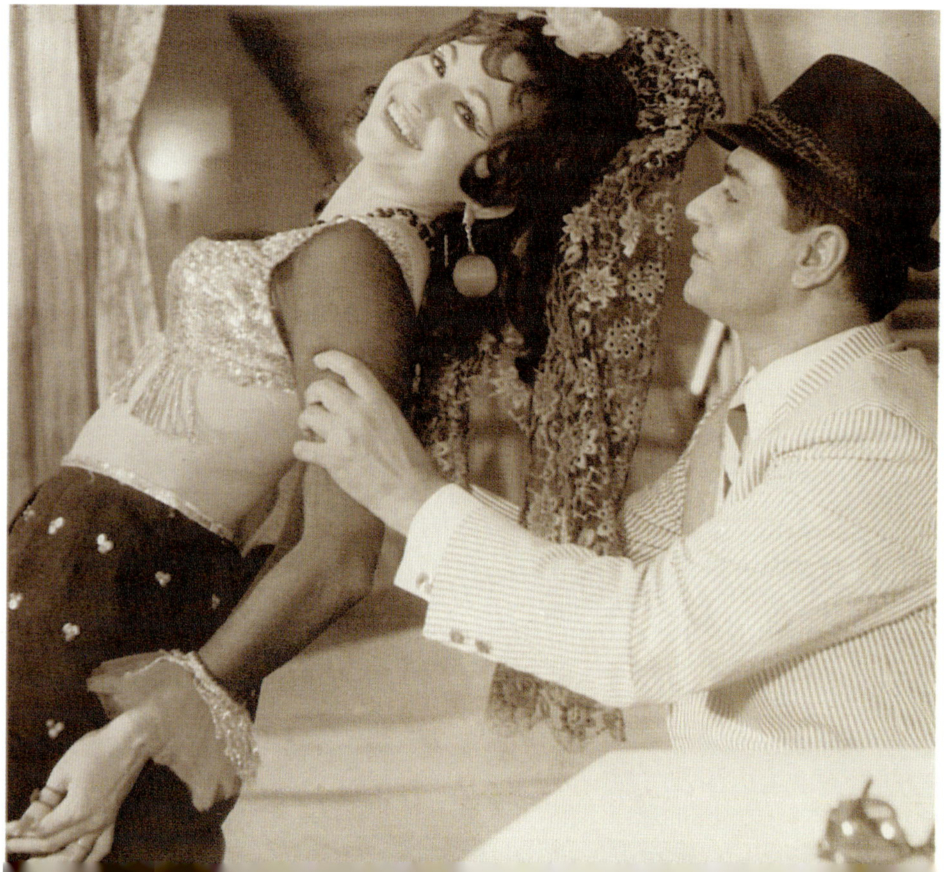

waists, tall, stork-type legs, and big breasts. They wear short dresses. Such advertisements are guilty of misinforming the audience.

Other advertisements play on the *recall effect* associated with imagery. A coffee advertisement shows a couple in foreplay who simply stop and sip the beverage. Coffee thereby is linked to the sex act and nudges the memory of the viewer when he sees the product. *Recall effect* also signifies the impact the advertisement has upon the audience.

The symbolism is meaningless and fails to arouse passion, but is obsessive, and hence pornographic. Though, these advertisements form only a minuscule portion of the new values agents are slipping into Indian society, they are widely accepted.

Dancing for God

The coin of globalisation has two sides to it: one, cultural convergence that opens up cultures, urges acceptance and lessens alienation; two, cultural reproduction, that is the change brought about in culture. This can often be so drastic that it is harsh against the centuries-old tradition in the country, causing generation conflict and identity crises.

Cultural convergence is seen in dance, music and art forms that have endured for centuries and have a strong erotic base. Indian dance exemplifies this across a broad spectrum of society. Dancing girls were as much a part of the *durbar* recreation as the *mujra* or wedding ceremonies were entertainment for the common man.

Dance also went hand in hand with the culture of prostitution and courtesans, common in ancient India. The higher class of courtesans was not looked down upon - even immortals enjoyed their company. The temple god, for instance, was considered a living being with his own court, wives, attendants and concubines. The *devadasis* were the temple dancers. However, they were not supposed to hesitate to bestow their favours on those whom the god desired to please, namely, the priests!

The number of *devadasis* in a temple was representative of the grandeur and prosperity of the temple. It has even been suggested that erotic representation on the temple walls of Khajuraho and Orissa belongs to the *devadasi* culture. The institutions of the *devadasis,* related to the fertility cults, degenerated with the rise of tantrism. It is believed that many temples ostensibly dedicated to Shiva, Surya or Vishnu were in reality tantric shrines which were sites of orgies.

The *devadasis* became popular in the medieval period. Temples had places specifically built for their

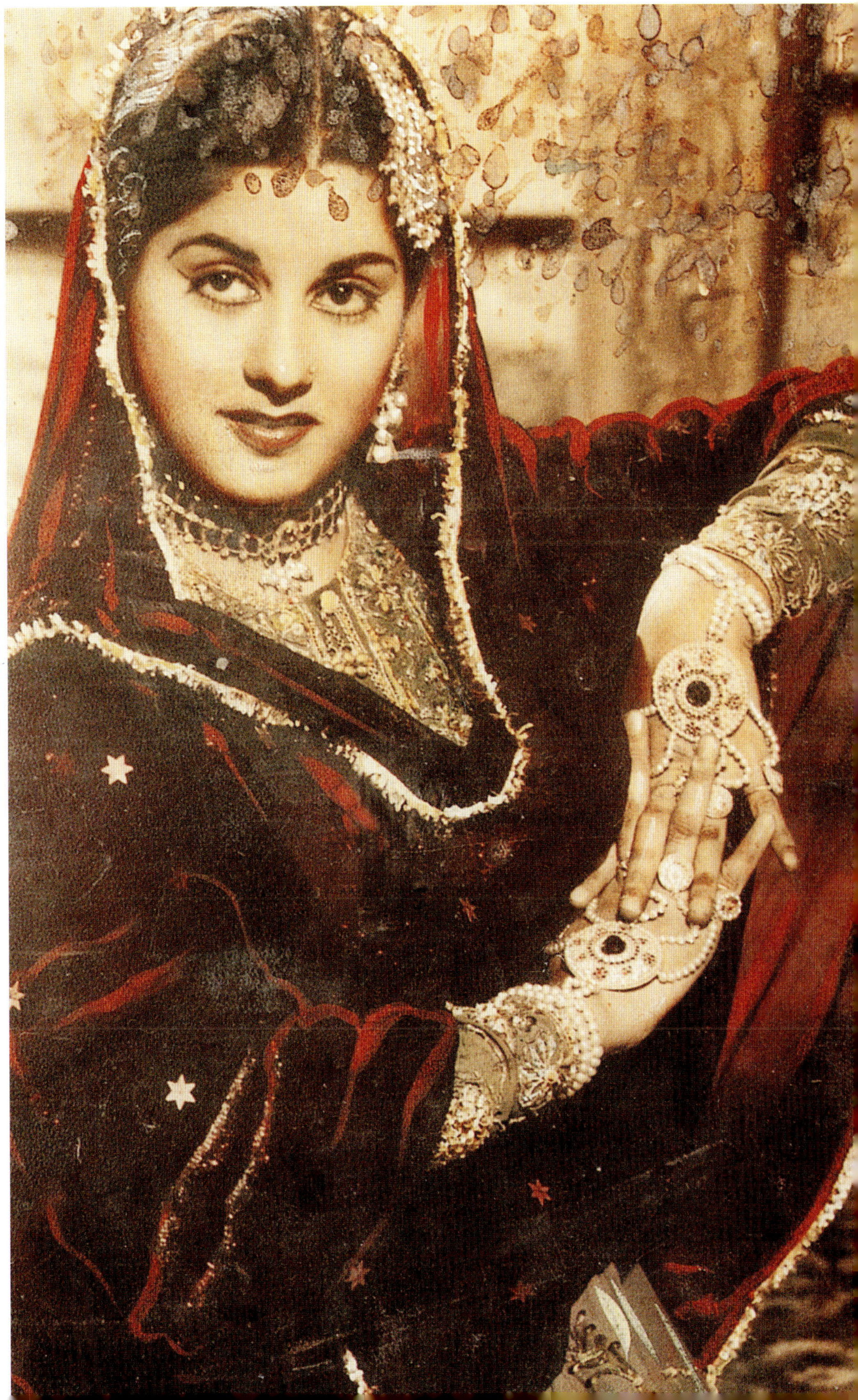

A still from the film *Chandni Chowk*. *Facing page, top:* Amjad Khan in a sex scene symptomatic of the stereotyped villians of mainstream Indian cinema. *Facing page, bottom:* Helen and Rajendra Kumar, stars of the 1960s.

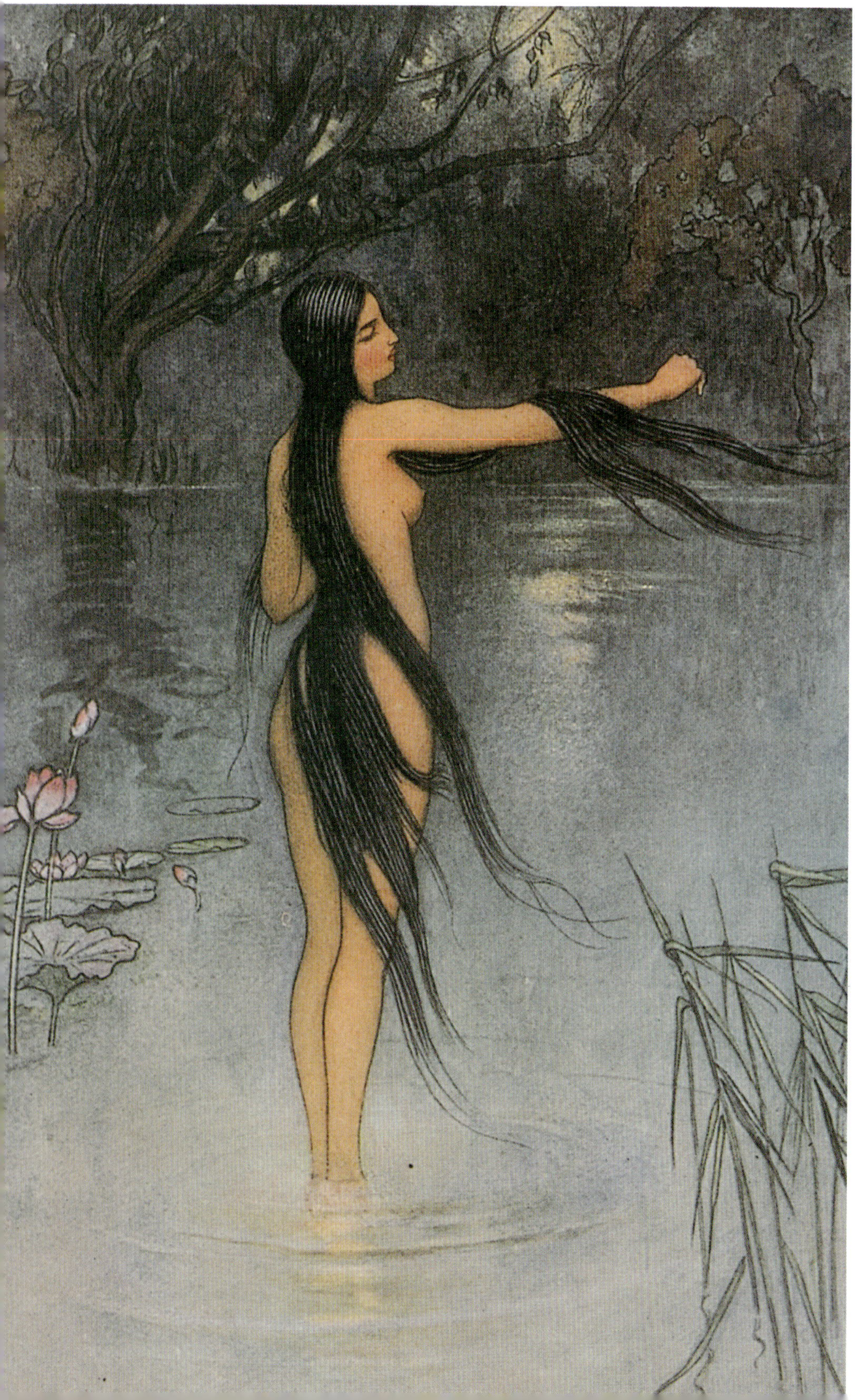

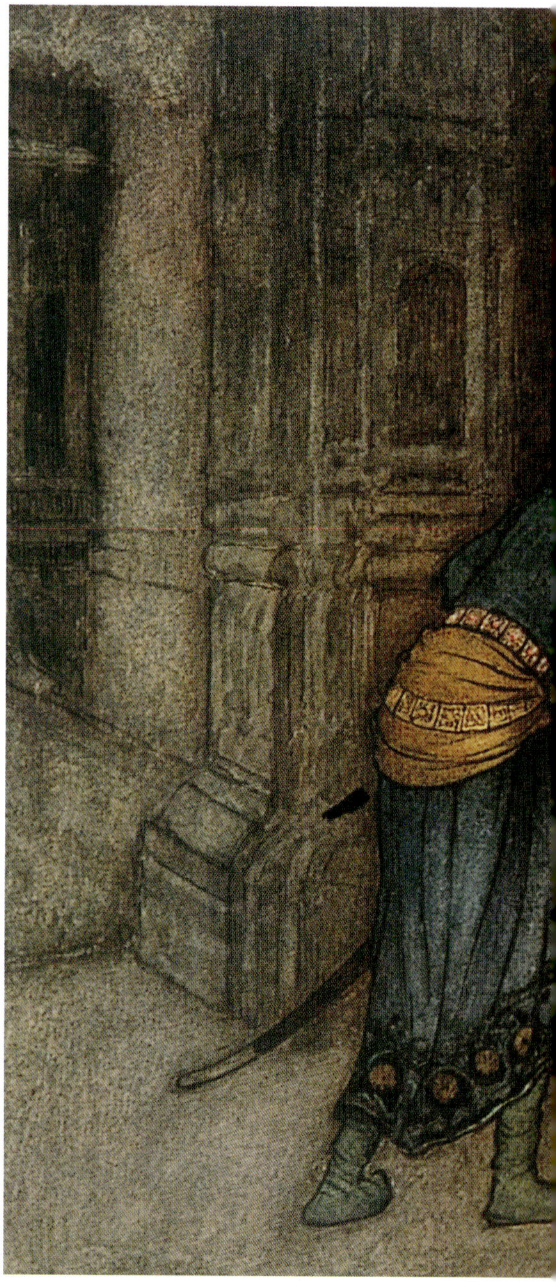

performances. The *devadasi* dancer treated God as a personified image and her relationship with the divine was intimate. Devdasis were not always from the lower classes. Often, rich and reputed families dedicated one of their daughters to the temple to fulfil a vow or to show their gratitude to God.

Sound of music

Music was another art form which provided an erotic language. However, in the case of music, erotica is not seen as much in classical high art as it is in popular genres. *Thumri* and *dadra* are two genres which moved from the classical to the *durbar* with easy facility.

Classical music had more to do with training of the voice and the grammar of music. However, folk music was for recreation and a part of popular culture. It adopted erotic images that could be sung to any beat and at any occasion. Monsoon songs, for example, are filled with erotic imagery. The *gopi* songs about Krishna are full of passion and love too. *Sawan ke geet* is another set of songs that is a repository of erotica.

Northern India is also familiar with the songs of Mirabai, with her longing to be one with the Supreme. But the songs of the Vaishnavites are more sensuous since they talk of human love. The *bhaktas* praised the female form and saw devotion essentially as

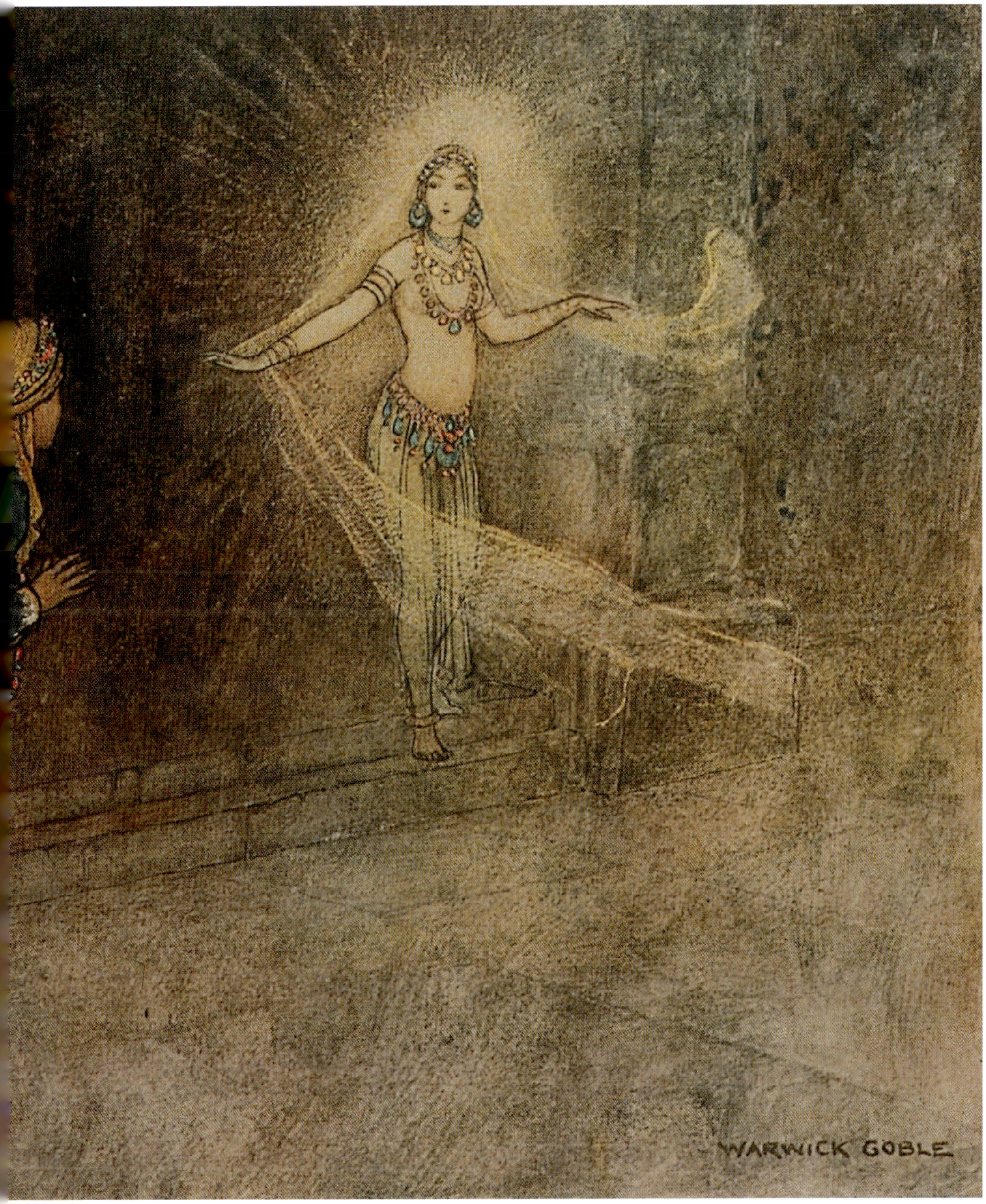

An angel of beauty stands revealed before an amazed sword-carrying male.
Facing page: The oldest image in the book: a nude bathing woman.

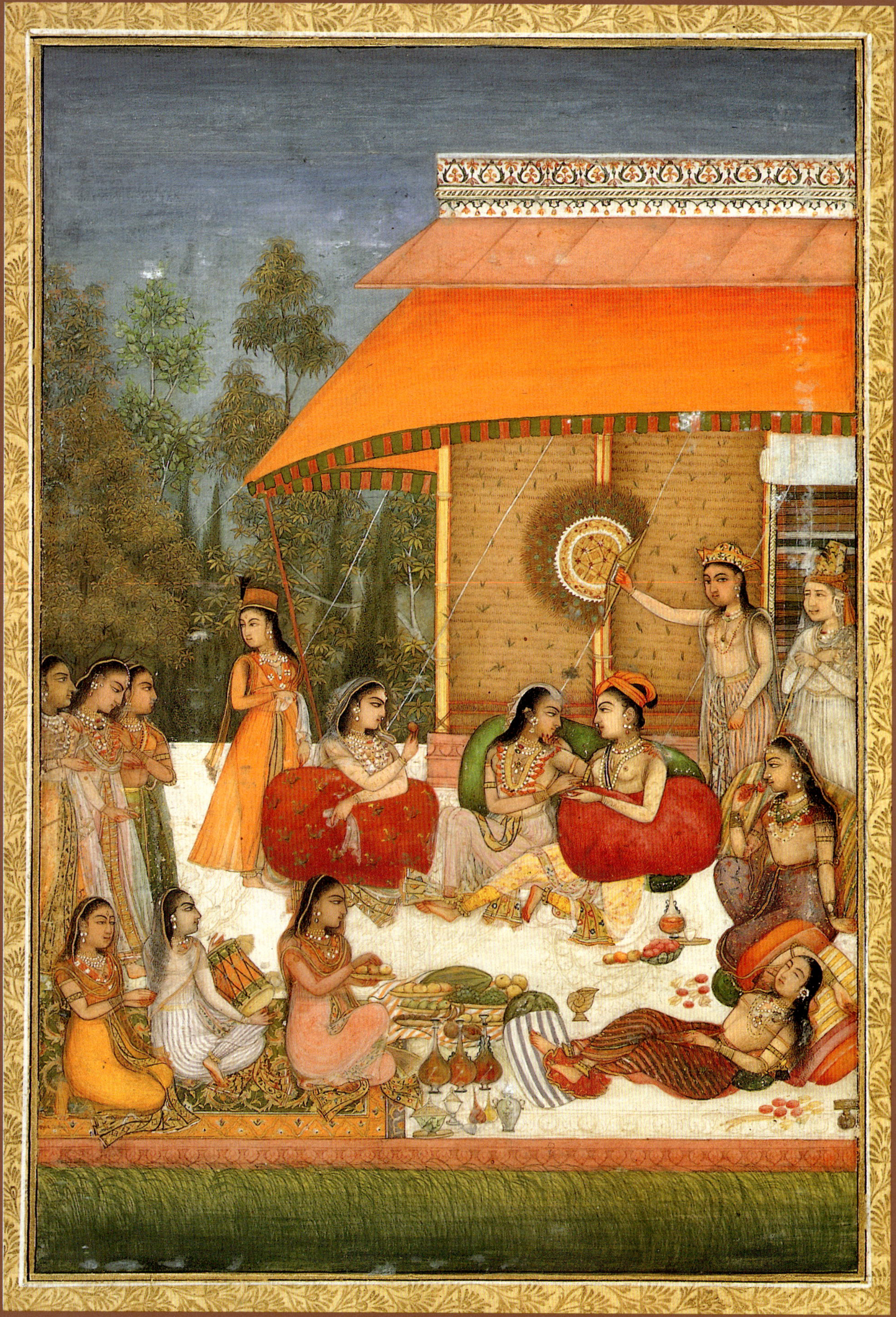

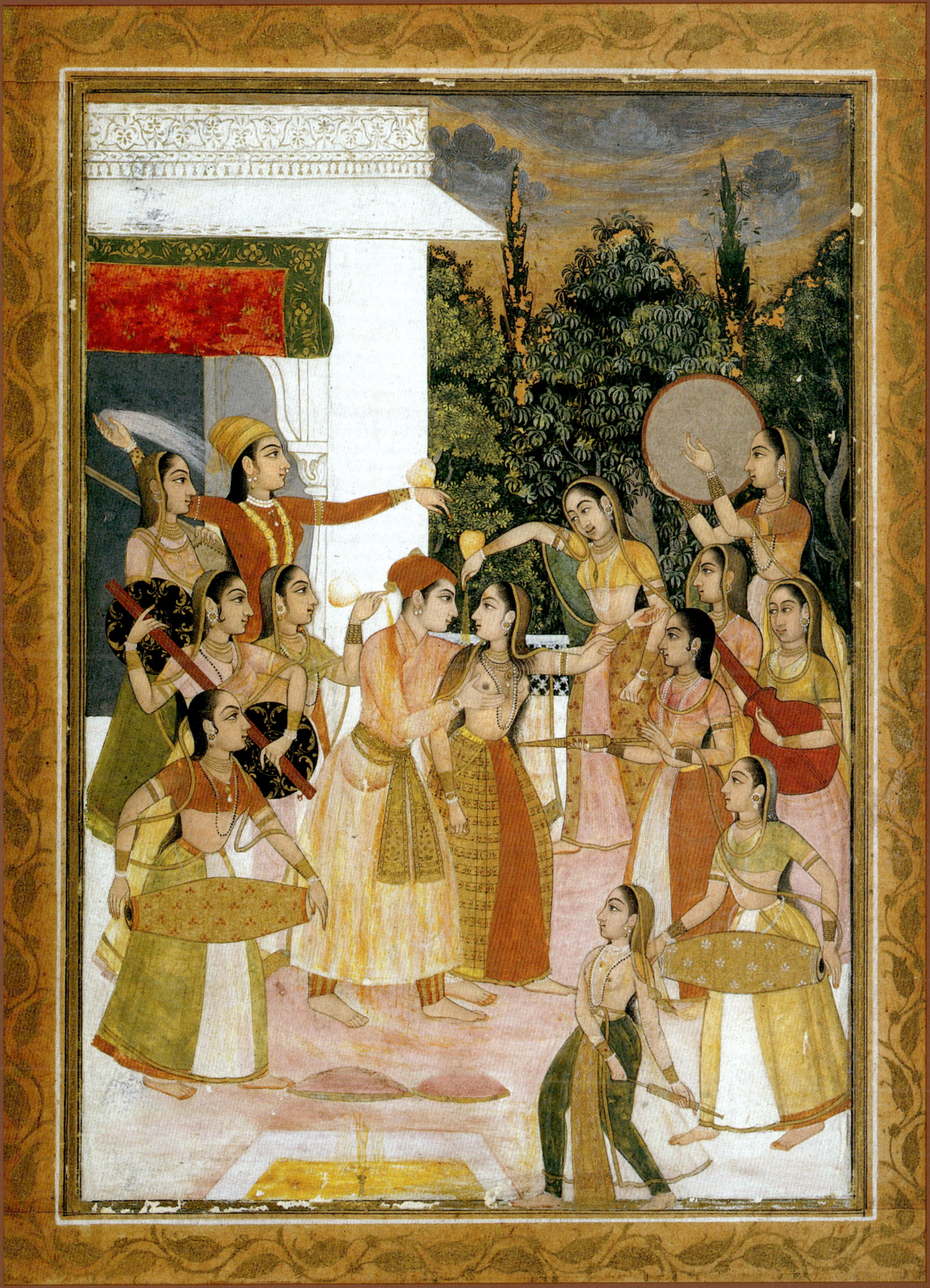

a surrendering of the human self to the divine. They too sang *geets* based on the love of Radha and Krishna. In fact, the Sanskrit poet, Jaidev, in his poetical work, *Geeta Govinda,* not only mentions Radha, but makes the love between Radha and Krishna central to his poetry. Their lovemaking is sexual though viewed by many as a mystical allegory. As Rustum J. Mehta says, 'While medieval India was pressing romantic love out of life, Indian religion was contemplating adultery.'

Both music and dance are an integral part of society today. Parties and weddings are unimaginable without them, as are car drives and homes without music. They are also inseparable from films and Bollywood.

In films, music has moved from being gentle, melodious and based on innocent love, to songs accompanied by pelvic thrusts, chest movements and a display of cleavages. Examples of such songs can be found in most movies and the Indian film industry, influenced by Hollywood, has started showing overt sexual imagery. Movies such as *Satyam Shivam Sundaram* and *Ram Teri Ganga Mailee* were among older movies that portrayed erotic scenes. Recent movies which showcased such explicit sexual images are *Fire*, *Aastha*, *Bandit Queen* and *Astitva,* to name a few. However, these films have looked into the social

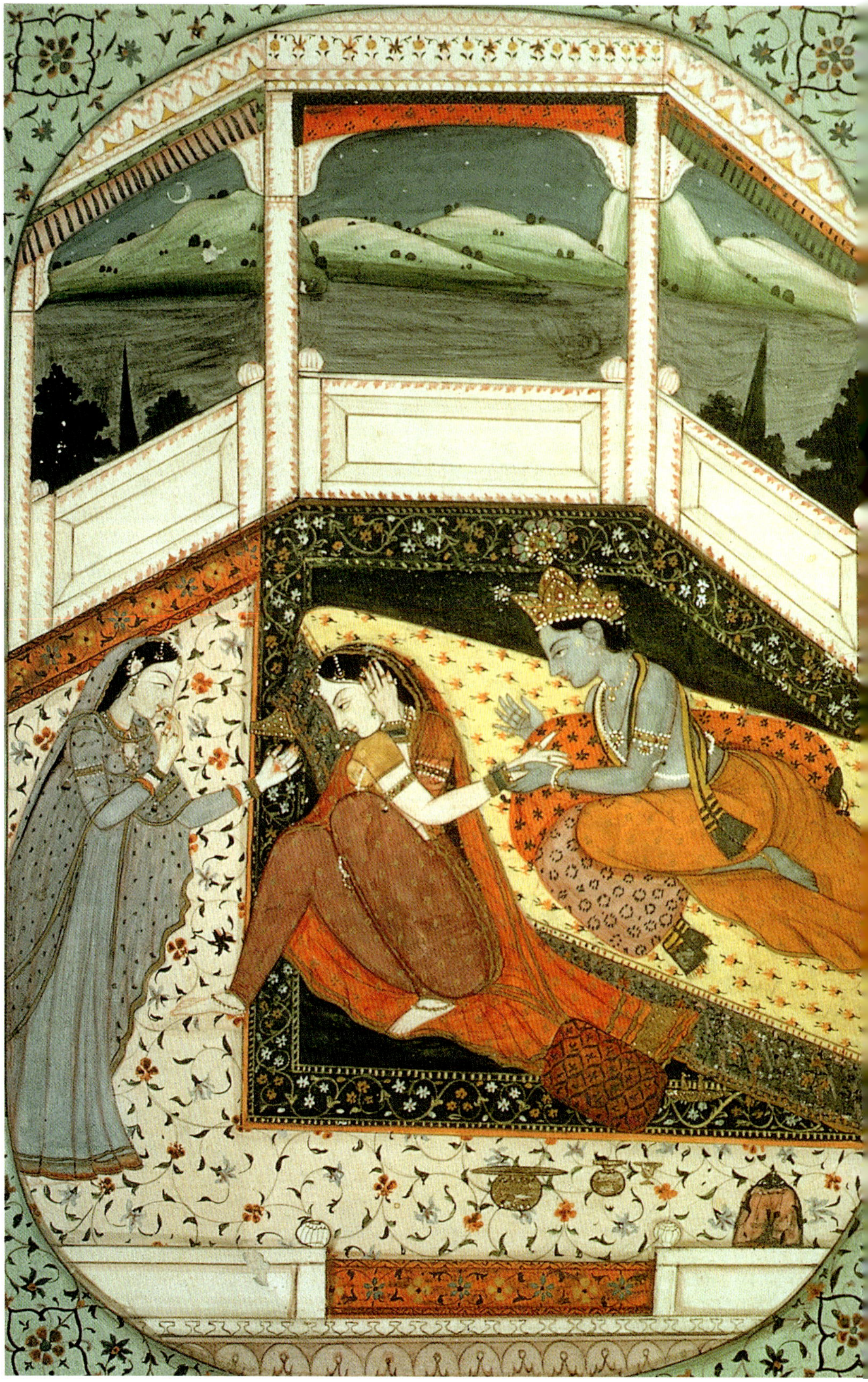

context of these scenes and carry a deeper meaning; thus they also have a greater impact. They almost comprise a reformist movement within the film industry and in society.

Films and media also reflect changes in social reality. They point to the fact that the notions of romance, of sensuality, have moved to a completely physical plane, far removed from the subtle sexuality of ancient Indian tradition.

Changing faces of women

The image of women has undergone a radical change since pre-Aryan society. With society becoming agriculturally driven, the woman became a minor goddess, a symbol of fertility. She attained divinity and was worshipped in the home and field as Mother Earth. During the medieval period, women became the playgirls of the gods and were viewed as that, though they were still respected. But with the acquisition of wealth and the ending of agricultural tilling, the woman's earlier sanctity was lost. She was turned into a vehicle for passion and lust. 'She became a commodity to be bought or bid for. Once bought she lost her individuality, her charm and her class,' says Rustum J. Mehta.

These negative and degrading images of the woman have been taken up as central themes in contemporary writings such as those of Bharati Mukherjee and Jaishree Misra. Jaishree Misra's novel, *Ancient Promises,* kicks off with the orthodox, male society in Kerala marrying off one of their boys to a girl from 'fast' Delhi society. The story goes on to describe the way the girl is treated and how she reacts when she eventually finds her ex-lover. With a baby being her primary responsibility, the book brings to life a woman's struggle to strike a balance between being socially accepted, being a mother, and living her life. It also shows changing attitudes towards women.

All this underlines the great transformation Indian literary writing has gone through. Earlier it was dedicated to God and his praises, to religious writings, and to the biographies of kings. Now, even fiction concentrates on social issues.

Popular ancient texts were based on themes quite different from contemporary writing. In prose, Kalidas's *Kumarasambhava* describes the passionate lovemaking of Parvati and Shiva. Bhavabhuti's *Malati Madhava* talks about the romantic love between Madhava and Malati. Bana, another writer, describes women who appeal to men in his book *Kadambari*. Dandin's *Dasa Kumara Charita* describes the beauty of Avanti.

Radhikaswantanamu, written by Mudupalani, is one of the most erotic

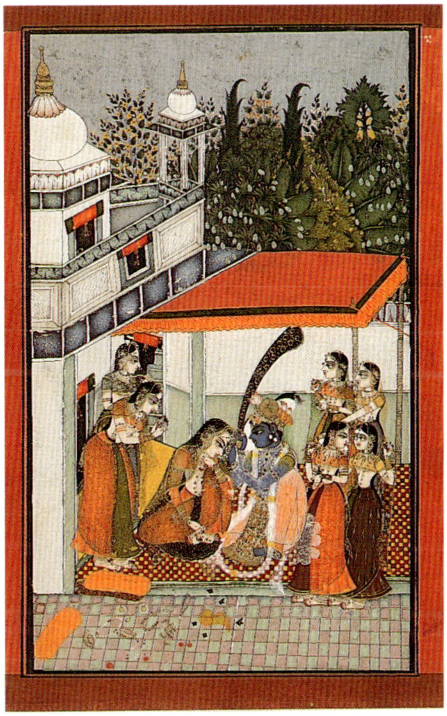

Krishna surrounded by *gopis.* *Facing page:* A lovelorn *nayika* in a Rajasthani miniature. *Previous page:* Miniature paintings show lovers surrounded by female friends who add a quaint charm to the whole scene.

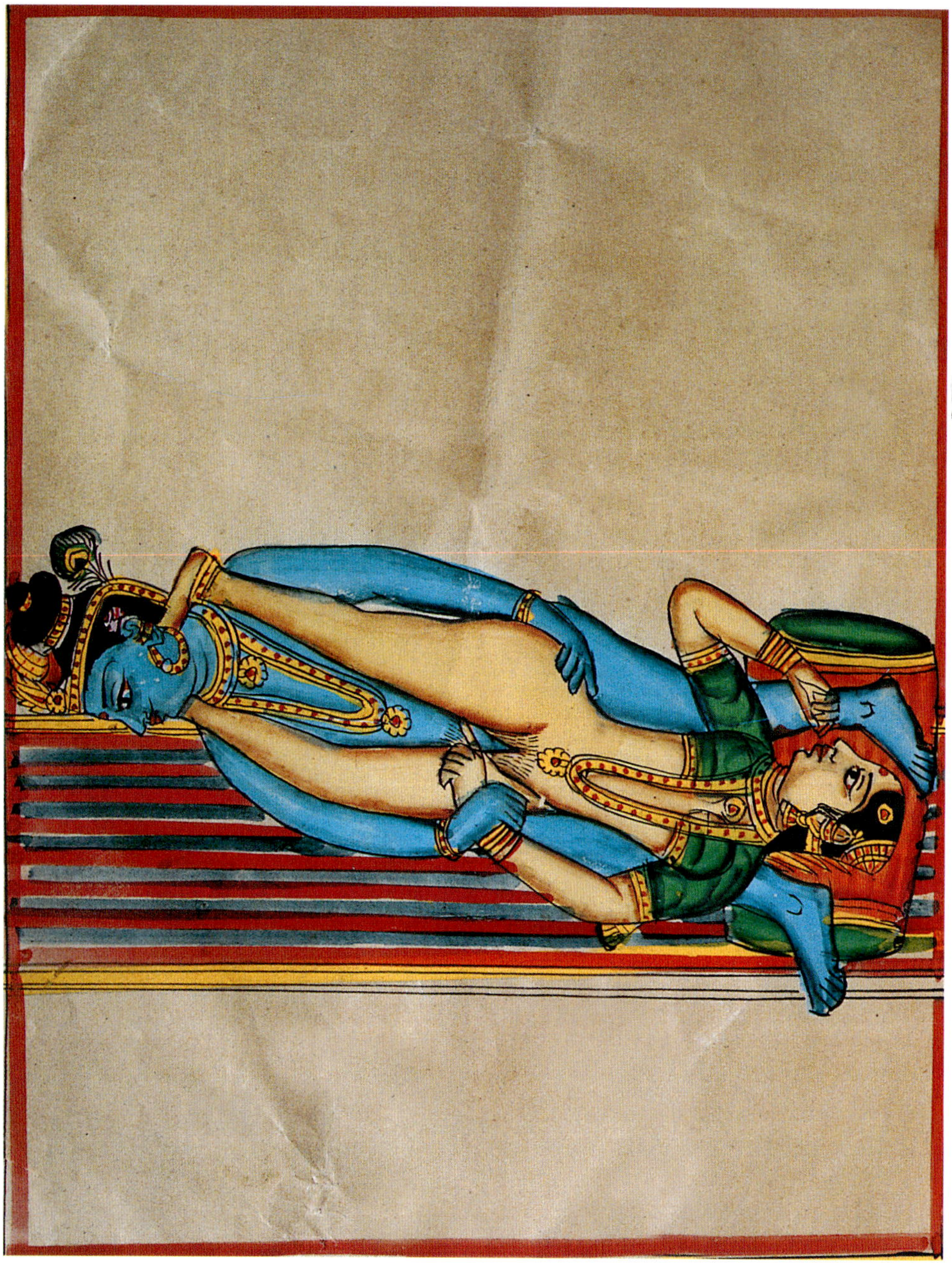

texts in Telugu. What is interesting is that the writer, Mudupalani, extols the beauty of the female form from a feminine perspective.

Sanskrit love poetry was at its height between the fourth and tenth centuries. The verses of Bhanudutt, the Sanskrit poet of the fifteenth century, in *Rasamanjari,* and in the *Rasakapriya* of Keshavdas, a Hindi poet of the sixteenth century, talk of passionate, illicit love. Apparently, it was the norm for the *nayika* or heroine, if married, to give her husband the slip and welcome her lover. 'Behind the Indian husband lurks the Indian lover, but it is in art and poetry rather than the joint Hindu family that he comes to life. To give the greatest stimulus – to excite, enchant and soothe – poets and painters dealt with ideal love,' reveals the *Koka Shastra*.

Literary art forms are often considered divorced from reality, as they are more or less fictionalised. But folk and tribal art are closer to reality and witness the merging of the *high* and *low* arts.

The boundaries between high and low art are as hazy as they are between *margi* and *desi Sangeet*. One can never say which comes first. Traditions filter down and move up. Therefore, the popular tradition of visual culture seen in the bazaar arts of Bengal, Orissa, Tamil Nadu, Andhra Pradesh and other states of India is an interface between craft and high art. This can be seen in the Orissi *Pattachitra* tradition. There is a *dasha-avatar* panel done on palm leaf where the surface has images of the ten incarnations of God, but when the leaf is turned, its underside contains images of couples in erotic love play. Whether these are for titillation or *bhakti*, one cannot say.

Miniature paintings

Indian miniature painting reached its highest point between the fourteenth and nineteenth centuries. During this period, much more than the act of sex, representation focused on the situations and problems of ideal lovers. Coital positions, as analysed in the *Koka Shastra,* were illustrated. In Orissa, sets of postures were even engraved with a stylus on palm leaves. In villages, these illustrated books came to be known as *bride books.* Many additions were made - some quite radical and with no reference to the imagery of the *Koka Shastra*. Nonetheless, these extremely

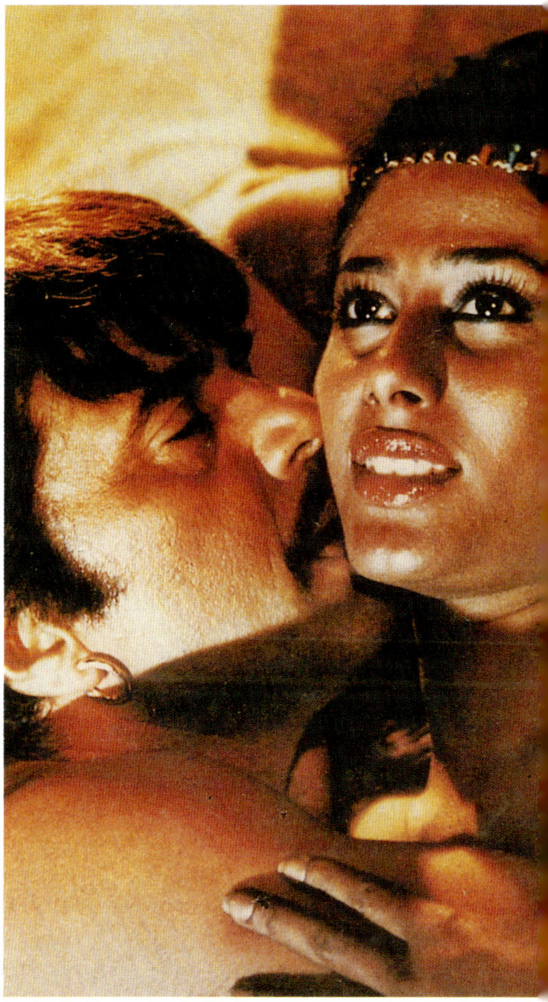

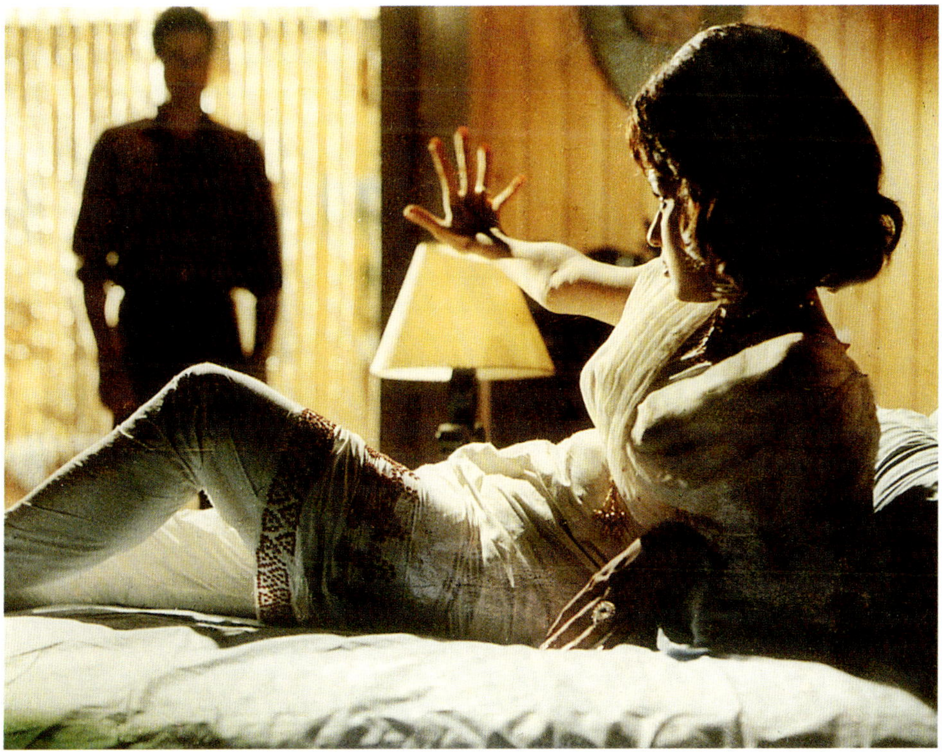

Actors Dharmendra and Smita Patil.
Left: A seduction scene from a Bollywood film of yesteryear.
Facing page: A Tanjore painting shows two lovers in an acrobatic posture.

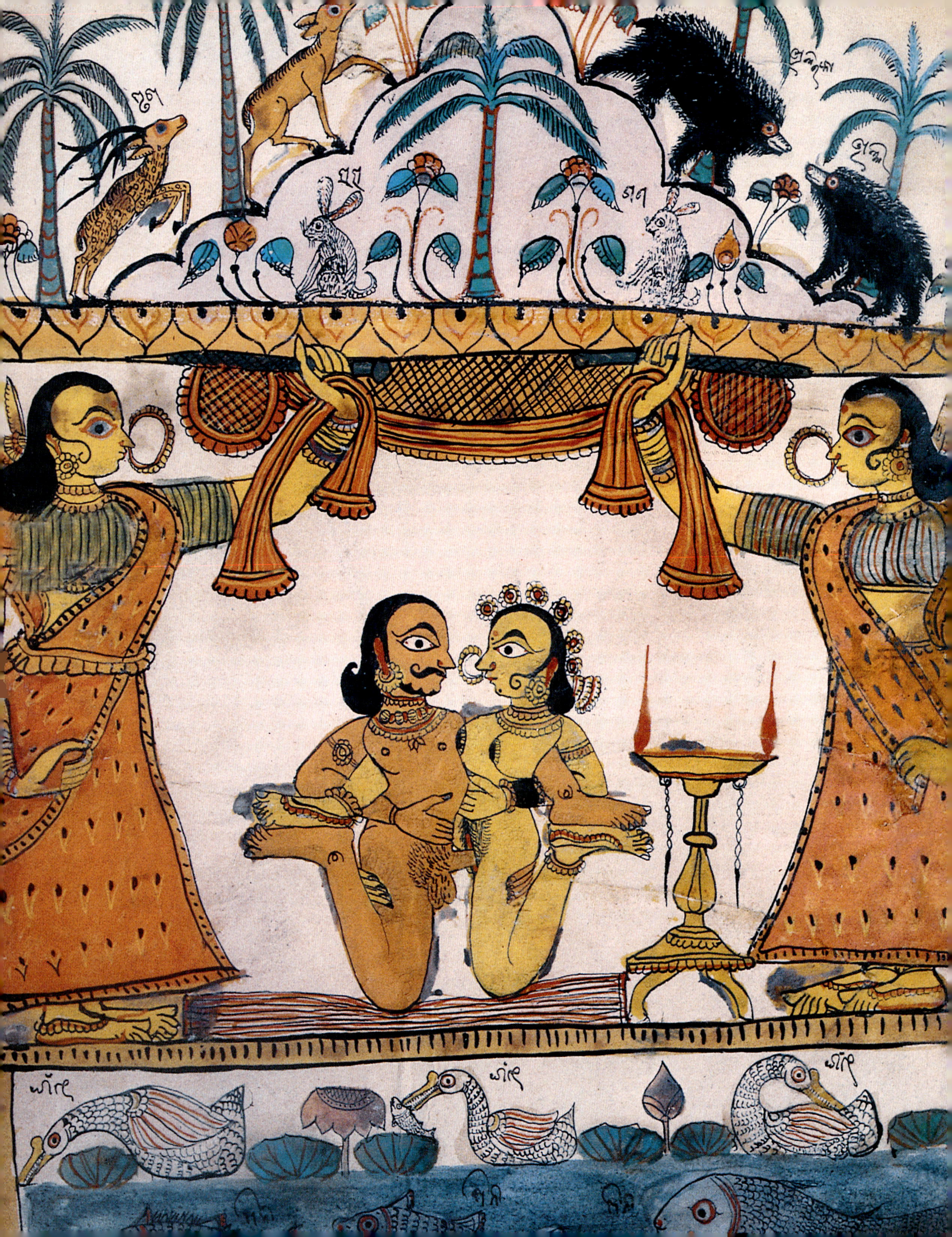

popular books were all given the generic name of *Koka Shastra*. The books were also found in Jodhpur in Rajasthan and in Kangra and Guler in the Punjab Hills. They had apparently been taken to these places for private viewing.

The production of such erotic books in the miniature tradition continued through the seventeenth and eighteenth centuries. Popular and provincial Mughal artists gave full vent to their fancies. The *Geeta Govinda* was lavishly illustrated in both Basohli and Kangra. Both versions of the *Geeta Govind* contain over 120 pictures. At least 100 of these depict various stages of romance; 10 show Radha and Krishna making love. Interestingly, the artist drew his inspiration from the idioms of the *Koka Shastra* rather than the *Kamasutra*.

But women in love, portrayed in the paintings of Punjab, central India and Rajasthan, were far removed from ordinary Indian women. They were imbued with aristocratic charm, but led a sheltered and repressed existence. These women were creatures of poetry and not of real life. So, it was only with the dancing girls and prostitutes that the Rajput princes experienced romance.

The tantric tradition too contributed a great deal to the usage of explicit imagery. *Shakti* worship in India found its root in non-violent feminine divinity. The *linga* and the *yoni*, as also the *ardhanarishwara* concept, were the important images Tantra loaned to erotica.

These are images of popular art in India, and they continue into the present though they have changed drastically. The gesture of the performative becomes the crucible of erotica. The performative and visual are associated with 'a new vulgarity which has come into dance', though dance is just one aspect that is seen as overtly perverted. There are other arts too which fall into the same category.

The idea of the erotic has become one that is unethical and disgusting. It has been caught in such a vicious circle of misinformation and lewdness that it is difficult for it to be accepted in society today.

India, once the land of the *Kamasutra*, which had a liberal and open attitude to human sexuality, has now become a more rigid and closed society. What could be the reason? Is it the influence of the West or a confusion about our own identity?

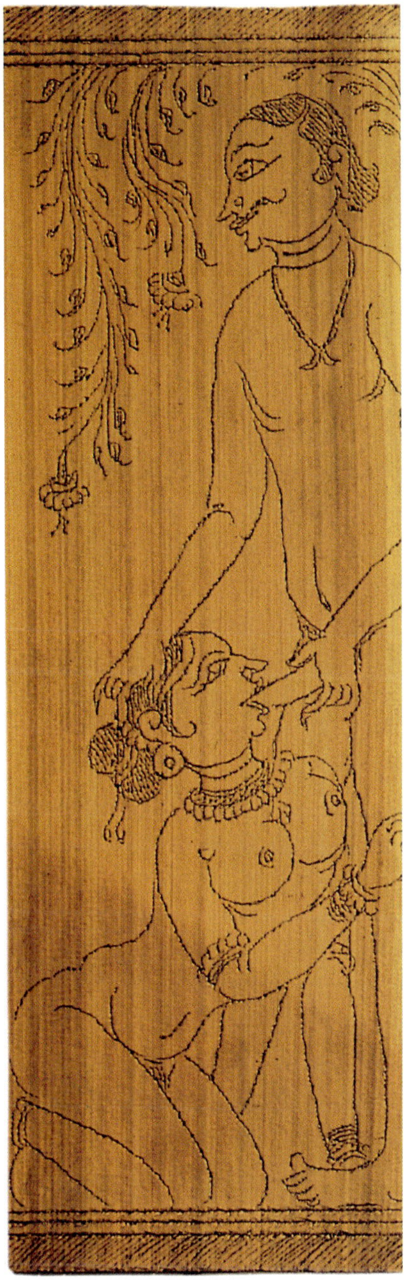

Coloured pen and ink sketches from Orissa showing fellatio. *Facing page:* Blissful union, as the *sakhis* (girlfriends) look on, amidst idyllic surroundings.

High Art

High Art

The celebration of life, sexual interplay, the decorative and the pleasurable have been central to both the visual and the performing arts of India. Undoubtedly, there has been a continuity of pleasure in Indian art. But somewhere between British prudery and Victorian primness this was neglected and suppressed. Not for long. Today, contemporary art practices are moving towards a cosmopolitan nature due to globalisation and intercultural communication.

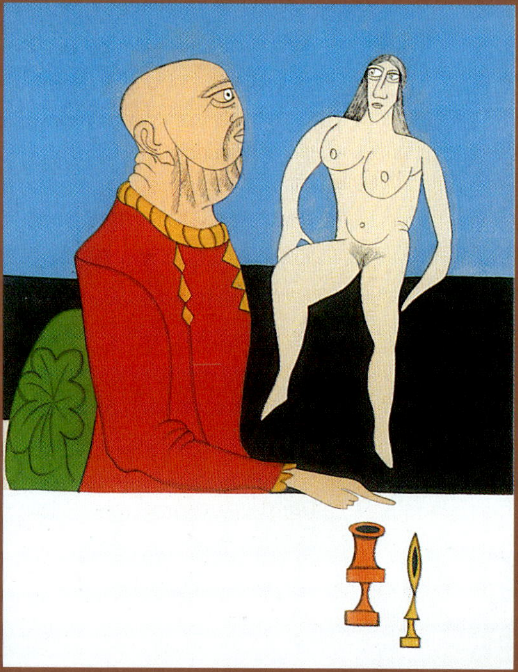

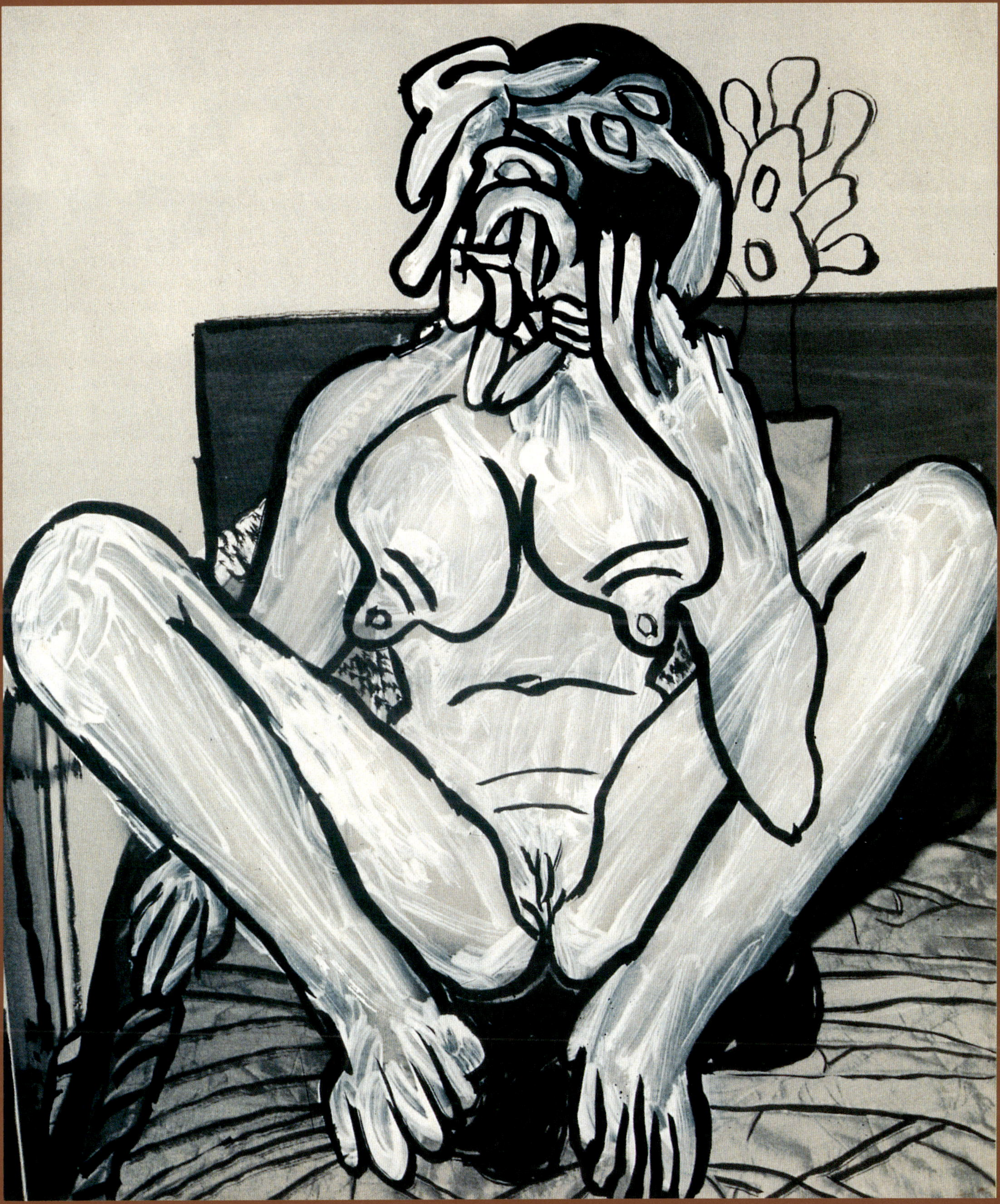

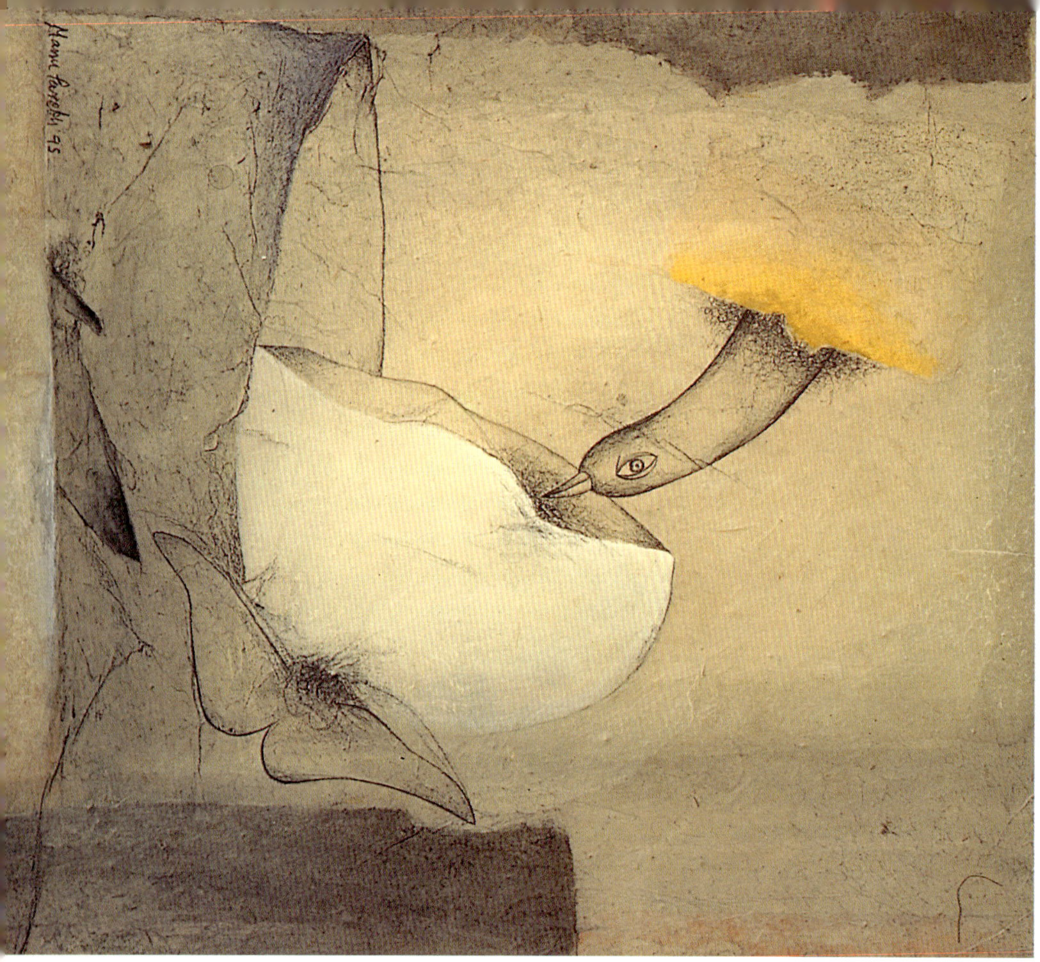

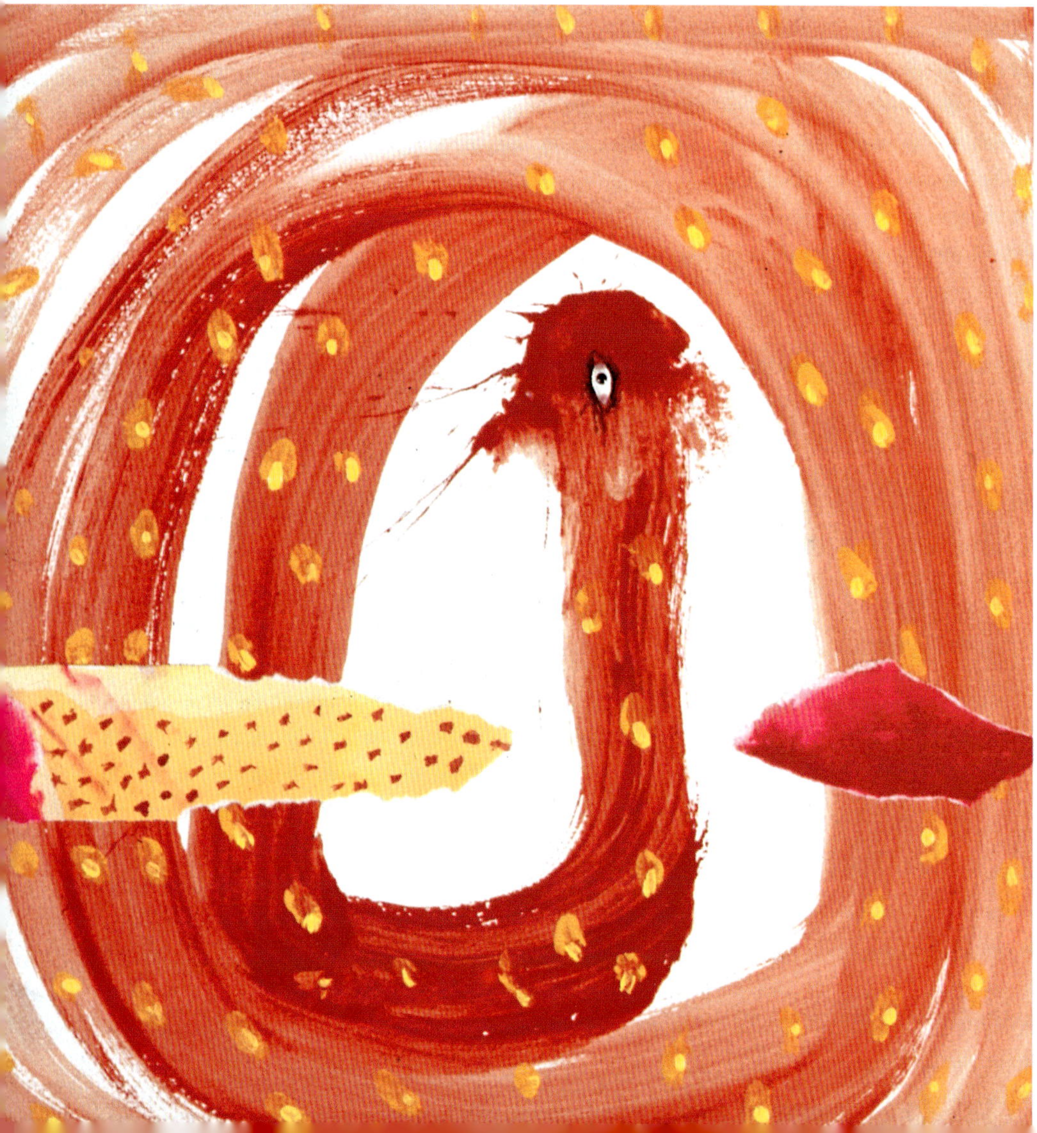

In the last couple of decades, Indian art has undergone significant changes and come under the sway of Western conceptual art. So, it is important to note the progress of the arts in the West. There, the first major movement was modernism, coming with a bang with the Viennese secession – the emergence of the Vienesse avant-garde. Klimt and Schiele, two prominent artists during this period, present two faces of the modern coin. Klimt concentrates on harmony through music and love, and Schiele focuses on the emancipated, plus the pain humans go through. Schiele drew from his past and his childhood, shadowed by an abusive father and filled with sorrow.

At the same time there was Picasso, one of the pioneers of cubism and modernism. Sexuality, and his physical relationships with different women, were directly reflected in his work. Picasso's *Les Demoiselles d'Avignon* revealed his reflections about women: their sexuality was dark and mysterious and associated with sexually transmitted diseases. A contemporary of his, Cezanne, focused on a different theme: the world around him, factories and industrialisation, were his preoccupations.

Surrealism and fantasy combined with erotica was the heady mix that came about with Sigmund Freud's influence. Max Ernst with his paintings, like *Oedipus Rex*, explored the erotic through his phantasmagoric imagery. Painters like him borrowed from Freudian theories. The concept that every man grows up to love his mother is painted down in Ernst's work. In the fable, Oedipus, unaware of the relationship he has with the woman he loves – his mother, wants to kill her husband – his father. When he finds out his relationship with the two, he punctures his eye. Ernst's painting shows two birds, the beautiful one representing the mother, and the one with the horns, symbolising the enemy or the father. Keeping to the same theme was Salvador Dali's *Metamorphosis of Narcissus*.

Then, there were artists like Mondrian who looked for harmony in a chaotic world, taking us back to Primitivism, a movement based on nature and harmony. Jean Dubuffet, who looked into crude, child and mad art, was its exponent.

The explicit body of art

At the same time there were artists from Latin America, such as Frida Kahlo, who were exploring the female identity, in terms of traditional customs and practices. Kahlo used her body to explore her identity both as a Mexican and a female. She became iconic for feminists like Lucy Irigay and Julia Kristeva.

With this came Marcel Duchamp and his readymades. They screamed that anything that was material could be art and anyone could be an artist. Finally, artists started believing in 'leaping into the void' and a movement of abstraction started in the visual and performative arts. Jackson Pollock, Barnett Newman and Mark Rothko were all names in Gestural Abstraction. They drew pictures that searched for a human identity in a chaotic world. Their large paintings evoked a sense of wonder about their position in a vast area. Fontana's famous slits were highly erotic and have been seen as portrayals of deflowering a woman. The slits in the canvas often look like the clitoris.

This led to geometric abstraction with Yves Klein as the central figure. He often used women models, dipping them in paint and dragging them across the canvas. Sometimes he invited the audience to view this style of painting and had a live band playing along with the performance. His women often pressed against the canvas, leaving impressions of their breasts and private parts.

Thus performance came to be linked with the arts. Yoko Ono, Yoshihara and Yayoi Kusama were

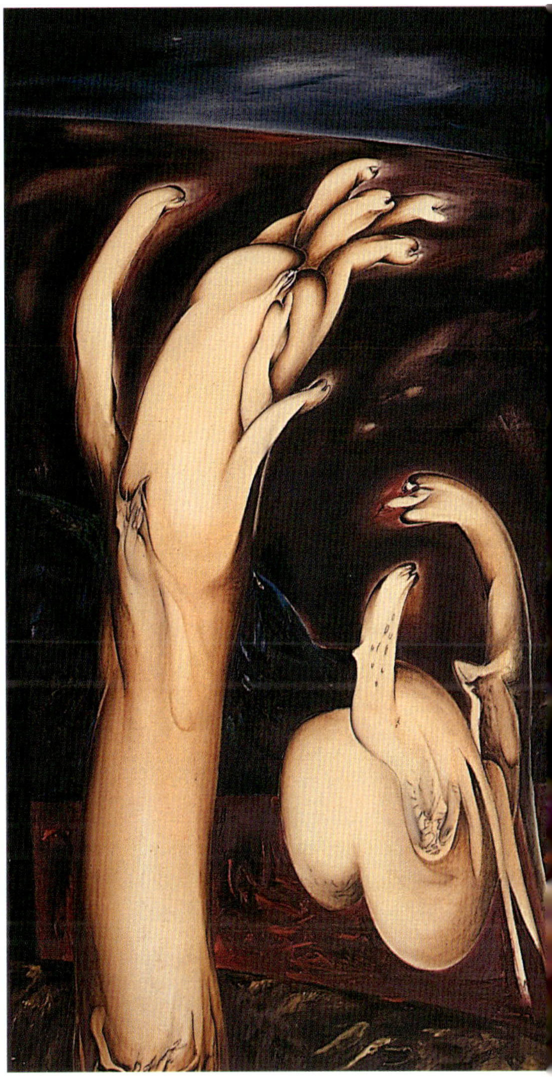

Manu Parekh's paintings try to create a rhythm of union.
Facing page, top: The images belong to a global consciousness even if they retain old themes.
Facing page, bottom: The old *kundalini* becomes the new snake.
Previous page: A painting by Francis Newton Souza.

performance artists who believed it was important for the artist to be a part of his work. Performance artists who are grotesque in their eroticism are Carolee Schneemann, Shigeko Kubota and Hannah Wilke. Carolee is seen nude on stage pulling out threads from her vagina. Kubota performs with a brush in her vagina, walking around the canvas, letting the paint drop. These sub-streams of art have drawn attention to the narcissistic theory that condemns certain cultural practices and is linked to the degradation of the feminine self. The performance arts summarise the use of primitivism in explicit body performance, where nudity was not a problem and helped position contemporary feminist manifestations.

Sexuality also loomed forth during the period of Neo-Expressionist and Neo- Surrealist art. These schools are highly exploited, but the media and every aspect of modern life are reflected within them. 'Whereas pop artists have mocked and glorified the icons of advertising and everyday consumer society,' says Arnason, 'many Neo-Expressionists pluck their imagery directly from the sleazy world of sex manuals, pulp romances and television soap operas, as well as from the more elevated sphere of high art, history and politics.'

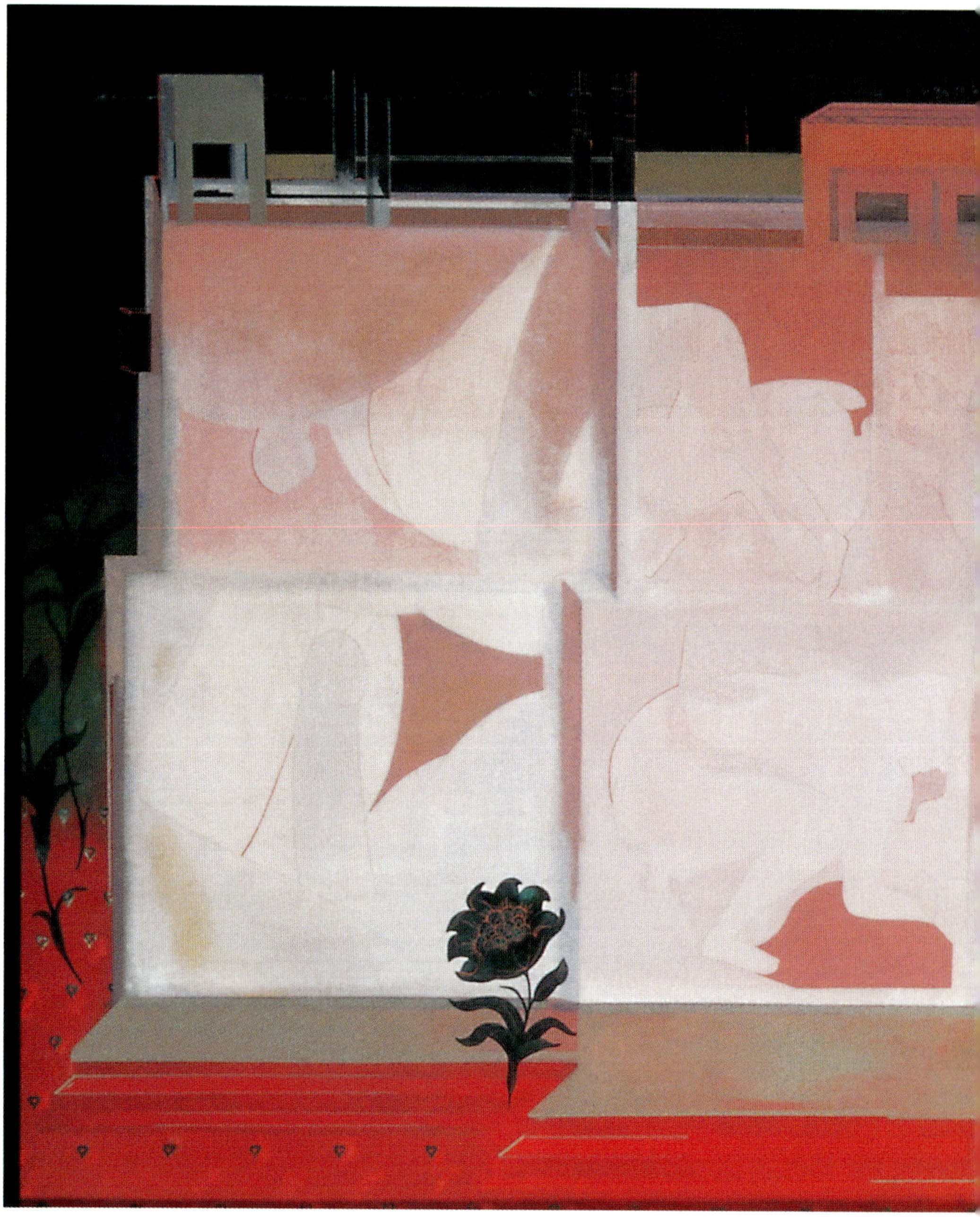

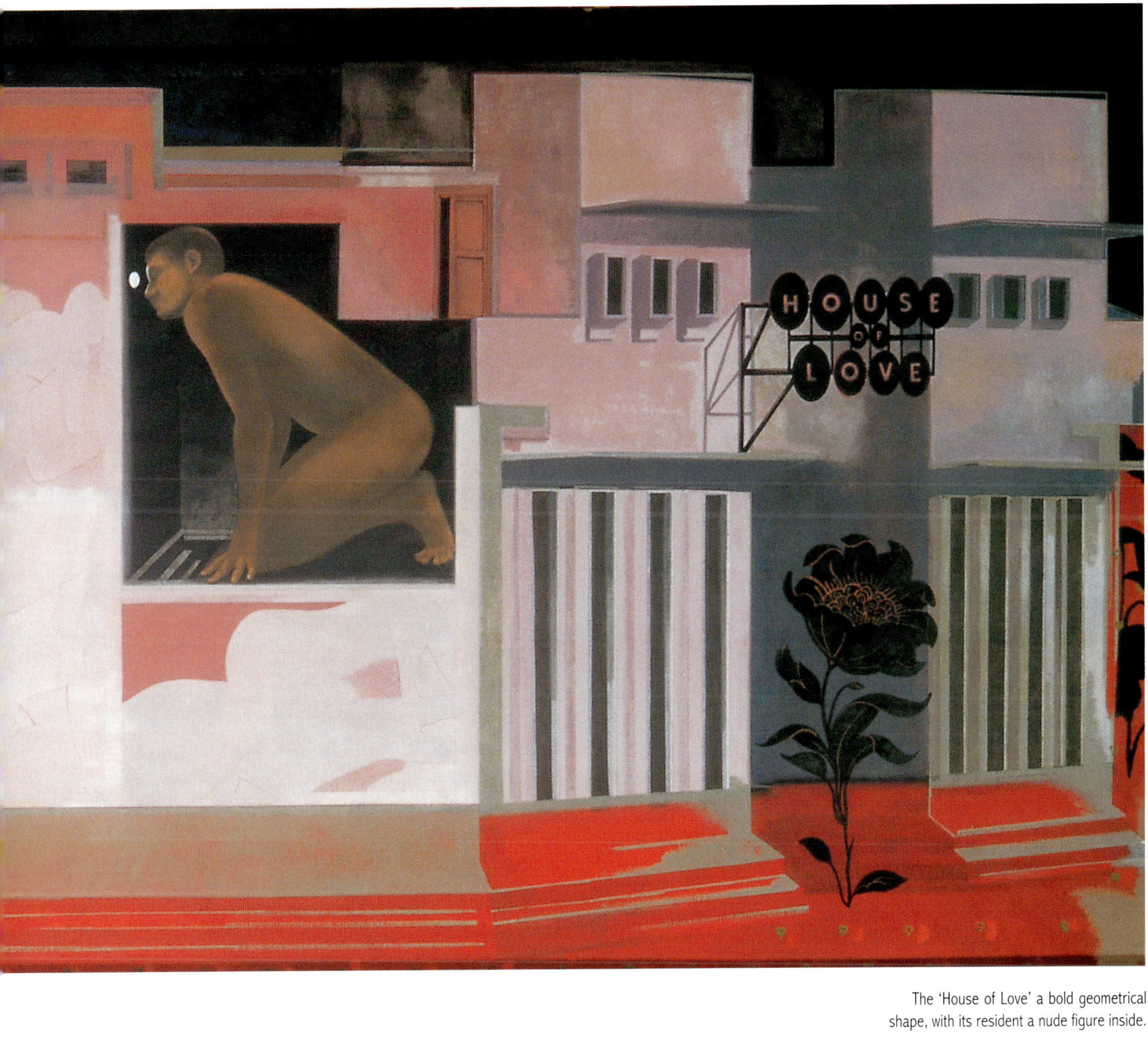

The 'House of Love' a bold geometrical shape, with its resident a nude figure inside.

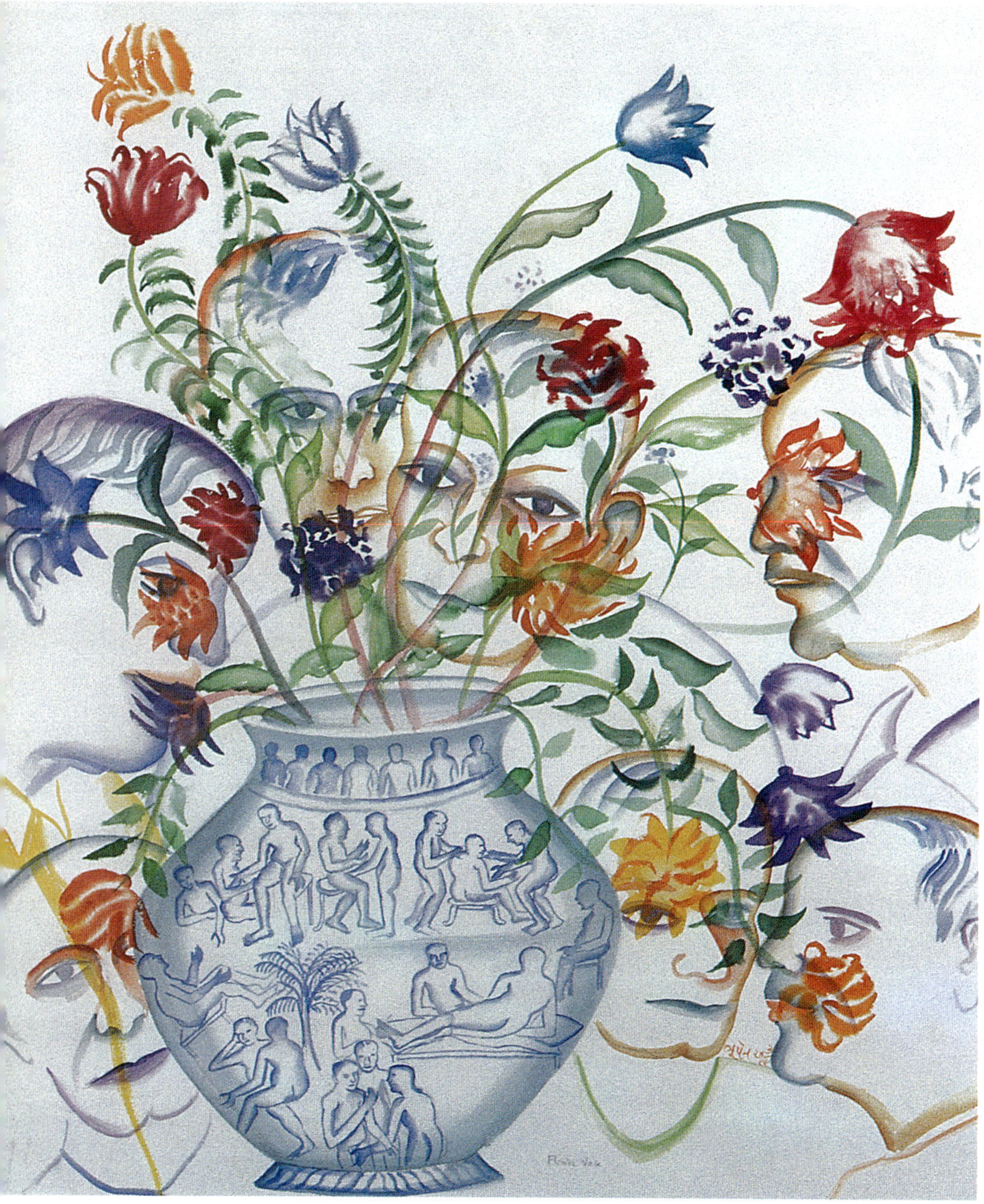

Rediscovery of Indian art

With the West as a reference point, the Indian contemporary artist can be fitted into several compartments. The first comprises those who are traditional in their representations. They paint landscapes and pretty pictures, and concentrate on the decorative arts. The second consists of those who trained and studied in the West. They were influenced by artistic trends in London, New York and Paris and were part of Western academic institutions. To this group belong the modern artists, led by Amrita Sher-Gil. After her, came a younger generation of artists of the 1970s, who were in a way paying a debt to tribal and folk art.

In between, were Raja Ravi Varma and his generation of artists who were a part of the process of change from the traditional to the modern.

However, from the 1990s, a slow rediscovery has begun. The artist of the nineties is vocal, comfortable with his identity, and has set out to discover Indian tradition. Yet these artists are also exposed to the West and belong, truly, to the new global consciousness.

The modernity and rediscovery of the Indian heritage holds different meanings for artists. Often they strike a balance between adapting to the 'modern' world, and the 'Indian' world. A lot of their work is rooted in ancient

A painting by Bhupen Khakar, the first artist to come out with a statement of sexuality.

Indian philosophies, religious and cultic practices. They then integrate these into their identity, and represent it in their art, speaking a universal language.

Upfront with sex

The artist who broke new ground in visual sexual representation is Baroda-based Bhupen Khakhar. He was the first contemporary Indian artist to admit the fact that he was homosexual. His art was at times autobiographical and brought out elements of sexuality that had gone underground with Victorian prudery.

Similarly, in the West, there was Robert Mapplethorpe who was open about his homosexuality. He did pioneering works on homosexual relations, and his art works show erotica through the representation of the world as a place for drugs and sexuality and exemplify his personal obsessions.

Another frank statement of sex was made after Independence. Francis Newton Souza painted large nude women displaying a great deal of frontal sexuality. He was highly exposed to the West, and the nudity he showed came from there.

Another artist, Ramachandran, interweaves myths and erotica. In his *Yayati* series, for example, he uses decorative imagery from ancient Indian art. His women are curvaceous, sensuous and earthy, and hark back to the Ajanta images.

Manu Parekh has a completely different view as he reflects on the human element. His emphasis is on the need for another being – a companion. His work creates a rhythm that comes about in union with another being. Sex, to him, is love and respect. It is not just an emotion but the basis of existence.

On the other hand, for Ranbir Singh Kaleka, erotic motifs are used to bring out 'sexuality with frontality'. For him painting an erect clitoris is a sharing of arousal. It is not pornography in the garb of high art. It is possible to make a painting where one need not conceal blatant sexuality. The image is complex and intricate nuances prevent it from being pornographic. He has found a new trajectory between traditional erotic motifs and the theories of Freud and Lacan.

Anish Kapoor, who now preceives himself as a British artist, takes eroticism to a more abstract level. He frequently uses orifices and tantric elements in his work. Erotica in Satish Gujral's work is portrayed through rams and women in the composition of his paintings. A certain sense of the animality of human behaviour is brought out.

There are other artists like S.H. Ara and Bendre who use the feminine body to define form and identity. Among well-known women artists, such as Nalini Malani, Rekha Rodwittiya, Vasundhara Tiwari and Arpita Singh, the female form is a leitmotif and the body, the means of cultural criticism.

Homosexuality in history

The exotic and the erotic (often the negatively erotic) mingle in theories that explain homosexuality. But what is not doubted is its presence through the ages. It is important to deal with lesbianism and homosexual relations as two separate issues since both have different levels of acceptance in society.

However, in general, both are unacceptable. This is in variance with the fact that they formed a significant part of Indian society in the past. The *Kamasutra* and other treatises of love mention that women turned bisexual or lesbian because they lived together in the harem. One must remember that the owner was the only male who was allowed in the ladies' chambers. Similarly, when kings and queens had bisexual or homosexual tendencies, those working for them were drawn into the act, either by choice or force. The last ruler of Awadh, Wajid Ali Shah, built a *pari khaana* or house of fairies devoted to 'his boys'.

In ancient temple sculptures and miniature traditions, homosexuality

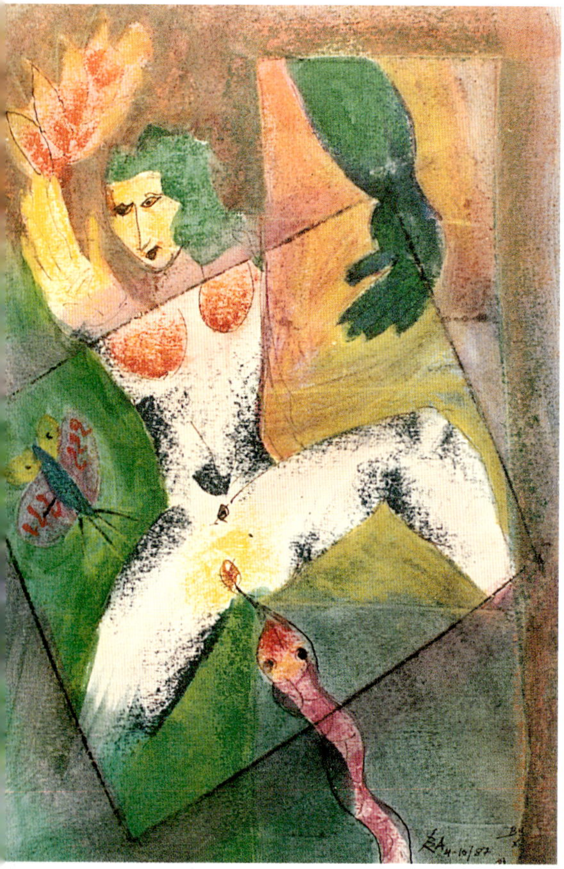

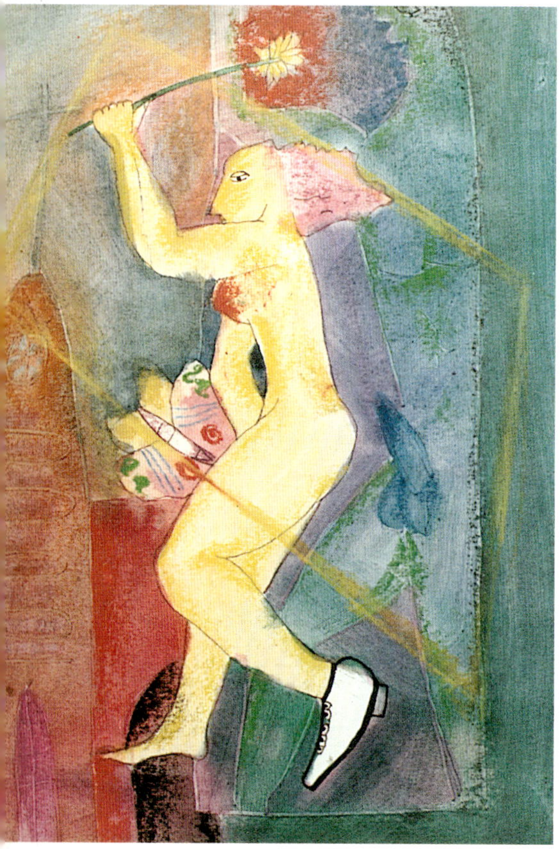

was very much in evidence. Relationships between two or more women were more common because polygamy was practised.

Historically, these homosexual relations were a part of society and were accepted with grace, probably because the elite practised them. The same elite defined norms, values and social behaviour. But today homosexuality has a new dimension.

The place of pleasure

Contemporary Indian artists speak a universal language which surfaces from their rooted Indianness. They find security in their identity whether they are homosexuals, feminists or just 'straight' artists with a high degree of eroticism in their work. This level of comfort with their sexuality leads to *vilas* or pleasure. Whether the art depicts pleasure or pain, it reflects a strong-rooted identity.

Pleasure is not a new theme at all. In the *Bhagvada Gita,* Krishna says: 'I am the pleasure within all beings.' Desire instigates pleasure. It is desire that expresses the nature of creation and is the only permanent reality. Indeed, *kama* is one of the four aims of life in ancient Indian philosophy. As the *Kamasutra* says: 'He who knows all the secrets of the erotic arts becomes chaste.'

Mystics in India have used a vocabulary of physical love. For the acme of pleasure is a metaphor of the infinite ecstasy of unity with the Godhead. Divine reality is often linked with physical love. The union of two bodies and its joy reflects the union of the *jivatma* with the *parmatma*. 'Mystics are erotic. They intuitively and profoundly understand the sensual pleasures of sexual love and prefer their experience of the divine merely because it is more delectable, more durable, more complete. It is the ambitious ones, not the mystics, who seek to place obstacles in the path of sexual love, since eroticism may become the means (perhaps the only one) of attaining liberation,' remarks Danielou.

Innumerable references to the erotic are found in ancient Indian texts. It is felt that love is the only path that leads to divine union. The *Briha-daranyaka* states that the Cosmic Being created the world because, by himself, he knew no joy. He wanted to be two. 'A man without desires never achieves anything. Everything that men have created has been done through the search for pleasure,' says the first law-giver of the Hindus, Manu.

It is widely accepted that eroticism is an integral part of self-realisation, not necessarily of marriage. Marriage is a social institution, part of the procreation process where the woman as a wife and mother is accorded

Top: The fullest acceptance of sexuality is such that it is reflected in every daub of paint and leads to artistic pleasure. *A painting by Babu Xavier.*
Bottom: A free imagination helps give new life to old ideas and forms. *A painting by Babu Xavier.*
Facing page: Two women in a close encounter.

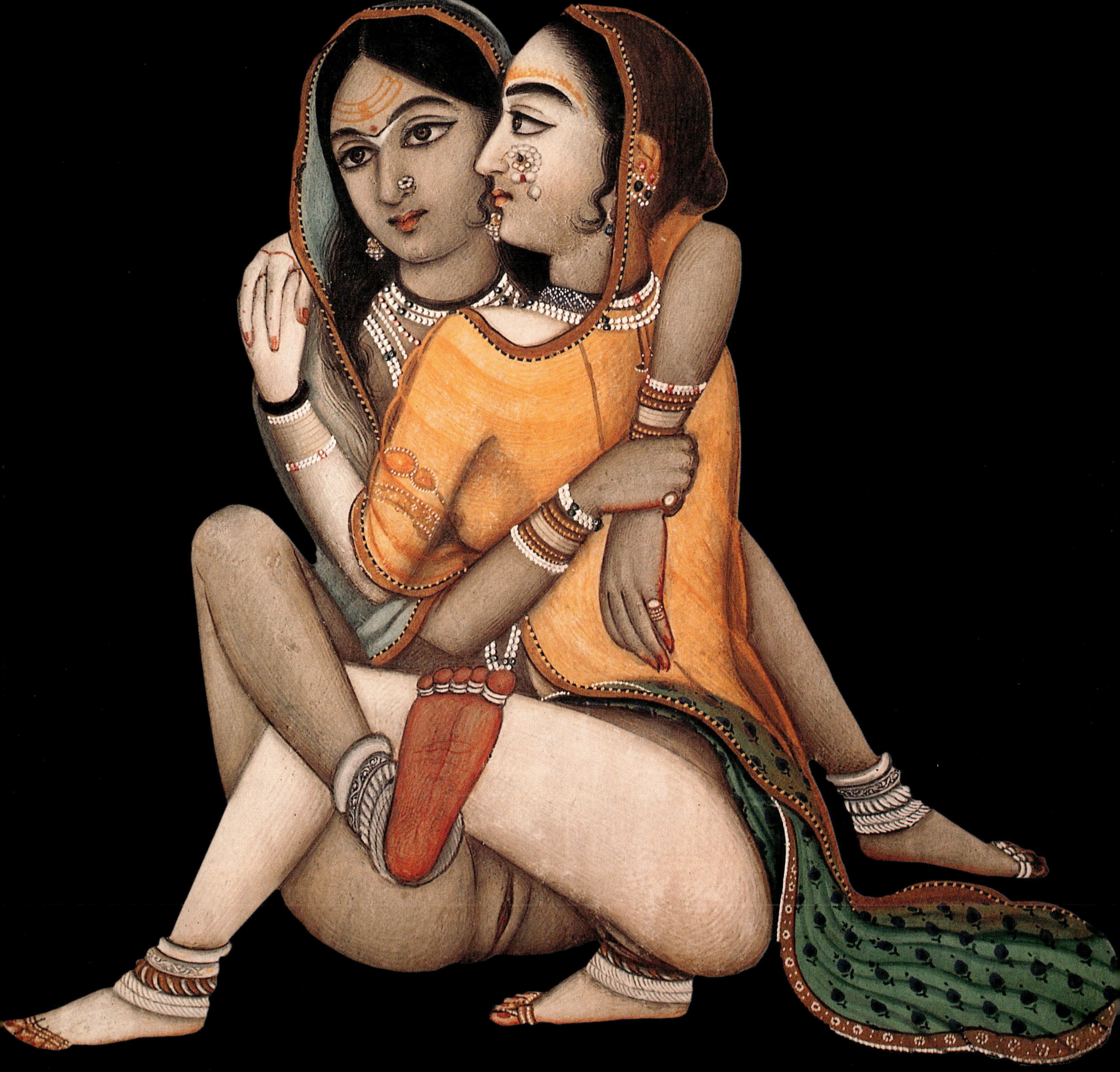

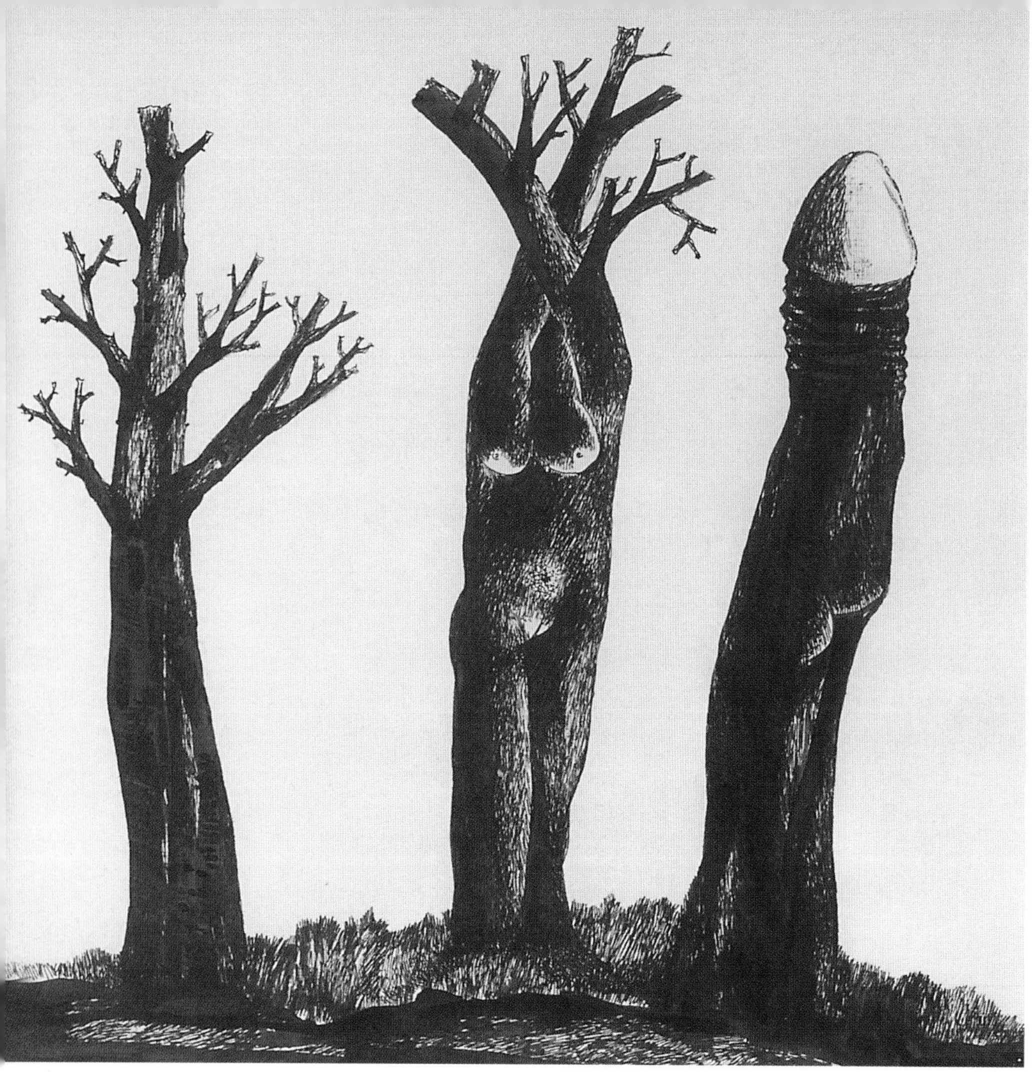

respect and a place in society. But a man and woman tied in holy matrimony may not be sexually fulfilled. It is only in complete fulfilment that there can be self-realisation. Love for that which does not belong to one (*parakiya*) is very different from love for that which belongs to one (*svakiya*). Quite often, in the Vaishnav *bhakti* tradition, the mystics and the poets actually idealise illicit love. Rukmini is the official wife of Krishna, and as the mother of his sons she has a lofty status. But it is Krishna's affair with Radha and his dalliance with the *gopis* that is constantly referred to. It is this love outside marriage which forms the inspiration for several texts, the poetry of the period, and even that of the later period.

An excerpt from the *Chandogya Upanishad* are direct pointers to the principle behind the experience of absolute pleasure in the sexual act itself.

Woman is the hearth,
the male organ is the fire,
The caresses are the smoke,
the vulva the flame,
Penetration the ember,
pleasure the spark.
In this fire, the gods sacrifice
semen
And a child is born.

From the *Shringara Rasa*, emerges the *bhava* of pleasure. The sensation of pleasure can be felt visually, or experientially. In the *Sankhya* philosophy the extreme sensation of pleasure reflects the infinite ecstasy of the individual when united with the divine. The *Shukra Niti* too emphasises the concept of pleasure. It says it is only through pleasure that social and economic circumstances are favourable, and it is through self-imposed limits that the pursuit of pleasure is made possible. 'As with forms of wealth, there are also forms of pleasure which run counter to duty, and upset the balance that makes the pursuit of pleasure possible, of which intrusions into others' pleasures are an example. This is why it is wrong to entertain a desire for another man's wife.'

The *Shukra Niti* of Shukracharya is one of the many Indian texts which is in part philosophical, and in part a manual of life. In it sexual desire, pleasure and love are given due importance as part of social behaviour. Indian erotica which spans decades of history, is seen frequently in the works of Indian visual artists. Since the erotic is an integral part of Indian philosophy, religion and cultural practices, elements of Indian erotica encompass Indian aesthetics and life with refinement, sophistication and elegance.

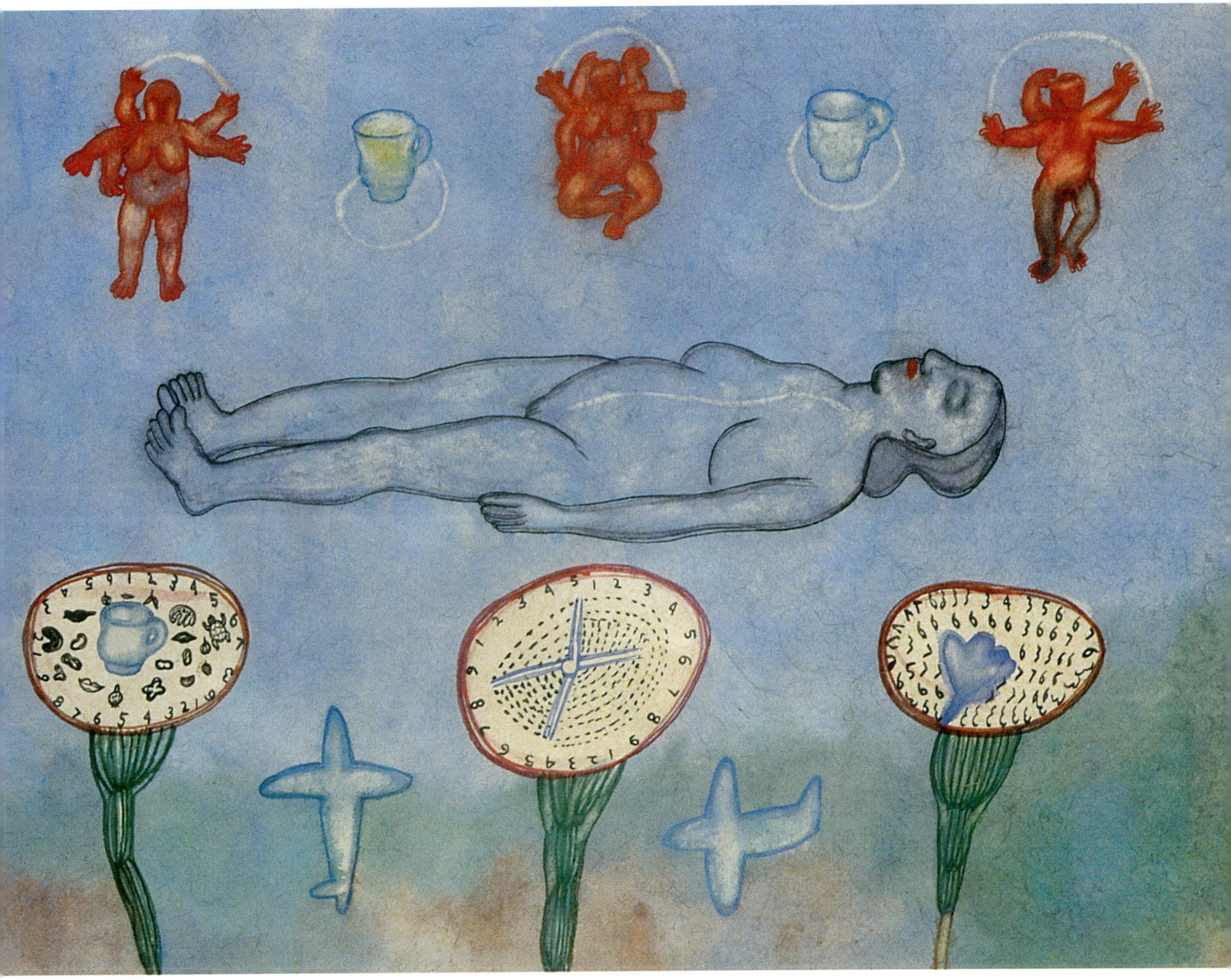

The levitating female as painted by Arpita Singh.

Facing page: Trees evoke fertility figures with their leafless branches and stumped ends.

Bibliography

PRIMARY TEXT

Ratimanjari of Jayadeva

Ratirahasya of Kokokka

Ratiramana of Sidhnagarjuna

Ratiratnapradipika of Shridevarajamaharaja

OTHER TEXTS

Agarwal, U., *Khajuraho Sculptures and Their Significance*, S. Chand & Co., Delhi, 1964.

Ajanta Painting, Lalit Kala Akademi, New Delhi, 1957.

Anand, M.R. *Kama Kala*. Skilton, London, 1958.

———. *Kama Kala*. Nagel, Geneva, 1963.

Anon, *Rati-sastra-ratnavalli* – Hindu Sexual Science, Madras,1905.

Arbuthnot, F.F. and Richard, F.B. *Ananga Ranga: Stage of the Bodiless One, the Hindu Art of Love*, Medical Press, New York, 1964.

Archer, W. *The Loves of Krsna*, New York.

Archer, W.G. *The Loves of Krishna in Indian Painting*, George Allen & Unwin Ltd., London, 1957.

———. *The Hill of Flutes*, George Allen & Unwin Ltd., London,1974.

Babulala, S.S. *Nagar Sarvaswam*, Eastern Book Linkers, New Delhi, 1994.

Banerjea, J.N. *The Development of Hindu Iconography*, University of Calcutta, Calcutta, 1956.

Basham, A.L. *The Wonder That Was India*, Macmillan & Co., New York,1954.

Basu, B.N. *The Kama Sutra of Vatsyayana*, revised by S.L. Ghosh, 10th ed., Medical Book Co., Calcutta, 1951.

Battacharya, H. ed. *The Cultural Heritage of India*, Vol. IV, the Ramakrishna Mission Institute of Culture, Calcutta.

Bhandarkar, R.G. *Vaisnavism, Saivism and Minor Religious Systems*. B.O.R.I., Poona, 1929.

Bhattacharya, T.P. *Maithuna Figures in Indian Art*, Lalit Kala Akademi, New Delhi, 1967.

Bhattacharyya, N.N. *History of Indian Erotic Literature*. Munshiram Manoharlal, New Delhi, 1975.

Bilhana, *Chaurapanchasika*, Oriental Book Agency, 1946.

Brown, W.N. *The Vasanta Vilasa*, American Oriental Society, New Haven, 1962.

Chandra, M. *The World of Courtesans*, New Delhi, 1972.

———. *The World of Courtesans*, Vikas Publishing, New Delhi, 1973.

Comfort, A. *The Koka Shastra and Other Indian Writings on Love*, George Allen & Unwin, London, 1964.

Comfort, A. *The Koka Sastra*. New York, 1965.

Coomaraswamy, A.K. *Introduction to Indian Art, Adyar, 1923.*

———. *The Dance of Shiva*, Asia Publishing House, 1948.

Dalmia, Y. *The Painted World of the Warlis*, Lalit Kala Akademi, New Delhi, 1988.

Dandin, *Dasakumaracharita*, Chicago, 1927.

Danielou, A. *The Phallus*, Inner Traditions International, Rochester, Vermont, 1993.

———. *Virtue, Success Pleasure and Liberation*, Inner Traditions International, Rochester, 1993.

Dasgupta, S. *A History of Indian Philosophy*, Cambridge University Press, London, 1969.

Dasgupta, S.B. *An Introduction to Tantric Buddhism*, (I.T.B.), University of Calcutta, Calcutta, 1950.

Dasgupta, S.N. and S.K. De eds. *A History of Sanskrit Literature* (Classical Period), Vol. I, Calcutta, 1947.

De, S.K. *Ancient Indian Erotics and Erotic Literature*, Mukhopadhyay, Calcutta, 1959.

Dehejia H.V. *Parvatidarpana*, Motilal Banarasidass, Delhi, 1997.

Desai, D. *Erotic Sculpture of India*, Tata McGraw-Hill, New Delhi, 1975.

———. *Relevance of Tantrism to Erotic Temple Sculpture*, Madhu, Delhi, 1981.

Donaldson, T. *Propitious—Apotropaic Eroticism in the Art of Orissa*, Artibus Asiae, 1975.

Dunuwila, R.A. *Saiva Siddhanta Theology*, Motilal Banarasidass, Delhi, 1985.

Dutt, M.N. ed. *Garuda Purana*, Ch. S.S., Varanasi, 1968.

———. *Markandeya Purana*, 1948; English translation by F.E. Pargiter, Bib. Ind., Calcutta, 1904.

Fouchet, M. *Erotic Sculpture of India*, Criterion Books, New York, 1959.

Frederic, L. *The Art of Indian Temples and Sculpture*, Harry N. Abrams, Inc., New York.

Gichner, L.E. *Erotic Aspects of Hindu Sculpture*, U.S.A, 1949.

Goldenberg, B.Z. *The Sacred Fire, The Story of Sex in Religion*, London, 1937.

Havell, E.B. *The Art Heritage of India*, Taraporevala's Publications, Bombay, 1964.

Hume, R.E. tr. *Upanishads, The Thirteen Principal Upanishads*, 2nd ed., revised, Oxford University Press, 1931.

Jayadeva *Gita-Govinda* with *Rasikapriya* and *Rasamanjari*, N.S.P., Bombay, 1949; English translation by. Lakshminarasimha Shastri, Madras, 1956.

Jolly, J. tr. *Narada-Smriti*, Oxford, 1889.

Jones, A. *Body Art / Performing the Subject*, University of Minnesota Press, Minneapolis,1998.

Kalahana *Rajatarangini*, B.S.S. 1892-94; English translation by. M.A. Stein, Motilal Banarasidass, 2 Vols., reprint 1961.

Kalidasa *Abhijnana-Sakuntalam*, edited and translated into English by C.R. Devadhar in *Dramas of Kalidasa*, Motilal Banarasidass,1966.

Kalyana-malla *Ananga – Ranga*, translated by Sir Richard Burton and F.F. Arbuthnot,Kama Sutra Society, Cosmopoli

———. translated by T.L. Ray, Medical Book Agency, Calcutta, 1944.

———. edited by Visnu Prasad Bhabdari, Kashi Sanskrit Series No. 9, Varanasi, 1923.

Keay John, *India, a History*, HarperCollins.

Kinsey, A. et al., *Sexual Behaviour in the Human Male*, W.B. Saunders, Philadelphia, 1948.

———.*Sexual Behaviour in the Human Female*, W.B. Saunders, Philadelphia, 1953.

Kinsley, D. *Tantric Visions of the Divine Feminine*, Motilal Banarsidass, Delhi, 1998.

Kokkoka, *Rati-rahasyam: Devidatta Sarmana Tippanikaya Vsadikrtya Sodhitam*,Tara Press, Benares, 1912.

———. *Rati-rahasyam: Srimat – Kancinatha – Krta – Dipikakhyaya Vyakhyaya Samudbhasitam*, ed. S.S.Ghildiyal, Bombay Sanskrit Press, Lahore, 1923.

Kraamrisch, S. *The Presence of Siva*, Motilal Banarsidass, Delhi, 1988.

Krishan,Y. *The Erotic Sculptures of India*, Artibus Asiae, 1972.

Lal, K. *Immortal Khajuraho*, Asia Press, Delhi, 1965.

———.*Erotic Sculpture of Khajuraho*, Asia Press, Delhi, 1970.

———.*The Cult of Desire – An Interpretation of Erotic Sculpture of India*, Asia Press, Delhi, 1996.

Leinhard, S. *Kokkoka – Ratirahasya*, Franz Decker, Stuttgart, 1960.

Maharaja, D. *Ratiratnapradipika*, edited by Liladhur Sarma, Benkateswar Book Agency, Calcutta, 1930.

Malavkagnimitram, in the *Dramas of Kalidasa,* 1966.

Malinowski, B. *Magic, Science and Religion and Other Essays*, 1948.

Marr, G.S. *Sex in Religion – A Historical Survey*, George Allen & Unwin Ltd., London, 1936.

Marris, P. and S.Thornham *Media Studies*, Edinburgh University Press Ltd., Edinburgh,1996.

Marsh, P. and D.Morris *Tribes*, Pyramid Books, London, 1988.

Matsya Purana, edited by Pandits of Anandaasrama, Poona,1907; English translation in 2 Vols., Allahabad, 1916-17.

Meyer, J.J. *Sexual Life in Ancient India – A Study on the Comparative History of Indian Culture*, vol.1, George Routledge & Sons Ltd., London, 1930.

———.*Sexual Life in Ancient India*,2 Vols. London, 1930.

———. *Sexual Life in Ancient India*, Vol 2, New York, 1930.

———. *Sexual Life in Ancient India*, Motilal Banarasidass, Varanasi,1971.

Misra, J. *Ancient Promises*, Penguin Group, Penguin Books Ltd., London.

Mitra, R. ed. *Agni Purana*, 3 Vols., Bib. Ind., 1873 – 79, Calcutta, English tr. Dutta, M.N., Calcutta, 1903.

Mookerjee, A. *Kali – The Feminine Force*, Thames and Hudson Ltd., London,1988.

———. *Tantra Art, its Philosophy and Physics*, Kumar Gallery, Delhi, 1966-67.

———. *Tantra Asana*. Ravi Kumar, Basel, 1971.

Mookerjee, A. and Khanna, M. *The Tantric Way*, Thames and Hudson Ltd., London, 1977.

Muttumanitalam, M.C. *Kokkokasastram*. Vidyarambham, Allepy, 1959.

Nagarjuna, S. *Ratisastra*, Translated by A.C. Ghosh, Seal, Calcutta, 1904.

Nandargirkar R. ed. and tr. *Raghuvamsa*, Gopal Narayana & Co., Bombay, 1981.

Narayana P.M. *Koka – sara – vaidyaka*,1937.

Nerurkar, V. R. ed. and tr. *Meghduta*, 4th ed., Bombay, 1948.

Nevile, P. *Nautch Girls of India*, Ravi Kumar Publishers, Paris, New York and New Delhi and Prakriti India, New Delhi, 1996.

O'Flaherty, W.D. *Siva: The Erotic Ascetic*, Oxford, 1996.

O'Sullivan, T.; J. Hartley; D. Saunders; M. Montgomery & J.Fiske, *Key Concepts in Communication and Cultural Studies*, Routledge, New York, 1996.

Padmasri *Nagarasarvasra*, Edited by Tasakhram Sarma, Gujarati Press, Bombay, 1912.

Panikkar, K.M. Intro. to *The Kamasutra of Vatsyayana*, English translation by R. Burton and F. Arbuthnot. Allen & Unwin Ltd., London, 1963.

Pavolini, S. *Ratimanjari of Jayadeva*. Giorn. Soc. Asiat. Ital. 17, 1904.

Prakash, B. *Khajuraho*. Taraporevala's Publications, Bombay, 1967.

Prakash, V. *Khajuraho*. Taraporevala's Publications, Bombay, 1967.

Rai, B.K. and Vidyarthi, L.P. *The Tribal Culture of India*, Concept Publishing Company, New Delhi, 1976.

Rangaswami, I.K. *The Kama Sutra of Vatsyayana*, Punjab Skr. Book Depot, Lahore, 1921.

Rao, T.A. Gopinatha *Elements of Hindu Iconography*, 2 Vols., Madras, 1914-16.

Rawson, P. *Erotic Art of the East*, Prometheus, New York, 1968.

———. *The Indian Cult of Ecstasy*, Thames and Hudson, London, 1973.

Ray, T. L. *Kokkokam and Ratirahasyam*, Medical Book Agency, Calcutta, 1960.

Sanyal, J.M. tr. *Bhagavata Purana*, N.S.P., 4 vols., Bombay, 1940; Translated into 5 vols., Dutta Bose & Co., Calcutta.

Saraswati, S.K. *A Survey of Indian Sculpture*. K.L. Mukhopadhyay, Calcutta, 1957.

Schneider, R. *The Explicit Body in Performance*. Routledge, London and New York, 1997.

Shah, S. ed. *Tribal Arts and Crafts of Madhya Pradesh*, Mapin Publishing Pvt. Ltd., Ahmedabad, 1996.

Skanda Purana Venkateswar Steam Press, Bombay, 1910.

Smedt, Marc de *The Kama Sutra: Erotic Figures in Indian Art*, Crescent Books, New York, 1980.

Smith, B. *Erotic Art of the Masters*, Gemini – Smith, La Jolla, California.

Stiles, K. and P. Selz eds. *Theories and Documents of Contemporary Art*, University of California Press, London, 1996.

Thomas, H.H. *The Theatre of the Hindus*, Susil Gupta, Calcutta, 1955.

Totajaya, Y. *The Kokkokam of Ativira rama Pandian*, Medical Book Co., Calcutta, 1949.

Unwin, J.D. *Sex and Culture*. Oxford University Press, London, 1934.

Upadhyaya, S.C. *Study in Ancient Indian Erotics*, J. Gujarat Res. Soc. 15, 1953.

Vatsyayana *Kama Sutra*, tr. S.C. Upadhyaya, Chas. Skilton, London, 1963.

———. tr. Sir Richard Burton and F.F. Arbuthnot, George Allen & Unwin, London, 1963

Vayu Purana, 2 Vols. Bib. Ind., Calcutta, 1880-88; Translated into Hindi by S.S. Acharya, 2 Vols., Sanskrit Janasthan, Bareilli, 1967.

Visnu Purana. Eng. Tr. H.H. Wilson, 5 Vols., London, 1864-70.

Wall, O. *Sex and Sex Worship*, St Louis, 1919.

Weston, J.L. *From Ritual to Romance*, Doubleday and Co., New York, 1957.

Woodroffe, S.J. *Sakti and Sakta*, Ganesh & Co. Pvt. Ltd., Madras, 1918.

Wright, T. *The Worship of the Generative Powers* – In Sexual Symbolism. New York., 1957.

Zanna, E. and Auboyer, J. *Khajuraho.* Hague, 1960.

ARTICLES

Danielou, A. "An Approach to Hindu Erotic Sculpture," *Marg*, II, No. 1, 1947-48.

Deva, K. "Temples of Khajuraho." *Ancient India*, No. 15, 1959.

Mookerjee, A. "Tantric Art," *The Times of India Annual.* 1965.

Murray, M.A. "Female Fertility Figures." *F.R.A.I.,* Vol.64,1934.

Panigrahi, K.C. "Obscene Sculptures of Orissan Temples," *P.I.H.C.*, VIII.

Rudra, A. "Temple Sculptures of India," *Conspectus,* Vol. 4, 1965

Sankalia, H.D. , "The Nude Goddess or 'Shameless Woman' in Western Asia, India and South-Eastern Asia," *Art. As.*, XXIII, 1960.

Tripathi, L.K. "Erotic Scenes of Khajuraho and Their Probable Explanation," *Bharati*, Bulletin of the College of Indology, Banaras Hindu University, No. 3, 1959-60.

Upadhyaya, S.C. "Literary Sources for a Study of Indian Erotics," *F.G.R.S.*, Vol. XVI, 1954.

Lance Dane: Page 18, 24, 26, 28, 31, 38, 40-41 (all 3 pictures), 43, 49, 50, 51 (2 pictures), 55, 56, 57, 58 (2 pictures), 61, 62, 63, 65 (3 pictures), 66, 67, 70 (bottom left), 72-73, 75 (2 pictures), 76, 77, 78, 79, 80-81, 82 (2 pictures), 83, 84, 85, 86, 87, 88, 89, 90-91, 92 (4 pictures), 93, 94 (bottom left), 98 (2 pictures), 99, 102 (right), 114, 116, 118, 122, 130-131, 138, 140, 150 (2 pictures), 160

Manu Parekh: Page 144 (2 pictures), 145

Nitin Bhayana: Page 142, 143, 146-147, 148, 153

Roli Collection: Page 9, 11, 16, 17 (2 pictures), 25, 29, 34, 35, 39, 42, 45 (2 pictures), 46, 59, 94 (top right), 95, 97, 100-101, 102 (left), 103, 104-105 (3 pictures), 110-111, 113, 115, 123, 132-133, 152

Satish Gupta: Page 130-131 (3 pictures), 139

Victoria and Albert Museum: Page 5, 7, 13, 14-15, 19, 32-33, 44, 47, 60, 68-69, 71, 127, 134-135 (2 pictures), 136-137 (2 pictures)

Werner Forman: Page 1,2-3, 20, 21, 23, 27, 30, 37, 74, 106, 107, 112, 120, 121, 124, 141, 151

The publishers wish to thank the following museums for their help and co-operation:
Chandigarh Museum; Crafts Museum, New Delhi; Dacca Museum, Bangladesh; Gwalior Museum; Indian Museum, Calcutta; Madras Museum, Egmore, Chennai; National Museum, New Delhi; Patna Museum, Bihar.
We also express our gratitude to Mr Noel Rands and Mr Kapil Dev Burman and other private collectors.

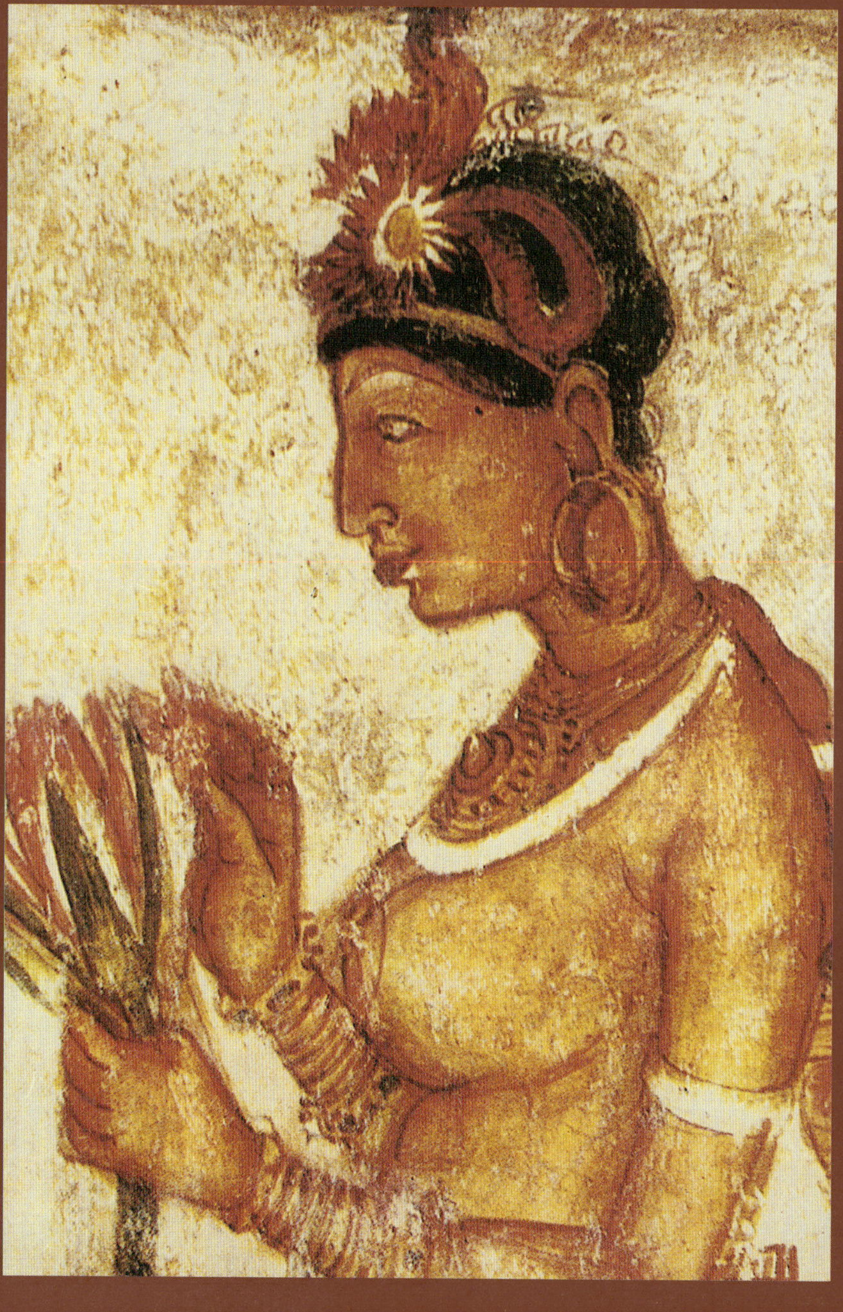